The Yearbook of Polar Law

The Yearbook of Polar Law

Editors-in-Chief

Gudmundur Alfredsson (*University of Akureyri, Iceland, and China University of Political Science and Law*)
Timo Koivurova (*Arctic Centre, University of Lapland, Finland*)

Editorial Board

Agust Thor Arnason (*University of Akureyri, Iceland*)
Nigel Bankes (*University of Calgary, Canada*)
Kees Bastmeijer (*Tilburg University, The Netherlands*)
Malgosia Fitzmaurice (*Queen Mary, University of London, United Kingdom*)
Lauri Hannikainen (*Erik Castrén Institute, University of Helsinki, Finland*)
Marie Jacobsson (*Ministry for Foreign Affairs of Sweden and University of Lund*)
Arngrimur Johannsson (*Polar Law Institute, Akureyri, Iceland*)
Rachael Lorna Johnstone (*University of Akureyri, Iceland, and University of Greenland*)
David Leary (*University of Technology, Sydney, Australia*)
Natalia Loukacheva (*University of Northern British Columbia, Canada*)
David VanderZwaag (*Dalhousie University, Canada*)
Laila Susanna Vars (*University of Tromsø, Norway*)
Lotta Viikari (*Faculty of Law, University of Lapland, Finland*)

Book Review Editor

Kamrul Hossain (*Northern Institute for Environmental and Minority Law, Arctic Centre, University of Lapland, Finland*)

VOLUME 8

The titles published in this series are listed at *brill.com/pola*

The Yearbook of Polar Law

Volume 8, 2016

Edited by

Professor Gudmundur Alfredsson (*University of Akureyri, Iceland and China University of Political Science and Law*)

Professor Timo Koivurova
(*Northern Institute for Environmental and Minority Law, Arctic Centre, University of Lapland, Finland*)

Special Editors for Volume 8

Professor Betsy Baker (*Vermont Law School and University of Alaska Fairbanks affiliate, USA*)
Dr. Mara Kimmel, Ph.D. (*Senior Fellow, Institute of the North, Anchorage, Alaska, USA*)

BRILL
NIJHOFF

LEIDEN | BOSTON

Typeface for the Latin, Greek, and Cyrillic scripts: "Brill". See and download: brill.com/brill-typeface.

ISSN 1876-8814
E-ISSN 2211-6427
ISBN 978-90-04-32436-7 (hardback)

Copyright 2017 by Koninklijke Brill NV, Leiden, The Netherlands.
Koninklijke Brill NV incorporates the imprints Brill, Brill Hes & De Graaf, Brill Nijhoff, Brill Rodopi and Hotei Publishing.
All rights reserved. No part of this publication may be reproduced, translated, stored in a retrieval system, or transmitted in any form or by any means, electronic, mechanical, photocopying, recording or otherwise, without prior written permission from the publisher.
Authorization to photocopy items for internal or personal use is granted by Koninklijke Brill NV provided that the appropriate fees are paid directly to The Copyright Clearance Center, 222 Rosewood Drive, Suite 910, Danvers, MA 01923, USA. Fees are subject to change.

This book is printed on acid-free paper and produced in a sustainable manner.

Contents

Editorial Note VII
Acknowledgements IX

In Memoriam – Walter B. Parker, 1926–2014

Tribute to Walt Parker 3
> *Harry Bader*

Support and Opposition: An Informal History of the Law of the Sea Convention in the United States and Alaska, Including a Tribute to Walter B. Parker 6
> *Mead Treadwell*

Responsible Resource Development in Alaska: A Developer's Perspective on the Red Dog Mine 20
> *Lisa Parker*

Research Articles

Respectful Neighbourliness: The United Kingdom's Arctic Approach 27
> *Rachael Lorna Johnstone*

From the High North to the Roof of the World: Arctic Precedents for Third Pole Governance 56
> *Simon Marsden*

Understanding Arctic Co-Management: The U.S. Marine Mammal Approach 76
> *Kathryn Mengerink, David Roche, and Greta Swanson*

The Greenland Self-Government Act: The Pitfall for the Inuit in Greenland to Remain an Indigenous People? 103
> *Bent Ole Gram Mortensen and Ulrike Barten*

An Agreement on Enhancing International Arctic Scientific Cooperation: Only for the Eight Arctic States and Their Scientists? 129
Akiho Shibata and Maiko Raita

The Impact of Choice-of-Law Rules in Cross-Border Pollution Damage Caused by Petroleum Spills from Offshore Rigs and Installations: The Case of the Barents Sea 163
Kristoffer Svendsen

The Recent Arctic Council Assessments: Influential Tools in Policy-Making in the Council and Beyond? 187
Małgorzata Śmieszek, Adam Stępień, and Paula Kankaanpää

The Nordic Welfare State and the Development of Northern Finland 214
Matti Niemivuo and Lotta Viikari

Poster Based Articles

How Satellites Can Support the Information Requirements of the Polar Code 247
Johnny Grøneng Aase and Julia Jabour

Essential Fish Habitat Regulation in the United States: Lessons for High Latitudes? 266
Aileen M. Nimick and Bradley P. Harris

Editorial Note

The Eighth Polar Law Symposium was held in the u.s. state of Alaska from September 23–26, 2015 to coincide with the United States Chairmanship of the Arctic Council. This was the first time the Polar Law Symposium, which was established in Iceland and returns there every three years, was held in North America. Colleagues and students from around the Arctic and the world convened first at the University of Alaska Fairbanks and then at the University of Alaska Anchorage for four days of presentations and discussions around the theme "The Science, Scholarship, and Practice of Polar Law: Strengthening Arctic Peoples and Places."

The conference theme combining science, scholarship and practice of law reflects the approach in Alaska to solving practical issues facing the country's only Arctic state. The theme also mirrors the approach that many groups are taking around the circumpolar north to build solutions to pressing challenges based on sound science in partnership with academic institutions and individuals dedicated to improving the legal system to meet those demands. Walter B. Parker, to whom this volume is dedicated, seamlessly combined all of those approaches in his life-long work to make life better for Alaskans, especially Alaska Natives, and to building strong international relationships in the Arctic, especially with Russia. His abiding interest in science was reflected in his time as a member of the us Arctic Research Commission. Just some of the many and inimitable ways Walt devoted himself to the state and to strengthening common ties around the Arctic are captured in the three essays that begin this volume: from Harry Bader, a xxx; from Mead Treadwell, the former Lieutenant Governor of the State of Alaska, and from one of Walt's daughters, Lisa Parker, who continues in the same vein of her father's service to the state as a Regent for the University of Alaska system.

The Polar Law Symposia continue to cast a broad net and to welcome new people into a collegial circle of academics and others. We learn from each other through lively interactions at the Symposia, through continued contact throughout the year, and in reading and sharing each others' work. This Yearbook is a prime venue for such exchanges. Ninety-five participants from a dozen countries gathered in Alaska in 2015, including a large number of representatives from us government agencies and Alaska Native organizations, and many practicing lawyers from around the state. We were honored to be able to present to our assembled international guests the range of issues facing the state of Alaska, and to hear visitors from abroad address ways in which those issues are presented and resolved in other Arctic countries.

All of the papers in this volume were presented in earlier form at the Eighth Polar Law Symposium. However, as did our predecessor, Professor Julia Jabour, host of the Seventh Polar Law Symposium in Hobart, we also take a step beyond the traditional boundaries of the Yearbook. **New in 2015**, the Symposium included a poster session for rising Arctic scholars to present their work, often together with their faculty mentors. Accordingly, this Volume 8 of the Yearbook of Polar Law contains a separate section for these shorter scholarly pieces, representing only some of the posters presented at the conference.

This support of emerging Arctic scholars is also in keeping with the work of the man to whom we dedicate this volume. Walt Parker was keenly aware that the state of Alaska has no law school and urged law professors visiting from out of state to help address the situation. He would have been pleased to see Seattle University launch the first graduate law opportunity in the state in 2015, allowing law students who start their studies elsewhere in the United States to complete the last year of their education here.

Betsy Baker and Mara Kimmel
Special Editors, Volume 8
Anchorage, Alaska
August 2016

Acknowledgements

Our first thanks go to Bridgette J. Cooper, a law student and journal editor at the University of Washington School of Law, who provided thorough and efficient line editing for every article in the volume.

Thanks, as well to Cindy Fester, Editor-Research Publications, University of Washington School of Law, for her invaluable and patient assistance at the height of the U.S. law school publishing season.

We are also grateful to all of you who provided peer review for your thoughtful, constructive and timely comments.

Finally, thanks go to our generous sponsors and partners, without whom the Eighth Polar Law Symposium would have been even more spartan than the rustic Alaska hospitality provided. The following law firms, Alaska Native Corporations, foundations, non-governmental organizations, and universities joined to support the Symposium, and publication of this Yearbook, through generous financial and in-kind assistance: Anchorage law firms Stoel Rives LLP, Landye Bennett Blumstein LLP; Davis Wright Tremaine LLP, and Perkins Coie; the Alaska Humanities Forum, Bristol Bay Native Corporation, World Wildlife Federation (WWF-Alaska), Alaska Pacific University, the University of Alaska–Anchorage (The Justice Center and Institute for Social and Economic Research), the University of Alaska–Fairbanks, Vermont Law School, and the University of Washington School of Law.

Betsy Baker and Mara Kimmel
Special Editors, Volume 8

In Memoriam – Walter B. Parker, 1926–2014

Tribute to Walt Parker

Harry Bader[a]

The large life of Walt Parker shaped the present character of Alaska, and determined its current course, more than any man since statehood. This is a strong statement wand yet it is easily defended with indisputable facts readily available to all.

PHOTO BY BOB HALLINEN / ALASKA DISPATCH NEWS ARCHIVE.

---

a Deputy Executive Director – Global Development Lab at U.S. Agency for International Development (USAID).

Walt's handiwork is evident in all aspects of Alaska. From commerce and transit, to the preservation of Arctic wilderness, to the availability of Alaska's rich resources, and the protection of the Alaskan quality of life, Walt's efforts transformed the 49th state.

In leading the state's transportation policy, Walt made the single most important decision any government leader has ever made shaping the life of all Alaskans. It was Walt Parker that argued and carried the day that the transportation system of a large and remote subcontinent is best served through the air rather than on land. And so it was his vision to put an airstrip in every community. To any casual observer, that course set in place the direction that has had a more profound impact upon the character of what it means to be Alaska than any other.

Walt, along with Esther Wunnicke, provided the blueprint for land selections that became the greatest American land conservation statute in history, the Alaska National Interest Lands Conservation Act. Together on the Federal-State Lands Commission, these two pioneers, simultaneously champions of preservation and development, helped shape the character of this state. The vast wilderness swaths of the Arctic, the Interior, and the Coast which are now forever protected are a testament to their collective endeavor. The mines, the mills, and the oil wells, which produce wealth shared by all Alaskans, are the product of Walt and Esther seeking balance for a viable state economy. If only Gifford Pinchot and John Muir had been able to get along as well as Esther and Walt, America would be a profoundly better place.

And, in one of our state's darkest hours, another governor, Governor Steve Cowper, turned to Walt Parker. Walt was named to chair the Alaska Oil Spill Commission. His investigation after the Exxon-Valdez disaster, led to changes in law and agency practice that we see today, and in the citizen oversight that is integrated into the monitoring and regulation of Alaska's waterways and marine resources. His work identified the ills of complacency and overconfidence. Walter Parker had faith in the power of transparency, accountability, and the involvement of the public as the great hallmark of effective democracy.

To ensure Alaskans had the means of self-government, Walt tirelessly advocated for a law school in this state. He worked to ensure that all Alaskans had access to both education and the ballot box. He cared deeply that Alaskans, whose homes were made millennia ago after crossing the Bering Land Bridge, were given the same access to opportunity as those who walk across the Anchorage airport sky-bridge to start their new lives. He was a friend to the refugee, the dispossessed, and the trafficked.

Walt Parker conducted himself with grace and understanding. He was also resolute. World War II and the Cold War were profound influences that shaped his character. He reflected on the realization that even good people, of noble intention, can make collective decisions that set into motion inevitable catastrophe. He understood that evil does exist, that civilization and morality are not relative, and there are those that must be vanquished in order that good may prevail.

How does one become so influential, so innately good? How does one become a man who could never ignore a friend or abandon a sled dog?

That answer lies in the bonds and love formed with an extraordinary spouse, his wife, Patricia. As much as Alaska needed Walt Parker at critical moments in its history, Walt needed his wife always. They shared a life and kept secrets. Walt never tired of telling the marvelous mystery of how such a petite woman could set a wolf trap so rapidly. I think, though I am unsure, that she may have kept this secret from him; at least he never revealed it to me.

Together they experienced Alaska, they built a homestead, they ran a trap line, and they raised a family. That family now continues to shape events in Alaska and elsewhere to this day, making our Great Land better.

Support and Opposition: An Informal History of the Law of the Sea Convention in the United States and Alaska, Including a Tribute to Walter B. Parker

Mead Treadwell[a]

Tribute to Walter B. Parker

Let me begin my remarks with a tribute to one of my mentors and friends, the late Dr. Walt Parker (August 11, 1926–June 25, 2014), a key figure in Alaska's understanding of the Law of the Sea negotiations and our state's participation in making use of the Convention in its early years. Before turning to a more detailed history of Alaskan and national interests in the Law of the Sea, I'd also like to talk about a subject that was as close to his heart as the Law of the Sea: bringing devolution of power to people where they live in the Arctic.

Walt came on my radar screen in the frenzy of completing the biggest writing assignment of my entire freshman year at Yale. The paper was about Alaska and the Law of the Sea, and the year was 1974. I was in the Yale library, piecing together things that had been happening in our bilateral relationships with Canada, South Korea, Russia, and Japan. I was also looking at multilateral efforts. At the time Alaska had eleven different international fisheries agreements, some of which survive today and some of which were replaced by the 200 nautical mile Exclusive Economic Zone soon to be established by Congress (Magnuson Act, later the Magnuson-Stevens Act, 1976), but authorized by the unratified Law of the Sea Convention. In the middle of this research I found a book that had just been published, titled *International Fisheries Regimes of the North Pacific (Alaska and the Law of the Sea)*[1] by Walter B. Parker. At that time, people involved with fishery issues in Alaska and the region were very frustrated. In Walt's book, he makes the argument for a stable world fisheries regime that puts power in the hands of coastal nations. His argument was that

---

a   President, PT Capital, Lieutenant Governor of Alaska (2010–2014), Chair, U.S. Arctic Research Commission (2006–2010).

1   Walter B. Parker, *International Fisheries Regimes of the North Pacific (Alaska and the Law of the Sea*, available at https://ntrl.ntis.gov/NTRL/dashboard/searchResults/titleDetail/COM74 11562.xhtml (National Technical Reports Library).

the coastal states would manage the fisheries best. At the time we had such freedom of the seas that many participant nations had different arguments about how much could be caught and who could catch it, and related issues. We did not, however, have a common management view. As another mentor, Wally Hickel,[2] said: if no one owns it, no one cares.

What we did, whether right or wrong, in response to these issues in the late 1970s, was to take ownership of our coastal fisheries within what would later be the exclusive economic zone. I would argue that fisheries management is much better today as a result than it was at the time.

In preparing for this presentation, I came across a report that had been written before Walt Parker's 1974 book. The July 1971 report was by Robert M. Goldberg, an associate professor with the University of Alaska Sea Grant Program and Walt Parker, Environmental Specialist, Federal Field Committee for Federal Planning in Alaska. The report covers the Sixth Annual Law of the Sea Institute held in Kingston, Rhode Island. Walt returned from that Institute and told Alaskans that they really needed to pay attention to this Law of the Sea business. He indicated that by extending the continental shelf area that is subject to national claims, a broader national sea makes shelf exploration more attractive and also enlarges any pollution control zone that begins at the edge of the territorial sea and it may greatly influence fisheries management and conservation through a larger exclusive fishery.

So early on in the Law of the Sea negotiations (the Third UN Conference on the Law of the Sea), Alaskans were thinking a lot about these issues and some were of the view that we really needed to reach a law of the sea agreement to address resource management issues. Other Alaskans who were very much involved were former Congressman Howard Pollock, who had been a leader at the National Oceanic and Atmospheric Association (NOAA) and very active during President Nixon's administration when Governor Hickel was Secretary of the Interior. Pollock argued that we needed to reach an international agreement on the law of the sea and of course it was President Nixon who laid out the arguments to begin conversations on the law of the sea.

But let me get back to Walt. After he saved my freshman thesis I became a reporter, covering Alaska politics. Walt Parker and Esther Wunnicke[3] showed up in the Legislature one day to explain what they had done on a federal-state

---

2 Walter J. Hickel, Governor of Alaska, 1990–1994 and 1966–1969, US Secretary of the Interior, 1969–1970. Hickel was an active advocate for the 200-mile limit to protect our fisheries; NOAA and national fisheries management were part of the Interior Department in his tenure there.

3 Esther Wunnicke (March 13, 1922–March 19, 2013), an Alaskan lawyer whose public service included the Alaska Human Rights Commission, Commissioner of the Department of Natural Resources, and Assistant State Attorney General.

committee to help carve up Alaska's lands and change the map of Alaska. You can take a look at the land regimes in this state, including the Alaska National Interest Lands Conservation Act (ANILCA) and the Alaska Native Claims Settlement Act (ANCSA) before that, and thank Walt and Esther for being the locals, being the leadership of the local teams, that made sure that Congress was listening to our local needs. I can't say Congress always listened. I love to complain that they don't listen – that's a common thing for Alaska's political leaders to say – but Walt was there. He was immortal before he was mortal, and he changed the map of Alaska. Walt helped establish many of our conservation units and parks in Alaska. He helped us extend the exclusive economic zone to 200 miles. In the work he did as leader of the Exxon Valdez Oil Spill Commission, to which he was appointed by Governor Steve Cowper in 1989, Walt helped us change the liability laws, establish citizen oversight and much stronger oil spill science, and mandate contingency planning. That Oil Spill Commission accomplished extraordinary work that endures today, even into the LOS debate when we talk about Article 234 of the LOS Convention.

After all that, Walt and I served together on a state commission to bring new technology to the oil spill world, and we worked together as the Prince William Sound Oil Spill Recovery Institute was started in Cordova. He always supported advancing "best available technology" in this realm. Then he was appointed to the US Arctic Research Commission, where he served from 1995–2001. As a US Arctic Research Commissioner he asked me to help the Commission do more to bring about and support arctic cooperation. We created an ad-hoc group of Alaskans on Arctic issues, which meets monthly to this day. I was then at the Institute of the North.[4] One day we were on the telephone with the US State Department because the US Military was saying in effect, "We want to help with these floods in the middle of Siberia but the Russian national government isn't asking for our assistance." Walt and I knew from our perspective in Alaska that the local governments in Siberia were in fact asking. The military and diplomatic leaders wanted to know "What can we do?" and we found ourselves educating our own foreign ministry on the infrastructure needs of eastern Russia.

After that experience Walt and I came back to the Arctic Council process, where we had been involved, and proposed a circumpolar Arctic Infrastructure Task Force that could begin to talk about shipping and many other issues. The result of that process was what Lawson Brigham likes to say was the first document negotiated word for word by the Arctic Council: the Arctic Marine Shipping Assessment (AMSA) 2009 Report. Walt really helped kick off that

---

4 More information about the Institute of the North is available a http://www.institutenorth
.org/about/mission-vision/.

process and I continued to push it after I replaced him in 2001 on the US Arctic Research Commission (I should say, after I took his seat, since no one could replace Walt). That is when he turned his energy to working as a Senior Fellow at the Institute of the North. AMSA was the first time the eight nations of the north sat down and articulated their common agenda for marine safety in the north. For that we can thank Walt Parker and the ministers who said this was an important exercise. Pretty much everything we have done on Arctic shipping we can trace to that seminal work, whether negotiating the mandatory Polar Code at the International Maritime Organization, or the eight Arctic states negotiating under Arctic Council auspices and agreeing to the legally binding Search and Rescue Agreement and the Oil Pollution Preparedness and Response Agreement, or the Arctic Council negotiations of the Science Agreement now underway. I want to thank Walt for his role in laying the foundation for all of those agreements.

Were Walt standing here today, he might ask if this room full of scholars and practitioners might help with completing the process of Devolution in the Arctic. He was a strong advocate for managing fish and game at a regional level in Alaska. I believe he would agree with those who look now at the transfer of ownership or management control of land in Greenland, Nunavut, and the Northwest Territories to local control from national control. I now find myself chair of a committee appointed by our governor and legislature called the Alaska State Lands Advisory Group (ASLAG). ASLAG is trying to respond to developments such as Canadian Devolution (and, to some degree, the Utah update to the "Sagebrush Rebellion," which seeks to move federal land to state control). While I find that an admirable goal I am not sure it is going to work in our political society but I do think there is more we can and must do to put the people who live in the region in control of what happens in their region.

The last thing I will say about Walt is this: he would be deep in a policy conversation and weave in some anecdote about running his trap line around Lake Minchumina. He worked with the Federal Aviation Administration out there and supplemented his income by trapping and running a dogsled. He was very active in the outdoors as long as he was alive. I thank you for remembering him here today.

An Informal History of the Law of the Sea Convention in the United States and Alaska

Now let me turn to the subject at hand, which is the UN Convention on the Law of the Sea. The Law of the Sea Convention, as you know, is a major international treaty and the United States is one of the few countries that have not joined it, which we can now only do by acceding to the convention. Frankly, much about the treaty has become more controversial since it was renegotiated in the Reagan Administration. Based on conversations I've had with people on both sides in the US Senate, I don't think ratification is likely to happen very soon. You can argue whether it should or shouldn't happen, but I can tell you based on my recent experience running for election to the US Senate that not ratifying the LOS Convention is considered to be one of the great accomplishments of the Tea Party movement in the United States. Whether you sympathize with the goals of the Tea Party or not (and I basically do), they have made this issue such an icon that many people believe that acceding to the treaty is transferring our sovereignty from the United States to the United Nations. Many moderate Republicans I know won't touch the issue. Thirty-five votes were necessary to keep it off of the Senate's treaty ratification schedule and thirty-five Republican senators signed a letter saying they didn't think it should happen in the lame duck session after the 2012 election.

Senator Dan Sullivan, our junior US Senator, Max Gruenberg, a representative to the Alaska Legislature, and a columnist has made something of this in the newspaper. Dan, Tea Party favorite Joe Miler and I were in several debates during the Senate Republican primary in 2014. I tried to remind Alaskans that, when the agreement was being negotiated, we went out and actually fought for a law of the sea convention. I tried to remind them that the convention's provisions helped give us control of our salmon fisheries, and helped give us the 200-mile Exclusive Economic Zone, among other benefits. Miller, one of my opponents, said he was shocked that I would ever put the economy of the Alaska before the sovereignty of the United States. After he had laid this blow on my chin, he gave me no time to respond because we cut to a commercial break. So I said to Miller, "Hey, this guy Sullivan was assistant secretary of state, and his job was to get it ratified. And Dan says "Oh, no, don't put me in the middle of it; I'm not for that treaty." And indeed he is saying he is not for that treaty now.

So this is the question I'll address in my remaining time: How did a treaty that the United States proposed, convened, and supported through over a decade of negotiations become so politically radioactive that is not going to get anywhere, given that it addresses such a critical topic?

Before I answer that question let me go back and talk a little bit about where Alaska was at that time. In 1972, the state of Alaska created a Commission on Law of the Sea. Its members included many people I have had the thrill of working with in my career: Bob Mulcahy, a State Senator from Kodiak; Fred Zharoff, a State House representative from Kodiak; Bob Thorstenson, a fish processor from Petersburg who had served as commissioner on what was then the International North Pacific Fisheries Commission (that commission reserved a seat for other fishing nations of the North Pacific, and while bringing all parties to the table is essential in management of a common pool resource, the INPFC was ineffective in my mind in terms of serving good fisheries management, as a consensus organization often produces a "lowest common denominator" between views); Phil Daniel of the United Fishermen of Alaska; Jeff Stephan, now with the United Fishermen Marketing Association in Kodiak; Dan O'Hara who is today Mayor of Naknek; and Chuck Meacham, Sr. who was the Director of International Fisheries for Governor Jay Hammond and worked with Governor Wally Hickel. This commission reported every year or so to the Alaska legislature on Alaska's positions on the Law of the Sea negotiations.

The Commission's report from 1978 was quite interesting. Its main argument was that the state should support the 200-mile Exclusive Economic Zone in order to strengthen our ground fisheries; an argument that would also benefit ground fisheries today in the Arctic. The landed value of fisheries in Norway, Russia, Canada, the United States [combined], is about 3.3 billion dollars a year by one estimate I've seen. When value is added, the economic impact is probably double that, by other estimates. At that time, the prospect of major Alaskan participation in ground fisheries was virtually new. Foreign fleets caught bottom fish, and to Alaskans, salmon was practically everything. The main outcome that Alaskans were pushing for with the Law of the Sea Convention was to ensure control of our salmon, by getting the international community to recognize that the coastal state ought to have control over anadromous fisheries, and that – by extension – foreign vessels fishing outside 12 miles ought not to be catching our salmon. This is an issue we are still facing in some ways today with driftnet fishing, almost a lifetime later (considering that many people in this room were born after 1975).

Another law of the sea issue important to Alaska at the time was oil transport by sea. The commission's report said that because the state was soon to be exporting major amounts of pipeline oil by tanker it had an incentive to minimize Law of the Sea impediments to tanker traffic. Nevertheless, the state's primary ocean resource concern was then, is, and always will be fisheries, with adequate protection and proper management of those resources off of Alaska shores. Accordingly, the report proposed that the law the sea agreement grant to coastal nations broad jurisdiction to promulgate and enforce measures to regulate activities within their exclusive economic zones that might adversely affect fishery resources. Included within this broad jurisdiction, the report said, should be the ability to regulate tanker traffic. At the same time, the Law of the Sea treaty should require all coastal maritime nations to work through appropriate international organizations to establish uniform coastal state rules for pollution controls. So this was our State's position in the late 1970s. Challenges of paying for spill prevention from ships in innocent passage continue today, but the Oil Pollution Act of 1990 (after Exxon Valdez, thanks in large part to Walt Parker) addresses some of the regulatory gap Alaskans bristled about in the 1970's.

What I'd like to highlight about these matters is that, for Alaska, and for the Arctic, I would say that we gained four big things from the treaty.

- The Exclusive Economic Zone and Fisheries
- Freedom of Navigation
- Article 234 and Pollution Prevention in Ice-Covered Areas
- A Process for Establishing Extended Continental Shelf Rights

1) *The Exclusive Economic Zone and Fisheries*. First and foremost regarding fishing, the principle was established in international law that coastal states have control over our anadromous fish. In addition, the 200 mile limit in and of itself addressed Governor Hickel's concern that if no one owns a resource, no one cares for it: the Exclusive Economic Zone basically said we "owned" it, that is, the coastal state had management authority over the offshore undersea lands and the fisheries resources they contained. We later "Americanized" our fisheries in the EEZ, and gained a larger economic stake in the fishery. By taking ownership, we didn't have scientists of one nation putting their numbers against the scientists of the other nation and getting to the least common denominator consensus approach on how many fish could be caught. Many studies in fisheries management have shown over the years that consistency in management theory is most effective over time. Now I'm not a scholar of that issue, but my point is that we have a relatively consistent management approach since the North Pacific Fishery Management Council took it on.

We have had relatively strong success with our fishery management council here in Alaska, but the toughest place where we have not had success has been in the North Atlantic. There the management council, in my view, puts economics ahead of conservation and still has a situation where several nations control the fisheries of a particular base. But nevertheless, the Law of the Sea Convention achieved something pretty important for Alaska. When I arrived here in the 1970s, it was mostly foreign nations that caught our fish and the Convention and 200 mile zone changed that. To Alaskans who say they oppose the Law of the Sea, I would say, "Take a look at what we gained because of these negotiations."

2) *Article 234 and pollution prevention in ice-covered areas*. A second thing we gained from the negotiations, and we didn't really realize how important it was

SUPPORT AND OPPOSITION

until later on, is Article 234. You just heard me read Mr. Meacham's point in the report to the legislature: Alaska's position was that the state ought to have some way to control tanker traffic passing by our shores. There was not a lot of tanker traffic passing by Alaska's shores in the 1970s. Frankly there is not a whole lot of tanker traffic right now, either, but we do have a situation where thousands of ships not in compliance with US spill prevention rules transit through Alaska's Aleutian Islands using innocent passage. My friends who work with the Coast Guard say we don't necessarily have a way – unless the vessel has left an American port – to require that the vessel be part of an oil spill contingency planning process. In fact, since the US Oil Pollution Act of 1990 was passed, it has taken us until last year (2014) to approve alternative contingency planning criteria in western Alaska and to begin the process of implementation.

A fascinating artifact of the Law of the Sea Convention discussion is the different position the United States and Canada take regarding what areas are international straits versus national waters. Canada takes the position that the Northwest Passage comprises internal waters while the United States views it as an international strait. A similar and even more difficult situation exists in Russia, which has declared the Northern Sea Route to be internal waters. Some people have suggested they play a "troll under the bridge" approach. Russia basically says to all vessels "You can't sail through there unless you pay for our icebreaker services, whether you need them or not, and that will cost you as much as $500,000 for a voyage." The internal vs. external waters impasse has been bridged, somewhat, by Article 234. Coastal states in areas where ice covered waters exist are clearly allowed to impose non-discriminatory measures to protect their environment and support marine safety, even to vessels in innocent passage. The U.S. has been reluctant to embrace this; given precedent it may set for innocent passage in other areas. Nevertheless, this plank in Law of the Sea may be Alaska's best bet to get needed oil spill response and icebreaker coverage paid for on its coasts.[5]

3) *Freedom of Navigation.* The U.S. stance on the Northwest Passage is just one of the ways in which the United States has continued to work for freedom in navigation. That goal – freedom of navigation – actually prevented us from protecting our fisheries for many years. My senior thesis in college examined how Japan sailed into Alaska's Bristol Bay in the 1930s, started scooping up our salmon outside 12 miles from Alaska's coast, the political reaction was

---

5   Mead Treadwell, *Will Arctic nations let Russia control Arctic shipping? Should they?* Harvard International Review, 36(3) 2015, available at http://hir.harvard.edu/will-arctic-nations-let-russia-control-arctic-shipping-should-they/.

strong; longshoremen along the entire west coast went on strike in support of our fishermen. President Franklin Roosevelt went to the State Department asking if the country could enforce a 200-mile limit. Alger Hiss was the State Department officer on this brief who wrote back, and I paraphrase his answer to FDR: "No, Mr. President, our Navy won't be able to sail through the strait of Gibraltar if we do take control of our fisheries." And so, in 1937 the United States set a policy path it was tied to for some 40 years until 1976. That is when the revolution that was the Law of the Sea Convention negotiations proposing a 200-mile Exclusive Economic Zone began to separate marine resource economic rights from freedom of shipping rights. And that's a pretty important distinction that happened in that negotiation as well. This is an outcome that I would argue conservatives should be very happy with.

4) *A process for establishing Extended Continental Shelf Rights.* A fourth thing that we got out of this treaty, one that Alaskans weren't contemplating at the time, was a process for extending undersea territorial rights, by making a submission regarding the Extended Continental Shelf (ECS) beyond the 200 mile limit in the Arctic and anywhere a country has a coastline. This is a huge potential addition to the area where the United States can exercise sovereign rights.

I had the opportunity to work on this issue, following my predecessor George Newton, as Chair of the U.S. Arctic Research Commission. When I approached the State Department in 2006 about Alaska's potential ECS, they told us, "Well, we have no money to go chart our claim." I replied, "Why don't you ask Congress for it?" and they said, "For us to ask Congress we would need the Office of Management and Budget (OMB) to sign off, and for the President to put the request in his budget and only then would we be allowed to talk about it." To which I said, "Well the Commission has made this charting a research priority, so the law allows me to talk about it with Congress right now."

So I went up to Congress, raised this issue in a Senate hearing, and fairly quickly, we received an $80 million appropriation, which paid for the US mapping efforts of the ECS, at times in cooperation with Canada, in the Artic and other places. Under the rules sent out in the Convention, the United States is now in the process of establishing its claim to an area that amounts to almost twice the size of California, even though we are not party to the Convention. This is an area where the United States will be able to designate who can explore and exploit the living and non-living resources of the ECS and require that they follow US rules for doing so, so that was a significant gain.

All of these things: freedom of navigation, Extended Continental Shelf rights, extending our laws offshore, and the incredibly important fisheries changes through the EEZ – are changes in legal thinking that happened because of the

SUPPORT AND OPPOSITION

Law of the Sea Treaty. However when the Alaska legislature was considering its Arctic Policy in 2015, there were more phone calls, email messages and constituents contacting the legislature to say, "Please keep Law of the Sea out of our Arctic policy because it's a United Nations treaty." Let me read one other thing that Mr. Meacham predicted in his 1980 report to the legislature on the Law of the Sea negotiations. He said,

> Whether the United State Senate will ratify the convention after signature by the Executive Branch is a serious question worth pondering. There are those who decry the end of the traditional freedom of the seas, who argue that the seabed authority dominated by the vast majority of our merging nations will overwhelmingly control marines' activities and [create?] a new UN for the oceans. The deep sea bed mining will be enormously expensive and perilous venture in which with the rewards but not the risks must be shared with developing nations which contribute nothing but demand the major benefits and there are those who argue that there will no longer be freedom to conduct marine scientific result nor sufficient freedom to transit for worships and straits in economic zones to protect our security and military objectives of our Nation. There are others who will violently object to having the US finance the Enterprise (the operating arm of the authority) to the tune of perhaps $25 million, so that it can compete with American deep seabed miners and there will be those who will object to the uncertainty of the repayment schedules on the interest free loans the government is compelled to advance to the Enterprise without knowing how to accurately evaluate the full financial obligation.[6]

Meacham, then Chairman and Executive Secretary of Alaska's Commission on Law of the Sea, went on to say that, even if the Law of the Sea convention never entered in the force (an outcome which he deemed quite remote) the myriad articles contained in the draft convention – all of which were agreed to by consensus over the years of the Law of the Sea conference sessions – would eventually be accepted as customary international law, that is to say as the supra-national norm. He said that this evolution into customary international law would likely occur in almost all areas except for those in which an entity was created by the treaty (the International Seabed Authority, the Enterprise, the Commission on the Limits of the Continental Shelf, the Tribunal on the Law of the Sea). On the issue of getting a 200-mile EEZ, he's certainly been

---

6   Author's note: Quotation not verified against original.

proven correct. Meacham understood that international organizations cannot come into existence through customary international law, but some principles can be established by state practice – use and acceptance.

My last point is that one reason we are at a stalemate in this country is because the Convention's proponents and its opponents don't want to talk to each other. I'll detail the points of disagreement in a moment, but the exact prediction that Mr. Meacham made in 1980 has truly come to pass. We have conservatives arguing that we don't need to sign on to the treaty and create these organizations because the good things in the treaty have already become customary international law.

That position does make it harder for our nation to establish the extent of our extended continental shelf (ECS) because, as a non-party to the Convention, it cannot appoint a member of the Commission of scientists that considers each submission; and may not be able to present a submission to it. The Commission on the Limits of the Continental Shelf established under the Convention does not consider maritime boundary disputes. It may be possible for the United States to work out its boundary differences with its neighbors on a bilateral basis (we have done that with Russia and have a quiet process moving forward with Canada over whether the Alaska-Canada boundary extends due north or in a northeasterly direction, perpendicular to the Beaufort headlands at the border) and then "unilaterally" declare extended continental shelf jurisdiction in the Arctic and other places. We essentially did that with the 200-mile limit. To be clear, maritime boundary disputes do not necessarily need to be resolved before assertion of the extent of a nation's ECS. We should make our ECS claim known, I'd argue, whether or not we ever join the convention, simply to put our marker down. I am uncertain whether I would argue for a unilateral declaration of our ECS. Our leverage to fix the most challenging parts of the convention may be lost if we do; there is not a rival claimant for most of what our ECS claim would be.

My closing argument and my challenge to you as scholars is to help us figure out a way to fix what have emerged as the knottiest challenges with the Law of the Sea. Treaty supporters do not want to make fixes; their attitude is that because joining the convention is the right thing, sooner or later, we'll get enough votes to pass it and move on. My argument is we can maybe do what we did when there was a similar stalemate in the 1970s when the question was, should we or should we not as a nation recognize the People's Republic of China (PRC)? As you may recall, those who opposed recognition (and I would argue that the Tea Party today is the lineal descendant of those opponents) said "Don't recognize those pinkos in China who run that lawless nation." And whatever our ideology was, we said there are practicalities here and we will recognize the PRC, but we will also pass the Taiwan Relations Act. That act side-stepped the disagreements in a way that has worked since the mid-1970s. Among other things the Act said that the United States will come to Taiwan's aid if anybody tries to unify Taiwan and China by anything but peaceful means. The Act made clear that the United States would always be there as an ally for Taiwan. My recommendation is that we study how to adapt that kind of approach to implementing law to Law of the Sea. This approach is worthy of legal scholarship.

The second thing I would argue in closing is that we should at least implement some parts of Law of the Sea in US law. Currently a considerable disagreement exists between Alaska and the federal government about revenue sharing in the Alaska Outer Continental Shelf. (States adjoining the Gulf of Mexico get a different, much larger, share of OCS revenue.) We might consider enacting provisions on revenue sharing in the area of the extended continental shelf, whether or not our submission is recognized. We might also include some of the arguments about pollution laws to make sure that we and only we control our pollution laws and not some other government. We can do certain things with our own sovereignty. On Article 234, I think we can take the best of Article 234 by working with coastal nations in the Arctic to establish a seaway.[7]

In addition, I think we need to address the International Seabed Authority (ISA) issues straight up. If you peel back the onion to understand why the United States is not acceding to the treaty, many conservative opponents have said, "we're not going to vote for this thing" because of the ISA. Accurately, they say, the ISA can "tax" activity by a nation in its ECS and require sharing of those revenues with all treaty members. (In principle, this means funds collected under the Law of the Sea could be used to support states that engage in terrorism.) This appears to be among the biggest problems conservatives (including myself) have with the treaty. As I see it, the ISA is an artifact of that old, discredited idea pushed during Law of the Sea negotiations by the so-called Group of 77 that because the oceans are owned by everybody, the UN should control all our fish and offshore resources, collect rents their use, and divide the rents among the people of the world. Frankly, that wasn't going to work. We ended up shrinking that "common heritage" approach to just the deep international seabed, and giving coastal states control of their adjacent seas. The Group of 77 approach, embodied in the ISA, is a tax for global government. I think the US should say we spend enough money on the oceans, we'll match the rest of world on this, we're just not going to participate in the ISA. Now I don't know if that can be done legally or not, but I would think legal scholars

---

7 Treadwell, *supra*, note 5.

should have that discussion because that's the biggest objection that many people have now to Law of the Sea treaty in this country. Maybe it means going back to the States Party to the convention and saying, let's make this a more voluntary organization. I don't know. I don't believe the world needs the ISA the way the treaty created it, and that's what's kept the United States from doing the other things in the treaty.

Article 234 was about the only answer in the Convention to a coastal state's interest in controlling tanker traffic off of its shores. Article 234 provides that, in traditionally ice-covered areas, a costal state may control for pollution prevention and enforce its pollution laws within the EEZ, provided it does so on a non-discriminatory basis.

So in essence Canada and the United States have an informal agreement to disagree on the status of the Northwest Passage but to allow the coastal state a say in regulating vessels that pass through traditionally ice-covered areas. The United States takes the position that our vessels can sail in the Northwest Passage without seeking permission and have some side letters with Canada to that effect. On the strength of the Law of the Sea convention, we have agreed that that if an Arctic coastal state wants to prevent pollution by requiring double-hulled tankers and requiring vessels to have contingency plans or icebreaker escorts, it can. And we should: contingency planning means the locals get involved, contribute priorities and local knowledge before a spill, not in the fury that can begin in the middle of the night if a spill actually occurs. Current federal law makes sure that tanker owners have to talk to the locals before they bring a tanker full of something thru only if those tankers are coming or going to a U.S. port; LOS allows us to extend that requirement to all vessels – even itinerants using innocent passage – but the USA has not taken advantage of this provision.

Those are things that Arctic residents of all of the five coastal states, plus Iceland, tell us they want. It has been a frustration of mine that the United States has never put forward the idea of how it would use Article 234. Frankly, if we were to do this, I think it would have great impact on getting us to a seaway in the Arctic that would lead to much better economics for all of us.

Finally, I would point out that it is very important that the current negotiations on science access, which Canada began in its chairmanship of the Arctic Council and the United States is trying to finish in its chairmanship, go forward. As former Chair of the Arctic Research Commission (USARC), I know that we have sensors at the North Pole that have collected a great data set. If the ECS submission process ends up indicating that Russia (or Denmark) has ECS rights in the North Pole and if we happen to be 10 feet off position, we would very likely have to get that country's permission to keep that sensor

SUPPORT AND OPPOSITION

there. During the time I was chair of the USARC, Russia turned us down on their EEZ access for science well over a dozen times. It's very important that we get reciprocity in the Arctic Ocean at least and, ideally, in the all of world's oceans, so that access to our ocean for research in our EEZ or our ECS is available to everyone else. I thought it was interesting that Meacham also predicted that this will be used as a reason to vote against the convention. I hadn't read Meacham's report at the time I held off my vote at the USARC arguing for ratification of the treaty, and I honestly believe it's one of those important things we can do for mankind right now is to keep access to the oceans for science.

These, then, are my challenges to you, the bottom line is simply, that proponents can try to steamroll the conservatives who object to joining the convention. You may outlive individual opponents but I don't think you're going to outlive the skepticism that conservatives have about this treaty unless we address some of these issues. Thank you very much.

Responsible Resource Development in Alaska: A Developer's Perspective on the Red Dog Mine

Lisa Parker[a]

Thank you for inviting me today to the Eighth Polar Law Symposium. I understand this is the first time the Polar Law Symposium has been held on North American soil making me honored and humbled that you would invite me to share a few thoughts.

This is an exciting time for Alaska and the Arctic. If my father, Walt Parker, were alive he would be at every meeting engaging in as many of the issues as possible. And he would have wondered why President Obama hadn't met with him while visiting earlier this month.[1] While he is not here with us physically he is still providing guidance to many he mentored, taught and loved.

Alaska, its people, and its beauty offer many opportunities. As Alaskans we fight hard to make sure this land we love is protected while allowing us the ability to maintain our lifestyle. While people in Washington DC and others give the impression that Alaskans believe in 'rape, ruin, and run' this is far, far from the truth. We treasure this land upon which we live and enjoy every day, which is why we remain – to continue to work to protect the land and the resources, and provide for our people.

Many of us have seen great change occur over the years – this change has impacted communities all around the state – from the smallest village to large metropolitan areas like Anchorage. For the indigenous Alaskans who have been here thousands of years – the change they have seen has been staggering. As a lifelong resident even I have noticed change in our landscape – more people, more roads, more homes, less open space – at least here in the Anchorage

---

[a] Lisa Parker is a member of the University of Alaska Board of Regents and President of Parker Horn Company, Soldotna, Alaska. She served as Government and External Affairs Manager for Cominco Alaska (Teck) from 1984 to 1991.

[1] The US Department of State hosted, and President Barack Obama attended, the Conference on Global Leadership in the Arctic: Cooperation, Innovation, Engagement and Resilience (GLACIER), in Anchorage, Alaska on 31 August 2015. See http://www.state.gov/e/oes/glacier/index.htm, accessed 13 July 2016.

area where I grew up. In the early 1990's I moved with my family to the Kenai Peninsula. I commented to my young son to observe what the area looked like then for over the years he might notice changes in the landscape. And there has been change, but with change also comes growth and opportunity – positive growth if done properly.

I was privileged early in my career to have the opportunity to help in developing the renowned Red Dog Mine in Northwest Alaska and work with the people of the NANA region.[2]

I would like to share a bit of the history – from the developer's perspective about this amazing project that after 25 years "... continues to be an economic engine for this remote Arctic region and ensures sustainable benefits for the region and its people."[3] What NANA and its leaders envisioned in the early 1980's when it established the partnership with Cominco (now Teck) serves as a positive model for how responsible economic development can be done while residents maintain subsistence lifestyles.

As background, NANA selected the Red Dog Mine area as part of its land entitlement under the Alaska Native Claims Settlement Act. After the people of the NANA region decided they wanted to develop the mine, they solicited proposals from a number of different companies. In the end NANA, as the landowner, selected Cominco to be the mine developer and operator entering into what is today called a 'landmark agreement.' This agreement has served as a model for indigenous people not only in many regions of the Arctic but also in the southern hemisphere.

After the Cominco-NANA agreement was signed, there were many hurdles to overcome along with the normal things that must be completed when attempting to develop a project – like completion of an environmental impact statement and obtaining permits, lots of permits. Some of the hurdles that needed to be overcome included finding financing for a road, port, and mine site facility; negotiating with the State of Alaska about the possibility of providing financing for the transportation infrastructure; determining what was going to be the most appropriate route to get the mine concentrates from mine site to the determined delivery point; getting access through a relatively new National Monument, Cape Krustenstern, one of the new conservation system units set up under the 1980 Alaska National Interest Lands Conservation Act; and then there was a boundary issue.

---

2   NANA Regional Corporation, Inc. (NANA) is a Regional Alaska Native corporation formed in 1971 under the Alaska Native Land Claims Settlement Act (ANCSA).
3   Petroleum News, North of 60 Mining News, 20 September 2015.

As I have learned from my friends in the Arctic, if you work together things can and will get accomplished. The respect and traditions I acquired from my Iñupiat friends I utilize every day.

The development of the Red Dog mine is a prime example of how, with collaboration and cooperation complex issues can be resolved. As I mentioned earlier, it began with the signing of the agreement in 1982 between Cominco and NANA. In general the agreement establishes targets for shareholder training and employment, provides preference for NANA subsidiaries, and established some key committees including the Subsistence Committee and the Management Committee consisting of senior management from NANA and Cominco.

This was followed by collaborating with the State of Alaska. Under the direction of Governor Bill Sheffield and with the approval of the Alaska State Legislature, the Alaska Industrial Development Authority[4] was given the ability to provide financing for the road and port facilities.[5] At the time Cominco did not have the financial resources to support the development of the entire project – road, port, and mine site facilities. The financial package, to provide a loan for the transportation infrastructure, was instrumental in making Red Dog a reality. The loan has been paid back and Red Dog continues to pay annual user fees to the State of Alaska for use of the DeLong Mountain Transportation System.

After completion of the environmental impact statement, the best route to get from Red Dog to the Chukchi Sea was through Cape Krusenstern National Monument. NANA, in working with the Congressional delegation, was successful in getting Congress to grant NANA a 100-year easement through Cape Krusenstern. I remember asking a friend of mine at NANA following passage "What happens after 100 years?" The response was "I'll be dead. Someone else will have to deal with it."

When the North Slope Borough was established in the early 1970's the Arctic Circle defined the southern boundary of the Borough. To my knowledge, that didn't create any conflict until NANA decided to develop its land at Red Dog. After considerable discussion the North Slope Borough agreed to adjust its boundaries by providing the land in the Red Dog region to the future Northwest Arctic Borough. While not required NANA and the North Slope resolved their issues before formal action was taken by the State's Local

---

4 The authority's name was expanded in subsequent years to the Alaska Industrial Development & Export Authority.
5 DeLong Mountain Transportation System.

Boundary Commission.[6] In Alaska it is the Local Boundary Commission that is empowered to create and alter municipal boundaries. During this stretch I remember it took time and on occasions it appeared Red Dog might remain part of the North Slope Borough. In the end the two regions agreed and the Local Boundary Commission approved the establishment of the Northwest Arctic Borough in 1987. The Northwest Arctic Borough boundaries are identical to the NANA regional corporation boundaries.

The final issue to resolve was what would be the taxes levied by the new borough on the mine. Instead of levying a tax, an agreement was reached with the borough for payment in lieu of taxes. The original policy stated that the borough would not enact an ordinance creating a property, income, production, or severance tax on operations or activities for a period of 14 years. Today the mine still makes payment in lieu of taxes.

It was only through collaboration and cooperation by many – Cominco (Teck), NANA, North Slope Borough, Governor Sheffield, Alaska State Legislature, the U.S. Congress, the Local Boundary Commission and residents of the NANA region – that development of this world class mine occurred. Initial ground breaking ceremonies took place at the Red Dog Port Site on July 3, 1986. In the span of 3 ½ years, in what I believe was remarkable time, everything that needed to be done to make this mine operational occurred.

During that time the facilities that were put in place included a port, a 52-mile road and all the necessary mine and port facilities. When I began working for Cominco in 1984 many in Alaska thought Red Dog would never become a reality. Five years later first concentrates were produced with over 50% of the employees Iñupiat from nearby villages in the NANA region.

Simultaneous to the construction of the road, port and mine facilities was the construction of two dams at the mine. A water dam for drinking water and a tailings dam to retain run off from the surrounding area. An interesting point: prior to the operation at Red Dog, fish could not survive in Red Dog Creek because of the natural run off from the mineralized hills. Cominco collects the run off from the surrounding area and diverts it into the tailings impoundment treating to drinking water standards prior to discharge. As a result, today Red Dog Creek supports healthy populations of Arctic Grayling and Dolly Varden trout.

The Red Dog Mine is something unique that was accomplished and has not been replicated. The agreement that was established 33 years ago continues and the relationship is strong. Red Dog serves as a model for how development can occur with the support and input from local communities. The NANA

---

6   The Local Boundary Commission was created by the Constitution of the State of Alaska.

region is one of the most economically and culturally unified political subdivisions in Alaska.

During a 25th anniversary celebration last year Teck's CEO stated "[t]he Red Dog partnership has set the standard for how resource development can create economic prosperity and opportunity while at the same time supporting tradition, culture, and heritage."[7]

Alaska and the Arctic are facing challenging times but I believe through cooperation, collaboration, and partnerships we can succeed and will be stronger. If we use the model developed and implemented by NANA and Cominco (Teck) there is no reason we won't succeed. As Mayor Reggie Joule said at the recent GLACIER conference, "[w]e have learned with diligence and oversight that you can balance resource development and still have the animals and the fish and the plants flourish."[8]

---

7   25th Anniversary of Red Dog, http://www.teck.com/news/stories/2015/25th-anniversary-of -red-dog, accessed 13 July 2016.

8   Shane Lasley, 'Mining News: Setting the standard. Teck continues to be recognized for its commitment to sustainable mining,' in *North of 60 Mining News*, Vol. 20 (38), Week of 20 September 2015, http://www.petroleumnews.com/pntruncate/355003928.shtml, accessed 13 July 2016.

Research Articles

∴

THE YEARBOOK OF POLAR LAW VIII (2016) 27–55

Respectful Neighbourliness: The United Kingdom's Arctic Approach

Rachael Lorna Johnstone[a]

Abstract

The United Kingdom has a longstanding interest in the Arctic and has recently begun to develop a set of guiding principles for its engagement in the region. Although the UK has a great deal to offer in terms of scientific research and expertise, it is missing an opportunity to engage more fully with issues of importance to the Arctic region.

Keywords

Arctic Council – Observer States – Non-Arctic States – British Arctic policy

1 Introduction

Notwithstanding a longstanding interest in Arctic exploration and scientific research, the United Kingdom (UK)[1] has been slow to develop a coordinated approach to the Arctic. Three different grand institutions of the State have recently sought to develop a set of priorities for British Arctic engagement: the Environmental Audit Committee of the House of Commons (EAC) in *Protecting the Arctic* 2012; the Government with *Adapting to Change: UK policy towards the Arctic* (2013); and the House of Lords Arctic Committee (HLAC) in

---

a Professor of Law, University of Akureyri, Iceland and University of Greenland. Email: rlj@unak.is.

1 The term 'UK' refers to the United Kingdom of Great Britain and Northern Ireland, and consists of four countries: England, Northern Ireland, Scotland, and Wales. The adjective 'British' is used to indicate matters pertaining to the whole UK (*i.e.*, including Northern Ireland).

© KONINKLIJKE BRILL NV, LEIDEN, 2017 | DOI 10.1163/22116427_008010005

Responding to a Changing Arctic (2015).[2] While some common concerns can be identified through the three reports, in particular climate change, there is no consensus on how these concerns should be addressed and no single set of principles to lead British Arctic cooperation.

This article will begin with a short introduction to British engagement in the Arctic before analysing each of the three reports in turn in light of the respective constitutional roles of their authors. The final section positions the British approach in light of the broader role that non-Arctic States play in Arctic relations and reviews the main emphases and implications of the British reports, as well as apparent gaps. The title derives from the emphasis of the Government on 'respect' and its self-identification as the Arctic's 'nearest neighbour,' the latter theme having been developed by the HLAC. The article tentatively concludes that: the stated policies of the current government are formulated as a response to the new criteria for observership at the Arctic Council; the UK has a great deal to offer in terms of scientific research and expertise but is missing an opportunity to support search and rescue in the Arctic; the priorities of the current government are mostly commercial in nature and promote 'responsible development' rather than 'sustainable development'; adaptation is preferred to mitigation of climate change; the sovereignty of Arctic States is a convenient foil against British responsibility for protection of the environment, respect for human rights and the rights of indigenous peoples, and prevention of corporate abuses; Scotland has been marginalised in the official British Arctic discourse; and although the UK has a number of interests in the Arctic, the region is not a priority as it faces stiff competition from British interests elsewhere.

2 British Engagement in the Arctic

British exploits in the Arctic stretch at least as far back as the British whaling voyages of the 16th century, the expeditions of explorers such as Franklin or the rather more successful John Rae in the 19th century, and the colonisation

---

2 United Kingdom, House of Commons Environmental Audit Committee, *Protecting the Arctic* Volume I, HC 171, London, The Stationery Office, Ltd., 2012 (EAC 2012); United Kingdom, HM Government, *Adapting to Change: UK policy towards the Arctic*, London, The Stationery Office, Ltd., 2013 (HM Government 2013); United Kingdom, House of Lords Select Committee on the Arctic, *Responding to a Changing Arctic*, HL Paper 118, London, The Stationery Office, Ltd., 2015 (HLAC 2015).

of Canada.[3] Strong historic and cultural ties exist also between the Nordic countries and the North of Scotland.[4] Yet when evaluating the UK's relevance in Arctic relations, of more significance are contemporary linkages and interactions, not least through the Arctic Council system; collaboration in Arctic science; and through the geography of interdependent climate, ocean currents, and ecosystems.

The UK participated in the Arctic Environmental Protection Strategy (AEPS) as an observer in a rather vague and *ad hoc* system before becoming one of the original observer States at the Arctic Council.[5] British researchers and research institutes have been active contributors in the working groups though perhaps not as active as they could be, owing to lack of committed funding.[6] The UK is also an observer at the Barents–Euro Arctic Council and the British National Environmental Research Council is a founding participant in the International Arctic Science Committee.

Nevertheless, despite British interest in and interests in the Arctic stretching back for centuries, the UK had not attempted to develop a coherent policy or strategy in respect of the region until 2013. The Arctic has always been overshadowed by more urgent concerns in other regions of the World where the UK plays an influential role: Commonwealth countries in Africa, Asia, and the Caribbean; Europe; and the Middle East.

A Polar Regions Unit was established within the Foreign and Commonwealth Office (FCO) in 1943. It was retitled as a 'department' around 2013 and is headed by Jane Rumble.[7] Its eight staff are ostensibly engaged at both Poles.[8] In practice, it is more focused on the Antarctic where the British tenaciously maintain their sovereignty ambitions. The Polar Regions Department is extremely low key and does not even have its own website.

Of the seven ministers within the FCO, one has responsibility for the Polar Regions. However, to indicate the gravitas of this portfolio, the same minister

---

3 *See* Alyson Bailes, "The Arctic's Nearest Neighbour? An Evaluation of the UK's 2013 Arctic Policy Document," *Arctic Yearbook* (2014): 381–383; Duncan Depledge and Klaus Dodds, "The UK and the Arctic: The Strategic Gap," *The Rusi Journal* 156(3) (2011): 73–74 for summaries.

4 Rachael Lorna Johnstone, "An Arctic Strategy for Scotland," *Arctic Yearbook* (2012): 116–117.

5 Malgorzata Śmieszek and Paula Kankaanpää, "Observer States' Commitments to the Arctic Council: the Arctic Policy Documents of the United Kingdom and Germany as Case Study," *Yearbook of Polar Law* 6 (2014): 378.

6 *Ibid.*, 384; *see also* HLAC 2015, *supra*, note 2, 99 and 104; and *see* text below at notes 102–103.

7 It remains a 'unit' in the EAC 2012 report, but is a 'department' in the HM Government 2013 report. The change in moniker was based on some internal restructuring within the FCO and had no substantive implications for staffing, budget or mandate.

8 EAC 2012, *supra*, note 2, 62.

is responsible also for overseas territories; conflict issues; consular affairs; protocol; ministerial oversight for FCO services; the Caribbean; Illegal Wildlife Trade; and the whole of Africa.[9] The incumbent's background and experience is notably lacking in any Arctic (or Antarctic) focus.[10]

In terms of visible presence on the diplomatic Arctic circuit, one can look back to 2013 and the first Arctic Circle meeting in Reykjavík to which there were three official British delegates. Responding to questions about this humble showing, the UK rather overcompensated in 2014. A team of sixty arrived, ten of whom spoke at the UK's 90 minute plenary while they filled the huge overhead in the meeting hall with the Union flag and planted three smaller (comparatively) Union flag-emblazoned banners on the stage proclaiming: "Technology is GREAT Britain"; "Science is GREAT Britain"; and "Business is GREAT Britain" respectively.[11] The British Ambassador to Iceland proudly declared to 1500 participants: "The British are here!"[12] The plenary was followed by an official British breakout session and through the three-day conference, the delegates wandered about amiably, ostentatiously bearing a red poppy over monochrome dark suits to ensure their affiliation was not in doubt.[13]

The UK reverted to a more modest contribution in 2015 with a fifteen-minute plenary in which only the British Ambassador and one representative from the FCO appeared; no flags were in evidence and it was too early in October for even the most patriotic to boast a poppy.[14]

3 Recent British Arctic Policy

In 2008, the Ministry of Defence prepared an Arctic Strategy but its contents are unknown.[15] Almost certainly devoted exclusively to 'hard security' issues,

---

9   "Parliamentary Under Secretary of State at the Foreign and Commonwealth Office," UK Government, Foreign and Commonwealth Office, accessed November 26, 2015, https://www.gov.uk/government/ministers/parliamentary-under-secretary-of-state--23.

10 *Ibid.*

11 "United Kingdom Country Session," Arctic Circle 2014, accessed November 26, 2015, https://vimeo.com/113049777.

12 *Ibid.*

13 "2014 Assembly Program," Arctic Circle 2014, accessed November 26, 2015, http://arctic circle.org/sites/arcticcircle/themes/ac/pdf/2014%20Program%20October%2030.pdf.

14 "2015 Assembly Program," Arctic Circle 2015, accessed November 26, 2015, http://arctic circle.org/sites/arcticcircle/files/2015ArcticCircleProgram01.pdf.

15 Baroness Ann Taylor, Speech delivered by the Minister for International Defence and Security, Joint NATO/Icelandic Government conference (Security Prospects in the High

the strategy was never published. The publicly released 2010 Strategic and Military Defence Review contained nothing on the Arctic.[16] Since then, reforms to the military over the past 5 years compromised the British Arctic capacity for security and search and rescue. The only maritime patrol aircraft were decommissioned in 2010 and two of the three air force bases in Scotland were closed. However, the most recent National Security Strategy and Strategic Defence and Security Review, published in November 2015, committed to the purchase of nine Boeing P-8 patrol aircraft (absent any competitive tender process or consideration of alternative suppliers) to be stationed in Scotland.[17]

Klaus Dodds and Duncan Depledge, of The Royal United Services Institute (RUSI), published a paper in 2011, arguing that it was time for a coordinated and formalised UK Arctic Strategy. The present author followed up in 2012 with a study of Scotland's unique Arctic interests and the potential benefits and pitfalls of a Scottish–Arctic strategy.[18]

While the British Government remained quiet, it was the EAC that undertook an investigation and consultation, publishing their report: *Protecting the Arctic* in 2012.[19] The Government delivered an official response in 2013, then swiftly released its own policy document, *Adapting to Change*.[20] The House of Lords established in turn its own Select Committee on the Arctic in 2014 (HLAC) which delivered its report, *Responding to a Changing Arctic*, in February of 2015 and the Government replied officially in July.[21]

North) Reykjavík, Iceland, January 29, 2009), accessed November 25, 2015, http://web archive.nationalarchives.gov.uk/+/http:/www.mod.uk/DefenceInternet/AboutDefence/People/Speeches/MinISD/20090129JointNatoicelandicGovernmentConference securityProspectsInHighNorthReykjavicIceland.htm.

16   United Kingdom, HM Government, Securing Britain in an Age of Uncertainty: The Strategic Defence and Security Review. CM 7948, London, The Stationery Office, Ltd, 2010.

17   United Kingdom, HM Government, *National Security Strategy and Strategic Defence and Security Review 2015*. CM 9161, London, The Stationery Office, Ltd, 2015, para. 4.49.

18   Johnstone, *supra*, note 4.

19   EAC 2012, *supra*, note 2.

20   United Kingdom, House of Commons Environmental Audit Committee, *Protecting the Arctic: Government Response to the Committee's Second Report of Session 2012–13*, HC 858, London, The Stationery Office, Ltd., 2013 (HM Government EAC Response 2013); HM Government 2013, *supra*, note 2.

21   HLAC 2015, *supra*, note 2; United Kingdom, HM Government, Government Response to the House of Lords Select Committee Report HL 118 of Session 2014–15: Responding to a Changing Arctic, CM 9093, London, The Stationery Office, Ltd., 2015 (HM Government HLAC Response 2015).

The titles already indicate diverging approaches. The EAC emphasises *protection*: perhaps unsurprising for a committee devoted to environmental concerns. In the report itself, efforts to *mitigate* climate change in the Arctic are prioritised, including reducing black carbon but most prominently, a call for a moratorium on Arctic hydrocarbons. The Government policy points to *adaptation* and a closer look suggests they want to 'adapt' to new business opportunities. The HLAC emphasises *response* which sounds more passive than *adapt* and implies that the UK should be following the lead from the Arctic, rather than taking the lead. However, a closer look at the substance of the report suggests a more ambitious and pro-active approach.

In all three reports, climate change is the lens through which the challenges facing the Arctic are viewed. However, while the EAC sought a cautious and precautionary approach to Arctic development, the Government and to a lesser extent, the Lords, were more eager to explore the opportunities presented to British interests.

3.1   *Protecting the Arctic* (*EAC*)

Select committees are appointed from and by the members of Parliament. They can be House of Commons, House of Lords, or joint committees with members from both Houses. There is even a select committee called the Committee of Selection whose job it is to select the members to sit on the other select committees.[22] The composition of select committees should mirror that of the House of Commons, *i.e.*, the largest parties in the House of Commons have the most seats on each select committee. Chairs are elected by the entire House of Commons but vote-trading and agreements between the various party whips mean that the committee chairs are shared between the parties proportionately to their respective numbers of members (MPs).

The EAC is a House of Commons committee and all of its members are sitting members of Parliament in that House. The Arctic report is based on an extensive inquiry, the title of which was also *Protecting the Arctic*, indicating the likely direction and emphasis on environmental protection even before any evidence was collected. During its inquiry, its chair was Labour MP Joan Walley.

Protecting the Arctic, has three main substantive chapters: Chapter Two: "The Impact of Climate Change on the Arctic"; Chapter Three: "The Risks to the Arctic from Increased Development"; and Chapter Four: "Governance

---

22   The members of the Committee on Selection is not selected in this manner but are elected by the entire House of Commons and, in practice, they are the party whips plus a chairperson from the ruling party.

of the Arctic". The approach of the EAC is to mainstream the principles of the Rio Declaration in British policy, both domestically and in international cooperation.[23] It pushes for efforts to mitigate rather than simply accept climate change, including, for example, measures to reduce emissions from shipping.[24]

The big headline is the call for a moratorium on further Arctic hydrocarbon development.[25] This is based on the aforementioned concerns to mitigate climate change and the ostensible impossibility of exploiting Arctic hydrocarbons while meeting the 2°C degree target.[26] According to the EAC, the moratorium should last until such time as the following are in place:

- Strengthened regulatory regimes; reducing the acceptable to risk to 'as low as possible' rather than 'as low as reasonably practicable';
- A pan-Arctic oil spill response standard;
- A strong civil liability regime;
- 'Peer-review' between hydrocarbon firms of operations and action plans;
- Further research on oil spill clean-up in the Arctic; and
- A 'sanctuary' over at least part of the Arctic.

However, even if the criteria set out by the EAC are met before offshore oil and gas activities proliferate, none of them answer the question of meeting the 2°C warming threshold.

The proposal for the sanctuary is a headline-grabber in its own right and is developed later in the report.[27] The report is rather vague on the point but given that there are already various kinds of reserves in the Arctic today and that the UK has limited options to influence decisions regarding sovereign territory, one must assume that the EAC intends a new marine sanctuary of some sort. There are already a number of protected areas onshore and offshore in the Arctic under the jurisdiction of the Arctic States.[28] The EAC suggests that the UK promote such an outcome through the Arctic Council, giving a

---

23   EAC 2012, *supra*, note 2, 5; *see also* "Rio Declaration on Environment and Development" *International Legal Materials* 31 (1992): 876.

24   EAC 2012, *supra*, note 2, 21–22.

25   *Ibid.*, 46–7.

26   *Ibid.*, 30.

27   *Ibid.*, 60–62.

28   *See* CAFF, "Protected Areas Index," Arctic Council, accessed November 26, 2015, http://www.caff.is/indices-and-indicators/protected-areas-index; and PAME, *Framework for a Pan-Arctic Network of Marine Protected Areas*, Akureyri, PAME International Secretariat, Arctic Council, 2015, Annex IV.

sense that it does not quite understand what the Arctic Council does – and does not do – or the UK's influence at that forum.[29] The UK's influence at the Arctic Council is predominantly through the working groups and it could (with a little more investment and coordination) support the scientific research into sensitive marine areas, or vulnerable marine species. For example, the Protection of the Marine Environment working group (PAME) has recently developed a framework for MPAs in the Arctic but any decisions to create these are fully within the domestic jurisdiction of the Arctic States.[30] PAME's framework does not address the area beyond national jurisdiction which is under review by the International Maritime Organisation (IMO). On shipping, the EAC champions 'sustainable development,' promotes a robust Polar Code (at that time, still being negotiated), and proposes the designation of particularly sensitive sea-areas (PSSAS) under MARPOL in the Arctic.[31]

The EAC likewise overestimates British influence in discussion of fisheries management. While recognising that Arctic fisheries are under coastal State jurisdiction, it proposes that "as an observer on the Arctic Council, the Government should also seek to influence Arctic states to regulate their fisheries sustainably."[32] Even if the Arctic Council were the right forum for such discussions, the Norwegians and the Icelanders may not take kindly to lectures from the British on fisheries management.[33] The UK is twice removed from Arctic fisheries management. First, as long as the UK remains in the EU, fisheries are managed through the Common Fisheries Policy and the UK does not negotiate or sit on regional fisheries management organisations in its own name but is represented through the EU institutions. Second, neither the British government nor the EU can have much influence on existing Arctic fisheries that are all well within the exclusive jurisdiction of the Arctic coastal States (*i.e.*, the 200nm exclusive economic zones).

The final headline from the EAC is that the British Government develop a formal 'Arctic Strategy' in consultation with the eight Arctic States.[34] Uniquely for Arctic Strategies, the EAC recommend that the UK's approach be built around the Rio Declaration and address, *inter alia*:

---

29   EAC 2012, *supra*, note 2, 62.

30   PAME, *supra*, note 28, 5.

31   *Ibid.*, 53 and International Convention for the Prevention of Marine Pollution from Ships, November 2, 1973, 1340 U.N.T.S. 62 (MARPOL).

32   EAC 2012, *supra*, note 2, 55.

33   *See also* text below at note 75.

34   EAC 2012, *supra*, note 2, 66–69.

RESPECTFUL NEIGHBOURLINESS

- The application of science and research to increase British influence on Arctic matters;
- A policy to ensure that hydrocarbon activities in the Arctic take place only once the criteria specified by the EAC (above) are met;
- The establishment of a sanctuary, excluded from hydrocarbon development;
- The protection of the Arctic from negative impacts of shipping through IMO, United Nations, and Arctic Council channels and supporting British investment in sustainable shipping in the Arctic;
- A commitment to sustainable fisheries management in the Arctic;
- The potential for a broader Arctic forum, under the United Nations;
- Interaction with Citizens Advisory Councils to allow local persons to participate in decision-making regarding hydrocarbon activity in the Arctic; and
- The potential for 'grand bargains' with other States on environmental issues.[35]

These are certainly not all considerations that would normally be found in a strategy.

The EAC clearly prioritised environmental protection which is hardly surprising in a committee dedicated to environmental affairs and built its work around the Rio Declaration. At times in the report, the EAC approached environmental protection without sufficient nuance and sensitivity to the peoples already in the Arctic and the current state of development, stating boldly (and wrongly) that, "[t]he Arctic region is one of the last true wildernesses on Earth."[36] This exemplifies a general conflation in the report of 'the Arctic' as one homogenous (and empty) zone.

3.2 Protecting the Arctic: the Government's Response

The Government made a formal response to the report in January 2013 rejecting outright the EAC's more ambitious proposals for environmental protection in the Arctic.[37] While supportive of efforts to reduce black carbon ship-source pollution through the IMO and European Union (EU),[38] the reply insists that energy security be prioritised over the calls for a moratorium on Arctic oil and gas.[39] Cautious regarding PSSAs or other zones with enhanced protection against pollution from shipping, the Government prefers to pursue a

35   *Ibid.*, 68–69.
36   *Ibid.*, 11.
37   HM Government EAC Response 2013, *supra*, note 20.
38   *Ibid.*, 4.
39   *Ibid.*, 5.

new implementing agreement under the Convention on the Law of the Sea (UNCLOS)[40] in respect of areas beyond national jurisdiction which may – after many, many years of negotiations – facilitate some kind of marine protected areas in the Arctic High Seas.[41] The Government is also deferential to Arctic State sovereignty. This is no mere exaggerated British politeness but a shrewd strategy that also ensures that it is the Arctic States that bear responsibility for the difficult things like consultation with local populations, environmental protection, liability regimes, and clean-up.[42] Their sovereignty: their responsibility. The Government has a more realistic understanding of the Arctic Council's reach and rejects the EAC's proposal to use that forum to pursue special fisheries management measures. The government instead emphasises the primary responsibility of the coastal States under whose jurisdiction the fisheries remain.[43]

The Government states its reluctance to develop an Arctic strategy *per se*, but commits to publication of an official Arctic Policy Framework.[44]

The EAC was openly 'disappointed' with the Government's response although it welcomes the plan to develop and publish the Arctic Policy Framework.[45] The EAC takes this as an invitation to reply and indicates that their comments should be taken into account in the development of the Framework.[46] They were not.

3.3 *Adapting to Change: UK Policy Towards the Arctic (Government)*

The official government Arctic policy paper, *Adapting to Change: UK Policy Towards the Arctic* was released in September 2013. It does not refer to the earlier EAC report. It was developed without any formal consultation with civil society.[47] It is not presented online amongst the twenty-two published 'policies' of the FCO but it is difficult to know if this is an oversight or rather

---

40 United Nations Convention on the Law of the Sea 1982, December 10, 1982, 1833 U.N.T.S. 397 (UNCLOS).

41 HM Government EAC Response 2013, *supra* note 20, 6 and 8–10.

42 *Ibid.*, 5–8.

43 *Ibid.*, 12.

44 *Ibid.*, 13–14; and HM Government 2013, *supra* note 2.

45 United Kingdom House of Commons Environmental Audit Committee, *Protecting the Arctic: The Government's response*, HC 333, London, The Stationery Office, Ltd., 2013 (EAC Response to Government Response 2013) 3–4 and 15.

46 *Ibid.*, 4.

47 *Ibid.*, 15.

reflects its lowly status within the FCO machinery.[48] The UK was the first of the observer States to publish or revise an Arctic policy following the agreement of new expectations regarding observers. At the Kiruna meeting in May 2013, the Arctic Council had both doubled the number of observer States and confirmed the clearer criteria for observership that had been proposed at the Nuuk ministerial in 2011. These include four-yearly reviews of observer contributions.[49]

The preposition of the UK's title is telling: the UK does not presume to be an Arctic actor but rather modestly looks *towards* the Arctic. The paper contains a lot of glossy pictures but is rather short on both descriptive and prescriptive content. It was expertly analysed by Alyson Bailes in 2014 but a review is necessary to set the scene for an examination of the HLAC report and to reach some general conclusions regarding the approaches of the three distinct organs of government.[50] The Government's policy paper is cautious in tone, sending a message to the Arctic States that there is nothing to fear from (continuing) British engagement in Arctic affairs.

It is in *Adapting to Change* that the UK is first presented as the Arctic's 'nearest neighbour' – a theme that is later pursued by the HLAC. The Government emphasises its contributions to Arctic science, bows to the sovereignty of the Arctic States, and is meek on military and defence issues.[51] It sets itself apart from the five Asian upstarts and Italy that had newly been admitted as Arctic Council observers by highlighting its longstanding participation as "an active and engaged Observer of the Arctic Council since its inception in 1996...."[52] However, despite the analysis by Dodds of British attempts to present the UK as a 'model observer,' it was Korea that the President of Iceland allegedly singled out as a 'model observer' in June of 2015.[53] (It is more likely that the President

---

48   "Policies" UK Government, Foreign and Commonwealth Office, accessed November 26, 2015, https://www.gov.uk/government/policies?organisations%5B%5D=foreign-common wealth-office.

49   *See Arctic Council Rules of Procedure*, as adopted by the Arctic Council at the First Arctic Council Ministerial Meeting, Iqaluit, Canada, Revised by the Arctic Council at the Eighth Arctic Council Ministerial Meeting, Kiruna Sweden, accessed November 26, 2015, https://oaarchive.arctic-council.org/handle/11374/940.

50   Bailes, *supra* note 3.

51   HM Government 2013, *supra* note 2, *e.g.*, 7, 10, 16, 22 and 29.

52   *Ibid.*, 13.

53   Klaus Dodds, "Adapting to Change: UK Policy Towards the Arctic" *Geopolitics & Security: Critical perspectives from Royal Holloway*, October 17, 2013, accessed November 26, 2015, https://rhulgeopolitics.wordpress.com/2013/10/17/adapting-to-change-uk-policy-towards -the-arctic-2/; HE Yun Byung-se, Minister of Foreign Affairs of the Republic of Korea, Dinner Remarks at the Commemorative Event to Mark 2nd Anniversary of ROK's

was blissfully unaware that the UK had first dibs on this moniker rather than that he made a deliberate attempt to snub the UK).

The UK policy accepts climate change as fact – not an unusual position in a European State but by no means guaranteed in the highest echelons of the British Government these days.[54] However, unlike the EAC, there is no proposal to mitigate. Further departing from the EAC approach, the Government policy supports 'responsible development,' a concept that is left undefined but is certainly not synonymous with 'sustainable development.'[55]

The 'vision' of UK Arctic engagement is wound around three themes: respect, leadership, and cooperation.[56] Respect is the leading concept here and is hammered home repeatedly.[57] Respect is further broken down into three sub-themes:

- *Respect for the sovereign rights of the Arctic States to exercise jurisdiction over their territory;*
- *Respect for the views and interests of people who live and work in the Arctic and call it home;*
- *Respect for the environment, its fragility and its central importance to the global climate.*[58]

The phrasing of the first sub-theme is careless and misleading. It suggests on the one hand that the Arctic States only enjoy sovereign *rights* in their territory when in law they hold *sovereignty* – a much more extensive concept. On the other hand, it is silent as to respect for the *sovereign rights* that States have in their exclusive economic zones and continental shelves beyond territorial waters; these are not technically State *territory*. (In fairness, this may only be

---

Accession to Arctic Council, July 7, 2015, accessed November 26, 2015, http://www.mofa .go.kr/webmodule/htsboard/template/read/engreadboard.jsp?typeID=12&boardid=14137 &seqno=315432&c=&t=&pagenum=1&tableName=TYPE_ENGLISH&pc=&dc=&wc=&lu =&vu=&iu=&du=.

54   HM Government 2013, 3; *see* also, *e.g.*, Mehdi Hasan, "Why is Climate Change Denier Owen Paterson Still in His Job?" *Huffington Post*, November 2, 2014, accessed November 26, 2015, http://www.huffingtonpost.co.uk/mehdi-hasan/uk-floods-owen-paterson_b_4767153 .html.

55   HM Government 2013, *supra* note 2, 7; *see* also below note 113 (on definitions of sustainable development).

56   *Ibid.*, 7–8.

57   *See* also Bailes, *supra* note 3, 11 (suggesting the report contains "almost comically frequent assurances of 'respect'").

58   HM Government 2013, *supra* note 2, 7.

apparent to a pedantic international lawyer with politicians and international relations experts seeing only a general deference to Arctic States' powers.)

The second sub-theme is interesting in its generalised approach to the views and interests of 'people' not 'peoples' without the usual nod to the unique rights and interests of indigenous peoples. The implication is that "the views and interests of all people who live and work in the Arctic" are equal, whether they be indigenous, longstanding settler communities, or migrant workers. International and constitutional law say otherwise. It is not until the following chapter that two paragraphs appear on 'indigenous peoples' (sic): so general that they appear almost *cliché*.[59] "The UK will respect the views, interests, culture and traditions of Arctic indigenous peoples and promote the participation of indigenous peoples in decision-making."[60] Nevertheless, participation should not be mistaken for endorsement of the principle of free, prior, and informed consent.[61]

Not having any recognised indigenous peoples of its own within the British Isles puts the UK in an awkward position *vis á vis* indigenous rights. It could, without any direct internal costs or obligations, support unambiguously the most progressive interpretations of indigenous rights.[62] However, its eagerness to demonstrate the requisite deference to Arctic *State* sovereignty makes it impossible to take a strong position as it can appear as an unwarranted interference with matters that some Arctic States continue to view as largely internal matters. The unqualified use of the plural form – *indigenous peoples* rather than *indigenous people* – suggests that there might be a softening of the British rejection of 'collective rights' of groups (including indigenous groups).[63] On the other hand, the drafters may have preferred simplicity and brevity over detailed and potentially contentious exposition in a policy document without legal force.

Respect for the environment can hardly trigger objections though the failure to engage at all with the EAC's report raises some questions about the genuineness of the government's commitment.

---

59   *Ibid.*, 14.
60   *Ibid.*
61   *Ibid.*
62   The UK has no recognised indigenous peoples but it has linguistic minorities in Scotland, Wales, Cornwall and Northern Ireland.
63   Compare United Nations General Assembly, Record of the 107th plenary meeting, September 13, 2007, UN Doc. A/61/PV.107 (in which the British ambassador to the United Nations uses the term 'indigenous peoples' with a lengthy qualifying explanation in the context of the adoption of the United Nations Declaration on the Rights of Indigenous Peoples).

On leadership, the UK pays homage to the Arctic States' pre-eminent role in Arctic governance but points to British influence through international bodies of significance in the Arctic; these include climate change negotiations, regulation of shipping, and management of black carbon.[64] The paper also emphasises British contributions to scientific research and involvement in industry and NGO participation.[65]

The section on cooperation is short and vague (a total of 56 words) and suggests little more than that the UK continue to 'cooperate' with Arctic States, indigenous peoples and unspecified 'others.'[66]

Unsurprisingly for an Arctic Council observer, the official policy is to support UNCLOS and the sovereign rights of the Arctic States (notwithstanding the imprecise wording noted above) and to back the Arctic Council as the key regional forum for Arctic issues.[67] Confirming its credentials as a 'good' observer, it rejects the call for a comprehensive Arctic Treaty which by 2013 was already a moot point.[68]

British military capacity is played down but stability in the Arctic region is a priority (as it presumably is for everyone else aside from arms manufacturers and nihilist terrorist organisations). The UK highlights the 'central' role of NATO as well as its own participation through the Arctic Security Forces Roundtable forum.[69] This short paragraph on security is discreetly tucked into the chapter rather misleadingly called 'the Human Dimension.' This chapter is in fact focused on State and institutional security rather than human security.[70]

The UK reiterates its support for a new implementing agreement under UNCLOS to protect the environment of areas beyond national jurisdiction that it earlier raised in its response to the EAC. It also supports in principle the possibility of marine protected areas under the OSPAR convention.[71] The UK, an archipelago with a long history of seafaring nations, is a leader in law of the sea both in scholarship and in policy development through, for example, the IMO.

Having already told the EAC that a moratorium on Arctic offshore oil and gas would not get British support, the Government again prioritises energy

---

64   HM Government 2013, *supra* note 2, 8, 18 and 25.

65   *Ibid.*, 8.

66   *Ibid.*

67   *Ibid.*, 13.

68   *Ibid.*, 14.

69   *Ibid.*, 13.

70   *See also* Bailes, *supra* note 3, 6–8.

71   *Ibid.*, 20 and Convention on the Protection of the Marine Environment of the North-East Atlantic, September 22, 1992, 2354 U.N.T.S. 67 (OSPAR); *see* also text above at note 41.

security.[72] However, while it recognises its ongoing dependence on the Norwegian oil and gas supply and supports, ostensibly for this reason, the development of Norwegian hydrocarbons, the Government then snubs Norway by 'strongly supporting' the International Whaling Commission's moratorium on commercial whaling.[73] It also rather bravely raises the seal product ban, stating that it 'implements' the EU directive (since revised) without wading into its merits.[74]

The Government is aware of its limited influence on Arctic fisheries management.[75] Some reference to Svalbard and differences of opinion regarding Norwegian jurisdiction and competing interpretations of the Spitsbergen Treaty could have been included here but the policy paper carefully circumvents potential disputes on this as most other sensitive issues (seal product ban and whaling moratorium aside). As a result, it iterates only the UK's internal 'overriding principle' of fisheries management that fishing activity be managed in light of precautionary and ecosystem-based approaches with only a nod to the desirability of 'cooperation between all interested States' that is presumably a subtle reference to the potential for fisheries in the Central Arctic Ocean.[76]

The time had come for the House of Lords to get in on the act.

3.4   *Responding to a Changing Arctic (House of Lords)*

The HLAC spent months in consultation through open written submissions and hearings with experts. The report takes up the theme of the UK as the Arctic's 'nearest neighbour,' using this expression six times. However, like the government policy paper, the HLAC report does not even reference the EAC report. The Lords' report is mostly descriptive – containing rather good, succinct analyses of geopolitical, economic and environmental trends and downplaying the 'conflict' narrative.[77] In general, it is a lot more ambitious than the government policy paper and promotes a much more active role for the UK in Arctic governance.

---

72   HM Government 2013, *supra* note 2, 24.

73   *Ibid.*, 20 and 24.

74   *Ibid.*

75   *See* text above at note 33.

76   HM Government 2013, *supra* note 2, 21.

77   *E.g.*, HLAC 2015, *supra* note 2, 47 (recognising the dual functions of 'military' investment in the Russian Arctic for NSR development and search and rescue).

The big headline from the report is the call for a British ambassador to the Arctic and a more conspicuous presence in Arctic geopolitics more generally.[78] An ambassador could coordinate the interests of different government departments and be a bridge between British scientific and commercial endeavours and their Arctic counterparts.[79] The HLAC proposes, with rather more gusto than anything in the government's rather timid policy, that "the UK should be positioned as the premier partner for Arctic states and other interests in Arctic cooperation."[80] It laments what it views as a reactive approach of the government to Arctic affairs, asks it to be "more strategic, better coordinated, and more self-confident and proactive" and suggests that British Arctic involvement could become marginalised by other States 'with less experience' but more direct approaches.[81] Almost certainly, China is at the forefront of these concerns.

The report reaches four main, broad conclusions: "the Arctic is strategically important for the UK"; "the Arctic has the potential to bring increasing benefits to the British economy"; the UK is geophysically connected to the Arctic through climate and weather; and it is connected through biodiversity and shared waters.[82]

The HLAC appears ruffled by the lowly status of observers within the Arctic Council system. In the report, the Lords requests the Arctic Council to make "observers such as the UK feel encouraged and incentivised to participate proactively".[83] It appeals to the Arctic Council not to become (remain?) an exclusive club, stating that: "The rest of the World has a legitimate interest in the Arctic...."[84] Foreshadowing the concerns it later expresses regarding the newcomers on the Arctic scene, it subtly implies that all observers are not equal and they might be treated differently for different purposes.[85]

The report's presentation of the climate change science is both clear and detailed and, like the government, the HLAC accepts climate change as fact and further warming as inevitable.[86] There is no concern with mitigation.[87]

---

78   *Ibid.*, 103.
79   *Ibid.*, 105.
80   *Ibid.*, 94.
81   *Ibid.*
82   *Ibid.*, 92–93.
83   *Ibid.*, 54.
84   *Ibid.*, 54–55.
85   *Ibid.*, 54.
86   *Ibid.*, 14–30.
87   *E.g., ibid.*, 17.

The examination of climate change impacts on the Arctic serves as the background to the social, economic, and environmental analyses that follow.

Departing from the EAC, the Lords points out that "the Arctic is not a pristine, untouched wilderness" though this is perhaps stretching the submission of Frances Wall who stated more cautiously: "[t]he first thing to say is that the Arctic is not necessarily pristine."[88] It is not necessarily all contaminated beyond repair either and there are vast wilderness areas that might still merit protection from human interference. Mirroring the government, the HLAC also avoids the use of 'sustainable development', preferring instead to promote the pursuit of "balanced and responsible economic development in the Arctic."[89]

Although describing the inadequacy of current knowledge and technology to recover spilled oil in the Arctic, the HLAC rejects a moratorium on Arctic drilling, suggesting rather a cautious approach. The report indicates a belief that the current, low hydrocarbon price will be sufficient to slow things down.[90] However, relying on market forces to govern Arctic oil and gas seems a risky game: just as they rapidly declined, so they can equally rapidly rise. The HLAC enthuses about mineral development in the Arctic and the benefits for indigenous populations through employment opportunities and local government income.[91] It supports British mining companies and advises them to "engage proactively and effectively with local residents" (indigenous or not) but does not refer to free, prior and informed consent and avoids any touchy questions about resource and land claims or even benefit sharing.[92]

The HLAC is realistic about commercial shipping possibilities, recognising that fewer miles does not necessarily equate to lower costs and it reflects on the dangers to insufficiently prepared cruise vessels and environmental impacts from heavy fuel oil, emissions and ballast water.[93] The Lords also recognises the IMO as the appropriate forum to address the environmental risks, in particular through the Polar Code.[94]

Search and rescue is lacking in the Arctic and the HLAC sees that this is an area in which the UK can take an active part and make a very welcome contribution.[95] However, defence organisation and procurement decisions

---

88   *Ibid.*, 70.
89   *Ibid.*, 73.
90   *Ibid.*, 76–78.
91   *Ibid.*, 78–80.
92   *Ibid.*, 80.
93   *Ibid.*, 80–87.
94   *Ibid.*, 86.
95   *Ibid.*, 87.

over the past five years have seriously hampered capability for British search and rescue in the Arctic. There is competence and experience but currently no maritime patrol aircraft since the NIMROD were taken out of service in 2010: "the UK is blind in the Arctic".[96] This message seems to have been heard by the government which promised nine new patrol aircraft in November 2015.[97] Search and rescue as well as oil spill preparation and clean-up are areas where the UK has extensive experience and substantial resources which could be of great benefit, especially in the North-Atlantic. Greenland and Iceland have vast areas of ocean to cover and almost no resources to do so. If the UK wants to find something to offer the Arctic, some way of putting itself on the Arctic map and highlighting its relevance, this is it.

The HLAC identifies the Arctic Ocean as a 'semi-enclosed sea' which will no doubt be welcomed by five Arctic Ocean littoral States (A5) as it bolsters their pretensions as its chief managers.[98] It also follows the A5 in supporting a moratorium on High Seas fishing in the Central Arctic Ocean and argues that the UK should be included in negotiations towards a regional fisheries management organisation (possibly through the EU).[99]

The HLAC recognises the significant scientific contribution of British institutions to Arctic research but proposes that it be better coordinated, including with the introduction of a new Arctic research programme.[100] The report reaches a fair conclusion that British scientific research in the Arctic (and indeed the Antarctic) is respected and valued.[101] Nevertheless, there is concern about poor British participation in Arctic Council working groups and this is, in part, related to insecurity of funding.[102] UK representatives had attended only two of eighteen working group meetings and seven of sixteen task force meetings.[103] Greater UK involvement in Arctic science requires investment

---

96   *Ibid.*, 87 and 109–110 (quoting Luke Coffey).

97   National Security Strategy 2015, *supra* note 17, 6.

98   HLAC 2015, *supra* note 2, 9.

99   *Ibid.*, 87–90.

100   *Ibid.*, 61 and 101. A new programme was meant to be announced at the end of October 2015 although it had not, at the time of writing, transpired: "Tip of the Iceberg" *International Innovation*, accessed November 26, 2015, http://www.international innovation.com/tip-of-the-iceberg-2/.

101   HLAC 2015, *supra* note 2, 94.

102   *Ibid.*, 99–104.

103   *Ibid.*, 104; *see also* Sebastian Knecht, "New Observers Queuing Up: Why the Arctic Council Should Expand – and Expel" *The Arctic Institute*, April 20, 2015. Accessed November 26, 2015, http://www.thearcticinstitute.org/2015/04/042015-New-Observers -Queuing-up.html.

RESPECTFUL NEIGHBOURLINESS   45

from the UK; but the HLAC report had earlier indicated that it did not feel the
British contributions were received with sufficient appreciation.[104] This then
leads to the aforementioned proposal for a more robust British Arctic presence, led by an ambassador and a fully formed strategy (albeit possibly under
another name) – "bolder [than the government policy] in presenting the UK as
a premier partner in the Arctic".[105] The report concludes by once more remind-
ing the reader that "the UK is the Arctic's nearest neighbour and the Arctic is
the UK's neighbourhood."[106]

3.5 Responding to a Changing Arctic (the Government's Response)

Before the government had the opportunity to formulate an official response, a
general election in May 2015 returned a Conservative overall majority and thus
removed the moderating influence of the Liberal Democrats from the government. When the response came, the government rejected the calls to appoint
an Arctic ambassador or to firm up a 'strategy'.[107] However, it did commit to
boosting British visibility in Arctic affairs by sending a UK delegation to all
the Arctic Council ministerial and Senior-Arctic-Official meetings and to be
present at major Arctic fora, including the Arctic Frontiers and Arctic Circle
meetings.[108]

   The government reiterates its respect for Arctic sovereignty by making
it "absolutely clear that overall leadership for Arctic stewardship rests primarily with all eight Arctic States and the people [sic] within those States."
Nevertheless, it once more affirms the UK's status as the Arctic's 'nearest neighbour' and sets itself apart from the newcomers through length of service, stating that: "The UK has been a full and active Observer to the Arctic Council
since its establishment in 1996."[109]

   Much of the response concerns industrial opportunities. The government
says: "Ensuring the sustainable development of the Arctic is part of the overall governance framework of the Arctic, which rests with the sovereign Arctic
States."[110] This a very carefully worded statement that manages to weave in the
popular language of sustainable development without actually promising to

---

104   HLAC 2015, *supra* note 2, 54–55: *see* text above at note 83.
105   *Ibid.*, 105–107.
106   *Ibid.*, 113.
107   HM Government HLAC Response 2015, *supra* note 21, 14.
108   *Ibid.*, 3–4.
109   *Ibid.*, 13.
110   *Ibid.*, 8; *see also* 3 (expressing satisfaction that the Arctic Council addresses environmen-
      tal protection and sustainable development).

do it: sustainable development is desirable but it is the responsibility of the Arctic Eight, not the UK. Rather, the UK government "is committed to promoting responsible commercial development."[111] It further explains this as "engagement with, and respect for, the local communities; respecting the environment in which the company intends to operate, including taking responsibility for their actions and preparing for the worst; understanding the risks to the environment and local communities; and sharing the understanding of the environment that they do have."[112] This is not sustainable development.[113]

Moreover, there is no recognition in this section of the rights of indigenous peoples over natural resources, the principle of free, prior and informed consent, or benefit sharing. The support the UK government expresses for involvement of indigenous peoples in 'decision-making' is tied to the Arctic Council and scientific research and in any case, is only support for 'participation' or 'cooperation'.[114] When it comes to resources, indigenous communities are subsumed into 'local communities' or (worse still) 'stakeholders'.[115]

---

111   *Ibid.*, 9.

112   *Ibid.*

113   *Compare, e.g.*, the definitions of sustainable development in the Brundtland Report: "development that meets the needs of the present without compromising the ability of future generations to meet their own needs": United Nations General Assembly Resolution 42/187, *Report of the World Commission on Environment and Development, 'Our Common Future,'* December 11, 1987, UN Doc. A/RES/42/187; and of the International Law Association: "The objective of sustainable development involves a comprehensive and integrated approach to economic, social and political processes, which aims at the sustainable use of natural resources of the Earth and the protection of the environment on which nature and human life as well as social and economic development depend and which seeks to realize the right of all human beings to an adequate living standard on the basis of their active, free and meaningful participation in development and in the fair distribution of benefits resulting therefrom, with due regard to the needs and interests of future generations.": International Law Association, *Sustainable Development: New Delhi Declaration of Principles of International Law Relating to Sustainable Development*, Resolution 3/2002 Annex, New Delhi, April 2002, preambular para. 13; and most recently of the United Nations General Assembly detailing 17 sustainable goals built upon its three dimensions: economic, social and environmental: United Nations General Assembly Resolution 70/1, *Transforming our World: the 2030 Agenda for Sustainable Development*, September 25, 2015, UN Doc. A/RES/70/1. *But see* HM Government HLAC Response 2015, *supra* note 2, 8 (where the "UK's commitment to sustainable development" is promoted in the context of scientific cooperation with indigenous communities) and 10 (where 'sustainable development' is referred to rather obliquely in respect of the mining industry).

114   HM Government HLAC Response 2015, *supra* note 21, 7–8.

115   *Ibid.*, Chapter 5.

RESPECTFUL NEIGHBOURLINESS   47

The management (and sustainability) of resource development, including hydrocarbons and minerals, is left very much in the hands of the Arctic States with the government only loosely supporting a few non-binding sets of corporate social responsibility guidelines.[116] UK Trade and Investment (the governmental department that supports British businesses investing abroad and seeks foreign investment in the UK) sees a role for itself in assisting British businesses in meeting any requirements set by Arctic States in order that they might be competitive.[117] It also seeks to promote British businesses in the Arctic and elsewhere, especially mining firms through 'UK mining capability messaging'.[118] This rather odd expression is found in no other government publication and presumably means marketing of British mining firms. UK Trade and Investment's assistance with regulatory compliance and 'encouragement of the highest standards' of corporate social responsibility are reduced to a 'UK unique selling point' when touting for Arctic business although they are also declared, without any real grounds, as "a clear demonstration of the UK's commitment to sustainable development both in the Arctic and elsewhere".[119]

Following general British policy on freedom of navigation, the government supports the IMO as the key forum for shipping regulation *vis á vis* protection of the marine environment and human safety.[120] It also views the IMO as the appropriate body to examine the need for marine protected areas in the Arctic high seas, most likely through an implementing agreement on areas beyond national jurisdiction.[121]

Search and rescue is a responsibility that "rests squarely with the Arctic States".[122] No doubt, this wording was meant to reiterate the polite deference to Arctic sovereignty and sovereign rights that permeates the response as well as the government's own policy. However, it comes across as rather blasé: the UK insists on the rights of its ships to sail in the Arctic but in the event of a crisis, it is the Arctic States and their populations who must come to their aid. As already mentioned, the UK has extensive resources and experiences to offer in the North Atlantic where they are sorely needed. It is possible that the 'discussions' to which the government modestly refers on Arctic search and

---

116   *Ibid.,* 9–10: these include the Voluntary Principles on Security and Human Rights in the Extractive Industries; the Extractive Industries Transparency Initiative; and the Equator Principles.

117   *Ibid.,* 10.

118   *Ibid.*

119   *Ibid.*

120   *Ibid.,* 11–12.

121   *Ibid.,* 12 and *see* text above at note 41.

122   *Ibid.*

rescue will evolve into meaningful cooperation. The nine P-8 aircraft that are on their way give the UK capacity to take this forward.[123] First and foremost committed to the protection of the nuclear deterrent (to be renewed and stationed in its existing Scottish base), these aircraft could also be put to use in civilian search and rescue operations. The rationale for the purchase is cased in 'hard security' terms, but their application in search and rescue is mentioned as an additional benefit.[124]

Notwithstanding the government's commitment in the reply to active participation in major Arctic conferences, the UK barely appeared at the 2015 Arctic Circle meeting, with a very modest 15 minute plenary in which the Ambassador to Iceland made a brief introduction and the Chief Scientific Adviser to the FCO presented a report on British Arctic research.[125] The governmental UK Science and Innovation Network and the Arctic Institute jointly hosted a breakout session that had no ostensible British focus.[126] Scotland had a more visible presence as an eclectic group of architects, artists, and a journalist hosted a breakout session inquiring into a 'Possible Arctic Scotland?'[127] It is impossible to determine whether the FCO made a concerted effort to tone down the British presence at the Arctic Circle or whether there was simply too much competition for space with the new observer States – some of whom hosted lavish functions for approximately 2000 attendees. Almost certainly, both factors were at play.

4   A Quiet, Respectful, Reliable Neighbour

Perhaps the biggest question of all is why a State should develop an Arctic strategy at all. What does it seek to gain from it? This is easier to answer for the Arctic States who developed their strategies in response to a perception of unwanted interference in their affairs, sought to defend their sovereignty and sovereign rights, and insisted that disputes, real or imagined, would be

---

123   *Ibid*; National Security Strategy 2015, *supra* note 17, 6.

124   "PM Pledges £178 Billion Investment in Defence Kit" UK Government, Prime Minister's Office, Press Release, November 23, 2015, accessed November 27, 2015, https://www.gov.uk/government/news/pm-pledges-178-billion-investment-in-defence-kit.

125   2015 Assembly Program, *supra* note 14.

126   *Ibid.*

127   *Ibid.* Neither the MEP nor the lecturer listed on the programme attended.

handled amongst themselves or through established legal processes.[128] There was a collective message of "We've got this!" and "Hands off!". More recently, the Kiruna rules for observers contain a veiled threat to recall the observer status of any entity that challenges the Arctic States' legitimate authority.[129] Observership was never officially 'permanent' and it would have taken only one Arctic State to exclude an observer either temporarily or permanently, but the language of 'permanent' observers was commonplace and until recently was used on the Arctic Council's own website.[130] The new criteria introduce a four-yearly review of each observer entity and clarify that observers are welcome only for as long as: they support the Arctic Council; they recognise the sovereignty and sovereign rights of Arctic States; they recognise the existing legal regime (especially law of the sea); they respect indigenous peoples and other Arctic inhabitants; they contribute, including financially, to indigenous participation; demonstrate interest and expertise of relevance to the Arctic Council; and they show interest and ability to support the Arctic Council, including through global institutions.[131]

Observer States must not be perceived as encroaching on domestic affairs or Arctic States' vested rights and powers. However, to maintain their observer status, they must at the same time demonstrate Arctic interests and expertise and ability to support the Arctic Council. In short, they must convince the Arctic States and permanent participants that they have more to offer than to gain from the Arctic. A succinct Arctic policy is a fairly direct and simple way to establish credentials.

Following the UK government, Germany and South Korea published their Arctic positions in November and December 2013 respectively.[132] France issued a tamely named 'Science plan 2015–2020 of the French Arctic Initiative' (a quasi-autonomous 'scientific monitor for the Arctic') in 2014 that expanded upon a 2012 report of the Institute for Ecology and Environment.[133] A more

---

128   Lassi Heininen, *Arctic Strategies and Policies: Inventory and Comparative Study*, 2nd ed. (Akureyri: Northern Research Forum & University of Lapland, 2012).

129   AC Rules of Procedure, *supra* note 49.

130   *See* Piotr Graczyk and Timo Koivurova, "A New Era in the Arctic Council's External Relations? Broader consequences of the Nuuk observer rules for Arctic governance" *Polar Record* (2013), accessed November 26, 2015, doi: 10.1017/S0032247412000824.

131   AC Rules of Procedure, *supra* note 49, para. 36 and Annex II, paras. 5–6.

132   Germany, Federal Foreign Office, Germany's Arctic Policy Guidelines: Assume Responsibility, Seize Opportunities, Berlin, 2013; Republic of Korea, Arctic Policy of the Republic of Korea, Seoul, Korea Maritime Institute, 2013.

133   France, French Arctic Initiative, *Science Plan, French Arctic Initiative 2015–2020*, Paris, Centre National de la Recherche Scientifique, 2014; Robert Chenorkian and Mireille

comprehensive Arctic policy or strategy is expected soon.[134] Japan released an Arctic policy at the Arctic Circle meeting in Reykjavík, in October 2015.[135] Italy is the most recent Arctic Council observer to release a statement on the Arctic, although the title of its document, *Verso una strategia Italiana per l'Artico*, indicates that this is a work in progress and not to be considered definitive.[136] These documents all present their respective States as contributors to the Arctic, in particular through scientific research and partnership in industrial development. They placate Arctic sensibilities regarding sovereignty and authority by emphasising respect for international law and by downplaying or omitting hard security issues.

However, a published strategy or policy is not the only way to meet the requirements of the Kiruna rules and may not even be a welcome one.[137] China is nurturing its Arctic influence not only through the Arctic Council but also by investment in bilateral relations with the Arctic States;[138] yet it has not indicated any plan to publish a comprehensive Arctic strategy or policy document.[139] If it has an internal Arctic policy framework, it is not making this public.

Given the constraints of the Kiruna rules and the niceties of international relations, it is not surprising that the UK's Arctic policy lacks critical analysis or novelty. The tough questions can be asked by the Houses of Parliament and their relevant committees but the government plays a more diplomatic game. The Kiruna criteria help explain the repetition of the themes of 'respect' and British contribution to Arctic science. The British approach is to walk the fine line between presenting a message that the Arctic 'needs' the UK (or at

---

Raccurt, et al., *Prospective Recherches Polaires, Paris*, l'institut écologie et environment, 2010.

134   Ambassador of the Republic of France to the Republic of Iceland, personal communication to the author, January 16, 2016.

135   Japan, *Japan's Arctic Policy*, Tokyo, Headquarters for Ocean Policy, 2015.

136   Italian Ministry for Foreign Affairs and International Cooperation, *Verso una strategia italiana per l'Artico*, December 2015, accessed 15 February 2016, http://www.esteri.it/mae/ it/politica_estera/aree_geografiche/europa/artico.

137   *See, e.g.*, the response in Canadian newspaper, the *National Post* to suggestions that Scotland might develop an Arctic Strategy: Randy Boswell, "Scottish MP Pipes Up with Arctic Claim", *National Post*, November 29, 2011, accessed February 16, 2016, http://news .nationalpost.com/news/canada/scottish-mp-pipes-up-with-arctic-claim.

138   For example, a free trade agreement between China and Iceland was signed in 2013: Iceland Ministry for Foreign Affairs, "Free Trade Agreement between Iceland and China", accessed 15 February 2016, https://www.mfa.is/foreign-policy/trade/free-trade -agreement-between-iceland-and-china/.

139   *See* Sanna Kopra, "China's Arctic Interests" *Arctic Yearbook* (2013): 107–124.

RESPECTFUL NEIGHBOURLINESS

least benefits from British investment in science and industry) and reassuring the Arctic States that it will not abuse its position to exercise control or interfere with Arctic governance. Mostly self-aware[140] of its colonial history and former great-power status, the UK seeks to present itself as a responsible and reliable neighbour that will quietly assist and support the Arctic as called upon without interfering with the Arctic States' internal affairs or their collective governance through the Arctic Council.

In terms of Arctic relations, the government in the UK may be right in preferring quiet diplomacy in the Arctic – not something for which it is famous in other regions of the World. Its long-term cooperation and investment in Arctic science is certainly more welcome than yet another be-suited ambassador to add to the platform at international conferences. It could, on the other hand, increase cooperation in search and rescue and make itself genuinely indispensable in the North Atlantic.

The UK is deferential to Arctic sovereignty. One can imagine the Arctic States' ambassadors all nodding appreciatively but in Judge Huber's famous words, 'responsibility is the corollary of sovereignty.'[141] You want sovereignty; you get responsibility. Search and rescue, environmental standards, oil spill preparedness and clean-up, respect for the rights of indigenous peoples, human rights protection, and corporate behaviour are all 'sovereign' concerns of the Arctic States and hence their responsibilities. This leaves the British government to continue to promote commercial opportunities (including shipping) for British firms while ensuring the externalities remain in the Arctic. The government uses the term 'indigenous peoples' without its usual caveats but nonetheless leaves the rights of indigenous peoples in the hands of the Arctic States.

The EAC's references to the 'pristine Arctic' and the 'last true wilderness' were rebutted by the Lords[142] and it certainly suits the government to promote an image of the Arctic as a site of industry. The sustainable development called for by the EAC is watered down to 'responsible development' or 'responsible, commercial development'.[143] Climate change science is accepted but the government's policy priority is unambiguously energy security before

---

140   Let us consider the Arctic Circle 2014 plenary session an aberration.

141   Island of Palmas case (Netherlands v United States of America) 1928, Permanent Court of Arbitration, Arbitrator: Huber, Reports of International Arbitral Awards, 2 (1928): 829, 839.

142   EAC Response to Government Response 2013, *supra*, note 45, 7; EAC 2012, *supra*, note 2, 11; HLAC 2015, *supra*, note 2, 11; and *see* text above at note 88.

143   HM Government 2013, *supra*, note 2, 7; HM Government HLAC Response 2015, *supra*, note 21, 9; and *see* text above at notes 55 and 111.

mitigation.[144] Calls to mitigate climate change by the EAC, including with a moratorium on Arctic drilling, are met with an acceptance of climate change as *fait accompli* with the question turning to how to how to respond and adapt to climate change: including responding by profiting from new commercial opportunities.[145]

The UK hosts some of the best research universities and institutions in the World and will continue to invest in Arctic science. The message from the HLAC that the UK must better coordinate its Arctic science and plan in advance to facilitate full participation in the Arctic Council's Working Group meetings is an important one to which the National Environmental Research Council, a key funder of Arctic science, will hopefully respond. A new polar research vessel is being built in Merseyside and another may be commissioned in a few years.[146]

It would be wrong to single-out the UK for avoiding the most contested or challenging issues like climate change, sustainability, and participation of indigenous and other communities given that even the Arctic States' own strategies steer clear of strong commitments on these points.[147] Likewise, non-Arctic States' Arctic policies and statements tend to avoid hard security issues, but clues can be derived from their military and defence reports. In the British case, the periodic strategic defence and security reviews indicate priority areas of concern and changes of emphasis over time. Russia, mentioned briefly as a partner in the 2010 defence review, re-emerged as a bogeyman in 2015, in particular with reference to its annexation of the Crimea and continuing interference in the Ukraine and its (lawful) military flights and vessels 'near' British airspace and territorial waters.[148] Nevertheless, 'the Arctic' is not presented as a region *per se* (*cf.*, the Middle East or Eastern Europe) of military concern.[149]

The efforts of the three British organs of government analysed above all take a strong centralised approach and do not examine the regional questions, in particular, the special position of Scotland and the extensive powers and interests of the devolved Scottish government, for example, over implementation

---

144   HM Government EAC response 2013, *supra*, note 20, 5; HM Government 2013, *supra*, note 2, 24; and *see* text above at notes 39 and 72.

145   *See* text above at notes 54 and 86–87.

146   Tip of the Iceberg, *supra*, note 100.

147   *See, e.g.*, Heininen, *supra*, note 128.

148   *E.g.*, National Security Strategy 2015, *supra*, note 17, paras. 3.19–3.21; 4.14; 5.27 and 5.45; *Compare Securing Britain in an Age of Uncertainty* 2010, *supra*, note 16, paras. 4.E.2 and 5.8.

149   *But see ibid.*, para. 4.47: a select group of Marines will be trained in 'Arctic warfare capabilities'; this is an interesting word-choice in preference to a more general 'cold-weather' warfare capabilities.

of the EU Common Fisheries Policy, environment, energy, transport (including non-military ports) and economic development. The contents of the three papers examined are sufficient to show that the Arctic cannot be examined only in foreign policy terms. The exclusion is partly structural: the Scottish National Party (SNP) (ruling party in Scotland since 2007) had, until the 2015 general election, very few seats in the Parliament at Westminster. Hence, there were no members on the EAC in 2013 (nor any members from Northern Ireland) and the SNP refuses on principle to take seats in the unelected House of Lords.[150] There is no Scottish minister in the FCO and this is almost impossible now with a Conservative government which has a solitary MP representing a Scottish constituency. The opportunity to consult with the Scottish government during the UK government's development of its Arctic policy was not taken.[151] The Lords, having received evidence from a number of experts based in Scottish institutions, only mentions Scotland explicitly in the context of its hydrocarbon industry but they propose that the government consult with the devolved administrations (which can be read as Scotland in particular) when or if it develops a full strategy.[152]

The exclusion of Scotland is unlikely to have been accidental and must be read in light of the respective campaigns in the run up to the Scottish referendum on independence that was held in September 2014. Neither the EAC nor the government wanted to give any support to the view that Scotland might have distinct foreign affairs interests or competences. While this might be understandable from a short-term, domestic, political point of view, it detracts from the quality of the exercises and also fuels calls for Scotland to develop its own Arctic policy.[153] Notwithstanding the vote in 2014 by a comfortable 10% margin to remain united, the UK may not be the Arctic's nearest neighbour for long.

Besides failing to look inwards at devolved competences within the UK, the three reports fail to look outwards: referring to the EU in a limited manner, for example, in relation to fisheries competence, but with no effort to engage with the EU's own Arctic policies. The EU's formal political engagement can be traced back to a Parliamentary Resolution in 2008, the Commission's

---

150   There were three MPs representing Scottish constituencies on the EAC in 2013, all from the Labour party, a strongly unionist party.

151   Alyson Bailes and John MacDonald, "The Future of UK Arctic Policy: a stronger, more inclusive, approach?" *Scottish Global Forum*, March 23, 2015, accessed November 26, 2015, http://www.scottishglobalforum.net/the-future-of-uk-arctic-policy.html.

152   *Ibid.*; HLAC 2015, *supra*, note 2, 77, 106, and 113.

153   Bailes and MacDonald, *supra*, note 151; Johnstone, *supra*, note 4.

communication in reply and the Council's response.[154] Since then, its three main organs (Parliament, Commission, and Council) have become ever more sophisticated in their approaches and have backed down from the Parliament's original call for a protectionist Arctic treaty comparable to that for the Antarctic. The Commission released another Joint Communication to the Council and Parliament of 2012 on the Arctic and at the time of writing, this is under review.[155]

This omission stands in marked contrast to Italy's Arctic strategy-in-progress which is carefully tuned to the broader European agenda and Germany's published Arctic policy that weaves Germany's own Arctic influence through the EU.[156] A referendum is likely to be offered to British citizens on continued UK membership of the EU in 2016 but when the EAC was consulting and reviewing and when the government was preparing its own policy, a 'Brexit' was not an imminent prospect.[157] Even if by 2015 when the House of Lords was finalising its conclusions that seemed a real possibility, a better integration and assessment of EU priorities, if only to show where they complement or differ from the UK's interests would have improved the utility of all the reports.[158] More attention on the EU, and especially its Northern Periphery Programme, would have also directed London's attention to Scotland which is an active partner of the Nordic States in EU regional programmes.[159]

---

154   EU Parliament, Resolution of 9th October 2008 on Arctic Governance, OJ C 316 E 41, December 11, 2008; EU Commission, Communication from the Commission to the European Parliament and the Council: the European Union and the Arctic Region, COM(2008) 763 final, November 20, 2008; EU Council, Council Conclusions on Arctic Issues, 2985th Foreign Affairs Council meeting, December 8, 2009.

155   EU Commission, Joint Communication to the European Parliament and the Council: Developing a European Union Policy towards the Arctic Region: progress since 2008 and next steps, [SWD(2012) 1982 final], June 26, 2012; see also Andreas Østhagen and Andreas Raspotnik, "The EU's Arctic Policy: Eventually Getting Somewhere?" The Arctic Institute, April 22, 2015, accessed Nov. 26, 2015, http://www.thearcticinstitute.org/2015/04/042215 -EU-Arctic-Policy-Getting-Somewhere.html.

156   Verso una strategia, supra, note 136; see also Rachael Lorna Johnstone and Federica Scarpa, "Little Italy: Seeking a Niche in International Arctic Relations," Nordicum-Mediterrean 11(1) (2016); Germany's Arctic Policy Guidelines, supra, note 132, 15–16.

157   'Brexit' is the common abbreviation used in the UK for a 'British exit' from the EU.

158   Alyson Bailes, personal communication to the author, November 15, 2015; see also Timo Koivurova et al., "The Present and Future Competence of the European Union in the Arctic," Polar Record (2011), accessed November 26, 2015, doi: 10.1017/S0032247411000295.

159   John MacDonald, "The Case for a Scottish Northern Strategy," Scottish Global Forum Working Paper, (forthcoming 2016) 11.

It is also necessary to consider the UK's interests in the Arctic in light of its commitments elsewhere. The UK may well be the Arctic's nearest neighbour but the Arctic is not the UK's nearest neighbour. This is not solely a geographical matter. Of course, France, Ireland, and the Netherlands are all much closer. It is also a geo*political* matter. The UK still has its fingers in too many pies elsewhere for the Arctic to be prioritised. And perhaps that is very welcome to the Arctic Eight who are quite happy for observers to observe and fund Arctic research – as long as they keep their opinions to themselves.[160]

---

160 *See* Sanjay Chaturvedi, "Geopolitical Transformations: 'Risking' Asia and the Future of the Arctic Council" in *The Arctic Council: Its Place in the Future of Arctic Governance*, ed. Thomas Axworthy, Timo Koivurova and Waliul Hasanat (Rovaniemi: Northern Institute for Environmental and Minority Law, et al., 2012) 225, 249.

From the High North to the Roof of the World: Arctic Precedents for Third Pole Governance

Simon Marsden[a]

Abstract

This article analyses the potential to apply legal and policy instruments from the 'First Pole', (the Arctic), to the 'Third Pole,' (the Himalayas/Tibetan Plateau) – the Antarctic is the 'Second Pole.' The Third Pole shares many environmental challenges with the Arctic: territorially both are comprised of nation states with domestic agendas; the issues of climate change, development and energy security are also common to both, and have transboundary dimensions. While acknowledging the contextual differences between Arctic states in the North and those with territory in the highest part of Asia (and the world), the growing relationship between them, institutions which regulate their affairs, and these shared challenges suggest there is opportunity to develop Third Pole environmental governance. The article reviews Arctic Council arrangements, focusing upon the South Asian Association for Regional Cooperation, and South Asia Cooperative Environment Program as reform platforms. It finds potential exists if political will is forthcoming, particularly on the part of China and India.

Keywords

Third Pole – Arctic – environmental governance – reform

1 Introduction

In a seminal article in the *Journal of Environmental Law* in 2015, the current and past Directors of the University of Lapland Arctic Centre and an experienced colleague (Koivurova, Kankaanpää and Stępién) significantly comment: "there

---

[a] Professor, Flinders Law School, Australia. simon.marsden@flinders.edu.au.

FROM THE HIGH NORTH TO THE ROOF OF THE WORLD

are good reasons to argue that the governance frameworks that have evolved in the Arctic are of relevance for environmental governance in other regions."[1] Making reference to the role of Indigenous people, a long history of regional (or perhaps *cross regional* given an inter-continental focus) environmental protection, and "functions and frameworks of international cooperation"[2] as examples, the potential to consider the Arctic Council (AC) as a legal transplant of "innovative environmental protection" is canvassed.[3]

What areas of the world could benefit from the experience of the AC? The current article considers the much neglected and under-researched 'Third Pole, the Himalayas/Tibetan Plateau, as the best candidate.[4] The Arctic ('First Pole') has many more similarities with the Third Pole than it does with the Antarctic ('Second Pole'); these similarities include national territory, transboundary watercourses, and a human population requiring environmentally sustainable development. Koivurova *et al.* acknowledge key differences between the Arctic and Antarctic,[5] and furthermore state: "the example of Arctic regional cooperation shows that flexible structure and a lack of rigid, unadaptable internal design can be critical in allowing regional organisations to learn."[6] Examining

---

1 Timo Koivurova, Paula Kankaanpää, and Adam Stępién, "Innovative Environmental Protection: Lessons from the Arctic," *Journal of Environmental Law* 27 (2015): 285, 286. In the previous *Yearbook of Polar Law*, Loukacheva, after reviewing the external relations of the Arctic Council also asks the question: "Does that mean that the Council will become an even more important player globally?" *See* Natalia Loukacheva, "Development in the Arctic Council," *The Yearbook of Polar Law* VI (2015): 340, 347.

2 *Ibid.*

3 *See* Alan Watson, *Legal Transplants: An Approach to Comparative Law* (University Press of Virginia, 1974). Neither Koivurova *et al.*, nor the present author apply the approach of legal transplants (a notion largely of comparative law); however there is a significant scholarship and potential to consider this further in an international law context also. There is also opportunity to use precedents from national law to inform international law; *see* Jonathan B. Wiener, "Something Borrowed for Something Blue: Legal Transplants and the Evolution of Global Environmental Law," *Ecology Law Quarterly* (2001): 27, 1295–1372. Space constraints prevent detailed exploration or application of the concept here, which will be considered in future work.

4 Aside from the NGOs involved in the Third Pole directly – *see* note 41 below – there have been very few events highlighting the importance of the Third Pole. Recent examples include the 15th "Festival Culturel du Tibet et des Peuples de l'Himalaya," with a theme of "the Third Pole," Maison du Tibet, Paris, June 13–14, 2015; Arctic Circle Assembly, October 16–18, 2015; "'Third Pole:' science diplomacy and transnational connections between Tibet, the Arctic and Antarctic," International Association of Tibetan Studies, June 19–25, 2016.

5 Koivurova *et al., supra*, note 1, 288–289.

6 Koivurova *et al., supra*, note 1, 286.

the type and form of institution responsible for transboundary environmental governance in the Third Pole will be an important consideration for the viability of any legal transplant, and the "learning" or "adaptive governance"[7] needed for success.

The Third Pole is primarily the Himalayas/Tibetan Plateau,[8] and related river systems,[9] including the Hindu Kush Mountains ranging from Central Asia to Kashmir at the Pakistan/India border. However it also includes the Pamir of Tajikistan, Karakoram of Afghanistan and Pakistan, and the Kunlun Mountains bordering the Tibetan Plateau in East Asia. It is high altitude compared with the high latitude of the Arctic and Antarctic. Given the challenges of earthquake-prone geology, climate change, water management, resource extraction, infrastructure development, and Indigenous/minority rights, there is a need to improve transboundary governance as many of these matters affect more than one state in the sub-region. Whatever the differences between environmental governance of the first two poles, applicable mechanisms have so far managed the diverse interests of participating states even if, (as discussed in the next section), they may in the eyes of some commentators have done so poorly.[10]

---

7   Koivurova *et al., supra*, note 1, 287–288.
8   The following definition provides more detail: "The Himalayas are the product of intense mountain building activity in the Cretaceous, Tertiary and Pleistocene periods. They extend for 3200 km from the 'Pamir Knot', on the Afghanistan border in the northwest, across the northern part of the Indian subcontinent in an arc. The main range of the Himalayas (the Great Himalayas) includes, from Afghanistan, Pakistan, India, Nepal and Bhutan Himalayas, which include mountains such as Mount Everest – 8848 m, Kanchenjunga – 8579 m, Makalu – 8470 m, Dhaulagiri – 8425 m, Annapurna – 8091 m, and Gosainthan – 8010 m." *See* United Nations Environment Programme and Development Alternatives, *South Asia Environment Outlook 2009*: UNEP, SAARC and DA, 2008, 4.
9   In relation to rivers, it is noted that: "Some of the world's largest river systems are in the South Asia. The River Indus originates in China and flows to Pakistan. The Ganga-Brahmaputtra river systems originate partly in Bhutan, China and Nepal and flow to Bangladesh and India. The Indus is one of the world's greatest river systems, measuring 3,180 km, from its source to the sea. The Ganga stretches for about 2,525 km and the Brahmaputtra – the third great Himalayan river, stretches for about 2 900km flowing through Tibet, India and Bangladesh. Many minor rivers that originate from the Himalayas and drain into Bangladesh, through Nepal and India. The Ganga, Brahmaputtra and Meghna are the major rivers in Bangladesh." *See South Asia Environment Outlook 2009, ibid.*, 4.
10   *See* Falk Huettmann, "Introduction: Why Three Poles and Why Protect Them," in *Protection of the Three Poles*, ed. Falk Huettmann (Springer, 2012), 3. Huettmann's more positive opinion of the effect of the Antarctic Environmental Protocol may have something

In the Arctic, the AC[11] and *Svalbard Treaty* (ST)[12] are the primary mechanisms for transboundary governance. These are significant for the following reasons: the AC has programs relating to climate change, pollution, risk, biodiversity, and other matters with a focus on environmental protection that developed from the Arctic Environmental Protection Strategy (AEPS);[13] the ST regulates the activities of foreign states on Norwegian national territory, also paying specific attention to environmental protection under implementing law.[14] Both permit sustainable development of natural resources in accordance with applicable policy or regulatory frameworks.[15] Only the AC is considered here, but the ST is also a significant example of multilateral environmental governance.[16]

In contrast, the environmental governance of the 'Second Pole' (the Antarctic) is largely irrelevant to either the First or Third Poles, and not only for the fact that issues of territorial sovereignty are so different.[17] While the *Environment Protocol* to the *Antarctic Treaty* contains annexes on protected areas, fauna and flora and environmental impact assessment (EIA) which are similar in some ways to the AC arrangements;[18] unlike in the Arctic or Himalayas/Tibetan Plateau, there is currently no place for sustainable development in Antarctica.[19]

---

to do with the absence of a sustainable development focus. He comments [my emphasis]: "This treaty has been in existence since 1961, with 47 signatory nations, and *has halted many negative impacts so far.*" *Ibid.*, 20.

11   *See* Declaration on the Establishment of the Arctic Council, Joint Communique of the Governments of the Arctic Countries on the Establishment of the Arctic Council, 35 ILM 1385–90 (1996), Ottawa, September 19, 1996 ("Ottawa Declaration").

12   The Svalbard Treaty (Paris, 9 February 1920) 2 LNTS 8; UKTS (1924) 18 in force August 14, 1925.

13   Koivurova *et al.*, *supra*, note 1, 286.

14   Svalbard Environmental Protection Act; Act of June 15, 2001 No.79 Relating to the Protection of the Environment in Svalbard.

15   Timo Koivurova and Pamela Lesser, *Environmental Impact Assessment in the Arctic: A Guide to Best Practice* (Cheltenham: Edward Elgar Publishing, 2016).

16   *See* Diana Wallis and Stewart Arnold, ed., *The Spitsbergen Treaty: Multilateral Governance in the Arctic*. Arctic Papers No 1. Note that this recognises the rights of a wide range of signatories, which include the Third Pole states China, India and Afghanistan.

17   Koivurova *et al.*, *supra*, note 1, 289.

18   Protocol on Environmental Protection to the Antarctic Treaty (Madrid, 4 October 1991), 30 ILM 1455 (1991), in force January 14, 1998. *See* Annexes I, II, and V.

19   For space reasons, the article will also not consider multilateral environmental agreements relevant to the Arctic and Third Pole, nor other potential precedents, such as from mountain or riverine environments globally, or the other Asian sub-regions.

While there is evidence of exploitable resources,[20] until 2048 when the 50 year Antarctic mining moratorium ends, no development is permitted, sustainable or otherwise.

The primary research question of this article is: to what extent do existing environmental governance frameworks in the Arctic have relevance in the Third Pole Asian sub-region? Given interest in the Arctic by Asian states, answering this question will highlight the benefits of this interest and in turn greater involvement by Arctic states in improving environmental governance in the Third Pole. The question therefore focuses on how institutional frameworks can be adapted, and how observer status may not only benefit the Arctic, but also the Himalayas/Tibetan Plateau, in developing an effective new Third Pole regime to manage transboundary issues.[21] These issues are also without question extremely difficult to manage, with added complexities that are arguably much greater to resolve than at either of the other two poles, and that in part may explain the limited legal and political reform discourse to date. Huettmann summarises the challenges as follows:

> The fact that conflict zones of global relevance, such as Pakistan, Afghanistan, and Tibet, are located in this region, further speaks to the complexity, the global role, and the impact of the third pole. The global forces China and India are also directly involved in the Hindu Kush–Himalaya region. As do the other two poles, the third pole involves huge, global economies and human wealth. Adding the third pole to our (Western) worldview naturally changes the center of the global perspective and universe, from Europe and North America right into Asia, and makes it less symmetrical and less convenient to manage.[22]

Following this first introductory section, the structure of the paper is as follows: the second section will describe further what the Third Pole is, explain why it is

---

20   Note in particular China's "scientific research" efforts. Michael Atkin, "China's interest in mining Antarctica revealed as evidence points to country's desire to become 'Polar Great Power'," ABC News, January 21, 2015.

21   See generally the following series of books on the issue: Helmut Breitmeir, Oran R. Young, and Michael Zürn, Analysing International Environmental Regimes: From Case Study to Database (Cambridge: MIT Press, 2006); Edward L. Miles, Steiner Andresen, Elaine M. Carlin, Jon Birger Skjaerseth, Arild Underdal, and Jorgen Wetterstad, Environmental Regime Effectiveness: Confronting Theory with Evidence (Cambridge: MIT Press, 2002); and Oran R. Young, ed., The Effectiveness of International Environmental Regimes (Cambridge: MIT Press, 1999).

22   See Huettmann, supra, notes 10, 15.

FROM THE HIGH NORTH TO THE ROOF OF THE WORLD

important and what the law can do to protect it; the third section will analyse what transboundary governance is currently in place in the sub-region, in particular the South Asian Association for Regional Cooperation (SAARC) and the South Asia Cooperative Environment Program (SACEP); the fourth section will consider relevant Arctic precedents, notably the arrangements under the AC, analysing what lessons the Arctic may provide for Third Pole environmental governance, in particular with the involvement of China and India, and generally the role of observers across the Arctic and South Asian institutions; conclusions will follow.

2 What is the Third Pole, Why is it Important, and Can the Law Protect it?

Legally and politically, the Third Pole consists of the Tibet Autonomous Region of China (East Asia); Nepal, Bhutan and parts of other states, notably India, Pakistan and Afghanistan (South Asia); and also Tajikistan (Central Asia).[23] Geographically, it is a series of mountain ranges and plateaus, including the Pamir, Karakoram, Himalayas and the Tibetan Plateau. It is similar to aspects of First and Second Poles: it comprises high altitude terrain in contrast to high latitude terrain and seas; climate change,[24] water management,[25] resource extraction, infrastructure development and Indigenous/minority rights and security[26] are significant issues. It is dissimilar because despite numerous

---

23 *See* the United Nations Geoscheme for examples of sub-regional classification in Asia: http://unstats.un.org/unsd/methods/m49/m49regin.htm#asia (accessed November 4, 2015).

24 In 2009, the South Asia Environment Outlook Report for the United Nations Environment Program commented: "South Asia is very vulnerable to climate change. Impacts of climate change have been observed in the form of glacier retreat in the Himalayan region, where the approximately 15,000 glaciers will likely shrink from the present total area of 500,000 km^2 to 100,000 km^2 by 2035. These glaciers form a unique reservoir, which supports perennial rivers such as the Indus, Ganges and Brahmaputra, which, in turn, are the lifeline of millions of people in South Asian countries (Bangladesh, Bhutan, India, Nepal, and Pakistan)." *See* South Asia Environment Outlook 2009, *supra*, note 8, xi.

25 *See* Ruby Moynihan and Bjørn-Oliver Magsig, "The Rising Role of Regional Approaches in International Water Law: Lessons from the UNECE Water Regime and Himalayan Asia for Strengthening Transboundary Water Cooperation," *Review of European, Comparative and International Environmental Law* 23 (2014): 43.

26 *See* for example, Karen Morton, "Climate Change and Security at the Third Pole," *Survival: Global Politics and Strategy* 53(1) (2011): 121–132.

watercourses, it is entirely terrestrial unlike the other two poles,[27] which either comprise, or are surrounded by, the Arctic and Southern Oceans respectively. It is hence located north of the Equator and a considerable distance from the closest seas, the Indian and Pacific Oceans. Significantly for the purposes of this article, there is no environmental governance framework comparable to the more developed treaty-based and other arrangements in the Arctic and Antarctic.

Recent coverage in the media emphasises the significance of the Third Pole Asian sub-region, the connections with the other poles, environmental concerns, and the need for effective governance. The following examples are illustrative: "Three poles: The Arctic, Antarctic and Himalayas all connect,"[28] "Himalayas at risk in hydro dam water grab,"[29] "Jammu-Pak border might have oil and gas, says ONGC,"[30] "China may build rail tunnel under Mount Everest, state media reports,"[31] "Man-made earthquakes cause seismic rumblings,"[32] "Obama: We're All for the Asian Infrastructure Investment Bank ... [if it] incorporates strong financial, social and environmental safeguards."[33] The first example highlights the relationship between the poles, and the following examples the resource and infrastructure issues. In connection with infrastructure, whether the Everest (also known as Mt. Chomolungma or Sagarmatha) rail tunnel is ever built, transboundary and other long-distance railways are a key part of the export of Chinese development across Asia, and a major reason

---

27   Note that both the Third Pole and the Arctic have a large number of transboundary watercourses; in relation to the Arctic, rivers are shared between the Nordic states and Russia for example. *See* "Chapter 1: Drainage Basins of the White Sea, Barents Sea and Kara Sea," *in* United Nations Economic Commission for Europe Convention on the Protection and Use of Transboundary Watercourses and International Lakes, *Second Assessment of Transboundary Rivers, Lakes and Groundwaters* (United Nations, 2011).

28   Falk Huettmann and Ashok Roy, "Three poles: The Arctic, Antarctic and Himalayas all connect," *Alaska Business Monthly*, June 1, 2013.

29   J. Vidal and K. Dasgupta, "Himalayas at risk in hydro dam water grab," *New Zealand Herald News*, August 13, 2013.

30   S. Prashant, "Jammu-Pak border might have oil and gas, says ONGC," *Business Standard*, February 7, 2014.

31   Haroon Saddique and Jason Burke, "China may build rail tunnel under Mount Everest, state media reports," *The Guardian* (London), April 9, 2015.

32   R.A. Lovett, "Man-made earthquakes cause seismic rumblings," *Cosmos Magazine*, March 24, 2014.

33   Ian Talley, "Obama: We're All for the Asian Infrastructure Investment Bank ... [if it] incorporates strong financial, social and environmental safeguards," *Wall Street Journal*, April 28, 2015.

FROM THE HIGH NORTH TO THE ROOF OF THE WORLD 63

why environmental safeguards of international financial institutions are so important, and potentially supportive of international law.[34]

As noted towards the end of the first section of this article, any Third Pole regime must contend with the interests of states traditionally in conflict for land and resources; these include India and Pakistan, and India and China, where boundary disputes are a continuing issue.[35] To date however, with the partial exception of transboundary water resources,[36] there has been little if any legal, policy, or governance scholarship in relation to the transboundary environmental governance of the Third Pole *as a whole*, despite the significance to millions of people directly or indirectly.[37] Some scientists have also been scathing in their condemnation of what attention has been given to date and the role of the law and lawyers. Huettmann states:

> ...we do not have a legal system that truly allows for fast, fair, low-cost, and uncomplicated policy changes, as is required for an adaptive management framework to perform...Nor do we have (polar) lawyers and judges who truly understand ecology or act accordingly....[38]

He continues, with a nod in the direction of the research question of this article:

---

34 Simon Marsden, "Environmental Assessment of Cross-Border Development: China and the Third Pole," *Journal of Environmental Assessment Policy and Management* 18: 165009-1 (2016): special issue on Environmental Assessment in South Asia.

35 Tsering Topgyal, "China and India's Border Dispute Rises to Dangerous New Heights," *The Conversation*, September 26, 2014.

36 Moynihan and Magsig, *supra*, note 25.

37 Nakul Chettri, Arun B. Shrestha, Yan Zhaoli, Birendra Bajracharya, Eklabya Sharma, and Hua Ouyang, "'Real World' Protection for the Third Pole and its People," *in* Falk Huettmann, ed., *Protection of the Three Poles* (Springer, 2012), 113–133.

38 Huettmann, *supra*, notes 10, 12. Huettmann is positive towards the role of Indigenous peoples and the environment, and in the context of the Third Pole particularly, the role of non-western religions. While Indigenous peoples have a direct role in AC governance, space considerations mean that any transplant of the Indigenous Permanent Participants from the AC to Third Pole governance is not canvassed here, and will be considered in future research. Similarly, the influence of religion on the law – in the Third Pole in particular – is largely absent. He comments: "...other religions, notably the Hindu, Buddhist, and indigenous views, tend to treat the Earth as one vehicle and thus provide much more holistic concepts...These perspectives are dearly needed if we want to contend with the poles, the snow, ice, climate, and environmental niche in any relevant form and fashion, and if we want to keep them for future generations." *Ibid.*, 19.

The last thing we need, however, are more regulations and laws that do not work and a legal model of "quick-fixes" that presents bizarre cornucopia and a mosaic of failed policies...Laws without funding and enforcements cannot work; virtually all lawyers know it, yet they do nothing against it, while species increasingly close the distance to their own extinction. It is here where Western society and its culture has failed us so badly again; the United States and its elite law schools are in the lead here. We were fed the idea that more rules, more regulations, and more laws would provide us with a secure and stable fix, making things better (= "makes sense"). But this concept clearly failed in regard to climate change, human welfare, and in most environmental and wilderness applications.[39]

Clearly lawyers – including this academic one – must do better if we are to respond effectively to these issues, translate science to practical policy solutions, and ensure that they are working via the legal system. Whether lawyers have neglected Third Pole governance issues because they are seen as too difficult is not clear; however attention has overwhelmingly been given by scientists[40] and non-governmental organizations to date,[41] and this has generally not addressed regulatory issues. This needs to change as future pressures include further development of the transboundary rivers originating in the Tibetan Plateau for hydroelectricity; India, Pakistan, Nepal and Bhutan plan 400 dams, and China 100 for instance.[42] The extraction of oil and gas is also cause for considerable concern given the lack of experience of either practice

---

39   Huettmann, *supra*, notes 10, 23. The alternative, which is beyond the scope of this article, is ecological/earth jurisprudence, also known as "wild law" or "earth justice," and which takes an ecocentric rather than anthropocentric view of and approach to the environment. *See* Christopher Stone, *Should Trees Have Standing: Law, Morality and the Environment* (Oxford: Oxford University Press, 2010); Cormac Cullinan, *Wild Law: A Manifesto for Earth Justice* (Green Books, 2011); Peter Burdon, ed., *Exploring Wild Law: The Philosophy of Earth Jurisprudence* (Wakefield Press, 2011).

40   *See* for example, K. Hewitt, "Karakoram Glaciers and Climate Change," in *Glaciers of the Karakoram Himalaya: Glacial Environments, Processes* (Springer, 2014) 291.

41   Note the work in particular of the (ICIMOD), based in Kathmandu; Third Pole Environment (TPE), based in Beijing; and The thirdpole.net, based in London.

42   Kieran Cooke, "The Dams of India: Boon or Bane?" *The Guardian* (London), March 17, 2014. 160 dams proposed for Assam specifically.

FROM THE HIGH NORTH TO THE ROOF OF THE WORLD 65

or regulation in this sub-region.[43] And finally climate change will continue to occupy the minds of many in the sub-region as elsewhere.[44]

3 What Third Pole Sub-Regional Transboundary Frameworks Currently Exist?

While sub-regional environmental governance of other parts of Asia is slowly developing,[45] the Third Pole is one of the few sub-regions without such a framework. However regimes do exist in South Asia, even though environmental governance of the Third Pole is not the primary focus and these can provide a starting point. The first is framed by an international treaty for a transboundary river between India and Pakistan that is over 50 years old, the Indus Waters Treaty.[46] The second is the SAARC Framework Agreement for Energy Cooperation, which recognises the "common benefits of cross border electricity exchanges," and supports the "development of efficient conventional and renewable energy sources including hydropower."[47] The third, and most significant, is the South Asia Cooperative Environment Program (SACEP), with the same Parties as SAARC, a formal arrangement to promote regional cooperation. The fourth is part of the global cooperative initiative of the United Nations Environment Program Regional Seas Program,[48] although unlike other sub-regions that are part of this initiative,[49] it is not, currently at least,

---

43   Prashant, *supra*, note 30.

44   For an example of action, *see* the Declaration on Control and Prevention of Air Pollution and its likely Transboundary Effects for South Asia, adopted at the Seventh meeting of the Governing Council of SACEP, Malé, April 1998.

45   Examples include: Western, Central, South East and North East Asia, *see* Simon Marsden, *Environmental Regimes in Asian Sub-regions: China and the Third Pole* (Cheltenham: Edward Elgar Publishing, 2017).

46   Indus Waters Treaty (Karachi, September 19, 1960).

47   Recitals 2 and 4, SAARC Framework Agreement for Energy Cooperation (Electricity), (Kathmandu, November 27, 2014).

48   The Arctic Ocean has been considered as a candidate to be part of this program, *see* Sébastien Duyck, "Legal issues related to options for a regional seas-type arrangement for the Arctic Ocean," *Northern Institute for Environment and Minority Law* (2014).

49   Such as the Caspian Sea, the Red Sea/Gulf of Aden, and the Arabian Gulf, which are regulated respectively by the: Framework Convention for the Protection of the Marine Environment of the Caspian Sea (Tehran, November 4, 2003), 44 ILM 1 (2005), in force August 12, 2006; the Regional Convention for the Conservation of the Red Sea

framed by an international agreement (the South Asian Seas[50]); SACEP is the secretariat of the South Asian Seas Program.

SAARC was formed by Charter 1985 by the following states: Bangladesh, Bhutan, India, Maldives, Nepal, Pakistan and Sri Lanka; Afghanistan joined later.[51] Most are in the Third Pole sub-region, agreeing to promote "peace, stability, amity and progress in the region."[52] In relation to the issues addressed, the Charter makes no mention of the environment in either the recitals or articles, but is focused above all on "fostering mutual understanding, good neighbourly relations and meaningful cooperation."[53] The SAARC Convention on Cooperation on Environment was however signed during the Sixteenth Summit, has been ratified by all Member States, and entered into force with effect from 23 October 2013. It identifies 19 areas for cooperation in the field of environment and sustainable development "through exchange of best practices and knowledge, capacity building and transfer of eco-friendly technology in a wide range of areas related to the environment."[54] The implementation of the Convention has been entrusted to a Governing Council, comprised of the Environment Ministers of Member States.

SAARC was furthermore preceded by SACEP in 1982, emphasising the importance of sustainable development and cooperative action to address environmental degradation and other issues. SAARC has the same members as SACEP, and in July 2004 signed a Memorandum of Understanding (MOU) with it.[55] Because of its membership and objectives, SACEP acknowledges that

---

and Gulf of Aden (Jeddah, 1982), ECOLEX B7 p. 982:13, in force August 20, 1985 ("Jeddah Convention"); and the Regional Convention for Cooperation on the Protection of the Marine Environment from Pollution (Kuwait, April 24, 1978), in force July 1, 1979 ("Kuwait Convention").

50 "South Asian Seas," *United Nations Environment Programme*, accessed November 4, 2015, http://www.unep.org/regionalseas/programmes/nonunep/southasian/default.asp.

51 Charter of the South Asian Association for Regional Cooperation (SAARC) (Dhaka, December 18, 1985).

52 *Ibid.*, recital 1.

53 *Ibid.*, recital 2.

54 "Area of Cooperation," *South Asian Association for Regional Cooperation*, accessed November 4, 2015, http://saarc-sec.org/areaofcooperation/cat-detail.php?cat_id=54. This followed the SAARC Environment Action Plan adopted by the Third Meeting of the SAARC Environment Ministers (Male, October 15–16, 1997). It identified some of the key concerns and established parameters and modalities for regional cooperation. Since its adoption in 1997, a number of measures have been implemented by the Regional Centres.

55 Memorandum of Understanding on Cooperation in the Field of the Environment between the South Asian Association for Regional Cooperation (SAARC) and the South Asia Cooperative Environment Program (SACEP). The strengthening of the SAARC/

FROM THE HIGH NORTH TO THE ROOF OF THE WORLD

it is "an appropriate forum for action on transboundary environmental issues." The Hindu Kush Himalayan belt is recognised by SACEP for its biodiversity, comprising 10% of the world's flora. It acknowledges however that the region is prone to natural disasters, with over 60% of the world's disaster-related deaths in the 1990s. Apart from efforts to address natural disasters, including recent earthquakes in the sub-region,[56] the majority of its work has so far gone into coastal and marine issues, rather than addressing specifically Third Pole concerns.

However in 2014, at the 18th SAARC Summit Declaration in Kathmandu, the heads of government expressed concern in relation to disasters[57] and climate change,[58] and: "directed the relevant bodies/mechanisms for effective

---

    SACEP partnership was underscored by the Kathmandu Declaration, made on January 25, 2007 at the Tenth Governing Council of SACEP, accessed November 6, 2015, http://www .sacep.org/?page_id=556.

56   J. Boone, "Afghanistan and Pakistan earthquake death toll will rise, say officials," *The Guardian* (London), October 27, 2015.

57   Note that the SAARC Agreement on Rapid Response to Natural Disasters was signed at the Seventeenth Summit (Maldives, November 10–11, 2011) and will come into force once ratified by all members. The establishment and implementation of the SAARC Natural Disaster Rapid Response Mechanism under this agreement will institutionalise regional cooperation in the critical area of response following natural disasters. This followed, pursuant to the Malé Declaration, a "Comprehensive Framework on Disaster Management 2006–2015" which was adopted in 2006 to address the specific needs of disaster risk reduction and management in South Asia. The Framework is also aligned with the Hyogo Framework of Action (2005–2015). Member States are in the process of preparing their respective National Plans of Action for implementation of the Regional Framework and thereafter, an Expert Group Meeting will harmonize the national reports and articulate a Regional Plan of Action.

58   Climate change was the theme of the Sixteenth Summit (Thimphu, April 28–29, 2010) which adopted the "Thimphu Statement on Climate Change." This outlines important initiatives to strengthen and intensity regional cooperation. The Inter-governmental Expert Group on Climate Change established by the Thimphu Statement is required to monitor, review progress and make recommendations to facilitate its implementation, reporting to the SAARC Environment Ministers. The background to this Statement was the Fourteenth SAARC Summit (New Delhi, April 3–4, 2007) which expressed "deep concern" over the global climate change and called for pursuing a climate resilient development in South Asia. During the Twenty-ninth session of the SAARC Council of Ministers (New Delhi, December 7–8, 2007), the Council felt that given the vulnerabilities, inadequate means and limited capacities, there was a need to ensure rapid social and economic development to make SAARC climate change resilient. Pursuant to this decision, a Ministerial Meeting on Climate Change was held in Dhaka on July 3, 2008 preceded by an Expert Group Meeting on Climate Change on July 1–2, 2008. The Ministerial Meeting adopted the

implementation of SAARC Agreement on Rapid Response to Natural Disasters, SAARC Convention on Cooperation on Environment and Thimphu Statement on Climate Change...";[59] "renewed their commitment to substantially enhance regional connectivity...through building and upgrading roads, railways, waterways infrastructure, energy grids, communications and air links..."; "emphasized the need for linking South Asia with contiguous regions, including Central Asia...";[60] and "directed the relevant SAARC bodies and mechanisms to identify regional and sub-regional projects in the area of power generation, transmission and power trade, including hydropower, natural gas, solar, wind and bio-fuel, and implement them with high priority with a view to meeting the increasing demand for power in the region."[61]

In order to make comparisons with the AC governance framework it is also necessary to briefly consider the institutional arrangements of SAARC and SACEP. The SAARC Charter describes the institution as an *organisation*,[62] and the fact that it has entered into numerous agreements in relation to matters such as trafficking, terrorism, narcotics, criminal matters, child welfare and the environment indicate that it may in fact have legal personality.[63] SAARC has in recent years expanded to include observers in its governance framework; at the Delhi 2007 summit for example, seven countries joined: China, the USA, Mauritius, the EU, Japan, South Korea and Iran;[64] this trend was followed by the admission of additional observers since.[65] The inclusion of the

---

"Dhaka Declaration and SAARC Action Plan on Climate Change." For more information, *see* "Area of Cooperation," *supra*, note 55.

59   Kathmandu Declaration, Eighteenth SAARC Summit, Kathmandu, Nepal, November 26–27, 2014, para 14 (environment).

60   *Ibid.*, para 8 (connectivity).

61   *Ibid.*, para 9 (energy).

62   SAARC Charter, *supra*, note 51.

63   The ICJ in the *Reparation Case* established the parameters for this, which has been considered extensively since and is beyond the reach of this article, and not essential given that the legal transplant currently under consideration (AC) is presently without international legal personality anyway. In relation to the AC, *see* Duyck, *supra*, note 48, 3, and the examples given of other institutions (including Asia Pacific Economic Cooperation) together with options for the AC. *See* also Eric C. Ip, "The Power of International Legal Personality in Regional Integration," United Nations University-Comparative Regional Integration Studies Working Papers, W-2010/4, with another Asian example (the Association of South East Asian Nations).

64   Suk Deo Muni and Rajshree Jetly, "SAARC: The Changing Dimensions." United Nations University-Comparative Regional Integration Studies Working Papers, W-2008/8: 20.

65   *See* Kathmandu Declaration, *supra*, note 59, where the member states "...welcomed the participation of Observers from Australia, the People's Republic of China, the Islamic

FROM THE HIGH NORTH TO THE ROOF OF THE WORLD

USA (a member and currently chair of the Arctic Council), and China (with sovereignty over Tibet) is particularly significant. Muni and Jetley furthermore believe there is potential for China to become a full member in the future, supported by Pakistan, Nepal, Bangladesh among others;[66] while this is yet to happen it would have a major influence on the potential future governance of the Third Pole.

In relation to SACEP, it ambitiously describes itself as an *inter-governmental organisation* on its website;[67] however, other than memoranda of understanding and declarations, it does not appear to have concluded any international agreements. Significantly, distinct from most of the other regional seas,[68] there is no agreement for the Indian Ocean, which suggests international legal personality is absent. This is not necessarily problematic for making comparisons with the AC, for as will be seen this has also never had the status of an organisation in international law, and indeed it was preceded by a *strategy* (AEPS) not dissimilar to the *program* (SACEP) basis of the current arrangement. Organisational collaboration with other institutions is an essential component of the work of both SAARC and SACEP, and indeed between them.[69] Article 1(h) sets out the objective of the *SAARC Charter*: "to cooperate with international and regional organisations with similar aims and purposes";[70] the Mission of SACEP is "to work closely with all national, regional, and international institutions, governmental and nongovernmental, as well as experts and groups engaged in such co-operation and conservation efforts."[71]

Republic of Iran, Japan, the Republic of Korea, Mauritius, the Union of Myanmar, the United States of America, and the European Union at the Summit. In furtherance of earlier decisions on establishing dialogue partnership with States outside the region, the Leaders appreciated the Study undertaken by the SAARC Secretariat to review and analyze the engagement with the existing Observers to establish dialogue partnership. The Leaders directed the Programming Committee to engage the SAARC Observers into productive, demand-driven and objective project based cooperation in priority areas as identified by the Member States."

66   *Ibid.*, 21.
67   *South Asia Co-operative Environment Progamme*, accessed November 6, 2015, http:// www.sacep.org/; *see* Colombo Declaration on the South Asia Cooperative Environment Program, February 25, 1981.
68   Jeddah and Kuwait Conventions, *supra*, note 49.
69   Memorandum of Understanding, *supra*, note 55.
70   SAARC Charter, *supra*, note 51.
71   SACEP website, *supra*, note 67.

4 Arctic Precedents: Arctic Council Governance

AC governance[72] provides potential precedents in analysing what legal transplants, lessons, or learning experiences may be relevant to the Third Pole. While acknowledging different contextual constraints, the AC, SAARC, and SACEP all involve Arctic and Asian states as observers, and have a focus upon transboundary environmental governance. As outlined in the previous section, three aspects are particularly relevant in the comparative analysis: the areas of focus (such as the environment, water management, resource exploitation, climate change and natural disasters); the institutional structure (notably degrees of flexibility, and treaty making abilities); and collaboration opportunities (with related organisations within the sub-region, and those in the Arctic), including the opportunity for observers to contribute to regime building based upon their experience elsewhere.

The AEPS preceded the 1996 establishment of the AC.[73] It emphasised six key threats (persistent organic contaminants, radioactivity, heavy metals, noise, acidification and oil pollution); outlined applicable international treaties; and specified additional actions. Four working groups were established: Conservation of Arctic Flora and Fauna, Protection of the Arctic Marine Environment, Emergency Prevention, Preparedness and Response and the Arctic Monitoring and Assessment Programme. The latter, and large-scale scientific assessments in general[74] as supported by different communities, has been a core function and learning experience:

> The outcomes of the learning process – the focus on large-scale scientific assessments, the building up of the Arctic epistemic community and the particular way the assessments are conducted in the Arctic Council – constitute lessons in their own right. These might be useful for other regional forums looking for a viable niche, where they could position themselves most effectively in terms of influence on decision-making at various levels.[75]

---

72 For an overview of meanings and interpretations which is beyond the scope of this article, *see* Cécile Pelaudeix, "What is 'Arctic Governance'? A Critical Assessment of the Diverse Meanings of 'Arctic Governance'," *The Yearbook of Polar Law* VI (2015): 398.

73 Arctic Environmental Protection Strategy, 30 ILM 1624 (1991).

74 *See* for example the 2004 Arctic Climate Impact Assessment and the 2013 Arctic Biodiversity Assessment.

75 Koivurova *et al., supra*, note 1, 287.

FROM THE HIGH NORTH TO THE ROOF OF THE WORLD

The Ottawa Declaration clearly emphasises the areas of focus: "issues of sustainable development and environmental protection in the Arctic;"[76] to "oversee and coordinate the programs established under the AEPS;"[77] and to "oversee and coordinate a sustainable development program."[78] There are now 6 working groups with the addition of the Sustainable Development Working Group, and a working group to manage an Action Plan to Eliminate Pollution in the Arctic. The subject areas of most of these groups are also relevant in Third Pole context. Governance arrangements also include practical measures like contextualised EIA guidance for development projects;[79] and in 2011 and 2013, search and rescue, and oil spill treaties were finalised, negotiated under the auspices of the AC,[80] which "may also lead to new legally binding agreements in the foreseeable future;"[81] agreements on biodiversity and EIA for example, are common to arrangements in various parts of the world, and may follow.[82] The flexibility to do this (and significance) is reported by Koivurova *et al.*, in the following terms:

> In fact, the Arctic appears to counter the general trend of states seemingly being more reluctant than before to concluding treaties. This is primarily a consequence of the attention currently given to Arctic climate change and its impacts, highlighted in ACIA findings, especially the anticipated increase in various human activities in the region. As a result, there is a heightened focus on the adaptation of Arctic governance to a new climate change-driven reality in such areas as Arctic maritime navigation, oil spills or fisheries. The fact that the Arctic Council – at its core a soft law body – was capable to serve as a catalyst for binding agreements shows how its structural flexibility allows it to react to changing

---

76   Ottawa Declaration, *supra* note 11, article 1(a).

77   Ottawa Declaration, *supra* note 11, article 1(b).

78   Ottawa Declaration, *supra* note 11, article 1(c).

79   AEPS, *Guidelines for Environmental Impact Assessment (EIA) in the Arctic*, Finnish Ministry of the Environment (1997), accessed Nov. 8, 2015, www.unece.org/fileadmin/DAM/env/eia/documents/EIAguides/Arctic_EIA_guide.pdf.

80   Agreement on Cooperation on Aeronautical and Maritime Search and Rescue in the Arctic (signed in Nuuk on May 12, 2011, entered into force January 19, 2013) 50 ILM 1119 (2011) (SAR Agreement); Agreement on Cooperation on Marine Oil Pollution, Preparedness and Response in the Arctic (signed in Kiruna on May 15, 2013), accessed November 8, 2015, www.arctic-council.org/eppr (Oil Spills Agreement).

81   Loukacheva, *supra*, notes 1, 343.

82   In the Asia context, *see* Marsden, *supra*, note 45.

international environment within which it functions, displaying the ability for adaptive learning.[83]

Under the Ottawa Declaration, Members, Permanent Participants, and Observers all have key roles.[84] In 2013 observer status was granted to a number of significant Asian states, including the Third Pole nations: China and India.[85] Solli *et al.* report that application procedures were amended prior to the consideration of the new Asian observers, to ensure that their interests in the Arctic were consistent with the status quo, existing standards and their potential to contribute.[86] The application of the so-called "Nuuk criteria" to China and India was an important part of the process.[87] These were followed by instructions for engaging observers in the working groups, the "Observers Manual."[88]

In relation to structure and form, a key aspect of the AC emphasised in the Ottawa Declaration was that it was "established as a high level *forum*."[89] The significance attached to this was apparent from the process leading up to the Declaration, with the USA particularly opposed to the AC being given the status as an intergovernmental *organisation*. If this had occurred the AC would have had legal personality, bringing with it the ability to enter into international agreements on its own account.[90] Nonetheless, the AC has developed recently, in particular with the establishment of a Permanent Secretariat in 2013 in Norway; and notwithstanding the absence of *international* legal

---

83 Koivurova *et al., supra*, note 1, 307–308, footnote in quote deleted.

84 Ottawa Declaration, *supra* note 11, articles 2 and 3.

85 Per Erik Solli, Elana Wilson Rowe, and Wrenn Yennie Lindgren, "Coming into the cold: Asia's Arctic interests," *Polar Geography* 36(4) (2013): 253–270.

86 *Ibid.*

87 Sanjay Chaturverdi, "Geopolitical Transformations: 'Rising' Asia and the future of the Arctic Council," in Thomas S. Axworthy, Timo Koivurova, and Waliul Hasanat, ed., *The Arctic Council: Its Place in the Future of Arctic Governance*, Conference Proceedings, Munk-Gordon Arctic Security Program and University of Lapland, January 17–18, 2012.

88 Arctic Council, Arctic Council Observer Manual For Subsidiary Bodies (Kiruna, May 12, 2013) Senior Arctic Officials Report to Ministers (Kiruna, Sweden May 12, 2013), accessed November 8, 2015, www.arctic-council.org/index.php/en/document-archive/category/425-main-documents-from-kiruna-ministerial-meeting?download¼41780: observer-manual.

89 Ottawa Declaration, *supra*, note 11, article 1.

90 Duyck, *supra*, note 48, 2–3. *See also* Yoshinobu Takei, "The Role of the Arctic Council from an International Law Perspective: Past, Present and Future," *The Yearbook of Polar Law* VI (2015): 349, 353–356.

FROM THE HIGH NORTH TO THE ROOF OF THE WORLD

personality, Duyck notes that to enable it to perform its functions effectively, Norway afforded it *domestic* legal personality.[91] Furthermore, based on recent developments noted above, there is optimism that full institutional maturity is not far off:

> All these initiatives show that the Council has evolved from its advisory mandate into a more important body able to react and be responsive to the most calling issues facing the Arctic both in terms of political and practical significance. The Council is not a talking-shop any more. Reforms of the Council also show that it is becoming an influential player in the institutional structure of Arctic governance; its agenda is becoming clearer in dealing with questions of common responsibilities and concerns. In the future, the Council may even gradually evolve into a fully-fledged international organisation.[92]

The potential development of international legal autonomy is a significant aspect of the lessons for other organisations (such as SACEP), and the AC Secretariat will be a key component as it "bears much responsibility for communication *and outreach work* [my emphasis] for the Arctic Council."[93] The role of observers is a key part of inputting this outreach work, as the perspectives observers bring both potentially infuses the work of the AC in the Arctic, and enables lessons to be drawn and applied in other contexts. Article 3(b) of the *Ottawa Declaration* states: "Observer status in the Arctic Council is open to: (a) non-Arctic states; [and] (b) inter-governmental.... organisations global and regional.... that the Council determines can contribute to its work." Added to the observer triggers in the South Asian organisations cited above, this is a potential means of establishing relationships between the AC on one hand, and SAARC and SACEP on the other; or indeed between the AC and non-Arctic states.

Because of their economic and geographical significance, the role of China and India is crucial to developing governance of the Third Pole. The Tibetan plateau is part of China and has developed rapidly over recent years; China has

---

91   *Ibid.*, 3. Duyck notes also that the Indigenous Peoples Secretariat of the AC is also without international legal personality and similarly depends on national legal personality to carry out its functions.

92   Loukacheva, *supra*, note 1, 343.

93   Magnús Jóhannesson, "New Development: The Arctic Council Secretariat: Remarks to the Sixth Symposium on Polar Law/University of Akureyri, October 11, 2013," *The Yearbook of Polar Law* VI (2015): IX, XII.

observer status with both the AC and SAARC. A large part of the Himalayas is located in India; India is a member of SAARC, and has observer status on AC. Both of these states are therefore well placed to recognise the links between the First and Third Poles, and the need to address environmental protection and climate change issues, as well as economic development. The Indian PM Modi's visit to Beijing in May 2015 may indicate a thawing of relations,[94] which is positive for any new initiatives. In addition, China's domestic economic decline and India's rise may strengthen cooperation between them, particularly in the light of China's westward advance enabled by the Asian Infrastructure Investment Bank, which will fund major initiatives and must therefore incorporate effective safeguard mechanisms.[95]

5   Conclusions

The question to be answered in this article is: to what extent do existing environmental governance frameworks in the Arctic have relevance in the Third Pole Asian sub-region? The short answer is to a considerable extent. The findings are that AC governance in content, form and outreach has significant potential to enhance existing Third Pole institutions and develop transboundary governance. The areas of focus of the AC overlap to a major degree with those in the Asian sub-region, with concerns for environmental protection in general, water management, energy development and climate change (among others) shared by the AC, SAARC and SACEP. The institutional structures of the AC – formal and informal – have elements of both SAARC and SACEP, with a new Permanent Secretariat and the promulgation of two treaties strengthening the 'forum' considerably, even if it still lacks international legal personablity. The subject matter of these treaties should be of interest to all SAARC/SACEP members, regardless of whether they are coastal states; SAR and oil spills have relevance to terrestrial areas and can be adapted, especially given the disaster-prone nature of South Asia.

The shared observer/member status of certain states, in particular the USA (a SAARC observer and AC member), enables the application of lessons from the Arctic to the Third Pole context, particularly if the initiative is taken

---

94   "China and India call on rich countries to step up climate change efforts." *The Guardian* (London) May 15, 2015; D.R. Chowdhury, "Why Modi's India is warming to China," *South China Morning Post*, September 17, 2015.

95   Asian Infrastructure Investment Bank, *Environmental and Social Framework* (Consultation Draft) August 15, 2015. For discussion, *see* Marsden, *supra*, note 34.

during the current US Chairmanship to reach out to Third Pole states and institutions by promoting environmentally sustainable development in the sub-region. The European Union (EU) (which includes AC states Denmark, Finland and Sweden – and the close EU connections with Iceland and Norway), also has SAARC observer status; it can also do more to engage with this sub-region, as it has recently in the Arctic. SAARC itself already cooperates with over 20 intergovernmental organisations – one of these is the European Commission – and could apply for AC observer status to inform its own work and that of its members.

Most significantly perhaps, the experience of China and India as observers within the AC, added to knowledge of the impacts of climate change upon their own mountainous terrain, can inform their approach to Third Pole issues. Hydro-electric development in a geologically unstable sub-region with heavy dependence upon downstream water supplies is not to be undertaken lightly, particularly as these supplies are increasingly depleted through global warming. Similarly, potential oil and gas development without a regulatory framework already in place to contend with transboundary and domestic issues, is a huge risk for the environment, notwithstanding the extremely challenging geopolitics. The export of Chinese development across Asia and globally in particular poses major threats to the environment of the Third Pole, no matter how willing the other Third Pole states are to accept Chinese assistance. Environmental and other safeguards must not be compromised in the face of future development, but as is often the case, political will on the part of the key players is needed for lessons from AC governance to be effectively applied by existing South Asian institutions.

Understanding Arctic Co-Management: The U.S. Marine Mammal Approach

Kathryn Mengerink,[a] *David Roche,*[b] *and Greta Swanson*[c]

Abstract

Co-management is an effective tool through which Alaska Native communities can pursue self-governance and self-determination in regards to marine mammal resources. In the Arctic, co-management typically aims to promote environmental conservation, sustainable resource use, and equitable sharing of resource-related benefits and responsibilities. This paper traces a variety of co-management regimes and other international management frameworks, and posits that co-management of subsistence resources is not just a legal issue or a governance issue, but rather, it is an issue of human rights and environmental justice. It concludes that co-management regimes are most successful when they integrate frameworks for shared responsibility, and build long-term relationships on mutual trust and strong legal agreements.

Keywords

co-management – subsistence – environmental justice – human rights

---

a Senior Attorney & Director, Ocean Program, Environmental Law Institute and Academic Coordinator & Lecturer, Scripps Institution of Oceanography.
b Staff Attorney, Environmental Law Institute.
c Pro Bono Attorney, Chesapeake Legal Alliance and Visiting Attorney, Environmental Law Institute.

UNDERSTANDING ARCTIC CO-MANAGEMENT 77

List of Abbreviations

AEWC	Alaska Eskimo Whaling Commission
ANO	Alaska Native Organization
CAA	Conflict Avoidance Agreement
ESA	Endangered Species Act
FWS	U.S. Fish & Wildlife Service
MMC	Marine Mammal Commission
MMPA	Marine Mammal Protection Act
NMFS	National Marine Fisheries Service

1 Introduction†

In the Alaskan Arctic, as in other regions of the far North, indigenous peoples have made their living for thousands of years from available terrestrial and marine resources.[1] Alaska Native cultures are intertwined with their environments and rely on an in-depth understanding of the natural world, including indispensable traditional knowledge of Arctic species and ecosystems.[2] The cultures, economies, and natural systems of the U.S. Arctic have experienced significant changes over the last fifty years, including oil development on the North Slope in the 1960s and international regulation of subsistence harvest of whales.[3] In addition, a suite of legal and regulatory decisions have profoundly affected who can utilize, manage, and control the marine environment. These environmental and human use changes have accelerated in recent years as climate change dramatically alters the Arctic environment and opens up new areas for development. The U.S. federal government has responded to these changes with corresponding policies that seek to achieve a number of

---

† The authors wish to thank the many members of the Alaska Native community who have provided us with insight and expertise. In particular, we wish to thank Carolina Behe (Inuit Circumpolar Council-Alaska) for her input and guidance on this chapter.

1 *See, e.g.*, David E. Wilkins, American Indian Sovereignty and the U.S. Supreme Court: The Masking of Justice (University of Texas Press, 2010).

2 Inuit Circumpolar Council – Alaska, Alaskan Inuit Food Security Conceptual Framework: How to Assess the Arctic From an Inuit Perspective: Summary Report and Recommendations Report (2015), http://www.iccalaska.org/servlet/content/home.html.

3 Jessica Lefevre, "A Pioneering Effort in the Design of Process and Law Supporting Integrated Arctic Ocean Management," *Envtl. L. Reporter* 43 (2013): 10893, http://www.aewc-alaska .com/uploads/Jessica_CAA_Article.pdf.

sometimes conflicting objectives, including ensuring long-term sustainability of the environment, upholding its trust obligations to Alaska Natives, and supporting economic development. In the face of these changes, the roles of Alaska Natives in shaping development decisions take on heightened importance.

After the introduction, Part II of the paper introduces the concept of co-management and the fundamental rights of Alaska Natives under U.S. law. It describes how co-management can support tribal self-determination, while enabling the federal government to fulfill its trust responsibility to tribes and responsibility to effectively manage public resources. Part III of the paper examines the federal legal framework under which Alaska Natives co-manage marine mammals in the Arctic. In particular, it discusses the legal and regulatory structure of marine mammal co-management under the Marine Mammal Protection Act (MMPA)[4] and international law, and the structure and implementation of co-management agreements under such regimes. With an eye toward Alaska Native self-determination, Part IV explores opportunities, constraints, and best practices for co-management agreements. It discusses both legal strengths and limits of the existing system on the books, and how co-management can support self-determination of indigenous peoples, pointing to the need for future research on what works and what does not in practice. The two overarching lessons are that co-management is most successful when it involves shared responsibility, along with long-term relationships built on mutual trust and strong legal agreements.

2 Co-Management and Alaska Native Rights

The principle of self-determination is recognized by the United Nations Declaration on the Rights of Indigenous Peoples as a people's right to "freely determine their political status and freely pursue their economic, social and cultural development."[5] The Inuit Circumpolar Council-Alaska – a non-profit organization that represents Inuit from Alaska in domestic and international forums – considers meaningful involvement in managing subsistence resources to be a core principle of Alaska Native food security, culture, and basic human rights.[6] Self-determination for indigenous people is a right that is

---

4 *See* Marine Mammal Protection Act, 16 U.S.C. §§ 1361–1421h [hereinafter "MMPA"].

5 United Nations Declaration on the Rights of Indigenous Peoples, G.A. Res. 61/295 U.N. Doc. A/RES/61/295, Art. 3 (Sept. 13, 2007), http://www.un.org/esa/socdev/unpfii/documents/DRIPS_en.pdf.

6 ICC – Alaska, *supra*, note 2.

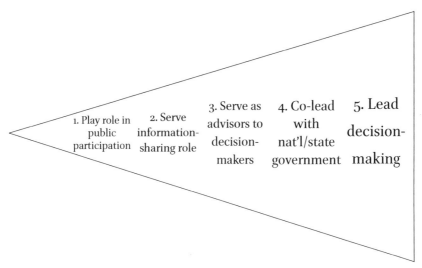

FIGURE 1   *Strength of Laws and Policies to Support Inuit Self-Governance.*

recognized globally and is of the utmost importance for subsistence resource governance and environmental justice in Alaska.

Alaska Native rights under federal law can be evaluated over a spectrum: from Alaska Native government having full authority over resources and decision-making at one end of the spectrum to legal regimes that provide Alaska Native communities with minimal opportunity to participate in the management of resources at the other (Figure 1). Despite efforts by Alaska Native communities to advance self-determination, in practice, the Alaska Native role in resource management tends to fall somewhere in the middle of this spectrum.

Co-management – in all of its iterations – is an effective tool through which Alaska Native communities can pursue self-governance and self-determination in regards to marine mammal resources. In the context of this paper, co-management of marine resources refers to an approach that shares management power between the federal government and Alaska Native communities.[7] More broadly, co-management is a pluralist approach to managing natural resources that incorporates two or more social actors to negotiate, define, and guarantee among themselves a shared arrangement of management functions for a given territory or set of resources.[8]

---

7   Eric Smith, "Some Thoughts on Co-Management," *Hastings W.-Nw. Journal Envt'l L. & Pol'y* 4 (1996): 1.
8   Grazia Borrini-Feyerabend et al., *Co-Management of Natural Resources: Organizing, Negotiating and Learning-by-Doing* (2007), https://portals.iucn.org/library/efiles/documents/

2.1   *Co-Management Opportunities*

In the Arctic, co-management typically aims to promote environmental conservation, sustainable resource use, and equitable sharing of resource-related benefits and responsibilities.[9] If designed and implemented in the right way, some scholars contend that co-management is better equipped than less collaborative approaches to respond to rapid Arctic change because co-management intertwines social and ecological relationships to create a flexible, iterative management regime.[10] In this way, co-management is viewed as a tool for adaptive management in a rapidly changing environment.

Arctic co-management can enhance democratic representation of indigenous groups within larger states.[11] The empowerment of indigenous communities to use their own strategies and to participate meaningfully in co-management can promote community stability and self-sufficiency.[12] Alaska Native communities have built upon their traditional knowledge system over many generations and continue to obtain daily information of the environment. This intimate relationship with and access to the environment provides unique knowledge and vested interest in ensuring sustainability.[13] It is thus important that local values, priorities, and traditional knowledge are utilized in Arctic marine resources management,[14] and one way to achieve such utilization is through appropriate co-management systems.

Additionally, co-management is praised from the perspective of social justice because it increases decision-making agency for communities, recognizing that management of traditional food resources are central to Alaska Native culture. The Inuit Circumpolar Council-Alaska identified inadequate

---

    2000-082.pdf. *See also* Fikret Berkes, "Evolution of Co-Management: Role of Knowledge Generation, Bridging Organizations and Social Learning," *Journal Envt'l. Mgmt.* 90 (2009): 1692, 1692.

9   *See* Berkes, *supra*, note 8.

10   Derek Armitage et al., "Adaptive Co-Management for Social–Ecological Complexity," *Frontiers in Ecology & Env.* 7 (2009): 95; Claudia Notzke, "A New Perspective in Aboriginal Natural Resource Management: Co-Management," *Geoforum* 26 (1995): 187.

11   Jessica Shadian, "Of Whales and Oil: Inuit Resource Governance and the Arctic Council," *Polar Record* 49 (2013): 392.

12   Fikret Berkes et al., "Collaborative Integrated Management in Canada's North: The Role of Local and Traditional Knowledge and Community-Based Monitoring," *Coastal Mgmt.* 35 (2007): 1.

13   Armitage, *supra* note 10.

14   Marine Mammal Commission, Review of Co-Management Efforts in Alaska (2008), http://www.mmc.gov/wp-content/uploads/mmc_comgmt.pdf [hereinafter "MMC"].

UNDERSTANDING ARCTIC CO-MANAGEMENT

co-management as a primary driver of food insecurity.[15] To enhance food security, the Inuit Circumpolar Council-Alaska recommended bolstering co-management systems,[16] such as those set up for marine mammal management discussed in the next section.

2.2 *Co-Management Challenges*

While there are substantial opportunities related to co-management regimes, challenges arise as to inter-governmental, regional, and civil society stakeholders gaining new powers and rights related to resource management.[17] State and non-state actors may collaborate roughly as formal equals, although of unequal capacity and resources in practice.[18] These incongruences can lead to a process that is long, expensive, and indecisive.[19]

Another important consideration is knowledge co-production based on the utilization of traditional knowledge and science, which is a challenging aspect of adaptive co-management.[20] While traditional knowledge has made a "demonstrable difference" in many management strategies and has shown its utility in countless settings, it faces obstacles like inertia and inflexibility.[21] Here, inertia means resistance to change given unfamiliarity of traditional knowledge to some systems of management.[22] Inflexibility refers to specific objections to incorporating traditional knowledge, such as unreliability or lack of reproducibility.[23] Further, the dynamic nature of traditional knowledge

---

15   ICC – Alaska, *supra*, note 2.

16   *Id.*

17   Shadian, *supra*, note 11.

18   Bradley Karkkainen, "Marine Ecosystem Management and a 'Post-Sovereign' Transboundary Governance," *San Diego Int'l Law Journal* 6 (2004): 113, 124; Stella Spak, "The Position of Indigenous Knowledge in Canadian Co-Management Organization," *Anthropologica* 47 (2005): 233.

19   Borrini-Feyerabrand et al., *supra*, note 8.

20   Aaron Dale and Derek Armitage, "Marine Mammal Co-Management in Canada's Arctic: Knowledge Co-production for Learning and Adaptive Capacity," *Marine Pol'y* 35 (2011): 440; Thomas Thornton and Adela Scheer, "Collaborative Engagement of Local and Traditional Knowledge and Science in Marine Environments: A Review," *Ecology & Soc'y* 17 (2012): 8.

21   Henry Huntington, "Using Traditional Ecological Knowledge in Science: Methods and Applications," *Ecological Applications* 10 (2000): 1270.

22   *Id.*

23   *Id.*

across time, regions, and communities must be considered for successful integration into co-management arrangements.[24]

In addition to conceptual challenges and considerations, systems of collaborative governance often involve the interaction of several legal drivers, making it important to delineate rights, roles, and responsibilities. Laws and policies establishing the framework for collaborative governance and Alaska Native self-governance that are particularly important to marine mammal resources in the U.S. Arctic are outlined in Table 1.

TABLE 1   *Examples of Legal Drivers for Inuit Role in Marine Resource Management in u.s.*

Legal Driver	Overview
Section 119 of the Marine Mammal Protection Act (MMPA)	Section 119 of the MMPA allows the Secretaries of the Interior and Commerce to enter into cooperative agreements with Alaska Native organizations for the purpose of co-management of subsistence use by Alaska Natives.[a] A Memorandum of Agreement for Negotiation of MMPA Section 119 Agreements (2006) elaborates upon the functions of the co-management agreements.[b] Among its guiding principles, the Memorandum of Agreement recognizes that, to the extent allowed by law, Alaska Natives should have "full and equal participation" in decisions that affect "the subsistence management of marine mammals."[c] Section 119 is the primary legal mechanism for enforceable marine mammal co-management agreements.[d]
Executive Order 13,175	Executive Order 13175, Consultation and Coordination with Indian Tribal Governments, built from federal trust responsibility to tribes, establishing formal government-to-government consultation requirements, requiring that all federal agencies (but not state or local entities) consult with tribes "in the development of Federal policies that have tribal implications.

24   Henrik Moller et al., "Combining Science and Traditional Ecological Knowledge: Monitoring Populations for Co-Management," *Ecology & Soc'y* 9 (2004): 1.

Legal Driver	Overview
Executive Order 13,689	Executive Order 13689, Enhancing Coordination of National Efforts in the Arctic, focuses broadly on mechanisms to enhance coordination among the various actors in the Arctic.[e] The Order calls upon the federal government to promote collaboration where possible with Alaska Native tribes and Alaska Native organizations.[f]

a 16 U.S.C. § 1388.
b Memorandum of Agreement for Negotiation of MMPA Section 119 Agreements, U.S. Dep't. of Commerce, U.S. Dep't. of Interior, and Indigenous Peoples Council for Marine Mammals (2006), http://www.ipcommalaska.org/pdfs/Umbrella%20Agreement.pdf.
c *Id.*
d In addition to Section 119, Section 504 provides co-management authority to the Alaska Nanuuq Commission for polar bears. Prior to the enactment of Section 119, Section 112 formed the basis for co-management with the Alaska Eskimo Whaling Commission. The legal authorities are discussed in detail in Part III.
e *Enhancing Coordination of National Efforts in the Arctic*, Exec. Order 13689, 80 Fed. Reg. 4191 (Jan. 21, 2015).
f *Id.*

The MMPA and Executive Orders are a subset of laws and policies that interact to form a complex system of engagement. Other components of the system include public participation requirements under the National Environmental Policy Act[25] and the Administrative Procedure Act,[26] along with other substantive laws like the Endangered Species Act (ESA)[27] that can influence Alaska Native rights to access marine mammal resources. This increasingly complex system can stress the capacity – and patience – of tribal participants in collaborative governance.

2.3 *Summary*

Simply put, co-management faces challenges. However, the opportunities for sustainable and just governance embodied by co-management make it worthwhile to discuss how best to overcome those obstacles. The research reviewed above generally demonstrates that effective co-management regimes are better at adapting to rapid Arctic change, they are better at incorporating the best

25 42 U.S.C. §§ 4321–4347.

26 5 U.S.C. §§ 551–559.

27 16 U.S.C. §§ 1531–1544.

available information into management decisions, and they are better at creating sustainable environmental practices. The question then is how can legal frameworks authorize or mandate management systems that transcend information sharing and become true co-management systems that, among other things, satisfy the U.S. government's tribal trust responsibilities related to subsistence resources that are central to Alaska Native culture.

3 Legal Framework for Marine Mammal Co-Management in the U.S. Arctic

Marine mammal co-management in Alaska is characterized by two overlapping objectives. First, the main goal held by all the parties involved is to sustain species populations at healthy levels. The MMPA embodies this objective with its primary purpose of achieving optimal population sizes. Second, parties share a goal to support subsistence, which is crucial for the survival of remote Alaska Native communities. The communities themselves have first-hand knowledge of what is at stake, and provisions in the MMPA strive to create management systems that incorporate community perspectives into shared management systems. However, while co-management has moved toward those objectives, "further progress is essential to satisfy the goals" of the MMPA.[28] There are gaps in the legal framework and the manner in which co-management is implemented in practice,[29] leading to the critical question – how can we bridge those gaps to optimize co-management regimes in the future?

This section aims to get at that question by reviewing key laws and regulations authorizing co-management of marine mammals. It then reviews how these laws influence management of different species. The goal is to discern variations among different marine mammal co-management approaches in order to identify features of effective co-management systems in the Arctic.

3.1 Marine Mammal Protection Act

The MMPA of 1972 is the primary mechanism for conserving marine mammal species, including those that are essential subsistence resources for Alaska Native communities.[30] A strong conservation provision at the heart of the MMPA places a general moratorium on the taking of marine mammals.[31]

---

28 MMC, *supra*, note 14 at iv–v.
29 *Id.*
30 MMPA, 16 U.S.C. §§ 1361–1421h.
31 MMPA, § 101(a).

UNDERSTANDING ARCTIC CO-MANAGEMENT

However, the MMPA provides an exemption for take by Alaska Natives,[32] which allows for subsistence practices and underscores the importance of co-management. Specifically, Indians, Aleut, and Eskimo peoples who reside in Alaska and dwell on the coast of the North Pacific Ocean or the Arctic Ocean can take marine mammals as long as it is for subsistence purposes or for the making and selling of traditional handicrafts and is not conducted in a wasteful manner.[33] Thus, there are four major elements for subsistence take: (1) membership in a tribe; (2) dwelling on the North Pacific/Arctic coast; (3) taking for subsistence or traditional handicrafts; and (4) not conducting take in a wasteful manner.

3.1.1 Co-Management Authorities under MMPA

The evolution of authority for co-management agreements under the MMPA is important because it demonstrates a legislative endorsement of co-management as a means of effective resource management in Alaska. Co-management was not originally a mechanism explicitly provided for in the MMPA. The first co-management agreement between a federal agency and Alaska Native Organization (ANO) was entered into under Section 112, which authorizes broadly described "cooperative agreements" to carry out MMPA purposes.[34] Section 112 is general and does not include discussion of co-management or shared responsibility.

In 1994, Congress amended the Act, establishing a provision for cooperative agreements between the federal government and Alaska Native Organizations in order "to conserve marine mammals and provide co-management of subsistence use by Alaska Natives."[35] This provision – Section 119 – has formed the basis for all of the co-management agreements that came after it, including polar bear co-management. Section 119 explicitly contemplates grants to ANOs to develop "marine mammal co-management structures," along with shared responsibilities for monitoring, data gathering, and research.[36]

Senator Ted Stevens, who helped develop the 1994 amendments concerning Alaska, explained that Section 119 "would allow the Alaska Native community to conserve marine mammals and protect their historic harvest rights to marine mammals."[37] The Marine Mammal Commission (MMC), an independent

---

32 MMPA, § 101(b).

33 Id.

34 MMPA, § 112.

35 MMPA, § 119.

36 MMPA, § 119.

37 Senator Stevens (AK). "Marine Mammal Protection Act Amendments of 1994." Congr. Rec. Mar. 21, 1994.

federal agency that oversees marine mammal conservation policies and programs of federal agencies, stated that a "cooperative effort to manage subsistence harvests that incorporate the knowledge, skills and perspective of Alaska Natives is more likely to achieve the goals of the MMPA than management by federal agencies alone."[38] Therefore, through Section 119, the 1994 amendments to the MMPA codified the progress made under the less explicit Section 112, representing an endorsement of co-management of marine mammals with Alaska Natives.

Sections 112 and 119 are not species-specific and provide significant latitude for when, why, and how cooperative agreements are arranged. Section 504 takes a different approach by specifically targeting polar bear management, building on Section 119 authorization. It provides a legal basis for a "cooperative management agreement" with the Alaska Nanuuq Commission for the management of the taking of polar bears for subsistence purposes.[39] For the "shared authority" to occur, the Alaska Nanuuq Commission must (1) enter into a Section 119 agreement; (2) meaningfully monitor compliance by Alaska Natives; and (3) comply with the agreement and the Act.[40]

Such is the general landscape of co-management under the MMPA: Section 112, with its emphasis on cooperation is the genesis of co-management under the Act. Section 119, enacted in 1994, affirms a commitment to co-management of trust resources. Finally, Section 504 provides more concrete legal language in relation to the Alaska Nanuuq Commission's co-management of polar bears. As the backstop to these agreements, if Alaska Natives challenge a regulation, stock assessment, determination of depletion, or finding of unmitigable adverse impacts on subsistence take by oil and gas activities, the federal government bears the burden of showing that the regulation or determination is supported by substantial evidence on the record.[41] Thus, the general system is that marine mammals are co-managed under the MMPA, but the federal government makes the final management decisions, with the burden of proof shifting to the federal government if Alaska Native tribes disagree.

In sum, Congress passed the amendments to protect the rights of Alaska Native communities while protecting species. With the policy aims stated clearly in the MMPA and by policy-makers, the important questions become whether and how co-management agreements under the MMPA facilitate sustainability of resources and Alaska Native self-determination.

---

38   MMC, *supra*, note 14 at 1.

39   MMPA, § 504.

40   *Id.*

41   MMPA, § 101(b).

UNDERSTANDING ARCTIC CO-MANAGEMENT 87

3.1.2   Co-Management Agreements Under the MMPA

Two federal agencies share co-management authority based on the species at issue. With authority delegated by the Secretary of Commerce, the National Marine Fisheries Service (NMFS) of the National Oceanic and Atmospheric Administration (NOAA) co-manages all cetaceans, seals, and sea lions.[42] With delegated authority from the Secretary of the Interior, the Fish and Wildlife Service (FWS) co-manages walrus, polar bears, and sea otters.[43] NMFS and FWS take different approaches to co-management, and these differences provide an opportunity to explore strengths and weaknesses and learn how best to design optimal co-management.

An overview of the scope of responsibilities of NMFS and FWS will set the stage for examining the specifics of certain agreements. First, both agencies provide grants to ANOs for the purpose of co-management, with the details of those grants spelled out in a cooperative agreement in accordance with Section 119. FWS establishes yearly cooperative agreements with the Alaska Nanuuq Commission and the Eskimo Walrus Commission.[44] In the past, it also had agreements with the Alaska Sea Otter and Stellar Sea Lion Commission.

In contrast, in addition to providing funding through a grant agreement, NMFS has long-term cooperative or co-management agreements with seven Alaska Native organizations: the Alaska Eskimo Whaling Commission (AEWC), Alaska Beluga Whale Commission, Aleut Marine Mammal Commission, Alaska Native Harbor Seal Commission, Aleut Community of St. George Island, Aleut Community of St. Paul Island, and Ice Seal Committee.[45] These NMFS agreements provide the broad framework under which both parties agree to achieve co-management objectives. They are amended as needed and exist outside the bounds of the funding agreement.

The first instructive point is based on agreement structure, rather than agreement substance. NMFS not only provides funding through grant agreements but also enters into long-term co-management agreements under Section 119.[46] FWS, on the other hand, utilizes the cooperative agreement as a

---

42   MMPA, § 3(12)(A)(i).

43   MMPA, § 3(12)(A)(ii).

44   Cooperative Agreements, Fish & Wildlife Serv., accessed July 21, 2016, http://www.fws.gov/alaska/fisheries/mmm/agreements.htm.

45   *See Co-Management of Marine Mammals in Alaska*, NOAA, https://alaskafisheries.noaa.gov/pr/comanagement.

46   *See, e.g.,* Agreement between NMFS and ABWC for Co-Management of the Western Alaska Beluga Whale Population (1999), https://alaskafisheries.noaa.gov/sites/default/files/abwcagrefinal.pdf [hereinafter "ABWC Agreement"]. Because the agreement between AEWC and NMFS was initially established under Section 112, it has been and

grant agreement under Section 119 and does not create an additional long-term agreement spelling out the nature of the co-management relationship.[47]

After a formal management or funding agreement is adopted, it is possible to develop management plans. These plans outline elements that can change, such as catch quota, without necessitating a new agreement altogether. NOAA has created management plans with many of its co-management bodies, including the AEWC, the Alaska Beluga Whale Committee, the Aleut Marine Mammal Commission, and others.[48] FWS has not consistently entered into management plans with its marine mammal co-management partners.

3.1.2.a   *NMFS Co-Management Agreements*[49]

The agreements themselves have different provisions that delineate the scope of the co-management system and the relationship between the ANO and NMFS. Across the NMFS agreements, the provisions address seven key topics: (1) research, which includes population monitoring, biosampling, tagging, and other types of research; (2) harvest monitoring; (3) regulation; (4) allocation; (5) enforcement; (6) education and communication; and (7) consultation and dispute resolution.

3.1.2.a.i   AEWC Agreement

While many of the NMFS co-management agreements have substantial similarities, one in particular stands out – the Cooperative Agreement with the AEWC, which gives the AEWC considerable authority for management and

---

continues to be called a cooperative agreement. The other NMFS agreements are named "co-management agreements." While the names are different, NMFS considers the terms "co-management agreement" and "cooperative agreement" as having the same meaning. Personal communication with NMFS official (Jan. 29, 2016).

47   *See, e.g.,* Alaska Nanuuq Commission Co-Management of Polar Bears, Federal Grants, http://www.federalgrants.com/Alaska-Nanuuq-Commission-Co-Management-of-Polar -Bears-36488.html.

48   *See, e.g.,* Aleut Marine Mammal Commission and NMFS, Steller Sea Lion and Harbor Seal Co-Management Action Plan (2015), http://www.aleutmarinemammal.org/action nmfsaction2015.pdf.

49   NOAA's agreement with the Alaska Eskimo Whaling Commission is called a "cooperative agreement," which reflects the creation of the agreement under § 112 rather than § 119. *See* Cooperative Agreement between NOAA and AEWC (2013), https://alaskafisheries.noaa .gov/sites/default/files/aewc2013.pdf [hereinafter "AEWC Agreement"]. NOAA does not distinguish between the term "cooperative agreement" or "co-management agreement." Personal communication with NOAA personnel (Jan. 2016). Therefore, we refer to these agreements generally as "co-management agreements."

enforcement.[50] Under the agreement, the AEWC generally manages the bowhead hunt with oversight from NMFS.[51] The AEWC determines allocation of permitted strikes among villages and reports to NMFS all strikes and landings.[52] Regarding enforcement, the AEWC enforces the take limits and allocations, and collects civil monetary penalties from whaling captains if violations occur.[53] If there is a dispute over a strike or other enforcement provision, NOAA and the AEWC consult. If the dispute is not resolved, it goes to an administrative law judge, then to the NOAA Administrator, who may also assess penalties.[54]

Comparing and contrasting the AEWC agreement with other agreements highlights some elements that may be instructive in designing optimal co-management systems. Like other NMFS agreements, the AEWC agreement provides for the development of a management plan, which sets out principles of conservation, subsistence harvesting, use, monitoring and reporting, research, public involvement, and enforcement.[55] The ANOs are primarily responsible for inspection and reporting, with NMFS personnel participating in data collection. NMFS and the ANOs share research and day-to-day management responsibilities.

The primary difference between the AEWC agreement and the other NMFS agreements is how management and enforcement roles are shared between the federal agency and the ANO. The AEWC has an enhanced role that includes the authority to collect assessments and levy civil penalties, establishing the AEWC as the key actor throughout the management process, from policy development to implementation to enforcement. This role has allowed the AEWC to play a large part in domestic management.[56]

The AEWC's leadership role in the management of bowhead whales however predates and indeed, extends beyond the four corners of the management agreement itself, exerting an influence even at the international level. Three examples are important to highlight. First, the AEWC has collaborated with the U.S. government on the international stage serving as part of the US delegation at the International Whaling Commission meetings where annual bowhead

50 *See* AEWC Agreement, *supra*, note 56.

51 *See id.*

52 *Id.*

53 *Id.*

54 *Id.*

55 *See, e.g.,* ABWC Agreement, *supra*, note 52.

56 *See* David S. Case & David A. Voluck, *Alaska Natives and American Laws*, Chapter 8: Subsistence (Univ. of Alaska Press, 2012), 323.

whale quotas are set.[57] Second, and in the same vein, the AEWC has served as a "cooperating agency" under the National Environmental Policy Act for environmental impact assessment related to bowhead whale take, which supports U.S. decision-making regarding the international bowhead quota.[58] Third, as is discussed in further detail in Section III(a)(iii), the AEWC has long collaborated with the oil and gas industry to minimize conflict between the bowhead whale harvest and oil and gas activities.

It is also important to note the success of this co-management system: over the course of the three decades it has been in operation, the bowhead whale population has thrived. The Western Arctic population, once decimated by commercial harvest, is now estimated at 6,400–9,200 whales and growing at a rate of 3.2% annually.[59] It is in fact approaching the levels of the pre-commercial whaling population estimate.

3.1.2.a.ii Other NMFS Agreements

In addition to differences in the language of the agreements themselves, there are differences in governance among the NMFS agreements that are important to point out. These differences fall into three general categories: (1) how the co-management body is structured; (2) when consultation occurs and what triggers it; and (3) how management plans are developed.

Regarding co-management body structure, some of the ANOs include broader representation within the co-management body. For example, the Alaska Beluga Whale Committee itself "includes Federal, State and local government representatives," with membership set forth in by-laws.[60] For certain votes within the Committee (such as harvest allocation), only the Alaska Native representatives participate.[61] The Beluga Whale Committee is solely responsible for drafting management plans.[62] This approach has been praised

---

57 International Whaling Commission (IWC), North Slope Borough, accessed March 31, 2016, http://www.north-slope.org/departments/wildlife-management/other-topics/iwc-and -aewc/iwc.

58 NMFS, Draft Environmental Impact Statement for Issuing Annual Quotas to the Alaska Eskimo Whaling Commission for a Subsistence Hunt on Bowhead Whales for the Years 2013 through 2017/2018 (2012).

59 NOAA Fisheries, Office of Protected Resources, *Bowhead Whale* (Balaena mysticetus), accessed March 31, 2016, http://www.nmfs.noaa.gov/pr/species/mammals/cetaceans/ bowheadwhale.htm.

60 ABWC Agreement, *supra*, note 53.

61 Personal communication with ABWC co-management representative from Dec. 2015 (notes of discussion on file with authors).

62 ABWC Agreement, *supra*, note 53.

UNDERSTANDING ARCTIC CO-MANAGEMENT 91

as a successful mechanism to enable collaboration between agency scientists and traditional knowledge holders.[63]

Meanwhile, other ANOs consist only of tribal representatives. Management plans are drafted in co-management committees consisting of ANO and NMFS representatives. For example, the Ice Seal co-management committee (set up to guide the "joint and separate management actions by the [Ice Seal Committee] and NMFS") consists of "five management regional Representatives of [the Ice Seal Committee] and three members from NMFS."[64] The Aleut Marine Mammal Commission agreement, among others, has a similar co-management committee structure.[65] These committees develop the management plans that determine how the resource is governed.

Consultation between federal agencies and Alaska Native tribes is a complex issue both within Alaska generally and specifically as it relates to co-management and co-management agreements. At the outset, it is important to briefly describe the over-arching nature of consultation in Alaska. As introduced earlier, under Executive Order 13,175, Consultation and Coordination with Indian Tribal Governments (EO 13,175), the federal government must consult with tribal governments when making decisions that may affect tribal interests, a requirement stemming from the trust relationship the federal government has with tribes.[66] While there is overlap in purpose, co-management and consultation under EO 13,175 are separate processes and can be viewed as two distinct mechanisms used to enable federal agency and Alaska Native collaboration.

However, the practical operation of the regime is quite complicated since under EO 13175, federal agencies must consult on a government-to-government basis with tribal officials and *authorized intertribal organizations*."[67] While this consultation right lies with tribal governments, the inclusion of authorized intertribal organizations in the Executive Order indicates that other organizations – like marine mammal co-management bodies – could be authorized by tribes to engage in consultation on behalf of (or alongside of) tribal governments.

---

63   Personal communication with ABWC co-management representative from Dec. 2015 (notes of discussion on file with authors).

64   Agreement between the Ice Seal Committee and NMFS for Co-Management of Alaskan Ice Seal Populations (2006), https://alaskafisheries.noaa.gov/sites/default/files/agreement1006.pdf.

65   Agreement between the Aleut Marine Mammal Commission and NMFS (2006), accessed March 31, 2016, https://alaskafisheries.noaa.gov/sites/default/files/ammc06.pdf.

66   EO 13175, *supra*, note **Error! Bookmark not defined.**

67   EO 13175, *supra*, note 29 at § 1(b) (emphasis added) (definition of "Indian tribe").

While consultation is an important right, co-management on paper and in practice is a more robust system of shared management responsibility for certain resources.[68] Consultation, meanwhile, is a more general requirement that in practice falls far short of collaborative management.[69] However, co-management bodies can engage in consultation with their federal co-management counterparts and, in fact, all of the co-management agreements require consultation under specific circumstances. It is an open discussion whether the type of consultation called for within co-management agreements is the same type of consultation that is spelled out under the Executive Order,[70] an issue that is beyond the scope of this paper. The takeaway message is that co-management agreements require "consultation" under a specific set of circumstances. However, debate swirls about how this consultation authority interacts with consultation under the Executive Order and general tribal authorizations to ANOs that form the basis of co-management.[71]

Under the Beluga Whale Committee agreement, consultation is required before "assertion of federal management authority" and for research activities, and is conducted on an "as-needed basis concerning matters related to the management of Western Alaska beluga whales which either party believes are suitable for such consultation."[72] Specific scenarios envisioned include "matters which have the potential to affect any Western Alaska beluga whale stock or the Native subsistence hunting" of the whale population, along with any changes to the language of the MMPA, Endangered Species Act, or regulations.[73] The Ice Seal Committee agreement calls for consultation on a routine basis, and includes consultation before contact with the media, regulation and enforcement, species listing, and research.[74] The Aleut Marine Mammal Commission agreement's consultation provisions are substantially similar to the Ice Seal Committee agreement, with the addition that it requires consultation at least once per year.[75]

---

68 *See* Jordan Diamond, Greta Swanson and Kathryn Mengerink, "Rights and Roles: Alaska Natives and Ocean and Coastal Subsistence Resources," *Florida A&M Univ. L. Rev.* 8 (2013): 219.

69 *See id.*

70 *See* Consultation Report, *supra*, note 29 (discussing big "C" and little "c" consultation).

71 *See id.*

72 ABWC Agreement, *supra*, note 53.

73 *Id.*

74 Ice Seal Agreement, *supra*, note 70.

75 AMMC Agreement, *supra*, note 71.

UNDERSTANDING ARCTIC CO-MANAGEMENT 93

To summarize, while there is variation as to the circumstances that trigger consultation obligations, across all of the agreements, consultation provisions appear relatively strong in that they usually allow consultation when it is desired by either party. However, none of the agreements addresses how consultation actually occurs in practice, or how it interacts with government-to-government consultation as described under EO 13,175.[76]

The final major variation in the agreements is how management plans are developed and finalized. Both the AEWC and the ABWC are primarily responsible for drafting management plans, with oversight from NMFS for compliance. For the Aleut Marine Mammal Commission and the Ice Seal Committee, the management plan is drafted by the co-management committee, which consists of both Alaska Native representatives and NMFS.

3.1.2.b   *FWS Co-Management Agreements*

FWS awards annual grants to further the activities of the Alaska Nanuuq Commission and the Eskimo Walrus Commission. The grants are used to fund, among other things: "commission co-management operations; biological sampling programs; harvest monitoring; collection of Native knowledge in management; coordination on management issues; cooperative enforcement of the MMPA; and development of local conservation plans."[77] The nature of the FWS agreements as grant agreements combined with the absence of long-term cooperative agreements emphasizes the financial arrangements of the federal government and ANOs rather than shared management.

However, while the agreements themselves fall short of establishing long-term written commitments that specify how co-management will be achieved, both have had some success in practice. In particular, the Alaska Nanuuq Commission has a strong role in domestic and international management as set out in the MMPA, rather than by a subsidiary agreement. As discussed previously, Section 504 of the MMPA provides the Alaska Nanuuq Commission with shared authority for polar bear management.[78] This section is premised on an international agreement – the Agreement on the Conservation and Management of the Alaska-Chukotka Polar Bear Population, signed by Russia

---

76   *See* Environmental Law Institute & Marine Mammal Commission, Handbook: Model Alaska Native Consultation Procedures (2016), accessed March 31, 2016, http://www.mmc.gov/wp-content/uploads/model_consultation_procedures_handbookfinal.pdf (discussing procedures to structure consultation).

77   Cooperative Agreements, *supra*, note 50.

78   MMPA, § 504.

and the u.s. in 2000.[79] The agreement provides for representation by the Alaska Nanuuq Commission, which gives it a unique role in establishing overall take limits and other restrictions on the taking of polar bears at the international level.[80] In the absence of such leverage from international agreements, though, a co-management system based only on an annual grant agreement could undermine the long-term collaboration needed to sustain a healthy, shared management system.

3.1.3 Other MMPA Provisions for Alaska Native Participation

In addition to providing a subsistence exemption, the MMPA prioritizes subsistence uses when offshore oil and gas development occurs in the Alaskan Arctic. Under the MMPA, oil and gas activities must not have an "unmitigable adverse impact" on the availability of marine mammals for subsistence use.[81] The activities also must have no more than a "negligible impact" on marine mammal populations.[82] To avoid a determination of unmitigable adverse impact, regulations may require companies to develop Plans of Cooperation that set forth mitigating measures, along with Letters of Authorization or Incidental Harassment Authorizations for incidental take.[83]

A Plan of Cooperation, Letter of Authorization, or an Incidental Harassment Authorization should trigger consultation with Alaska Native communities when subsistence resources are at risk. Under FWS and NMFS regulations, they must include procedures to work with subsistence hunters and measures to avoid impacts and ensure availability of subsistence species.[84] However, the regulations do not require negotiated agreements.

When applying for a Letter of Authorization, FWS regulations may require applicants to consult with affected communities and develop mitigation measures.[85] Similarly, Incidental Harassment Authorization regulations require applicants to consult with affected communities if activities may impact subsistence. If a community raises concerns that the proposed activities

---

79   Agreement between the Government of the United States of America and the Government of the Russian Federation on the Conservation and Management of the Alaska-Chukotka Polar Bear Population (2000), http://pbsg.npolar.no/en/agreements/US-Russia.html.

80   *See id.*

81   MMPA, §§ 101(a)(5)(A), (D).

82   *Id.*

83   *See* 50 C.F.R. §§ 18.124(c)(4), 216.104(a)(12).

84   *Id.*

85   Incidental Take Regulations, u.s. Fish & Wildlife Serv., http://www.fws.gov/alaska/fisheries/mmm/itr.htm.

UNDERSTANDING ARCTIC CO-MANAGEMENT 95

may adversely impact subsistence, the applicant "must address conflict avoidance issues through a Plan of Cooperation."[86]

While MMPA provisions for oil and gas development do not require negotiated agreements with Alaska Native communities, the AEWC Conflict Avoidance Agreement (CAA) demonstrates the effectiveness of engaging private stakeholders with subsistence hunters to reach agreements about trust resources. Under the CAA process, every year, "whaling captains contemplate how the year's exploration and development work, as planned by the offshore companies, can be coordinated and carried out so as not to interfere with the fall bowhead whale migration and their critical fall whale harvest."[87] The CAA negotiated agreement has been successful for all parties involved, and demonstrates an apt model for the potential breadth of co-management to include collaboration with other resource stakeholders. Foremost in the CAA process success are the principles on which it is based. The CAA process is based "on the recognition that in situations where conflicts are localized and relatively unique: (a) immediate stakeholders may be the most-qualified candidates for identifying effective solutions; (b) well-crafted and appropriately peer-reviewed scientific research is a key element underlying decision-making; and (c) formally recognizing local residents as stakeholders in the decision process provides a sense of control in a setting where the outside forces of change can appear overwhelming."[88]

These principles can have application beyond CAAs or formal MMPA Plans of Cooperation, and could be incorporated into co-management. The main lesson for co-management is that shared authority between stakeholders with overlapping but not identical interests can lead to optimal conservation outcomes. When combined with the other MMPA lessons, the principles of the CAA point toward the need for co-management structures that truly share authority in practice, rather than just in name.

3.2 *Endangered Species Act*

While the MMPA and executive orders are the primary avenues for co-management between Alaska Natives and the federal government, the ESA and implementing regulations also provide a role for Alaska Natives in management of marine mammals.[89] The ESA generally prohibits take for all listed species, including many marine mammals, and establishes critical habitat

---

86   50 C.F.R. §§ 18.118(a)(6) (Chukchi Sea), 18.128(a)(6) (Beaufort Sea).
87   Lefevre, *supra*, note 3.
88   *Id.*
89   *See* Endangered Species Act, 16 U.S.C. §§ 1531–1544 [hereinafter "ESA"].

for some of those species. However, the ESA gives Alaska Natives a subsistence exception to the prohibition on take and critical habitat activities in some instances. Under ESA Section 10(e), subsistence activities may only be regulated if such takes "materially and negatively affect[] the threatened or endangered species."[90] Before regulating, there must be notice and hearing in the affected judicial districts. Secretarial Order No. 3225, which implements the subsistence exception in Alaska, provides an avenue for cooperative management to avoid regulations. It states that "the goal of the Departments will be to work collaboratively with Alaska Natives to craft cooperative agreements that will conserve the species, fulfill the subsistence needs, and preclude the need for regulations."[91]

For the most part, the ESA has succeeded in this objective – the MMPA and the co-management agreements largely preclude the need for additional regulation of subsistence species. For listed species like bowhead whales and ice seals (among others), NMFS found that subsistence take does not materially or negatively impact the species and thus does not regulate subsistence take under the ESA.[92] A contrasting example is the Cook Inlet beluga whale population, for which subsistence hunting is prohibited due to depletion findings under the MMPA and ESA.[93] Generally, however, ESA provisions concerning take and critical habitat designations are subsumed by the MMPA co-management agreements for subsistence take of marine mammals. As the ESA Secretarial Order indicates, successful management of listed marine mammals in Alaska relies on the federal government "work[ing] collaboratively with Alaska Natives to craft cooperative agreements."[94]

3.3   *International Agreements*

As discussed above, some of the variance in how co-management agreements are structured is attributable to the international framework for governance of specific subsistence resources. In particular, U.S. international obligations under both polar bear and whale treaties also influence the management of marine mammals in Alaska.

90   16 U.S.C. § 1539.

91   Dep't. of the Interior, Secretarial Order 3225, Endangered Species and Subsistence Uses in Alaska (supplement to Secretarial Order 3206) (Jan. 19, 2001).

92   *See* Alaska Seals, NOAA, accessed March 31, 2016, https://alaskafisheries.noaa.gov/pr/seals.

93   Cook Inlet Beluga Whales NOAA, accessed March 31, 2016, https://alaskafisheries.noaa.gov/pr/ci-belugas.

94   Secretarial Order 3225, *supra*, note 97.

3.3.1 International Whaling Convention

The United States is party to the International Convention for the Regulation of Whaling.[95] Article V(1) of the Act authorizes the International Whaling Commission to set a schedule for harvest limits; the Schedule sets harvest limits for various purposes, including for subsistence whaling. The United States implements this treaty through the Whaling Convention Act of 1949.[96] Based on the harvest limits, NOAA establishes a yearly limit by regulation. Regulations under the Whaling Convention Act codify the AEWC co-management agreement provisions for management of the whale hunt.[97] The AEWC's enforcement authority originates under the IWC, NOAA implementing regulations, and its co-management agreement with NMFS.

3.3.2 Polar Bear Agreements

The MMPA implements the United States' obligations under the Multilateral Conservation of Polar Bears Agreement[98] and the Agreement on the Conservation and Management of the Alaska-Chukotka Polar Bear Population between Russia and the United States (2000). Among the goals of the 1973 agreement are the protection of ecosystems of which the bears are a part and management of polar bears according to sound conservation practices.[99] Although generally prohibiting take of polar bears, the Agreement allows taking "by local people using traditional methods in the exercise of their traditional rights and in accordance with the laws of that Party; or wherever polar bears have or might have been subject to taking by traditional means by its nationals."[100] The 2000 agreement affirms those principles and sets up a management structure that includes the Alaska Nanuuq Commission as a voting member, and is codified by Section 504 of the MMPA, as described above. The Alaska Nanuuq Commission's unique enforcement authority derives from the international agreements, Section 504, and its co-management agreement. Other key features of Section 504 and connected MMPA provisions include requiring the United States government and the Nanuuq Commission representative to agree upon a position during international negotiations under the

---

95   International Convention for the Regulation of Whaling, Jan. 1964, 161 U.N.T.S. 2/24.

96   64 Stat. 421; 16 U.S.C. § 916.

97   50 C.F.R. § 230.

98   Agreement on the Conservation of Polar Bears, Nov. 15, 1973, 27 U.S.T. 3918, T.I.A.S. No. 8409.

99   Polar Bear Agreement, Art. II (1973), http://sedac.ciesin.org/entri/texts/polar.bears.1973 .html.

100   *Id.* at Art. III.

2000 treaty.[101] In addition, it states that FWS is authorized to pass regulations that accept a Nanuuq Commission ordinance related to harvest restrictions.[102] This approach is a unique example of putting the ANO in the driver seat for the development of federal regulations and policies.

3.3.3 Northern Fur Seals

The Fur Seal Treaty of 1911, signed by Russia, the United States, Great Britain, and Japan, was the earliest treaty to address marine mammal conservation, and was developed in response to the devastation of the northern fur seal population by commercial sealing.[103] The Treaty prohibited at-sea hunting of fur seals, managed the on-shore harvest, and protected aboriginal rights to subsistence harvest.[104] The Fur Seal Act of 1966 and the MMPA implemented the treaty in the United States.[105] Additionally, agreements under the treaty provide support for certain activities of the St. George and St. Paul tribal governments.[106]

The Fur Seal Act and MMPA continue to authorize subsistence harvest of the northern fur seal. NMFS issues regulations that estimate the subsistence harvest of northern fur seals by Alaska Natives of the St. George and St. Paul Islands and establishes an upper limit for subsistence take. The subsistence harvest regulations are developed in consultation with the affected Alaska Native communities.[107] Relying in part on the provisions of the co-management agreements, the regulations provide for continued cooperation between NMFS and Alaska Native hunters to manage and monitor the harvest.

3.3.4 Summary of International Agreements

Some of the variation in co-management agreements under the MMPA is attributable to international treaties that provide ANOs with substantial authority. In particular, the AEWC and the Alaska Nanuuq Commission are empowered through a formal role at the international level, and their enforcement authority derives in part from that role. It is interesting to note that the AEWC and Alaska Nanuuq Commission agreements are the strongest on paper (and likely in practice). Both agreements aim to conserve the subsistence resource while

---

101   MMPA, §§ 505, 506.

102   MMPA, § 503.

103   Convention Between the United States, Great Britain, Japan and Russia Providing for the Preservation and Protection of the Fur Seals, July 7, 1911, 37 Stat. 1542.

104   *Id.*

105   Fur Seal Act of 1966, Pub. L. No. 89–702, 80 Stat. 1091 (1966).

106   *See, e.g.,* 16 U.S.C. § 1166.

107   *See, e.g.,* 79 Fed. Reg. 65327 (Nov. 4, 2014); 50 C.F.R. § 216.72(b).

UNDERSTANDING ARCTIC CO-MANAGEMENT

providing native communities with an effective role that enhances their right of self-determination.

4   Lessons Learned from U.S. Marine Mammal Co-Management

How do all of these agreements, treaties, and regulations work in practice? It varies substantially among marine mammal species. Identifying which variations are beneficial is the key to understanding how to build stronger legal regimes that protect both resources and native rights. This section reviews how marine mammal co-management varies across species to provide insight into what works and how co-management can most effectively achieve its goals of sustaining resources and supporting the self-determination of indigenous peoples.

The MMPA recognizes the singular importance of subsistence resources to Alaska Native communities, along with the goal of resource protection, by providing for co-management agreements that share management authority between federal agencies and ANOs. While the agreements themselves all are rooted in the same MMPA provision for the most part, they diverge from trunk (structure of the agreement) to stem (how much authority is vested with the ANO) to leaves (specific provisions regarding consultation, among other things). In addition, other co-management examples, such as AEWC's CAA and the influence of international agreements on domestic co-management, provide instructive points for effective regimes. This review explores five essential elements that are important in understanding how to best design and implement co-management in the Arctic:

- Legal authority for the co-management agreement;
- Structure of the co-management agreement;
- Management and enforcement authority;
- Co-management body structure and management plan process; and
- Consultation and dispute resolution within the co-management process.

In addition, and at the heart of co-management success is the need to design a system that establishes long-term collaboration based on trust. Key take-away points from this research include the following:

First, for marine mammals, co-management agreements are structured as a longer-term legal document (NMFS) or a shorter-term grant (FWS). Both have the potential to sustain resources, though the longer-term legal agreements could encourage unobservable investments (a theory supported by economic literature).[108] In this case, unobservable investments could include long-term relationship-building, a key part of co-management and other forms of cooperative environmental management, like consultation.[109]

Second, legal authority for co-management in Alaska varies to some degree. AEWC was established under the more general Section 112 and the Alaska Nanuuq Commission's co-management approach is further specified under Section 504, while all of the other agreements are designed under Section 119 only. However, the AEWC and the Alaska Nanuuq Commission also operate under international agreements and implementing regulations that bolster their role as partners in co-management, supporting self-determination. Additional regulations (or legislation) that bolster shared authority for Section 119 agreements could provide a similar impetus for more robust self-determination (e.g., enhanced enforcement authority).[110]

Third, as a result of the different sources of legal authority, enforcement capabilities also vary. Generally, AEWC and the Alaska Nanuuq Commission have the strongest management and enforcement authority. In fact, the MMC determined that Alaska Native partners do not have enforcement authority under section 119; it therefore recommended that Congress amend the MMPA to give co-management partners authority to enforce harvest limits.[111] Since enforcement is a core element in the shared management of a resource, it is important to think about a legislative or regulatory fix to enhance self-determination.

Fourth, the structure of the co-management bodies varies. For example, the Beluga Whale Committee includes government representatives, while most other ANOs are comprised solely of Alaska Native representatives. In addition, these bodies provide differing approaches for stakeholder involvement and defining who is at the table when developing management plans. There are positives and negatives for the different approaches – representation of all parties within co-management bodies seems to be a step forward for shared authority and relationship-building. However, it could result in a less unified body that faces gridlock on difficult issues. No matter how a co-management body is structured, it is imperative that Alaska Native representatives have a preeminent role in shaping policies related to subsistence resources.

---

108   *See, e.g.*, Oriana Bandiera, Contract Duration and Investment Incentives, 5 *J. of European Econ. Ass'n* 953 (2007).

109   *See* Consultation Report, *supra*, note 29.

110   *See* MMC, *supra*, note 14.

111   *Id.* at 15.

Fifth, provisions for consultation and dispute resolution vary and generally do not contain a detailed description of how and when they will occur. Of particular concern is the relationship between the consultation that occurs under co-management agreements and the consultation that is called for under EO 13,175. With the existing lack of clarity between these two constructs, there is a possibility that co-management will be undermined by consultation under EO 13,175. The concern is that federal agencies could use consultation as an end-run around co-management when disputes arise. Furthermore, if agencies put more effort into consultation rather than co-management, it could shift federal-tribal relations from one involving mutual decision-making (co-management) into one that focuses more on information sharing (as often occurs with consultation in practice). More specific articulation of how consultation occurs and how it interacts with co-management within agreements or management plans could solve this problem, supporting healthy ecosystems and self-determination.[112]

5   Conclusion

Co-management of subsistence resources is not just a legal issue or a governance issue. Rather, it is an issue of human rights and environmental justice. As described by the Inuit Circumpolar Council-Alaska, co-management is an integral part of self-determination, which is essential for food security.[113] Food security, in turn, means many things, but at its core it is essential to the very culture of indigenous peoples in the Arctic.[114]

Thus, the stakes are high with co-management of subsistence resources. From this review, we learned that there are challenges and opportunities posed by co-management, some of which are based on the nature of shared governance, and some of which are based on the specifics of law and policy. In the U.S. Arctic, while law and policy is multifaceted, it is centered around co-management agreements under the Marine Mammal Protection Act. From those agreements, there appear to be multiple avenues for sustaining resources. But there are more clear paths toward maximizing self-determination, and in turn, supporting the human rights of indigenous peoples.

Co-management should be based on long-term legal agreements with strong provisions for shared authority. All stakeholders should be involved,

---

112   *See* Model Consultation Procedures, *supra*, note 82.

113   ICC-Alaska, *supra*, note 2.

114   *Id.*

but the Alaska Native voice should be given a greater say in times of disagreement. Finally, co-management should interact more clearly and strategically with other avenues for shared governance, like consultation, in order to avoid overwhelming the capacity (and patience) of tribal governments.

This legal review has focused on co-management on the books. While this paper explores some aspects of the legal framework for co-management, it only scratches the surface of what occurs in practice. Invariably some management regimes fall short of expressed goals and others are much more robust than what is indicated on paper. Further research into co-management on the ground – along with other methods of shared governance – is needed about the optimal way to implement strong, just agreements in practice.

Environmental justice and sustainability go hand-in-hand in the Arctic. Justice requires governance regimes that integrate and elevate the perspectives of indigenous peoples. Likewise, sustainability relies on traditional knowledge, which is best equipped to understand often remote and unforgiving Arctic ecosystems. For marine mammals, co-management is an essential avenue for pursuing these dual goals. However, co-management has had successes and failures influenced both by legal mandates and policies, as well as how institutions have implemented such laws and policies in practice. New and evolving approaches to co-management should learn from the lessons of existing co-management systems that federal agencies and ANOs that have spent 20-plus years designing and implementing.

There is no right answer about how to design a co-management system. But there is a right answer about whether justice and sustainability are crucial goals for environmental management, and co-management provides a mechanism to achieve them.

The Greenland Self-Government Act: The Pitfall for the Inuit in Greenland to Remain an Indigenous People?

Bent Ole Gram Mortensen[a] *and Ulrike Barten*[b]

Abstract

Are the Inuit in Greenland an indigenous people under international law? And what are the consequences of that categorization? This article focuses on the right to self-determination as the Inuit are recognized as an indigenous people; however, the Greenlanders have the explicit right to independence. The article concludes that the Self-Government Act can be regarded as the pitfall for the Inuit as an indigenous people. So far, nobody has fallen in; however, independence may mean an end to the status as an indigenous people. While the law might be considered relatively clear on this, the self-identification as an indigenous people will most likely not stop overnight.

Keywords

Indigenous people – Greenland – self-determination – self-government – Inuit people

1   Introduction

In 2009, the Greenland Self-Government Act[1] entered into force. It replaced the Home Rule Act that had been in force since 1979. The Self-Government Act

---

a   Professor, Department of Law, University of Southern Denmark.
b   Associate Professor, Department of Law, University of Southern Denmark.
1   Act No. 473 of June 12, 2009 on Greenland Self-Government. Greenland belongs to the Kingdom of Denmark (the realm), which constitutes itself as a sovereign state that has two sub-state entities, the Faroe Islands and Greenland. *See infra*, Section 4.

meant more control for the Greenlanders over their own affairs. It provides for recognition of the Greenlanders as a people with the right to self-determination under international law.

Kalaallit Nunaat, the Greenlanders' land, is made up of the island Greenland, the world's largest island and a large number of small islands. Who lives in Greenland? Some might answer the Greenlanders. Others will say Inuit. Some will add that the Inuit are an indigenous people. But are they really? International law is surprisingly unclear on the matter.

The answer whether the Inuit in Greenland are an indigenous people or not has far-reaching consequences. According to international law, an *indigenous people* has different rights than a *people* or a *minority*. Indigenous peoples have a certain right to self-determination; something that is denied to minorities and situations in which peoples' right to self-determination is farther reaching in scope. Indigenous peoples have special rights regarding living and non-living natural resources that are not awarded to other groups under international law. Depending on one's objective, there are thus good reasons to be regarded and treated as an indigenous people or simply a people.

It is important to note that the legal definition of the term *indigenous people* contains several criteria; some criteria being objectively observable and some subjective that need to be expressed by the members of the indigenous people.[2] This contribution focuses on the objective criteria and especially on the criterion of forming *non-dominant sectors of society*. It is on this point that the Self-Government Act contains a pitfall for the Inuit as an indigenous people. As the focus centered on this specific objectively observable point, the subjective self-identification is only mentioned in passing; however, this by no means signifies that the latter is a negligible criterion.

This contribution discusses the term *indigenous people* under international law before applying it to the Inuit in Greenland. The article briefly delineates between indigenous peoples on the one hand and peoples and minorities on the other, as this is the core issue in respect of the Inuit in Greenland. Are the Inuit a people, an indigenous people or an Inuit minority in Greenland?

This introduction concludes on a technical note. This contribution uses the terms definition and description interchangeably. This choice is due to a bewilderment of the authors at the general reluctance to use the term *definition*. The permanent Secretariat for Indigenous Issues has called art. 1 of International

---

2 Only the legal definition in international law is addressed in this article. More cultural understandings of belonging to an indigenous people are not dealt with.

THE GREENLAND SELF-GOVERNMENT ACT   105

Labour Organization (ILO) Convention No. 169[3] "a statement of coverage rather than a definition" and Martinez Cobo's description – Cobo himself underlines he is not *defining* but rather *describing* the term – an "understanding of the term."[4] To the authors' minds, the discussion below concerns lists of criteria. It makes no difference whether they are termed definitions or descriptions; the name does not determine the status as a source of international law.

2   The Term Indigenous People under International Law

The term *indigenous people* is a legal term arising from international law. It is a fairly recent term (half a century plus). International law recognizes many sources that are also applicable to indigenous peoples. Indigenous peoples are described in various sources, of which three are taken up in this contribution: (1) ILO Convention No. 169 which is a true binding source of international law; (2) Martinez Cobo's understanding of the term which is the generally accepted definition of an indigenous people but only a definition by an independent expert; and (3), the definition of the World Bank, which is not a binding source of international law at all. Nonetheless, the term is used by the World Bank in its every day work and accepted by concerned states, therefore making it relevant.

2.1   *The United Nations and Martinez Cobo*
Indigenous peoples have succeeded in establishing a platform at the United Nations. There is a Permanent Forum for Indigenous Issues[5] and, in 2001, the Special Rapporteur on the Rights of Indigenous Peoples started his work.[6] In the years 1995–2004 two decades for indigenous peoples were held.[7] In 2007,

---

3 C169 – Indigenous and Tribal Peoples Convention (No. 169)' entered into force on Sept. 5, 1991. It is available at http://www.ilo.org/indigenous/Conventions/no169/lang--en/index.htm. Accessed Dec. 14, 2015.

4 *See* Secretariat of the Permanent Forum on Indigenous Issues, 'The Concept of Indigenous Peoples,' January 2004, UN Doc. PFII/2004/WS.1/3, section 4 and 8.

5 Permanent Forum on Indigenous Issues. *See* http://undesadspd.org/indigenouspeoples.aspx; ECOSOC, 'Establishment of a Permanent Forum on Indigenous Issues,' 28 July 2000, UN Doc. E/RES/2000/22, accessed December 14, 2015.

6 Commission on Human Rights, 'Human Rights and Indigenous Issues,' April 24, 2001, UN Doc. Resolution 2001/57.

7 UNGA, 'International Decade of the World's Indigenous People,' February 18, 1994, UN Doc. A/RES/48/163; UNGA, 'Second International Decade of the World's Indigenous People,' February 24, 2005, UN Doc. A/RES/59/174.

the Expert Mechanism for the Rights of Indigenous Peoples was established.[8] It works as an advisory body for the UN Human Rights Council. Something that characterizes all these initiatives is that they do not have any direct consequences under international law. What comes closest to law is the UN Declaration on the Rights of Indigenous Peoples (UNDRIP)[9] which was adopted by the General Assembly in 2007 with 143 states voting in favour of it. Fifteen states did not vote at all or voted against the resolution.[10] Even though this is "only" a General Assembly resolution, it is the only globally applicable document specifically directed at indigenous peoples. The Declaration is quite broad in scope with over thirty articles of material rights. Some of those, however, confirm general human rights.

The Declaration aims to protect the special characteristics of indigenous peoples. These characteristics can be cultural, social, economic, and even political and thus cover many if not most elements of an indigenous people's way of life. The Declaration addresses very specific issues where modern society and the indigenous way of life meet. Thus, art. 12(1) of the Declaration on religious rights provides for the right to access religious and cultural sites in privacy. It also includes a right to repatriate human remains. Art. 12(2) obligates states to cooperate with indigenous peoples on the return of ceremonial objects and human remains that are in the possession of the state.

The Declaration is a milestone for indigenous peoples but it does not contain a definition or a description of the term *indigenous people*. This has been criticized by states with indigenous peoples;[11] however, the Secretariat of the Permanent Forum of Indigenous Issues has concluded that there is no need for a universal definition.[12] As will be shown below, this is very much the same for peoples and minorities.

The lack of a universally binding definition is not further discussed here but accepted as a fact. Instead, the definition of UN Special Rapporteur

---

8   Human Rights Council, 'Expert Mechanism on the Rights of Indigenous Peoples,' December 14, 2007, UN Doc. A/HRC/RES/6/36.

9   *See* regarding UNDRIP and Greenland Thomsen, Marianne Lykke, 'Greenland and the United Nations Declaration on the Rights of Indigenous Peoples' in Natalia Loukacheva 'Polar Law Textbook II' (2013) 242–265.

10 UNGA, 'United Nations Declaration of the Rights of Indigenous Peoples,' October 2, 2007, UN Doc. A/RES/61/295 and UNGA Voting Records, accessed December 14, 2015, http://www.un.org/en/ga/documents/voting.asp.

11 Hilario Davide, 'Supplement to the Report of the Facilitator on the Draft Declaration on the Rights of Indigenous Peoples,' 20 July 2007, annex I.

12 Secretariat of the Permanent Forum on Indigenous Issues, 'The Concept of Indigenous Peoples,' January 2004, UN Doc. PFII/2004/WS.1/3, section 8.

THE GREENLAND SELF-GOVERNMENT ACT

J.R. Martinez Cobo will be used. It is not binding, however, still a well-established definition.[13] Martinez Cobo defined – or rather described – an indigenous people in detailed terms as follows:

> Indigenous communities, peoples and nations are those which, having a historical continuity with pre-invasion and pre-colonial societies that developed on their territories, consider themselves distinct from other sectors of the societies now prevailing on those territories, or parts of them. They form at present non-dominant sectors of society and are determined to preserve, develop and transmit to future generations their ancestral territories, and their ethnic identity, as the basis of their continued existence as peoples, in accordance with their own cultural patterns, social institutions and legal system.[14]

Martinez Cobo introduced subjective and objective criteria that must all be fulfilled in order to live up to his description. The subjective element focuses on self-identification which has two aspects. Firstly, the group needs to consider itself as distinct from those parts of society that are now dominant in all or parts of the territory. Secondly, the group needs to have the will to preserve the distinct identity and culture which implies a conscious choice on behalf of the group.

Martinez Cobo thus introduces a temporal aspect. Martinez Cobo looks to the past in order to determine what is to be preserved for future generations. The objective elements concern aspects that can be observed from outside. The most important element in the context of this contribution is the status of forming a non-dominant part in society. Dominating a society is usually most easily identified as being in political power and thereby possessing the ability to shape society.

The second objective element is the historical continuity; in other words, a linkage to pre-colonial and pre-invasion societies. Martinez Cobo elaborates on the historical continuity which can be shown in different ways. For example, being direct ancestors of the very first inhabitants of the territory, a continuity in relation to culture which he takes to include religion, the way of living in a tribal community, the way of life, the means of livelihood, and occupation of one's ancestors' lands.

---

13   *Ibid.*

14   J.R. Martinez Cobo, 'Study of the Problem of Discrimination against Indigenous Populations,' 1986, UN Doc. E/CN.4/Sub.2/1986/7/Add.4, sections 379–382.

It is important to note that these are different ways of showing historical continuity and the continuity is arguably stronger the more of these criteria are fulfilled. However, it is also the case that the criterion of being the absolute first inhabitants of the territory is only of several requirements.

Martinez Cobo's definition offers a comprehensive description of an indigenous people which becomes clear once one considers other descriptions of the term *indigenous people*. Outside of the UN human rights context, the ILO and the World Bank have engaged primarily in discussion of the term. Both organizations deal with indigenous peoples on a daily basis; therefore, their approaches are deemed relevant even though they both have their weaknesses when it comes to the status of a source of international law.

2.2   The World Bank

The World Bank runs certain programmes that include indigenous peoples in the process of determining their own future in a globalized world.[15] It is therefore necessary to identify the group as such and the World Bank has described – again not defined – an indigenous people in Operation Policy 4.10 (2005) in its updated version of 2013.[16] The relevance of this description is drawn from the accepted applicability by states. Its weakness is arguably that it does not emerge from a source of international law.

Operational Policy 4.10 lists four criteria that need to be fulfilled to qualify as an indigenous people. As in the Martinez Cobo description, OP 4.10 contains subjective and objective elements. First, the group's member and others recognize a special indigenous identity.[17] It is noteworthy that recognition by the surrounding societies is necessary. Second, the group has an indigenous language. Third, the group has traditional cultural, economic, social or political institutions. Fourth, the group has a connection to its ancestors' land as such and the natural resources belonging thereto.[18]

This list of criteria is not controversial but on the contrary quite pragmatic. The criteria can be fulfilled to varying degrees[19] which allows for a flexible application of this description. At the same time it covers most of the elements of the Martinez Cobo definition and the definition in ILO Convention No. 169.

---

15   *See All Projects*, The World Bank, accessed Dec. 14, 2015, http://www.worldbank.org/en/topic/indigenouspeoples/projects/all.

16   OP 4.10 – Indigenous Peoples, July 2005, rev. April 2013, no. 4 (a).

17   OP 4.10 – Indigenous Peoples, July 2005, rev. April 2013, no. 4 (a).

18   OP 4.10 – Indigenous Peoples, July 2005, rev. April 2013, no. 4 (b)–(d).

19   OP 4.10 – Indigenous Peoples, July 2005, rev. April 2013, no. 4.

THE GREENLAND SELF-GOVERNMENT ACT

2.3   *The International Labour Organization*

ILO Convention No. 169 is one of the very few treaties on indigenous peoples[20] and is therefore of paramount importance when defining an indigenous people. The convention's arguable weakness is the low number of parties; only twenty-two states are parties to this convention. As Denmark, however, is a party, the definition has direct applicability for the Inuit in Greenland.[21] Although other nations have approved the treaty, Norway is the only Arctic Ocean coastal state to have ratified the ILO Convention.

Indigenous peoples are again defined by objective and subjective elements. Art. 1(1)(b) points at the ancestral relation with people who lived in the land or the geographical region at the time of conquest, colonization or the drawing of the current boundaries. Furthermore, the group must, disregarding its legal status, uphold some or all of its own social, economic, cultural, and political institutions. Art. 1(2) introduces the well-known subjective element of self-identification as a tribe or an indigenous people.

Important here is the upholding of the group's own institutions. It is unclear if these institutions must be upheld vis-à-vis modern state institutions, thereby fulfilling Martinez Cobo's requirement of forming a non-dominant part of society, or if these institutions can actually be the prevailing institutions in the modern society and applicable to the whole population. The wording seems to imply that both understandings can be correct. On the time aspect, it is again important to note that there is no requirement to be descendants of the very first inhabitants; nevertheless, the requirement looks to the ancestral relations with the group present at the time of colonization or conquest.

Comparing the three definitions it becomes clear that while the Martinez Cobo's description may be the most comprehensive, all three descriptions essentially point to the same elements: firstly, historical continuity with the groups present at the time of colonization; secondly, existence of traditional institutions which heavily implies existence of modern state structures; thirdly, *being* different; and finally – most importantly – self-identification relying on the past with a will for preservation of the identity in the future.

---

20   The old and for some states still applicable treaty is 'C107 – Indigenous and Tribal Populations Convention (No. 107),' which entered into force June 2, 1959.

21   The Danish government has in connection with the ratification of the Convention declared the original inhabitants of Greenland (Inuit) as the indigenous people within the meaning of the Convention. *See* the Danish Executive Order no. 97 of 9 October 1997 about the ILO Convention 169 of June 28, 1989 in relation to indigenous and tribal people in independent countries.

2.4 On the Term "Minority"

Just as the term *indigenous people* is not defined in binding international law, the term *minority* remains described in a working definition only. On a regional basis in Europe, the Framework Convention on the Protection of National Minorities[22] addresses minority issues directly. Global minority protection is solely based on art. 27 of the International Covenant on Civil and Political Rights.[23] In connection with art. 27, then UN Special Rapporteur Francesco Capotorti defined a minority in the following terms:

> A group numerically inferior to the rest of the population of a state, in a non-dominant position, whose members – being nationals of the state – possess ethnic, religious or linguistic characteristics differing from those of the rest of the population and show, if only implicitly, a sense of solidarity, directed towards preserving their culture, traditions, religion or language.[24]

Similarly to the Martinez Cobo definition of indigenous peoples, Capotorti's definition of a minority is generally accepted. There are a number of similarities between the two definitions. Both work with subjective and objective elements. Both groups *are* different and both groups *feel* different. The decisive difference between the two seems to be the historical continuity with the land and the traditions going back to pre-colonial times.

Within the Kingdom of Denmark, the Framework Convention covers only the German minority; not the Inuit in Greenland or the people on the Faroe Islands.[25] This is in line with the wishes of these two groups who do not wish to be regarded as minorities under the Framework Convention.[26] Thus, the minority issue should be closed; however, as will be referred to below, there

---

22 Opened for signature February 1, 1995. Entered into force February 1, 1998.

23 Adopted by the General Assembly resolution 2200A (XXI) of December 16, 1966. Entered into force March 23, 1976.

24 Capotorti, Francesco, 'Study on the Rights of Persons Belonging to Ethnic, Religious or Linguistic Minorities,' UN Doc. E/CN4/Sub2/384/Rev. 1, para. 568.

25 *See* the Danish declaration on Reservations and Declarations for Treaty No.157 Framework Convention for the Protection of National Minorities, accessed December 14 2015, http://conventions.coe.int/Treaty/Commun/ListeDeclarations.asp?NT=157&CM=8&DF=16/02/2015&CL=ENG&VL=1.

26 *See* the Ministry of domestic Affairs and Health: Denmark's second report under the Framework Convention for the Protection of National Minorities, May 2004, page 7, http://www.uvm.dk/~/media/UVM/Filer/Om%20os/PDF11/111031_dks_anden_rap_rammekon.pdf.

THE GREENLAND SELF-GOVERNMENT ACT

does not seem to be agreement among the different groups in Greenland on the approach of accepting only one single group of persons in Greenland. If there indeed is more than one group, there could possibly be talk of minorities in the sense of the Framework Convention.

2.5   *On the Term "People"*

International law sets out a third category: *a people.* There are primarily two approaches on the definition of peoples. The first, respecting states' territorial integrity and sovereignty, can be termed the territorial approach. Here, all persons within a given territory – usually the state – are considered to be one people. This approach characterized the era of decolonization. The second approach highlights the group's common characteristics. This approach was developed by independent experts under the UNESCO tutelage. This approach is very similar to the Martinez Cobo and Capotorti definitions on indigenous peoples and minorities respectively. It also contains subjective and objective elements. Common traditions and customs as well as the will to preserve these for future generations[27] are an example of these same criteria that are common to all definitions.

One of the few examples where this second approach is applied is Greenland. The Home Rule Act of 1978 recognized the Greenlanders as a "special nation[28] within the realm."[29] In 2004, the Danish Ministry of Foreign Affairs supported this view when it concluded that the Greenlanders are a people with the right to self-determination on the basis of their common characteristics.[30]

Lawyers, courts, governments and groups themselves have difficulties with the right to self-determination as its content and scope are not clearly defined. The only clear thing is that the right to self-determination is *not* a right that trumps all other rights. The right to self-determination must be balanced with a state's right to its territorial integrity.[31]

---

27   International Meeting of Experts on Further Study of the Concept of the Rights of Peoples, Final Report and Recommendations, Paris, February 22, 1990, UNESCO Doc. SHS-89/CONF.602/8, section 22.

28   The Danish original uses the term "folkeslag". The translation "nation" does not bear any of the connotations usually associated with nations under international law.

29   Act No. 577 of November 29, 1978 on Greenland's Home Rule.

30   Greenlandic-Danish Self-Government Commission report 1497/2008 on self-government in Greenland, Annex 7, pp. 375–378.

31   Res. 2625, principle V and indirectly art. 1(3) ICCPR which calls for all actions to be in conformity with the provisions of the UN Charter; among these the respect for the sovereignty and territorial integrity of the state.

It can, however, be most advantageous for a group to be able to define itself as a people. The right to external self-determination, in other words independence, is profoundly stronger (though not unlimited) for a people than an indigenous people.

2.6   *Intermediate Conclusion*

The discussion on definitions clearly shows that easy and exact definitions are hard to find, excluding legally binding definitions where the only example is the example of ILO Convention No. 169 on indigenous peoples. Along the lines of the Permanent Forum on Indigenous Issues, the Dutch Centre for Indigenous Peoples concludes that a universal definition is not needed as any given definition "will inevitably be either over- or under-inclusive."[32]

This might be the case with the Martinez Cobo description in a Greenlandic context. For that reason, the categories of peoples and minorities are included in the discussion because they offer a diverse view on the population in Greenland.

3   The Inuit in Greenland

The population of Greenland is overwhelmingly Inuit, who originally emigrated from Canada in several waves since the thirteenth century. The Inuit were not the first people to inhabit Greenland. When they first arrived in Greenland, the Paleo-Inuit of the Dorset culture and the Norse Vikings were already there; however, these cultures have long since ceased to exist and the Inuit are now the oldest existing ethnic group in Greenland. Genetic studies show that present day Inuit are direct descendants from the Thule-Inuit who came to Greenland in the twelfth century.[33] The fact that about eighty-eight percent of the population in Greenland is Inuit is unique in the Arctic context as Inuit in other states[34] are a numerical minority.[35]

---

32   "Definition of Indigenous Peoples," *Netherlands Centre for Indigenous Peoples*, accessed Dec. 14, 2015, http://indigenouspeoples.nl/indigenous-peoples/definition-indigenous.

33   Moltke et al., "Uncovering the Genetic History of the Present-Day Greenlandic Population," in *The American Journal of Human Genetics* 96 (2015), 1–16, p. 2.

34   However, in constitutive parts, such as Nunavut, the Inuit are not necessarily a minority.

35   *See* Katja Göcke, "Recognition and Enforcement of Indigenous Peoples, Land Rights in Alaska, the Northern Regions of Canada, Greenland, and Siberia and the Russian Far East," *The Yearbook of Polar Law IV* (2012): 287; *see also* Rebecca M. Bratspies, "Human Rights and Arctic Resources," *Southwestern Journal of International Law* 15 (2009): 262.

THE GREENLAND SELF-GOVERNMENT ACT   113

The large majority of the Inuit in Greenland have Greenlandic as a mother tongue. There is, however, a small minority of Inuit whose mother tongue is Danish. Greenlandic (Kalaallisut) is an Inuit language that belongs to the family of the Eskimo languages. Kalaallisut falls into three main variants: the dominating Western Kalaallisut with several dialects, the Eastern Kalaallisut and the Thule language. There are substantial differences between the variants and it is not necessarily possible to understand each other. It could be argued whether these are simply three dialects or three different languages.[36] The main part of the population masters both Kalaallisut and Danish to different degrees.   ·

According to section 20 of the Self-Government Act, Greenlandic is the official language in Greenland. It is not specified which variant is meant;[37] however, in practice Western Kalaallisut is used. In the Greenlandic public administration, Danish is often used a working language as many of the public servants do not speak Kalaallisut.[38]

Legislation exists which for one guarantees public service in the language of one's choice (Danish or Greenlandic) and for another preserves Danish in the public sphere.[39] In addition, the Greenlandic Language Act[40] aims at preserving knowledge of Greenlandic in the future as the language serves as a bearer of the traditional Greenlandic culture.

As explained below, Denmark treats the Inuit in Greenland as a closed group. This stands in contrast to the Inuit themselves, who seem to regard themselves as a single people or a single, indigenous people across all boundaries in the

---

36   Svend Kolte, *Kalaallit Oqaasii – Det Grønlandske Sprog i Inuit, kultur og samfund – en grundbog i eskimologi,* (Systime: 199), 86. The discussion on three dialects or languages shall not here be subjected to further treatment.

37   Forslag til Lov om Grønlands Selvstyre, as proposed on February 5, 2009 by the Prime Minister. Grønlandsk-dansk selvstyrekommissions betænkning 1497/2008 om selvstyre i Grønland.

38   It has not been possible to estimate the percentage of non-kalaallisut speaking public servants. Especially persons with master degrees come from Denmark in relatively large numbers. Many stay only a few years in Greenland. This "traffic" nearly seems a colonial approach. However, the many non-kalaallisut speaking public servants are in fact hired by the Self-Government. It is simply not possible to hire kalaallisut speaking academics in sufficient numbers.

39   Greenland Act No. 8 of June 13, 1994 regarding case management in public administration, as last amended by the Greenland Act No. 19 of November 22, 2011.

40   Greenland Act No. 7 of May 19, 2010 regarding the Language Policy.

Arctic.[41] The following analysis does not take this contradiction into account but follows the Danish approach and focuses on the Inuit in Greenland as a group on its own.

4 Greenland's Status in the Realm

Greenland first became part of the Danish realm in the eighteenth century, when Denmark-Norway began to colonize the island. The territory was at the time considered *terra nullius* even though an indigenous population already existed.[42] When the Danish-Norwegian kingdom ended in 1814, Greenland remained in the Danish realm.[43]

With the 1953 Danish constitution, Greenland ceased to be a colony and developed first as a county, later over a region with a certain degree of home rule to the self-governing territory it is today.

4.1 *The Self-Government Act*

In June 2009, the Self-Government Act entered into force which meant an expansion of the areas and competences of the Greenlandic parliament and government. Greenland, however, remains part of the realm. The Self-Government Act exhibits the classic separation of powers with judicial powers, a legislative power (Inatsisartut), and an executive power (Naalakkersuisut).

The Self-Government Act determines the powers of the self-government and the realm (in reality Denmark). Section 1(1) provides that the self-government has the legislative and executive power within the areas taken over by it. There are a number of areas where the self-government of Greenland itself decides if an area shall be taken over by the self-government. This take-over can happen in one of two ways. Section 3(1) states that those areas on list 1 of the Self-Government Act can be taken over simply by decision of the Greenlandic parliament. Section 3(2) states that the areas in list 2 are taken over after negotiations between the self-government and the Danish government.

---

41 Art. 1(3) and 1(4) of the Inuit Circumpolar Conference Declaration on Sovereignty in the Arctic, 2009, accessed February 9, 2016, http://www.inuitcircumpolar.com/uploads/3/0/5/4/30542564/declaration12x18vicechairssigned.pdf.

42 Göcke, *supra*, note 35 at 281.

43 The Treaty of Kiel between the United Kingdom of Great Britain and Ireland and the Kingdom of Sweden on one side and the Kingdoms of Denmark and Norway on the other side, dated January 14, 1814 in Kiel, Germany.

THE GREENLAND SELF-GOVERNMENT ACT

4.2   *Greenland's Independence*

The Self-Government Act's preamble expressly recognizes the Greenlanders as a people under international law with the right to self-determination. Section 21 of the act states that the decision on independence is made by the Greenlandic people. The actual process of independence has to be negotiated between the self-government and the Danish government. The agreement has to be endorsed by the Danish parliament and has to be adopted by the Greenlandic people through a referendum with a clear majority. Section 21 does not state what happens, when no agreement is reached or the agreement is not endorsed by the parliament or the population. The General Comments on the act, though, state that the Danish government must enter into the negotiations with the intent to actually reach an agreement. Thus, the negotiations must be held in a meaningful way and both parties must try to accommodate the other's wishes.[44]

The act does not include any conditions or requirements for the referendum. The implementation of the referendum is up to the Nallakkersuisut. In the General Comments, though, it is made clear that the referendum's result must show a clear wish for independence, so that no doubt about this will arise internationally.[45]

It can be argued that Greenland's independence so far is only a hypothetical case. Apart from the lacking economic basis to sustain a state, legal issues regarding independence also arise – issues that could stall or even uphold the process altogether. First, the Danish parliament, *Folketinget*, has to give its consent to the agreement on independence made between the Danish and the Greenlandic governments. Even though there is an expectation that honest negotiations take place, there is no solution as to what happens if the Folketing does not give its consent.

Second, the Self-Government Act is only that – an act. In theory, the Danish parliament *Folketinget* could adopt a new law on self-government in Greenland without the passage on independence. This is, however, unlikely for several reasons. For one, this would be in breach with many years of consistent support for Greenlandic independence by Danish heads of government. For another, taking back a promise such as this one raises serious issues under international law.

The preamble of the Self-Government Act speaks of the promotion of equality and mutual respect and the right to self-determination for the Greenlandic people. In addition, the good faith of Denmark would be called in doubt if

---

44   The explanatory notes on Greenland Self-Government bill, ch. 10.2.

45   The explanatory notes on Greenland Self-Government bill, ch. 10.2.

it acted contrary to all its previous statements and promises. While the Self-Government Act is not a unilateral declaration under international law *per se*, it functions very much like one.[46] The state of Denmark makes a unilateral promise to another actor. The promise is not only made in oral statements but actually written down in a law which surely must be seen as an expression of will on behalf of Denmark to bind itself. Other criteria such as a competent authority of the state expressing an opinion are also met. In consequences of viewing the promise of independence in the Self-Government Act as a unilateral declaration, the promise cannot be taken back under international law and the Greenlanders can rely on that promise in the future.

There is, of course, a very good reason not to accept the promise as a unilateral declaration. These declarations are made between two equal partners: two states. If one accepted vertical unilateral declarations, especially in the form of a national law, most laws could not be changed as they could be considered a retreat on a promise the state has made vis-à-vis its citizens. Therefore, unilateral declarations work horizontally between two states. The Greenlandic people are, of course, not on equal footing as the very core of the promise concerns its statehood. However, in response one can again point to the preamble which already recognizes a certain level of equality between Greenland and Denmark. Furthermore, as the very core issue is statehood for Greenland and the Self-Government Act recognizes the right to statehood (and thereby implies that all criteria of a state are fulfilled) it would again be contrary to good faith and previous promises to step back from the promise of independence.

5 The Inuit in Greenland as an Indigenous People under International Law

When the Denmark ratified ILO Convention No. 169 on Indigenous Peoples in 1996, it made a declaration recognizing the indigenous population (the Inuit) in Greenland as an indigenous people under the convention.[47]

---

46 For more details on unilateral declarations and their consequences under international law *see* Legal Status of Eastern Greenland (Denmark v. Norway), judgment of April 5, 1933, Permanent Court of International Justice, Series A/B, No. 53, s. 71 and Nuclear Tests Case (New Zealand and Australia v. France), Judgment of 1974 I.C.J. Reports, 253.

47 Order no. 97 of October 9, 1997, ILO Convention no. 169 of June 28, 1989 concerning Indigenous and Tribal Peoples in Independent Countries.

THE GREENLAND SELF-GOVERNMENT ACT

The Danish Supreme Court has explicitly stated that the Thule-Inuit in North-Western Greenland are not to be considered a tribal people or an indigenous people distinct from the Greenlanders as a whole under ILO Convention No. 169. Thus, the Thule-Inuit do not enjoy separate rights under the Convention.[48]

This judgment from 2003 follows up on the traditional Danish view which was already expressed in 1933, when Norway and Denmark disputed the domain over Eastern Greenland before the Permanent Court of International Justice.[49] Denmark saw then and still today regards the island as one unit with the population also being one group only.

The Inuit Circumpolar Council has criticized this approach.[50] In the following, two points will be discussed: First, whether the Inuit are a people or an indigenous people, and secondly, whether there are several indigenous peoples in Greenland. This last discussion is limited to indigenous peoples and only briefly touches upon the possible existence of minorities in Greenland.

5.1   *The Inuit as a People*

The short answer to the question, in how far the Greenlanders are a people, is given by reference to the preamble of the Self-Government Act, where it is stated that the Greenlandic people is a people under international law with a right to self-determination. This recognition is consistent with the territorial approach to defining a people.

When it comes to the approach that relies on common characteristics, the question is whether there is one people or possibly even several peoples. As with the discussion on the possible existence of several indigenous peoples, the important question arises: who does the group claiming to be a people compare itself to? It is decisive whether, for example, the Thule-Inuit compare themselves to other Inuit groups or to the Danes who make up almost ninety-eight percent of the population in the Danish Realm. This point of whether there exist several peoples in Greenland is of no practical value (for now), as no group within the Inuit community has claimed distinct status of a people.

---

48   Danish High Court, judgment of November 28, 2003 (cases 489/1999 and 490/1999).

49   Legal Status of Eastern Greenland (Denmark v. Norway), Judgment of April 5 1933, Permanent Court of International Justice, Series A/B, No. 53, p. 38.

50   Inuit Circumpolar Council (ICC): *Universal Periodic Review – Denmark 2011*. Joint Submission 2 – Greenland NGOs, Nov. 6, 2010. It can be found here: http://lib.ohchr .org/HRBodies/UPR/Documents/Session11/DK/JS2_JointSubmission%202-eng.pdf. Accessed Dec. 14, 2015.

When considering the overall claim of Greenlanders to be a people, matters are complicated by the fact that even though the vast majority of Greenlanders is Inuit and the two terms are often used as synonyms, they actually cover two different groups. The Inuit are covered by the term Greenlanders, but the term Greenlanders is wider in scope that includes those of non-Inuit origin. Basically, all persons with a Danish citizenship and residence in Greenland have democratic rights as Greenlanders. Nevertheless, as the Inuit make up about 90% of the Greenlanders, they would need to be considered to be the decisive group which must meet the criteria of being a people for Greenlanders as a whole to be a people. The remaining 10% of the population might make one or several minorities; something that is not examined here. The government has been describes as "a de facto ethnic government."[51]

The approach to defining a people through its common characteristics turns to a number of questions.[52] Most can be answered in the affirmative. The Greenlanders share ethnic and cultural characteristics, with small variants which are mainly explained by the fact that there are three main settling places in Greenland: The East, The West, and the Thule district in the North-West. As the argument could possibly be made that there are several languages instead of several dialects in Greenland, the common language is arguably a weak common trait. The Greenlanders are especially strong when it comes to fulfilling institutional criteria. They certainly exhibit a common economic life, political and social institutions, and a common legal system in place. These institutions could be argued not to be Greenlandic but Danish. This already touches on the core issues of this contribution – does the Self-Government Act make the Greenlanders distinct from everyone else in the Realm or does Denmark still retain the overall control. In any case, however, institutions are in place that would not leave a newly independent state in chaos; on the contrary, the new state would work with and within existing and functioning structures.

In short, the Greenlanders meet the characteristics approach to being a people, and they are also a people according to the territorial approach. The open question is, whether there exist minorities in Greenland; and, in case of an affirmative answer, which groups form one or several minorities within Greenland. This question on minorities is not pursued further in this

---

51 Mauro Mazza, "The Prospects of Independence for Greenland, between Energy Resources and the Right of Indigenous Peoples (with some Comparative Remarks on Nunavut, Canada)," *Beijing Law Review* 6 (2015): 321.

52 For the full list *see* International Meeting of Experts on Further Study of the Concept of the Rights of Peoples, Final Report and Recommendations, Paris, February 22, 1990, UNESCO Doc. SHS-89/CONF.602/8, para. 22.

THE GREENLAND SELF-GOVERNMENT ACT

contribution. Instead, the question now is, whether one can simultaneously be a people and an indigenous people – or whether there indeed are several indigenous peoples.

5.2 *The Inuit as one Indigenous People*

The Thule Inuit have made the argument that they are a group distinct from the other Inuit in Greenland. No conclusive answer can be given here; however, this claim informs the further discussion. There are three main points that are decisive in making a group an indigenous people. The first two points are intertwined: the group is distinct in a number of ways from those dominating society now. The two aspects are *being different* and then *not being the dominant society*. The third very important point concerns self-identification as an indigenous people. Application of these criteria to the Thule-Inuit is attempted further below. For now, all Inuit are examined as one single group.

Applying the Martinez Cobo definition to the Inuit in Greenland leads to the core question: does the Self-Government Act prevent the Inuit from being an indigenous people? The first of the criteria to be met is a historical continuity with pre-invasion or pre-colonial societies. It is important to note that this is not a requirement to be the original population in the territory but the important point in time is invasion or colonization. The Inuit living in Greenland today might have had problems living up to the original criterion as they descend from the Thule-Inuit and not the Norse Vikings or the paleo-Eskimos that were present when the first Thule-Inuit entered Greenland; however, they certainly fulfil the criterion of being descendants of the population present in Greenland when Danish colonization began.

The second criterion starts to cause a headache: being different from other sectors of the societies now prevailing in those territories. The Inuit are without doubt different from the colonizing Danes. However, are the Danes the now prevailing sectors of society? For one, the sheer dominance in numbers of the Inuit compared to the Danes seems to indicate that the Inuit prevail in society. This is, of course, a typical picture of a colony, where a small (external) minority is in power. In terms of political power one could argue that Danish standards, society and institutions prevail. Denmark has had control over Greenland. It has institutionalized Greenlandic society in the way modern states are organized. Self-government is still relatively new and Denmark still has control over a number of areas of Greenlandic interest. Such a conclusion, however, would be in opposition of the Self-Government Act which decidedly hands over political power to the Greenlanders and thereby primarily to the Inuit. Also, such conclusion would seem to indicate an acceptance of belonging to the Danish Realm. If the self-government is taken seriously, then the conclusion must be that the Inuit prevail in society which in turn means that they do not live up to this criterion on being different from prevailing sectors of society.

The criteria on self-identification and preservation of this identity in the future are equally difficult to determine. Here, a factor asserts itself that is worth taking into consideration but which complicates the picture. It may also try to answer whether the Inuit are dominant in Greenlandic society. Inuit are neither completely modern nor traditional in the sense that they are either/or. A modern lifestyle in one of the towns, where the majority of people live, does not preclude self-identification as indigenous. That said, the 13% of the Greenlandic population living outside of towns in settlements[53] are closer to what would commonly be understood to be traditional Inuit. A hint may be the 6.25% of the population who work in fisheries, hunting and agriculture.[54] However, this number does not only cover traditional Inuit ways of fishing, hunting and doing agriculture but also covers modern industrial ways of working. Another hint may be the number of whales or seals hunted per year.

Commercial whaling is generally prohibited.[55] One of the exceptions is aboriginal subsistence whaling, and the International Whaling Commission has set down quota for Greenlanders.[56] The current quota is 211 whales per year divided into detailed quota for the different kinds of whales.[57] In 2013, 192 whales were killed by Greenlanders on the Greenlandic East and West coasts.[58] How many people live off these whales cannot be accurately estimated.[59]

What all these numbers indicate is an informed guess at the best. Are the 6.25% minus a few who work in modern ways plus the families of those who do work in traditional ways of the real indigenous people in Greenland? They would certainly be those most affected if special rights based on the status

---

53   Statistics Greenland, Greenland in Figures, accessed December 14, 2015, http://www.stat .gl/publ/da/GF/2015/pdf/Greenland%20in%20Figures%202015.pdf, 12/10/2015, p. 9.

54   Statistics Greenland, Greenland in Figures, accessed Dec. 14, 2015, http://www.stat.gl/ publ/da/GF/2015/pdf/Greenland%20in%20Figures%202015.pdf, 12/10/2015, p. 16.

55   Based on the 1982 memorandum of the International Whaling Commission.

56   The International Whaling Commission uses the wording "aboriginal subsistence whaling". To what extent "aboriginal" may be different from "indigenous" shall not be discussed in this article.

57   "Aboriginal Subsistence Whaling," *International Whaling Commission*, accessed December 14, 2015, https://iwc.int/catches#aborig, 13/10/2015.

58   "Aboriginal Subsistence Whaling," *International Whaling Commission*, accessed December 14, 2015, https://iwc.int/table_aboriginal.

59   An analysis regarding the regulation of whaling and sealing cannot be accommodated sufficiently within the framework of this article.

THE GREENLAND SELF-GOVERNMENT ACT

121

of an indigenous people were taken away.[60] However, how many people must work in traditional ways for a whole people to count as indigenous? Almost 19% of the population work in the public administration.[61] Does that preclude the Inuit to be indigenous? When does a family live in traditional ways? Does that always require traditional housing? Or is it enough if traditions are kept alive?

Identification from the outside as well as self-identification cannot be based on clear cut criteria and numbers. Identity is shaped in everyday life and in a specific context. Identity is not fixed but develops over time, and it highly depends on *the other*.[62] *Othering* is a process, where one identifies what one is *not*. Self-identification in Greenland thus is complex, as the question is who *the other* is – the Danish society in Denmark? Danes in Greenland? Greenlanders in towns vs. those in settlements? There is no objective answer.

Inuit identity can best be imagined on a sliding scale where one end means no identification as an indigenous people and the other full identification as indigenous.[63] Most Inuit will find themselves between the two poles, but where exactly each individual Inuit is situated on the scale is a personal decision. No matter what outside decisions might be made, self-identification is likely not to be switched off from one day to the other.

Some of the same considerations regarding descent and self-identification apply in relation to the ILO definition. In addition, the definition requires that some or all social, economic, cultural, and political institutions are retained. It could certainly be argued that the modern political institutions are not indigenous to Greenland and the Inuit. Social, economic, and cultural institutions are inherently Danified, though especially cultural institutions retain their Greenlandic characteristics.

The definition offered by the World Bank seems to be the most useful of the definition, if indeed the goal is to define the Inuit as indigenous. The objective criteria which include original language, traditional cultural, economic, social or political institutions as well as the affiliation with ancestors' land and its

---

60   In how far the loss of status as an indigenous people under international human rights law would lead to an automatic refusal by the International Whaling Commission to allow for continued aboriginal subsistence whaling is not clear. The IWC seems to base its decisions in this regard on the Needs Statement and expert advice rather than on legal definitions.

61   Statistics Greenland, Greenland in Figures, October 2015, p. 16, accessed December 14, 2015, http://www.stat.gl/publ/da/GF/2015/pdf/Greenland%20in%20Figures%202015.pdf.

62   Sune Q. Jensen, "Othering, Identity Formation and Agency," *Qualitative Studies* 2 (2011): 63–78.

63   Self-identification as an Inuit does not automatically include identification as indigenous.

resources is partly fulfilled; by far all Inuit live in a traditional Inuit way; however, a part of the Inuit does.

Regarding the subjective element of self-identification, the World Bank takes not only the group itself into consideration but the surrounding society as well. There is no doubt that Inuit are commonly regarded as having an indigenous identity. What, however, also becomes clear is that international society does not distinguish between different Inuit groups but regards all Inuit in Greenland as one single group.

What the World Bank definition lacks is the status in society. Thus, the Inuit can still be regarded as indigenous under this definition even though they would be considered dominant parts of society under the Martinez Cobo definition. The World Bank definition, however useful it may seem, is the weakest source of international law – if one regards it a source of law at all.

The core issue in determining the existence of an indigenous people in Greenland is therefore the value of the Self-Government Act. Based on the above observation that the Self-Government Act is still relatively new and Denmark retains overall control, one would conclude that the Inuit indeed are an indigenous people. The larger the degree of self-government, with statehood as the ultimate goal, the weaker the argument in favour of the Inuit being an indigenous people becomes. Being different from dominating sectors of society does not work when one *is* society. This, however, leads to a further point that requires examination: treating all Inuit as one group does not do justice to the diversity within the Inuit population.

5.3   *Inuit as Several Indigenous Peoples*

Inuit culture is unquestionably different from Danish culture. Greenlandic culture is a mix of both. The argument has been made that the Inuit are so diverse that one cannot necessarily treat all Inuit in Greenland as one single group. At least the Thule-Inuit identify themselves as different from the rest of the Inuit in Greenland. They expressed this *inter alia* through the claims before the Danish High Court (see above). Taking language as the starting-point, there are at least three groups: the Western Greenlandic Inuit, the Eastern Greenlandic Inuit, and the Thule-Inuit.

Genetics show that all Inuit living in present day Greenland are related and descendants from the same Inuit. Nevertheless, different identities have developed. The arguments regarding whether Inuit sub-groups such as the Thule-Inuit can be considered indigenous peoples in their own right mirror the arguments when considering all Inuit as one single group.

Notwithstanding any claims of discrimination, one Inuit group has never colonized another. The colonizer is still Denmark. The problematic aspects

THE GREENLAND SELF-GOVERNMENT ACT

remain the dominant society factor. Again, if the Self-Government Act is to be taken seriously, the Thule-Inuit enjoy the rights under this act on equal footing with all other Greenlanders.

A reason for recognizing the Thule-Inuit in their own right would be that they are different from the governing Greenlanders. It is true that the largest portion of the Greenlandic population would be identified as Western Greenlanders, simply because this geographic region is the most populated area in Greenland. The Western Greenlandic dialect (or language) is the one most commonly used in public life. A compelling argument has been made by Terto Ngiviu in favour of the Thule-Inuit being an indigenous people.[64] Ngiviu shows the differences of culture, such as traditional hunting tools, clothing, women's role, kinship structures, and religion in the form of shamanism. Ngiviu convincingly shows the closer relationship of the Thule-Inuit with Canadian Inuit compared to other Greenlandic Inuit. Nevertheless, the question remains if the differences outweigh the similarities to such a degree that recognition as in indigenous people in its own right is justified.

Ngiviu argues for recognition in order to prevent the Thule-Inuit from becoming extinct due to the impact of political and economic change.[65] While one would expect more protection from a special status, it is by no means secured that the Thule-Inuit would receive more protection. Denmark and the international community have recognized the Inuit as a whole as an indigenous people already. If the Thule-Inuit were to be recognized in their own right, they would receive the exact same protection as they already enjoy as a part of all Inuit in Greenland.

The situation changes, of course, as soon as the status of indigenous people is lost to Inuit in Greenland in general. In this circumstance, it may well be worthwhile for the Thule-Inuit to seek protection as an indigenous people in its own right. However, the status of the Inuit as an indigenous people is most threatened by the self-government and the expansion of the same with ultimate statehood. If the Inuit in Greenland clearly become the dominating society, come into power and rule Greenland, then the Thule-Inuit would not be able to claim colonization by other Greenlanders. Thus, a key criterion of indigenous peoples is not fulfilled.

In the alternative, a path worth pursuing might be the minority path. There are also a number of criteria to be fulfilled; however, there is no requirement on descent and colonization. The Capotorti definition may be easier to fulfil

---

64   Terto Ngiviu, "The Inughuit of Northwest Greenland: An Unacknowledged Indigenous People," *The Yearbook of Polar Law* 6 (2015): 142–161.

65   *Ibid.*, at 149.

and instruments like the Language Charter and the Framework Convention may present useful tools. As long as Greenland is no independent state, any recognition of the Thule-Inuit under the Language Charter and the Framework Convention would have to be done by or at least pre-negotiated with Denmark.

5.4 *Intermediate Conclusion*

The Inuit in Greenland are in a difficult situation. On the basis of Martinez Cobo and the World Bank approaches, the Inuit cannot achieve independence and retain their status as indigenous people at the same time. The status as indigenous people comes with Danish control; vice versa, Greenlandic control over Greenland leads to the loss of the status as an indigenous people. In the context of the ILO, the status of the groups is not decisive. In addition, art. 1(2) of Convention no. 169 explicitly states that self-identification is a 'fundamental criterion' for establishing the existence of an indigenous people. As argued above, self-identification will not change overnight when Greenland becomes independent.

At the same time, the Greenlanders, and the largest part of the Greenlanders, the Inuit, fulfil the criteria for being a people. In the Self-Government Act, Denmark recognizes the Greenlanders as a people. In the ILO context, Denmark recognizes the Inuit as an indigenous people. Can the same persons be members of an indigenous people and a people at the same time? If one takes the diversity of Inuit into account (and disregards genetics), one could even add the layer of minorities. Can a person, for example a member of the Thule-Inuit, be part of the Greenlandic people, the Inuit indigenous people and the Thule-Inuit minority at the same time?

International law is not clear on the matter. While forum shopping is generally frowned upon, the UN Working Group on Minority Issues has stated that a person in one context can be a member of a minority and in another context member of a people.[66] Thus, it seems entirely possible to belong to different groups at the same time. As the three groups – peoples, indigenous peoples, and minorities – all have different rights, this conclusion leads to multiple right holders. The individual Thule-Inuit could individually claim special rights as a member of a minority and as a member of an indigenous people and together with other members of the group collective rights as an indigenous people and a people.

---

66   Working Group on Minorities. 'Commentary of the Working Group on Minorities to the United Nations Declaration on the Rights of Persons Belonging to National or Ethnic, Religious and Linguistic Minorities,' 4 April 2005. UN Doc. E/CN.4/Sub.2/AC.5/2005/2, para. 15.

6 The Relevance for the Inuit to be an Indigenous People

Under international law, different groups have different rights. A people has a right to self-determination which, under certain circumstances, probably includes a right to secession. According to the UN Declaration on the Rights of Indigenous Peoples, indigenous peoples have a limited right to self-determination which focuses on internal arrangements such as autonomy and self-government. Minorities do not enjoy the right to self-determination. However, there are international treaties in place which include very specific and detailed rights for members of minorities.

As an indigenous people, two paths are open and both can be taken at the same time. First, indigenous people can use the specific institutions established for indigenous people. This includes the UN Declaration on the Rights of Indigenous Peoples which has received widespread support but which is does not carry the legal authority of a treaty. The Declaration protects the way of living, the indigenous identity and culture, and access to the land and its resources; thereby covering the essential aspects of indigenous life.

Second, the other path is the larger human rights context, where there are far more treaties and institutions. On the downside, indigenous issues represent only some of very many issues that fight for attention of the international community. On this path, it is in theory not so important if one is an indigenous people or not. Human rights are applicable to all. No one needs to qualify for them. Politically, it can, though, be decisive to be an indigenous people as that can create the basis upon which claims can be built. Furthermore, some human rights, such as the prohibition on discrimination, are of more relevance than other human rights, like the freedom of association. Therefore, it can be important for indigenous peoples to be able to argue on the basis of being an indigenous people.

In the context of general human rights, the UN human rights treaty bodies, especially the Human Rights Council on the Committee on Economic, Social and Cultural rights, have shown strong tendencies to ask about the rights of indigenous peoples in the context of their respective convention.[67]

The ILO and the World Bank apply their definition to specific circumstances. It is therefore highly relevant for the Inuit to be recognized as an indigenous people in these contexts, as recognition under ILO Convention no. 169 and by the World Bank opens special rights, treatment, and programs.

---

67   *Arctic Human Development Report*, at 235, accessed December 14, 2015, http://www.svs.is/en/ahdr-ii-en.

The Inuit in Greenland are relatively well protected in Denmark, which is party both to the International Covenant on Civil and Political Rights (ICCPR) and the International Covenant on Economic, Social and Cultural Rights (ICESCR). ILO Convention no. 169 adds to this protection. Binding international law, therefore, protects the Inuit in one way or the other as an indigenous people.

The recognition of a people, on the other hand, is important if the goal is an independent Greenland. Peoples have the most extensive right to self-determination. This is already recognized in the Self-Government Act and it includes recognition of the Greenlanders as a people with the right to self-determination and the right to independence. Denmark, as the state losing territory in case of Greenlandic independence, has obligated itself to work constructively with the Nalaakkersuisut if and when independence is negotiated.

As linguistic minorities, not much would change for the Thule-Inuit and the Eastern Greenlanders in the case of independence. The Self-Government Act, through section 12, opens up the possibility for the Nalaakkersuisut to enter into international agreements. In theory, the linguistic minorities could be protected by the Language Charter or the Framework Convention. This, however, would be a long term project. It could also be argued that such categorization would draw sharp lines between the different Inuit groups that overall have more in common than divides them.

The status of Inuit as an indigenous people can have far-reaching consequences when it comes to fishing and hunting rights. As mentioned, Greenlanders are allowed to hunt a certain number of whales based on aboriginal subsistence whaling. It is questionable whether this were allowed to continue should the Inuit no longer identify themselves as indigenous or lose international recognition as an indigenous people.[68]

7 Conclusion

The question whether the Inuit in Greenland are an indigenous people is not easily answered. Several definitions of what constitutes an indigenous people have been used; each with its own value (or lack thereof) as a source under international law.

Nevertheless, the core question remains regarding the Self-Government Act. If one regards the Greenlanders as possessing effective control over their

---

68   This point on special rights regarding hunting, fishing and the use of the land warrants further discussion. However, this exceeds the scope of this contribution.

THE GREENLAND SELF-GOVERNMENT ACT   127

own affairs, then both the Martinez Cobo and the ILO definitions would refuse indigenous status to the Inuit in Greenland. One cannot dominate society *and* be an indigenous people at the same time. The World Bank is open to this possibility.

If one considers Denmark to be in effective control of Greenlandic affairs, then the Inuit are measured against the Danes and the overall answer would be that the Greenlanders still constitute an indigenous people. In any case, Greenland is without doubt in a long and slow process of severing ties with Denmark. Whether this also means that the Inuit define themselves less and less as indigenous can neither be presupposed nor can the contrary be proven at this point. Self-identification plays a vital role in indigenous issues and does not follow legal criteria.

The Inuit are also a people and as such have the right not only to self-determination but via the Self-Government Act also an explicit right to independence. The more a group decides on its own affairs, the less international protection it is granted. This is based on the inequality between the parties: a state on the one hand and a smaller, non-dominant group on the other.[69] When the dominating part, the state, recedes, the justification for special protection as offered by ILO Convention no. 169 or the UN Declaration on the Rights of Indigenous Peoples is weakened. The vacuum that the state leaves behind is filled by the group itself and thus there is no threatening power anymore.

The fact that the majority of Greenlanders lives in a modern society and has abandoned the traditional way of life raises serious issues regarding the status as indigenous people. This status seems to be based more and more on descent and self-identification then on objective criteria. In the alternative, can all Inuit be regarded as an indigenous people when only a small part of them fulfil the criteria of being an indigenous people?

A further question regarding the diversity within the Inuit population also arises. Genetically, there is only one Inuit group in Greenland. In addition, the common traits seem to outweigh the differences. On the other hand, self-identification points to different groups and at least for the Thule-Inuit a convincing argument for being a distinct group has been made.

---

69   For example, most civil and political rights are addressed to states, who are obliged to respect, protect and promote human rights. Human rights have always curbed the state's power vis-à-vis its own citizens. *See* Ed Bates, "History," in Daniel Moeckli, et al., ed., *International Human Rights Law*, 2nd ed. (Oxford University Press, 2014), 15–33; and Samantha Besson, "Justifications," in Daniel Moeckli, et al., ed., *International Human Rights Law*, 2nd ed. (Oxford University Press, 2014), 34–52.

Both views on the number of groups are legitimate. The question, though, that remains unanswered at this point is whether it would be more fruitful to speak of minorities instead of distinct indigenous peoples in Greenland. The avenue of minorities is a whole different matter which was not pursued here. What is clear, however, is that at the current time, it seems that little can be won for the Thule-Inuit to be recognized as an indigenous people in their own right. They already enjoy recognition as an indigenous people; albeit as part of the larger Inuit population in Greenland. The situation changes, once Greenland becomes independent.

The answer to the issue of the status of the Inuit in Greenland is far from satisfactory. International law is sparse, unclear and possibly simply not fitting reality. One clear observation, though, is that both the international community and Denmark identify the Inuit as indigenous and that the Greenlanders themselves take an active role within the institutions specializing in indigenous issues.

An Agreement on Enhancing International Arctic Scientific Cooperation: Only for the Eight Arctic States and Their Scientists?

Akiho Shibata[a] and Maiko Raita[b]

Abstract

At the Arctic Council's Iqaluit Ministerial Meeting in April 2015, the eight Arctic States decided to extend the mandate of the Task Force on Enhancing Scientific Cooperation in the Arctic (SCTF) in order to work toward a legally binding agreement on scientific cooperation. Based on the Oslo Draft of February 2015, this paper finds that the Agreement may improve the legal environment for Arctic science beyond current international law, including the law of the sea. The Agreement would lower the hurdles heretofore identified in international Arctic scientific cooperation, for example, the difficulties in accessing research areas and research facilities; and, the delays in border crossing procedures for entry and exit of scientists and their equipment and materials. Such an agreement is a good idea and should be promoted. However, non-Arctic States and their scientists may have an issue because the improved legal environment that is sought may benefit only the eight Arctic States and their scientists. In effect, the Agreement may create a two-category system where non-Arctic States and their scientists do not benefit from such improved environment. This paper examines whether they have substantial interests recognized under international law or by the Arctic scientific community by which they can claim certain benefits of the Agreement. We argue that the degree of benefits to non-Arctic States and their scientists under the Agreement should be commensurate with the degree of substantial interests accorded them by international law and by the Arctic scientific community.

---

a   Professor of International Law; Director, Polar Cooperation Research Centre (PCRC); Kobe University Graduate School of International Cooperation Studies (GSICS).
b   Master's course student, Kobe University Graduate School of International Cooperation Studies (GSICS).

Keywords

Arctic – scientific cooperation – agreement – improved legal environment – non-Arctic States

1   Introduction

At the Iqaluit Ministerial Meeting of the Arctic Council in April 2015, the foreign ministers of the eight Arctic Council member States, namely, Canada, Kingdom of Denmark, Iceland, Finland, Norway, Russia, Sweden, and the United States, decided to extend the mandate of the Task Force on Enhancing Scientific Cooperation in the Arctic (SCTF), "including to work towards a legally-binding agreement on scientific cooperation, with a view to completing its work no later than the next Ministerial meeting," acknowledging "the importance of scientific cooperation to the circumpolar region."[1] This paper examines the current state of negotiations on that agreement, proposed to be called the Agreement on Enhancing International Arctic Scientific Cooperation (hereinafter the 'Agreement'). The analysis is based on the Oslo Draft issued at the end of the fifth SCTF meeting,[2] February 2015, to highlight its legal significance and *problematique*. As of the time of writing this paper, the negotiations on the Agreement are still on-going with textual changes made at its sixth (Copenhagen in August 2015), seventh (Reykjavik in December 2015), and eighth (Washington, D.C. in March 2016) meetings of SCTF.[3] It is reported that, at its ninth meeting (Ottawa in July 2016), the eight Arctic States reached an agreement *ad referendum* on the new Agreement on Enhancing International

---

1   Iqaluit Declaration 2015 on the occasion of the Ninth Ministerial Meeting of the Arctic Council, para.44, available from the Arctic Council Secretariat Homepage, accessed April 1, 2016, http://www.arctic-council.org [hereinafter, unless otherwise noted, all Arctic Council related documents are accessed through this homepage as of July 15, 2016].

2   Agreement on Enhancing International Scientific Cooperation in the Arctic, Oslo Draft as of June 18, 2015 (on file with the authors) [hereinafter Oslo Draft].

3   "Scientific Cooperation Task Force (SCTF) meets in Copenhagen" (September 23, 2015); "Scientific Cooperation Task Force meets in Reykjavik" (January 20, 2016), Arctic Council Secretariat News and Events. Canada offered to host the ninth meeting in July 2016. This may well be the last meeting, considering the time necessary for the eight Arctic States to go through their respective internal procedures before their Foreign Ministers will be ready to sign the Agreement at the next Arctic Council Ministerial Meeting in Fairbanks in May 2017.

Arctic Scientific Cooperation.[4] Despite this dynamic nature of the subject matter, we considered it important to take stock of the discussion at this juncture based on the available text of Oslo Draft. This is because the focus of this paper, namely the relationship of this Agreement to non-Arctic States and their scientists, can be approached from its legal foundation, an examination on which may not necessarily depend on the technical interpretation of the final texts. On the other hand, it is still premature to examine other relevant and important provisions, particularly those on geographical and functional scope of the Agreement, as these provisions have not yet been disclosed to the public.

The main thrust of this paper is, first, to identify the potential legal significance of the new Agreement. It will be significant in improving the legal environment for conducting scientific activities in the Arctic among its Parties and their scientists who are their nationals. It would lower the hurdles heretofore identified in international Arctic scientific cooperation, for example, the difficulties in accessing research areas and research facilities and the delays in border crossing procedures for entry and exit of scientists and their equipment and materials. As our analysis demonstrates, this intended legal effect may establish a legal environment more conducive for Arctic science beyond what is currently provided by general international law, including the law of the sea as to marine scientific research in the Arctic Ocean, and other relevant regional and bilateral agreements and arrangements. As discussed below, the existing international law provides different legal environments for conducting scientific research in different geographical areas: land territories, territorial waters, exclusive economic zones (EEZ), the high seas, airspace, and outer space. The Agreement intends to improve such legal environments above and beyond the existing levels. The authors of this paper consider that this is a good idea and that the Agreement should be promoted.

However, there is an issue for non-Arctic States and their scientists as to the Agreement being applicable only to the eight Arctic States and their scientists. Non-Arctic States and their scientists may still have to work under the existing

---

4   "Task Force on Scientific Cooperation meets in Ottawa" (July 12, 2016), Arctic Council Secretariat News and Events. The eight Arctic States will go through their respective internal procedures to be ready for their Foreign Ministers to sign the Agreement at the next Arctic Council Ministerial Meeting in Fairbanks in May 2017.

legal framework, which has caused many difficulties and delays in their conduct of Arctic science. Some of these difficulties are identified during the fourth International Polar Year of 2007/2008.[5] In effect, we argue, the Agreement may establish what we call 'two-category system' where one category is the eight Arctic States and their scientists, who benefit from the Agreement's improved legal environment for conducting Arctic scientific research, and an inferior category is the non-Arctic States and their scientists, who do not benefit.

Therefore, we examine secondly whether non-Arctic States and their scientists have substantial interests recognized under international law, or by the Arctic scientific community, that enable them to claim certain benefits accorded in the Agreement. These potential benefits includes the possibility to:

- fully participate in the negotiation of the Agreement;
- become Parties to the Agreement;
- be accorded rights and benefits equal to those of the Parties even if they are not; and/or
- receive at least a cooperative attitude from the Arctic States Parties in the treatment of their scientists who conduct research in the Arctic.

We argue that the degree of benefits that non-Arctic States and their scientists may claim under the Agreement should be commensurate with the degree of substantial interests accorded to them by international law and by the Arctic scientific community.

There are other relevant and important issues involved in this Agreement, such as its geographical and functional scope,[6] the role of indigenous peoples

---

5 They are discussed in the Arctic Council's Senior Arctic Officials meetings in the context of Norwegian proposal on "Maximizing the Legacy of IPY." Norwegian Delegation to the Arctic Council, "Project proposal by Norway: Maximizing the Legacy of IPY" (2008): 3; Arctic Council Secretariat, "Maximizing the Legacy of IPY in the Arctic: A scoping study for the Arctic Council" (2009): 18–19. *See also* Hajo Eicken, "Internationally Coordinated, Cooperative Arctic Marine Science during the Fourth International Polar Year: Lessons for Future Arctic Ocean Science Agreements," in *Arctic Science, International Law and Climate Change*, ed. Susanne Wasum-Rainer, Ingo Winkelmann, and Katrin Tiroch (Springer, 2012): 285–298.

6 *See infra*, note 42.

ENHANCING INTERNATIONAL ARCTIC SCIENTIFIC COOPERATION 133

and their traditional knowledge,[7] intellectual property rights,[8] and a review process for its implementation.[9] Because of the reasons stated above, this

---

7 Oslo Draft Article 9: Traditional and local knowledge

  1. The Parties shall, in accordance with respective laws, [and] regulations, [procedures, policies, and international obligations,] encourage participants to take into account, as appropriate, traditional and local knowledge in the planning and conduct of scientific research and activities under this Agreement.

  2. [The Parties shall encourage indigenous and local communities, when appropriate, to render assistance in communication between holders of traditional and local knowledge and those participants conducting scientific research and scientific assessments under this Agreement.]

  [2 alt. The Parties (shall) encourage indigenous peoples to participate in scientific research and scientific assessments under this Agreement and then to use their traditional knowledge.]

8 [Oslo Draft Article 3bis by Russia

  The participants may conclude specific agreements to regulate issues pertaining to their joint activities, particularly the financing of joint activities, exploitation and use of scientific and research facilities, dispute settlements, protection and distribution of intellectual property rights created or transferred during any joint activity.]

9 [Oslo Draft Article 11 [Review]

  1. The Parties shall review annually the implementation of this Agreement, including successes achieved and obstacles to implementation. This review shall be carried out through the Senior Arctic Officials (SAOs).

  2. The Parties, through the SAOs, shall convene at least every five years a committee of individuals with appropriate science backgrounds to help assess the overall effectiveness of this Agreement and help determine the need for any amendments. The committee shall be composed of an equal number of representatives designated by each of the Parties. It shall consider information from Parties, Arctic Council Permanent Participants, and Arctic Council Observers, as well as any other relevant information that it deems useful, and shall provide recommendations on improving the effectiveness of this Agreement to the Parties' Ministers through the SAOs.]

  [Norway: Review and Meeting of the Parties.

  1. The Parties shall review on a regular basis the implementation of this Agreement, including successes achieved and obstacles to implementation. This review shall be carried in the Meeting of the Parties. The Parties shall consider information, as appropriate, from Parties, Arctic Council Permanent Participants, and Arctic Council Observers, as well as any other relevant information that it deems useful, and shall provide recommendations on improving the effectiveness of this Agreement.

  2. The Parties shall meet no later than one year after the entry into force of this Agreement as convened by the depositary, and from then on as decided by the Parties. Parties may elect to convene such meetings in conjunction with meetings of the Arctic Council.

paper will focus on the Agreement's subjective scope, namely, which entities can and should be legally considered as its subjects and beneficiaries.

2 The Two-Category System in the Oslo Draft

2.1 *A Brief History of the Negotiations*

As one of the legacies of the fourth International Polar Year (IPY), the Senior Arctic Officials (SAO) of the Arctic Council commenced discussion in 2008 on possible ways to improve access for scientists in the whole Arctic on a long-term basis.[10] The SCTF was established at the Kiruna Ministerial Meeting of the Arctic Council in 2013 to "work towards an arrangement on improved scientific research cooperation among the eight Arctic States."[11] Regarding this original mandate, it should be noted, first, that the expected outcome of the task force discussion was an 'arrangement' and, second, that the expected cooperation was 'among the eight Arctic States.' Under the co-chairmanship of Sweden, Russia, and the United States, the participants in the SCTF focused on the need to remove obstacles to collaborative Arctic science and to support its efficiency.[12] Participation in the SCTF is governed by the revised Rules of Procedure of the Arctic Council, in which non-Arctic States and intergovernmental and non-governmental organizations are invited to 'observe.'[13] The International Arctic Science Committee (IASC) made a presentation on how cross-border logistics had been made easier during the IPY. Key areas were

---

    3. Each Party shall designate a competent national authority as a responsible point of contact for this Agreement. The names of and contact information for the designated points of contact shall be included in an Appendix to this Agreement. Each Party shall promptly inform the other Parties in writing through its competent national authority or authorities and through diplomatic channels of nay changes to those designations.]

10   "Maximizing the Legacy of IPY in the Arctic: A scoping study for the Arctic Council," *supra*, note 4 at 19; Meeting of Senior Arctic Officials, Final Report, Torshavn, Faroe Island, October 19–20, 2010: 15; and Nuuk Declaration on the occasion of the Seventh Ministerial Meeting of the Arctic Council, Nuuk, Greenland, May 12, 2011, 3rd paragraph in the Section "Science and Monitoring."

11   Kiruna Declaration 2013 on the occasion of the Eighth Ministerial Meeting of the Arctic Council, Section on Protecting the Arctic Environment, 13th paragraph.

12   Task Force on Enhancing Scientific Cooperation in the Arctic, *Senior Arctic Officials' Report to Ministers, Iqaluit, Canada* (April 24, 2015): 10–11.

13   *See* Arctic Council Rules of Procedure (revised, 2013) and the consecutive articles on the SCTF in Arctic Council Secretariat News and Events for actual participants. Japan's participation as an observer State in the SCTF was sporadic and not well coordinated internally.

ENHANCING INTERNATIONAL ARCTIC SCIENTIFIC COOPERATION

identified where improvement is needed, such as: sharing of data; facilitating the cross-border movement of people, samples and equipment; and access to research areas and facilities. The SCTF then concluded, at about its third meeting (in Reykjavik, May 2014), that a high-level agreement would be the best mechanism to advance the objectives, and the group initially considered a draft memorandum of understanding.[14]

That draft, entitled Memorandum of Cooperation on Enhancing International Scientific Cooperation in the Arctic,[15] was a non-legally binding instrument that stipulated the intention of the governments of eight Arctic States as Participants to "raise the efficiency of scientific research in the Arctic through enhanced scientific cooperation" (Paragraph 1.2). For example, Paragraph 7 on Access to research areas provided that:

> The Participants intend to facilitate access to terrestrial, coastal, atmospheric, and marine research areas in the Arctic for the purposes of conducting cooperative Arctic scientific research activities, including the social and human dimension, under this Memorandum of Cooperation.
>
> Regarding marine research, the Participants intend to enhance their cooperation on the promotion and conduct of marine scientific research in the Arctic and in that context intend to use their best efforts to process applications to conduct marine and other scientific research in the Arctic as expeditiously as possible, in accordance with applicable national laws, regulations, and procedures and consistent with customary international law as reflected in the UN Convention on the Law of the Sea, in particular its provisions contained in Part XIII pertaining to marine scientific research.

Paragraph 12 provided that the memorandum "becomes operative upon signature by the Participants. . . ." There was also a proposal to have an annex, so that the memorandum itself would be kept on a general level and the specifications as to its follow-up would be included in the annex.

It was during the discussion on the draft memorandum at the May 2014 Reykjavik meeting that "a number of delegations felt that it would be preferable

---

14   Senior Arctic Officials' Report to Ministers (April 24, 2015), *supra*, note 11 at 10–11.

15   Memorandum of Cooperation on Enhancing International Scientific Cooperation in the Arctic (ca. May 2014) (on file with the authors).

to present a legally binding agreement to Ministers."[16] One of these was the Russia delegation, whose explanation was that

> [A legally-binding document] will enable the ministries and agencies in our countries responsible for carrying out such research to use their existing capacities in a more efficient way, [and also] a legally binding document could provide an opportunity to improve coordination and the process of getting different clearances within a country in order to carry out joint activities.[17]

Thus, the binding character of the Agreement was sought for domestic reasons by some Arctic States, including Russia. The co-chairs of the SCTF reported to the Iqaluit Ministerial meeting that

> [I]t became clear that addressing issues such as the movement of people and equipment across borders and access to research areas may require significant involvement from a wide range of government agencies and stakeholders ... [and i]t was agreed that resolution on these issues may benefit from the force of a legally binding agreement.[18]

It is worth noting in this context that the Russian delegation has been positively engaged in the negotiations and that this was well received by other members despite the political tensions occurring in 2014 and onward outside the Arctic.

The Oslo Draft resulted from this new direction toward a legally binding Agreement. As a fallout of this development, the thorny issue arose of the relationship of the Agreement to the non-Arctic States as its non-Parties, in part because the Agreement would become a treaty under international law, with its well-established doctrine of *res inter alios acta*.[19]

---

16   Report of the Co-Chairs to the Senior Arctic Officials, Task Force on Scientific Cooperation (October 2, 2014).

17   Statement of Yuri Tsaturov, Russia's Head of Delegation to the SCTF, "Interviews with SCTF Delegates" (March 26, 2015), Arctic Council Secretariat News and Events.

18   Senior Arctic Officials' Report to Ministers (24 April 2015), *supra*, note 11.

19   Malcolm N. Shaw, *International Law, Seventh Edition* (Cambridge Univ. Press, 2014): 672–674. *See infra*, note 34 and accompanying arguments.

ENHANCING INTERNATIONAL ARCTIC SCIENTIFIC COOPERATION

2.2   *Intended Legal Effect of the Agreement*

The Oslo Draft has the legal structure of a treaty, designating the contracting governments as 'Parties,' incorporating entering-into-force procedures (Article 13), and providing for legal obligations on the Parties to 'render assistance' to and/or 'facilitate' international scientific cooperation. Such obligations relate to the application of the most expeditious border crossing procedures for entry to and exit from the Parties' territories/jurisdictions of scientists, their equipment and samples (Article 4); access to data and sharing of data (Article 5); access to research infrastructure and facilities (Article 6); and access to research areas (Article 7). For example, in comparison to Paragraph 7 of the draft memorandum cited above, Oslo Draft's Article 7 on Access to research areas provides as follows:

> [1. The Parties, in accordance with and subject to their respective laws, regulations, [procedures, policies] and international obligations, shall facilitate access by the other Parties and their nationals to terrestrial, coastal, atmospheric, and marine research areas in the Arctic for the purpose of conducting cooperative Arctic scientific research activities.
>
> 2. The Parties shall process applications to conduct marine scientific research in the Arctic as expeditiously as possible, in accordance with and subject to applicable laws, regulations, [procedures, policies] and international obligations.]
>
> [Russia: Alternative version: The Parties shall render assistance in processing applications to conduct marine scientific research in the Arctic.]

It is important to emphasize that the Agreement does not intend to provide for a freedom of scientific research at the international law level in the Arctic under the sovereignty and jurisdiction of the eight Arctic States.[20] Instead, the intended legal effect is to have a certain degree of internationally agreed-upon control over the exercise of those States' regulatory powers that are recognized under international law as regards scientific activities in their Arctic territories and their water zones. The extent of this international control as provided in the Agreement seems to be still controversial among the negotiating Arctic States,

---

20   The Oslo Draft is still ambiguous as to whether it would also apply to "areas beyond the jurisdiction of any State" (*see* Norwegian proposal on Article 2 on Scope in the Oslo Draft). If the Agreement does become applicable to international scientific cooperation occurring in the high seas, the Area, and even outer-space, the freedom of scientific research of all States provided under the applicable international law must be the basis of any provision enhancing even further the scientific cooperation in those areas.

as shown by the Oslo Draft's use of different verbs, such as 'promote,' 'facilitate,' and 'render assistance,' to convey relative efforts to achieve the different levels of improved legal environment offered to other Parties. Controversy also seems to exist with the way the Oslo Draft refers to the domestic laws and policies of the Parties in providing for certain flexibilities in implementing these international efforts.[21] Yet, whatever the final outcome on the degree of this international control provided in the Agreement, the intention of the Parties is to improve the legal environment for conducting Arctic scientific research by legally binding them to exercise their regulatory powers in such a way as to lower the existing hurdles. The Agreement, when entered into force and appropriately implemented, will bring real benefits for international Arctic scientific cooperation.

The extent of the regulatory powers that the Arctic territorial and coastal States have over scientific activities, as recognized under existing international law, differs between the land area and the sea area. Within the sea area, it differs between, on one hand, the internal seas and territorial seas, and, on the other hand, exclusive economic zones (EEZs) and continental shelves. Unless otherwise provided by bilateral or regional treaties,[22] the territorial States

---

21   Oslo Draft Article 10 [Laws, regulations, procedures, and policies]

[Activities and obligations under this Agreement shall be conducted in accordance with and subject to the applicable laws, regulations, procedures, [and] policies[, and international obligations] of the Parties, and shall be subject to the availability of appropriated and other funds, personnel, and other resources.]

[Russia: Alternative version: Cooperation under the present Agreement shall be achieved in accordance with international obligations and national laws and regulations of the States of the Parties.]

[Norway: Alternative version: Activities and obligations under this Agreement shall be conducted in accordance with and subject to the applicable laws and regulations of the Parties and shall be subject to the availability of appropriated and other funds, personnel, and other resources.]

On the issue of international law referencing to domestic law, *see* Akiho Shibata, "International and Domestic Laws in Collaboration: An Effective Means to Environmental Liability Regime-Making," in *"L'être situé," Effectiveness and Purposes of International Law: Essays in Honour of Professor Ryuichi Ida*, ed. Shotarō Hamamoto, Hironobu Sakai, and Akiho Shibata (Brill, 2015): 193–213.

22   In the Arctic context, the application of 1920 Treaty of Spitsbergen over the Norwegian Svalbard Islands must be taken into account if the Agreement's geographical scope comes to include these islands. *See generally* Geir Ulfstein, *The Svalbard Treaty: From Terra Nullius to Norwegian Sovereignty* (Scandinavian University Press, 1995); E.J. Molenaar, "Fisheries Regulation in the Maritime Zones of Svalbard," *International Journal of Marine and Coastal Law* 27 (2012): 12–13.

ENHANCING INTERNATIONAL ARCTIC SCIENTIFIC COOPERATION

have full sovereignty in their land areas, including internal waters, to regulate foreign scientific activities in their territory, and any facilitation those States legally promise to offer specifically for Arctic science will improve the legal environment in conducting such activities. Bilateral science and technology cooperation agreements do not normally provide for specific obligations to facilitate access to land research areas or to facilitate movement of scientists and their equipment across borders. For example, the Japan-Russia Science and Technology Cooperation Agreement of September 4, 2000 provides in Article 4 that any details of cooperative activities may be stipulated in implementing arrangements between relevant scientific bodies of the Parties.[23] The Japan-Russia Committee established under that agreement at its twelfth meeting, September 2015, identified Arctic research as an area of interest for the Parties to strengthen their cooperation.[24] As yet, however, there are no legally guaranteed schemes to materialize such cooperation in the Arctic. We consider similar legal situation prevails in other countries under bilateral agreements.[25] Thus, for most countries and their scientists engaged in Arctic research in land areas, the facilitation provisions of the proposed Agreement will have a legal effect of improving the legal environment for conducting Arctic scientific research beyond that currently provided by international law, thus, benefiting international Arctic scientific cooperation.

Some scientists engaged in Arctic research may still hold on to a naive perception that the current cooperative schemes at the level of individual

---

23   Kagaku-Gijutsu Kyōryoku ni kansuru Nippon-koku Seifu to Russia-renpō Seifu tono aida no Kyōtei [Agreement between the Government of Japan and the Government of Russian Federation on Science and Technology Cooperation], signed and entered into force on Sept. 4, 2000, accessed Jan. 22, 2016, http://www.mofa.go.jp/mofaj/gaiko/treaty/pdfs/A-H12-1705.pdf (available in Japanese and Russian).

24   Gaimushō (Ministry of Foreign Affairs of Japan), Nichi-Ro Kagaku-Gijutsu Kyōryoku I-inkai Dai 12 kai Kaigō no Kaisai, Kekka [12th Meeting of the Japan-Russia Science and Technology Cooperation Committee, Results] (September 11, 2015), accessed Jan. 22, 2016, http://www.mofa.go.jp/mofaj/press/release/press4_002439.html (available in Japanese).

25   The exception seems to be the ones concluded by the United States. For example, Article 9 of the Agreement between the United States and Russia on Science and Technology Cooperation of 1993 provides for the Parties' obligations to facilitate entry into and exit from its territory of personnel and equipment, to promote appropriate personnel's travel to its relevant geographic areas, and to facilitate duty free entry for necessary materials and equipment relevant to the projects and programs under the Agreement. For examination of these bilateral agreements in the context of Arctic marine scientific research, *see* Betsy Baker, "Common Precepts of Marine Scientific Research Access in the Arctic," in Wasum-Rainer, Winkelmann, and Tiroch, *supra*, note 4 at 219–224.

researchers and institutions will be sufficient to conduct Arctic scientific cooperative activities. These arrangements may be informal or may be codified in memoranda of understanding (MOUs) at the institutional level. However, the Arctic Council members themselves found inherent limitations in the informal arrangements, and even in the institutional level MOUs, in enhancing international Arctic scientific cooperation. These arrangements were found particularly limiting when it comes to influencing the conduct of different governmental and local authorities, such as customs and the military. The intended legal effect of the Agreement is not to substitute for those cooperative arrangements at individual and institutional levels, but to provide a more stable legal environment where these arrangements would be effectively implemented. Scientists engaged in Arctic research would surely benefit from a more stable and secure legal environment conducive to Arctic scientific cooperation, which the Agreement intends to establish. In this sense, non-Arctic States scientists are legitimate stakeholders of the future Agreement.

The regulatory powers of the Arctic coastal states over marine scientific research in the Arctic Ocean are provided in the United Nations Convention on the Law of the Sea (UNCLOS), in particular, in Part XIII on Marine Scientific Research. While all States, irrespective of their geographical location, and competent international organizations have the right to conduct marine scientific research (Art. 238), the exercise of such right is circumscribed by the coastal States' authority to regulate, authorize, conduct, and consent (with or without conditions) to marine scientific research. In their territorial seas, Article 245 and other relevant provisions of UNCLOS provide a "complete control by the coastal State over marine scientific research."[26] Therefore, as to Arctic scientific cooperation in the territorial seas of Arctic coastal States, the Agreement would provide the same benefit as in the land territories, as explained above.

In the EEZ and on the continental shelf, the coastal States' authority is counterbalanced by the right of all States to conduct marine scientific research under a detailed consent regime (Articles 246–252), with specific conditions the researching State must comply with. These conditions include the provision of data and samples to the coastal States and the public availability of research results (Article 249). Most importantly, the coastal States shall, in normal circumstances, grant their consent for marine scientific research projects by other States that are "exclusively for peaceful purposes and in order to increase scientific knowledge of the marine environment for the benefit

---

26   Hideo Takabayashi, "Haitateki Keizai Sui-iki ni okeru Kagakuteki Chōsa [Marine Scientific Research in the Exclusive Economic Zone]," *Kokusaihō Gaikō Zasshi* [*Journal of International Law and Diplomacy*], 85–3 (1986): 44 (in Japanese).

ENHANCING INTERNATIONAL ARCTIC SCIENTIFIC COOPERATION 141

of all mankind." To this end, coastal States shall establish rules and procedures ensuring that such consent will not be delayed or denied unreasonably (paragraph 3 of Article 246). After another State has given the coastal State six months advance notice of its intention to conduct a marine scientific research project (Article 248), it is implied that the coastal State has consented to the project unless otherwise noted (Article 252). These provisions are intended to avoid arbitrary hindrance of legitimate marine scientific research in the EEZs and on the continental shelves;[27] therefore, UNCLOS already provides for an improved legal environment for research in those areas than is provided on the land territories or in the territorial seas. This legal situation is explicitly acknowledged by the negotiators of the Agreement, as in the eighth preambular paragraph of the Oslo Draft: "*Taking into account* the relevant provisions of the 1982 UNCLOS, in particular the provisions in Part XIII on marine scientific research as they relate to promoting and facilitating the development and conduct of marine scientific research for peaceful purposes."

Implementation of UNCLOS' relevant provisions, however, has not been uniform. This is because of the discretion allowed in those provisions of UNCLOS, particularly the coastal States' discretion to withhold consent for another State's research project in their EEZ and on their continental shelf (paragraph 5 of Article 246).[28] It has been widely recognized in academia that there was a room for improvement.[29] Also, at the policy level, the Arctic Ocean Review of 2013 (undertaken by the Protection of Arctic Marine Environment Working Group (PAME) of the Arctic Council, reporting to the Senior Arctic

---

27   *Ibid.*, at 17–32.

28   Montserrat Gorina-Ysern, *An International Regime for Marine Scientific Research* (Martinus Nijhoff, 2003): 599–618; Tullio Treves, "Marine Scientific Research", *Max Planck Encyclopedia of Public International Law* (2008), (online); Masahiro Miyoshi, "Haitateki Keizai Sui-iki ni okeru Chōsa Katsudō [Marine Scientific Research in the EEZ]," in *Nippon ni okeru Kaiyōhō no Shuyō Kadai [The Law of the Sea and Japan]*, ed. Tadao Kuribayashi and Takane Sugihara (Yushindō, 2010): 165–192 (in Japanese); Paul Gragl, "Marine Scientific Research," in *The IMLI Manual on International Maritime Law: Volume I: The Law of the Sea*, ed. Malgosia Fitzmaurice and Norman A. Martinez Guitérrez (Oxford University Press, 2014): 398, 423–425. *See also* United Nations, *Marine Scientific Research: A revised guide to the implementation of the relevant provisions of the United Nations Convention on the Law of the Sea* (United Nations, 2010).

29   Susanne Wasum-Rainer, "Conclusion of the Chair," in Wasum-Rainer, Winkelmann, and Tiroch, *supra*, note 4 at 307–310; Yoshinobu Takei, "Marine Scientific Research in the Arctic," in *The Law of the Sea and the Polar Regions: Interactions between Global and Regional Regimes*, ed. Erik J. Molenaar, Alex G. Oude Elfrink, and Donald R. Rothwell (Martinus Nijhoff, 2013): 348–351.

Officials) also identified the need for "an Arctic science instrument", beyond what UNCLOS and other relevant instruments now provide, to facilitate marine scientific cooperation and promote data sharing.[30] Article 7, paragraph 2, of the Oslo Draft on access to research areas (cited above) explicitly obliges the Parties to "process applications to conduct marine scientific research in the Arctic as expeditiously as possible." Article 5 on access to data, without distinguishing between data obtained from land areas and that from marine areas, provides that the "Parties . . . shall take all reasonable steps to facilitate access to data in connection with scientific research activities under this Agreement."[31]

Thus, it is clear that the intention of the negotiators of the Agreement is to improve the legal environment for conducting marine scientific research in the Arctic Ocean above that already provided by UNCLOS. This intention does not infringe on the usual caveat, as provided in Oslo Draft Article 12 *bis*, that "[n]othing in the present Agreement shall be construed as altering the rights or obligations of any Party under other relevant international agreements or international law", because the Agreement only provides for more specific ways to exercise the rights and implement the obligations already provided in UNCLOS.

The Arctic Council members negotiating the Agreement, therefore, intend it to have a significant legal as well as practical impact on Arctic science, improving the legal environment for conducting Arctic scientific research, both on land and in the sea, beyond that currently provided by general international law and relevant treaties. Because it will be signed by foreign ministers of the eight Arctic States, the Agreement will convey a strong message that Arctic science should not be hindered unreasonably. Article 11 on review provides

---

30   PAME, The Arctic Ocean Review Project, Final Report (Phase II 2011–2013) (Kiruna, May 2013): 14 (Recommendation 22): 87–93.

31   Oslo Draft Article 5: Access to data

[The Parties, in accordance with and subject to their respective laws, regulations, procedures, policies, and international obligations, shall take all reasonable steps to facilitate access to data in connection with scientific research activities under this Agreement.

The Parties shall render assistance to facilitate data distribution and data sharing by actions that may include, as appropriate and to the extent practicable, adhering to commonly accepted standards, formats and protocols, and implementing common sampling practices and reporting protocols.

The Parties also shall support full and open access to metadata and shall encourage open access to data and published research with minimum time delay, preferably online and free of charge or at no more than the cost or reproduction.]

[Russia: Alternative version: The Parties shall render assistance in scientific and technological data sharing among participants and open access of participants to metadata.]

ENHANCING INTERNATIONAL ARCTIC SCIENTIFIC COOPERATION

that the "Parties shall review annually the implementation of this Agreement, including successes achieved and obstacles to implementation" and that this review "shall be carried out through the Senior Arctic Officials (SAOs)."[32] In addition, the Parties will be able to make representation at the diplomatic level based on this Agreement if and when their Arctic scientists encounter difficulties that seem unwarranted under its provisions.[33]

2.3   *The Legal Nature of the Two-Category System*

The Oslo Draft, like the two previous agreements negotiated and adopted under the auspices of the Arctic Council,[34] does not contain an accession clause. At the beginning of its text, it lists the eight Arctic States and designates them as the 'Parties.' These elements indicate that the Agreement will be closed and no non-Arctic States will ever become Parties, unless through an amendment (Oslo Draft Article 12 *quarter*) adding an accession clause later on.

Under Article 36 of the Vienna Convention on the Law of Treaties (VCLT), if the Parties – namely the eight Arctic States – intend for the Agreement to accord a right to non-Arctic third States who are not Parties, the right may arise if the third States assent thereto. If the intent of the Parties to this effect is uncertain or imprecise, a third State may not invoke the benefit of a provision in the Agreement that it happens to find advantageous. Although a benefiting third State or group of States need not be explicitly stipulated in the Agreement, it is considered reasonable that they must be identifiable, because it is difficult to conceive that the intention to create a right can be totally disinterested and abstract.[35]

Under these conditions, it is difficult to interpret relevant provisions in the Oslo Draft as according to third States the legal right to claim, as against the Parties, the benefit of the improved legal environment for conducting Arctic

---

32   Oslo Draft Article 11 [Review], *see supra*, note 8.

33   Oslo Draft Article 12 on Disputes provides that "[a]ny differences arising from interpretation or implementation of the provisions of the present Agreement shall be resolved amicably by the Parties through consultations and negotiations."

34   Agreement on Cooperation on Aeronautical and Maritime Search and Rescue in the Arctic, done on May 12, 2011, entered into force on January 19, 2013; Agreement on Cooperation on Marine Oil Pollution Preparedness and Response in the Arctic, done on May 15, 2013, not yet in force. *See* Svein Vigeland Rottem, "A Note on the Arctic Council Agreements," *Ocean Development and International Law* 46 (2015): 50–59.

35   Olivier Corten and Pierre Klein, ed., *The Vienna Conventions on the Law of Treaties: A Commentary Volume I* (Oxford University Press, 2011): 932–935.

scientific research.[36] For example, Paragraph 1 of Article 7 on access to research areas (cited above) explicitly provides that the "access by *the other Parties and their nationals*" be facilitated (emphasis added). Similarly, an exclusionary intention is certain in Article 4 on entry and exit of persons, equipment and materials,[37] and Article 6 on access to research infrastructure and facilities,[38] which explicitly refer to "*the Parties*" and "*their nationals.*" This wording obviates any intention to extend the benefits of these two articles beyond the Parties and their nationals. On the other hand, Paragraph 2 of Article 7 (cited above) does not explicitly refer to "*other Parties and their nationals*" in regard to expeditious processing of applications to conduct marine scientific research. However, this provision, to say the least, is uncertain as to whether the

---

36   The relevant provisions of the Agreement almost invariably stipulate the obligation on the part of territorial and coastal States to 'facilitate' and/or 'render assistance to' international Arctic scientific cooperation taking place in their territories and water zones under their jurisdiction. The obligation of the territorial and coastal Parties to facilitate research does not automatically signify freedom of scientific research by other Parties. Instead, the other Party has the right to make a legal claim that such facilitation and/or rendering of assistance be materialized and extended to the Party and its nationals. It is this kind of right provided under the Agreement that is at issue here.

37   Oslo Draft Article 4: Entry and exit of persons, equipment and materials

      [The Parties shall apply, in accordance with and subject to their respective laws, regulations, procedures, policies, and international obligations, the most expeditious border crossing procedure possible to facilitate entry to, and exist from, areas under their jurisdiction of persons, research platforms, material, samples, data and equipment of the Parties and their nationals.]

      [Russia: Alternative version: Issues of entry/exit, as well as of stay in the territory of the State of a Party, of individuals being participants or representatives of the participants, and issues of import/export of equipment and samples used in joint activities within the framework of the present Agreement to/from the territory of the State of a Party shall be regulated in accordance with international obligations and national laws and regulations of the State of the respective Party.]

38   Oslo Draft Article 6: Access to research infrastructure and facilities

      [The Parties, in accordance with and subject to their respective laws, regulations, [procedures and policies], and international obligations, shall facilitate access by the other Parties to publically /government-financed research infrastructure and facilities for the purpose of conducting cooperative Arctic scientific research activities.]

      [Russian: Alternative version: The Parties shall render assistance in access of participants to national government research infrastructure and facilities for the purpose of conducting cooperative Arctic scientific research activities.]

Parties intend to extend such benefits to research vessels flying the flag of non-Arctic States or to projects organized and conducted by non-Arctic State nationals. Paragraphs 1 and 2 of Article 5 on access to data (cited above) are just as uncertain.

The Oslo Draft intends to cover 'joint activity,' defined as "cooperative activity conducted in accordance with the provisions of the present Agreement by participants from two or more *States of the Parties*" (emphasis added). 'Participant' in turn is defined as "a scientific and technological organization, institution, higher educational establishment, legal entity or individual of *the State of a Party*, or relevant public authority of *the State of a Party* when appropriate, involved in a joint activity" (emphasis added, Article xx on Use of terms). Although the overall legal structure of the Oslo Draft is still unclear as to how these two terms will be legally effectuated in the substantive provisions (for example, Article 7, cited above, does not use these terms), the proposed texts of the Agreement seem to limit its scope to the cooperative activities among the eight Arctic States and limit its benefits arising therefrom to their nationals, excluding the nationals from non-Arctic States.

It could happen that the Parties, in implementing the Agreement, would decide to enact or amend their relevant domestic laws and regulations to materialize the facilitation it requires, and such laws and regulations would most likely be applied to all persons or at least to all foreign scientists, irrespective of their nationality, under the jurisdiction of the Parties. For example, a Party, implementing its obligation under Article 7 on access to research areas (cited above), may enact an exemption from a permit requirement for entry into a designated research area for certain environmental studies in the Arctic. This legislation could well be applied to all scientists irrespective of their nationality. Such an improved legal environment implemented by the domestic laws and regulations of the Parties could be a positive, albeit indirect, legal effect of the Agreement, potentially benefiting even non-Arctic States' scientists. However, at the international law level, non-Arctic States have no legal means proactively to claim such benefits, or to make formal representation at the diplomatic level based on the Agreement if and when their scientists encounter difficulties in the actual application of such domestic laws and regulations.

It would also be difficult to use most-favored-nation clauses in bilateral commerce and navigation agreements between non-Arctic States and Arctic States to claim a not-less-favorable level of improvement than the Agreement provides. For example, Japan has commerce and navigation treaties with all of the eight Arctic States except Iceland, and some of these treaties provide for most-favored-nation treatment in relation to activities such as 'study and research'[39] or 'studies and investigation.'[40] However, the *ejusdem generis* rule providing grounds for such claim requires the subject matters addressed in the two treaties to be substantively similar.[41] Since the most-favored-nation treatment for research provided in commerce and navigation treaties is within the context of economic and commercial activities, it would be difficult in most cases to extend the benefits under the Agreement within the context of scientific cooperation to the beneficiary States (non-Arctic States) through the most-favored-nation clause. Furthermore, the 1954 Japan–Canada and 1958 Japan–Russia commerce agreements do not have any provision referring to study or research activities in the context of most-favored-nation treatment.

Thus, the non-Arctic States, as long as they are not Parties, would have no international legal basis to claim the Agreement's improved legal environment in conducting Arctic scientific research. The facilitation offered by the Arctic States Parties in conducting Arctic scientific research in their territories and the areas under their jurisdiction would extend only to 'joint activities' of the Parties, their nationals, and their participating researchers and institutions. Non-Party States and their nationals would be excluded; for example, the Parties would have no obligation to facilitate access to research areas in their territories to non-Arctic States' scientists. This legal situation that may be brought about by the Agreement is what we call a two-category system. One category is the Arctic States Parties and their nationals, with their Arctic scientific projects benefiting from the improved legal environment in conducting Arctic scientific research. The other category is non-Party States and their nationals, with their equally relevant projects not being able to benefit from

---

39   Treaty of Commerce and Navigation between Japan and Norway, signed and entered into force in 1957, Article 2: "Nationals of either Party, within the territories of the either Party: (a) shall be accorded most-favored-nation treatment in all matters relating to their study and research, the pursuit of their profession, and their commercial, industrial, financial and other business activities[.]" Texts accessed Jan. 22, 2016, http://www.mofa.go.jp/mofaj/gaiko/treaty/pdfs/A-S38(2)–148.pdf.

40   Denmark: Treaty of Commerce and Navigation, signed and entered into force in 1912, validity confirmed in 1952, Article 1, paragraph 1: "Shall, in all that relates to travel and residence; to the pursuit of their studies and investigation; to the exercise of their callings and professions, and to the prosecution of their industrial and manufacturing undertakings, be placed, in all respects, on the same footing as the subjects or citizens of the most favored nation[.]" Texts accessed Jan. 22, 2016, http://www.mofa.go.jp/mofaj/gaiko/treaty/pdfs/A-S38(1)-059.pdf.

41   *See* the International Law Commission's Draft Articles on Most-Favored-Nation Clauses, particularly its Articles 9 and 10 on *ejusdem generis* rule, *Yearbook of International Law Commission Vol. II, Part Two* (1978): 27–33.

ENHANCING INTERNATIONAL ARCTIC SCIENTIFIC COOPERATION   147

the Agreement and being left behind at the original legal situation that caused many obstacles and delays. These States would include Japan, Germany, and the United Kingdom, all of whom have long histories of substantial contributions to Arctic scientific activities and whose scientists have tremendous expertise in the field. In a relative sense, these non-Arctic States, their scientists, and their scientific projects may be relegated to an inferior category in Arctic science.

The potential creation by the Agreement of this two-category system may or may not be the negotiators' intention. Either way, considering the nature of the negotiations within a task force of the Arctic Council, the authors of this paper consider it to be the responsibility of the non-Arctic observer States and other interested observer organizations, such as the IASC, to raise their concerns during the negotiations. When they decide to raise the issue, it will be necessary for them to have an idea as to how and to what extent they and their scientists are to be treated in the texts of the Agreement. It is the argument of this paper that the way to address non-Arctic States and their scientists in the Agreement should be commensurate with the extent to which their legal and substantive interests, relevant to the issues dealt with in the Agreement, are recognized by the international community. In other words, what extent can we say that non-Arctic States and their scientists are substantially interested going beyond mere curiosity in the negotiations and in the substance of the Agreement?[42]

3   Non-Arctic States and Their Scientists as Substantially Interested Stakeholders

3.1   *Legal Interests Recognized by International Law, Including UNCLOS*
The Oslo Draft assumes that the Agreement will apply to scientific cooperative activities in the Arctic territories and water zones the Parties exercise their

---

42   This insight comes from our previous examination of the evolution of the Antarctic Treaty System in the 1970s and 1980s, when the legitimacy of the Antarctic Treaty Consultative Parties' authority to create Antarctic resource regimes was severely questioned by the outsiders. The Consultative Parties regained their legitimacy by proactively engaging States and international organizations substantially interested in Antarctic matters in the regime-making processes while keeping the 'curious' as observers. Akiho Shibata, "Japan and 100 Years of Antarctic Legal Order: Any Lessons for the Arctic?" *Yearbook of Polar Law* 7 (2015): 3–54.

sovereignty, sovereign rights, or jurisdiction consistent with international law.[43] Based on this assumption, and as explained above, the Agreement will impose a core obligation on those Arctic territorial and coastal States to exercise their sovereignty and jurisdiction so as to facilitate the Arctic scientific cooperative activities. This obligation is mutual among the eight Arctic States Parties having territories in the Arctic region although the actual extent of the obligation varies significantly, depending on the size of their Arctic territories and water zones and the scientific interests shown therein.

The non-Arctic States, on the other hand, will assume no obligation as to scientific activities occurring in their territories and the water zones under their jurisdiction. Because of this lack of reciprocity in the core obligation of the Agreement, non-Arctic States cannot be said to have the right to participate on an equal footing in the negotiations. The extent of the obligation to facilitate Arctic scientific activities in their territories and water zones ('promote,' 'facilitate,' and/or 'render assistance') and the extent of the flexibility allowed when implementing these obligations (referring to domestic laws and policies) are issues that only the eight Arctic States, with their direct interest as territorial States, can negotiate and finally decide. As long as the core obligation remains, the current negotiating forum of the Agreement, namely the SCTF, can be considered legitimate even though only the eight Arctic States can make decisions and the non-Arctic observer States are limited to making statements, submitting documents, and providing views on the issues under discussion.[44]

The Oslo Draft's Article 12 *ter* on cooperation with non-Parties provides that "[a]ny party may seek cooperation with States not party to this Agreement that may contribute to activities envisaged in this Agreement." This was copied from Article 17 of the 2013 Arctic Oil Pollution Response Agreement[45] and had not yet been materially discussed at the time of the Oslo meeting in February 2015. However, it implicitly conveys the idea that the non-Arctic States not party to this Agreement are passive subjects to be approached if and only if the

---

43   The two versions on geographic scope of the Agreement (Article 2) proposed by Russia and Norway both assume that the Agreement will apply to "any area over which a State whose government is a Party to this Agreement exercises sovereignty, sovereign rights or jurisdiction, consistent with international law."

44   Arctic Council Rules of Procedure (revised, 2013): para. 38.

45   Agreement on Cooperation on Marine Oil Pollution Preparedness and Response in the Arctic, *supra* note 33, Article 17: "Any Party may, where appropriate, seek cooperation with States not party to this Agreement that may be able to contribute to activities envisaged in this Agreement, consistent with international law."

ENHANCING INTERNATIONAL ARCTIC SCIENTIFIC COOPERATION   149

Arctic States Parties feel the need of their cooperation. This meager provision, which is the sole provision regarding non-Parties in the Oslo Draft, testifies that the draft's very nature concerns substantively only the eight Arctic States and their scientists. Since the Agreement intends to apply to 'joint activities' by scientists from different nationalities, the cooperation from other participating Parties and their scientists would greatly enhance the implementation of the Agreement. For example, Paragraph 2 of Article 5 on access to data (cited above) obligates the Arctic territorial States to facilitate data distribution and sharing in connection with multinational scientific activities undertaken in their territories. It would be the territorial States' primary responsibility to have an implementing domestic scheme to ensure that such data distribution and sharing would be actually effectuated, including encouragement of foreign scientists to abide by such a scheme. The cooperative attitude of the participating foreign scientists and their governments would greatly help in achieving the objective of this article. Yet the Oslo Draft does not foresee the need of such substantive cooperation from non-Arctic States or their scientists and fails to address 'joint activities' that involve them.

If future negotiations on the definition of 'joint activity' lead to its expansion to cover activities involving non-Arctic States and their institutions and scientists, the provision on cooperation with non-Parties will have a substantive legal significance for non-Arctic States. Even if the provision provides only for an obligation of Parties to "seek cooperation" from non-Parties, this alone, and the potential response of the non-Arctic States, would significantly enhance the effectiveness of the Agreement. As a consequence, the negotiators may need to recognize the legitimate interests of the non-Arctic observer States who are substantively engaged in Arctic international scientific activities, and those of other relevant observer organizations, in drafting the final provision on cooperation with non-Parties.

The potential for a two-category system is a matter of concern in regard to the special situation of improved legal environment for Arctic international scientific cooperation. This proposed legal environment is special because it goes beyond what is currently provided in general international law and relevant treaties, including UNCLOS and bilateral science and technology agreements. This special legal environment would be available to other Parties to the Agreement because the Parties, within their territories and water zones where international scientific activities occur, are obliged to exercise their regulatory powers over those activities in such a way as to promote them by, for example, facilitating access to research areas and facilitating the movement of personnel, equipment, and material. Abiding by the doctrines of *lex specialis* and *pacta tertiis nec nocent nec prosunt*, there is no legal obstacle to establishing such a special regime among the eight Arctic States by a treaty.[46]

The remaining legal question, for non-Arctic States and their scientists, as to the substantive content of the Agreement is whether there are legal interests recognized under international law that effectively allow them to claim treatment that is equal to that of the Arctic States and their scientists enjoyed under the Agreement. As examined above, the most-favored-nation clause in bilateral commerce and navigation agreements would hardly be a legal basis for such a claim.

UNCLOS may provide a legal basis for such claim, at least as to marine scientific research in the Arctic Ocean. Its Article 238 provides for the right to conduct marine scientific research of "all States, irrespective of their geographical location". Indeed, one of the Co-Chairs of the SCTF indicated, in the context of the SCTF discussion, that "the law of the sea gives important rights to all nations there [in the Arctic region], and the Arctic States fully recognize that fact."[47]

Article 311, paragraph 2, of UNCLOS safeguards the rights of non-Arctic States by stipulating that the agreements compatible with UNCLOS that may be concluded by some of its Parties (in this case by the eight Arctic States) would not affect the enjoyment by other States Parties (in this case, the non-Arctic States Parties) of their rights or the performance of their obligations under UNCLOS.[48] Under this provision, the non-Arctic States have a legitimate legal interest in overseeing the negotiation of the Agreement so that their rights under UNCLOS would not be affected by the Agreement. As explained above, the intended effect of the Agreement is not to infringe on or undermine the right under UNCLOS of non-Arctic States as regards their marine scientific research in the Arctic Ocean. Yet an issue still arises as to whether the way such a right may be exercised subject to the Arctic coastal States' regulatory authorities can legally be differentiated in favor of the Arctic States that are Parties to the Agreement.

---

46   *See* E.J. Molennar, "Current and Prospective Role of the Arctic Council System within the Context of the Law of the Sea," *International Journal of Marine and Coastal Law* 27 (2012): 553–595.

47   Evan T. Bloom, "New Arctic Frontiers in International Law and Diplomacy," Keynote Address at British Institute of International and Comparative Law, November 19, 2014 (on file with the authors).

48   Shabtai Rosenne and Louis B. Sohn, ed., *United Nations Convention on the Law of the Sea 1982: A Commentary Volume V* (Martinus Nijhoff, 1989): 243.

Part XIII of UNCLOS on marine scientific research is based on the fundamental concept of international cooperation in marine scientific research activities, including the encouragement of cooperation by different States and the wide dissemination of research results, as provided in its Articles 242 to 244.[49] The reference to "mutual benefit" in Article 242 emphasizes that all participating parties should benefit from such international cooperation, not only the researching States.[50] Article 243 provides for States' obligation to cooperate, through the conclusion of international agreements, to create favorable conditions for the conduct of marine scientific research in the marine environment and to integrate the efforts of scientists in studying the essence of phenomena and processes occurring in the marine environment. According to one authority, such agreements "on a basis of reciprocity [would provide for] simplified or less strict procedures for obtaining consent to do research in areas under their jurisdiction."[51] It is significant that the latter part of Article 243 extends the requirement of cooperation to that between groups of scientists and nongovernmental research institutions working in the field of marine scientific research.[52] Article 244 provides for States' obligation, in cooperation with other States, to promote the flow of scientific data resulting from marine scientific research.

The Agreement under discussion here can be seen as the effort of the eight Arctic States to implement these UNCLOS provisions in creating favorable conditions for the conduct of marine scientific research and in promoting the flow of scientific data specifically relating to the Arctic Ocean. In creating such a legal environment more conducive for marine scientific research, the relevant provisions of UNCLOS assume such cooperation to be open, rather than closed, to wide participation by those engaged in marine scientific research, requiring integration of research efforts of scientists and institutions from different States. At the same time, referring to "mutual benefit" these provisions suggest that such cooperative arrangements for specific marine areas extend to those States and scientists substantively interested in conducting scientific research

---

49 Alfred H.A. Soons, *Marine Scientific Research and the Law of the Sea* (Kluwer Law and Taxation Publishers, 1982): 238–246; Yoshifumi Tanaka, "Obligation to Co-operate in Marine Scientific Research and the Conservation of Marine Living Resources," *Zeitschrift für ausländisches öffentliches Recht und Völkerrecht* 65 (2005): 940–945.

50 Soons, *ibid.*, at 241.

51 *Ibid.*, at 242.

52 Shabtai Rosenne and Alexander Yankov, ed., *United Nations Convention on the Law of the Sea 1982: A Commentary Volume IV* (Martinus Nijhoff, 1991): 477, paragraph 243.7 (b).

in those areas. Betsy Baker, comprehensively analyzing these provisions under UNCLOS and other relevant agreements and practice, identified ten common precepts of marine scientific research in the Arctic that "will promote mutual benefit and international cooperation for *all who share an interest in peaceful marine scientific research in the Arctic Ocean*"(emphasis added).[53]

In the context of protection and preservation of marine environments, UNCLOS and the international practice as exemplified by regional seas programs encourage those coastal States bordering the specific seas in question to take the lead.[54] Many of the Arctic marine scientific research projects, including those organized and conducted by non-Arctic States and their scientists, relate to pollution of the Arctic marine environment.[55] Although the present authors do not share the view that the Arctic Ocean should be treated as a semi-enclosed sea (as defined in Article 122 of UNCLOS),[56] Article 123 of UNCLOS provides for "States bordering an enclosed or semi-enclosed sea" to coordinate their scientific research policies and to invite other interested States or international organizations to cooperate with them in such efforts. These provisions and many of the regional seas conventions suggest that the primary initiative in the protection of marine environment, including the coordination of marine scientific research policies for such purposes, should be taken by States bordering the specific seas.

In the context of scientific research on marine pollution, Article 200 of UNCLOS obliges "all States" to cooperate for the purpose of promoting studies,

---

53   Baker, *supra*, note 24 at 231–232 (emphasis added).

54   *See* Betsy Baker and Alison Share, "Regional Seas, Environmental Protection" (last updated March 2013), *Max Planck Encyclopedia of Public International Law* (online). For example, 1992 OSPAR Convention in its Article 8 provides for establishment of joint programs of scientific research among its Parties but is open for signature or accession only by those States bordering the maritime area covered by the Convention, those States located upstream on water courses reaching the same maritime area, and regional economic integration organization having at least one member satisfying such geographical criteria (Articles 25 and 27). Convention for the Protection of the Marine Environment of the North-East Atlantic, done on 22 September 1992, text accessed Jan. 22, 2016, http://www.ospar.org.

55   *Cf.*, Research menu "Arctic Ocean Environment and Climate Change," under the new Japanese government funded five year Arctic research project called ArCS (Arctic Challenge for Sustainability), accessed Jan. 22, 2016, http://www.arcs-pro.jp/en/project/collaborated/index.html.

56   William V. Dunlap, "The Arctic Ocean and the Regime of Enclosed and Semi-Enclosed Seas," in *International Boundaries and Environmental Security: Framework for Regional Cooperation*, ed., Gerald Blake et al. (Kluwer Law International, 1997): 105–119.

ENHANCING INTERNATIONAL ARCTIC SCIENTIFIC COOPERATION

undertaking programs of scientific research and encouraging the exchange of information and data acquired about pollution of the marine environment. Article 200 goes on to provide that all such States "shall endeavour to participate actively in regional and global programmes to acquire knowledge for the assessment of the nature and extent of pollution, exposure to it, and its pathways, risks and remedies." In other words, UNCLOS encourages all States willing and capable to join in programs of scientific research, even at the regional level, that will increase the knowledge about marine pollution in the area.[57] In the same vein, in the context of conservation of marine living resources in the EEZs, it is the prerogative of coastal States to determine the resource management schemes within their own EEZ; nevertheless, as to available scientific information and other data relevant to the conservation of fish stocks, Article 61, paragraph 5, of UNCLOS provides that such scientific results shall be contributed and exchanged "with participation by all States concerned, including States whose nationals are allowed to fish in the exclusive economic zone,"[58]

Therefore, the regional approach encouraged by UNCLOS does not signify an exclusion of States outside of the region and their nationals, particularly in the context of participating in and contributing to marine scientific research to acquire and share scientific knowledge of the particular marine environment. Consequently, even if the Agreement is considered a regional initiative led by the eight Arctic States, the relevant provisions of UNCLOS do not warrant exclusion of non-Arctic States and their scientists who are willing and able to conduct such research in that region. In this light, it would be against the spirit of UNCLOS to set up two different categories of States and scientists, one less favorable than the other, among those participating in the same international scientific endeavor in the Arctic Ocean. The legal environment should recognize that non-Arctic States and their scientists engaged in marine science have a legitimate interest in being treated on a par with the Arctic States and their scientists. In the context of marine scientific research, as Kristin Bartenstein recalls, "the reluctance to open Arctic cooperation to non-Arctic States... must be overcome in order to enable comprehensive cooperation."[59]

---

57   *See* Rosenne and Yankov, *supra*, note 51 at 90–93.

58   Satya N. Nandan and Shabtai Rosenne, ed., *United Nations Convention on the Law of the Sea 1982: A Commentary Volume II* (Martinus Nijhoff Publishers, 1993): 604–611.

59   Kristin Bartenstein, "The Arctic Region Council Revisited: Inspiring Future Development of the Arctic Council," in *International Law and Politics of the Arctic Ocean: Essay in Honor of Donat Pharand*, ed. Suzanne Lalonde and Ted McDorman (Martinus Nijhoff, 2015): 61–62. *See also* Dunlap, *supra*, note 55 at 113–114.

The underlying rationale for such non-discriminatory treatment of non-Arctic States and their scientists should be amplified, and even extended to terrestrial scientific research, in the case of the Arctic. This is because of the significance of Arctic science for the whole of humankind and the necessity, recognized by the Arctic scientific community, for open and truly international cooperation in Arctic scientific endeavors.

3.2   *Legitimate Expectations Endorsed by the Arctic Scientific Community*

Polar science has long been recognized as a special genre, leading to the launch of four truly international scientific endeavors in the past 140 years. These endeavors began with the first International Polar Year (IPY) of 1882–1883, which involved 11 nations sponsoring 14 polar research expeditions, together with 39 permanent observatories in 25 countries both in and outside of circumpolar regions cooperating in global research programs. The observations and data were made available to the whole world through a central commission.[60] The conceptual underpinnings of such scientific efforts were summarized by Karl Weyprecht, an Austrian physicist who assisted in organizing the first IPY. He declared that the Arctic regions offered opportunities unparalleled anywhere on the planet for scientific studies of the earth's physical and natural processes and that promotion of cooperation among nations was essential to the successful accomplishment of research in the Arctic.[61] These conceptual underpinnings remain true and have been strengthened, culminating in the fourth IPY of 2007–2008. Even today, the scope and scale of the polar research challenges lie beyond the capabilities of individual nations because polar processes extend across national boundaries and the scientific understanding from polar research is of worldwide relevance.[62] As a result, the fourth IPY "emerged as the largest internationally coordinated planetary research effort...with over 160 endorsed science projects assembled from the ideas of researchers in

---

60   E.F. Roots, "Co-operation in Arctic Science: Background and Requirements," in *Arctic Alternatives: Civility or Militarism in the Circumpolar North*, ed. Franklyn Griffiths (Science for Peace, 1992): 141–142.

61   *Ibid.*

62   ICSU IPY 2007–2008 Planning Group, *Framework for the International Polar Year 2007–2008* (November 2004): 9–10, accessed January 22, 2016, http://www.icsu.org/publications/reports-and-reviews/a-framework-for-the-international-polar-year-2007-2008/IPY-framework.pdf.

ENHANCING INTERNATIONAL ARCTIC SCIENTIFIC COOPERATION

more than 60 countries,"[63] including non-polar countries.[64] There is no indication whatsoever that these scientific efforts should be somehow differentiated by the geographic location of the participating nations or the nationality of the scientists who are engaged. Polar science, including Arctic science, has always been considered to be best achieved by the open and international character of its participation and cooperation.

The principle of scientific openness is enshrined in Article A.2 of the Founding Articles of the International Arctic Science Committee (IASC), a nongovernmental scientific organization composed of representatives of scientific organizations of member States. The IASC was established in 1990 with the aim to encourage and facilitate international consultation and cooperation for Arctic scientific research.[65] The principle of scientific openness means that any country engaged in significant scientific research in the Arctic can participate in decision-making for IASC activities, including the development of policies and guidelines for cooperative scientific research.[66] The IASC, therefore, recognizes "the important role of, and the need to work closely with, national scientific organizations from countries outside the Arctic region which have an active and continuing Arctic research programme."[67] As long as non-Arctic States' scientific organizations satisfy the above scientific criterion to become a member of the IASC's Council, they are entitled to participate on a par with the organizations of the original Arctic States Council members in its decision-making by consensus and in assuming other functions, such as becoming President of the Council and serving on its Executive Committee.[68] It is true that the Founding Articles were negotiated by the eight Arctic States

---

63   Ian Allison, Michael Béland, et al., The State of Polar Research: Statement from the International Council for Science/World Meteorological Organization Joint Committee for the International Polar Year 2007–2008 (WMO, 2009): 3, accessed Jan. 22, 2016, https://www.uam.es/otros/cn-scar/pdf/IPY_State_of_Polar_Research_EN.pdf.

64   See also "Maximizing the Legacy of IPY in the Arctic: A scoping study for the Arctic Council," supra, note 4 at 6.

65   Founding Articles for an International Arctic Science Committee (IASC), 1990, accessed Jan. 22, 2016, http://iasc.info/images/about/iasc-founding-articles.pdf.

66   IASC Handbook: 11, accessed Jan. 22, 2016, http://iasc25.iasc.info/images/history/IASC_Handbook.pdf. According to the IASC Rules and Procedures, "significant Arctic research" is an evidence of Arctic science activity in at least two major fields of enquiry, with published results in the international refereed science literature over a period of at least five years. Ibid., at 13.

67   Founding Articles for IASC, supra note 64, 5th preambular paragraph.

68   Louwrens Hacquebord, "How Science Organizations in the Non-Arctic Countries Became Members of IASC," in IASC after 25 Years, ed. Odd Rogne, Volker Rachold, Louwrens

and thus recognize their special regional interests and give them the original Council membership;[69] however, at the level of practical, nongovernmental coordination of scientific activities, the Arctic scientific community as represented by the IASC treats scientists and scientific bodies from non-Arctic States on a par with those from the Arctic States.

Therefore, the open, international character of Arctic science as pursued by the Arctic scientific community over the past 140 years should generate a legitimate expectation among scientists and research institutions willing and able to conduct Arctic science, irrespective of their nationality and their place of establishment and operation, that they be given equal opportunity with others to participate in Arctic cooperative scientific research. Any scheme for Arctic international scientific cooperation that may have the actual or potential effect, not based on their scientific merits, of discouraging certain categories of scientists should be considered contrary to the premises nurtured by the Arctic scientific community.

This legitimate expectation of equal participation in Arctic science by all willing and able scientists implicates legal and policy issues of their status and treatment under governmental regulations. Indeed, the fourth IPY identified, for example, access to and sharing of data and access to research areas and research infrastructure as its legacies; and it recognized the need of sustained actions in these areas to amplify the achievements of the IPY.[70] In this context, building on the IPY experience, the International Council for Science (ICSU) adopted in April 2010 a statement on "Universality of Science in the Polar Regions" that called on all parties conducting or influencing Arctic research to support continued and responsible access to all areas of the Arctic for research purposes and full, open and timely access to Arctic research data and information for research and educational purposes.[71] Because environmental changes in the Arctic region will have profound effects on human

---

Hacquebord and Robert Core (2015): 25, accessed Jan. 22, 2016, http://www.joomag.com/magazine/iasc-25-years/0102946001421148178?short.

69 Jacek Machowski, "IASC as Legal Framework of International Scientific Cooperation in the Arctic," *Polish Polar Research*, 14–2 (1993): 194–195; Odd Rogne with contributions from Robert W. Corell and Vladimir M. Kotlyakov, "Initiation of the International Arctic Science Committee (IASC)," in Rogne, Rachold, Hacquebord and Core, *supra*, note 67 at 9–20.

70 "Maximizing the Legacy of IPY in the Arctic: A scoping study for the Arctic Council," *supra*, note 4 at 3–5.

71 International Council for Science (ICSU), "Universality of Science in the Polar Regions," accessed Jan. 22, 2016, http://www.icsu.org/publications/icsu-position-statements/universality-polar-regions/download-statement.

ENHANCING INTERNATIONAL ARCTIC SCIENTIFIC COOPERATION

society around the world, the ICSU considers the observation, understanding, and sustainable management of the Arctic region as in "the common interest of all humanity." Thus, the open conduct of Arctic science and accessibility of scientific data and results will be a cornerstone of informed progress on the major Arctic challenges facing the global populace.[72] As its title demonstrates, the ICSU statement is premised on the universality of access by "all [parties] conducting... Arctic research," irrespective of nationality, with the support of those "influencing Arctic research," including governmental agencies with the authority to regulate access to research areas and infrastructure and data management.

These legal and policy issues regarding implementation of the principle of scientific openness have attracted attention in the Arctic Council. A scoping paper prepared by several scientists from both Arctic and non-Arctic States and international organizations stated that "an important and highly valuable legacy of IPY could be to reconsider access impediments in all regions of the Arctic, building on achievements made during IPY, and through intergovernmental consultations to improve the access situation for scientists in the whole Arctic on a long-term basis." They considered that "[t]his is a... demanding and politically complicated issue for which the forum and functions of the Arctic Council are uniquely situated."[73] At the workshop in June 2010, supported by the Arctic Council with participation from about 60 countries, there was even a suggestion to designate the Arctic Ocean as an 'Ocean of Science' and the Arctic as a whole as an 'Area of Cooperation,' with recommendations for increased efforts to enhance international access to research areas in the Arctic and research infrastructure and facilities relevant for the Arctic.[74]

These open discussions, supported by the Arctic Council but still within the Arctic scientific community, seem to endorse the above ICSU statement for the need of universal access to research areas and data sharing by all scientists engaged in Arctic science, irrespective of nationality. These academic discussions should generate a legitimate expectation among Arctic scientists and institutions that the Arctic governmental authorities accord them access to Arctic research areas, infrastructure, and data that is equal to that accorded others engaged in similar Arctic scientific endeavors. This legitimate

---

72   *Ibid.*

73   "Maximizing the Legacy of IPY in the Arctic: A scoping study for the Arctic Council," *supra*, note 4 at 19.

74   Chair of the International Polar Year, "Chair's Report from the Workshop on the legacy of the International Polar Year," Doc.9.1 AC-SAO Torshavn, Faroe Islands, October 19–20, 2010: 12–13.

expectation would negate a legal or policy scheme that allows governmental authorities to treat discriminately a certain category of scientists engaged in Arctic international scientific cooperation.

It can be concluded that the principles of openness and of universality in Arctic science as endorsed by the Arctic scientific community should generate a legitimate expectation among the scientists and research institutions who are willing and able in conducting Arctic science that they be treated on a par with others engaged in similar Arctic scientific endeavors. Such equal treatments would extend *inter alia* to: equal participation in decision-making regarding Arctic international scientific policies; equal opportunities to participate in Arctic scientific cooperative activities; and equal treatment by the governmental authorities in allowing access to Arctic research areas, infrastructure, and data. In the particular context of the negotiations on the Agreement under discussion here, this legitimate expectation endorsed by the Arctic scientific community means that non-Arctic States' scientists and research institutions should be treated on a par with those from Arctic States in enjoying an improved legal environment for conducting their research; that is, they should be equally facilitated by measures taken to implement the Agreement. The two-category system that may be set up under the Agreement, differentiating two categories of scientists based on their nationality, should be considered contrary to the principles of scientific openness and universality in Arctic science.

4   Conclusion

A new Agreement on Enhancing International Arctic Scientific Cooperation, expected to be signed by foreign ministers of the eight Arctic States in May of 2017, will be a significant legal instrument that will improve the legal environment for conducting Arctic scientific research activities over and beyond the current situation provided by existing international law, including the law of the sea. The Oslo Draft of the Agreement as of February 2015 provides legally binding obligations on the eight Arctic States Parties, for example: to facilitate access to research areas in the Arctic; to process applications to conduct marine scientific research in the Arctic as expeditiously as possible; to apply the most expeditious border crossing procedure for entry to and exist from areas under their jurisdiction in the Arctic for scientists, their equipment, and samples; and to support full and open access to metadata obtained from Arctic research. A greater and deeper scientific understanding of the rapidly changing Arctic and its implications is needed now more than ever, and thus this

Agreement enhancing Arctic international scientific cooperation should be strongly promoted.

Yet, because the Agreement will most likely be concluded only by the eight Arctic States, the well-established doctrine of *res inter alios acta* under the law of treaties raises the issues that non-Arctic States may not benefit from this improved legal environment. First, the legal nature of the core obligation of the prospective Parties under the Agreement does not seem to allow non-Arctic States to claim an equal right to participate in the negotiation of the Agreement. The Agreement is not intended to provide for freedom of scientific research in the Arctic; instead it allows a certain degree of internationally agreed-upon control over the exercise of States' regulatory powers over scientific activities in their territories and water zones under their jurisdiction. Under the Oslo Draft, the degree of such international control can be negotiated and agreed-upon only by the eight Arctic States. At the same time, however, because the Agreement also applies to research in the Arctic Ocean, the non-Arctic States who are parties to UNCLOS do have a legitimate interest in overseeing negotiations so that their rights relating to marine scientific research under UNCLOS would not be affected by the Agreement. The observer scheme in the SCTF, allowing non-Arctic observer States and other relevant observer organizations such as the IASC to submit their views, would guarantee their oversight. There may be a need for more active involvement of non-Arctic observer States in the drafting of a provision on cooperation with non-Parties[75] in the Agreement, especially if the Agreement comes to cover cooperative activities involving scientists and research institutions from non-Arctic States, as suggested below.

Secondly, the Oslo Draft is of particular concern for non-Arctic States and their scientists who are substantially engaged in Arctic science because it may create a two-category system in Arctic international scientific cooperation, benefiting only the Arctic States Parties, their nationals, and their joint scientific cooperative activities and leaving non-Arctic States, their scientists, and their research projects outside the ambit of the Agreement. The two-category system implicates multiple layers of differentiation between the two categories of entities, some of which may have a legitimate claim to be treated on a par with others, based on their legal interest recognized under international law and on a legitimate expectation endorsed by the Arctic scientific community. Under the provisions of UNCLOS relating to promotion of marine scientific research and sharing of the resulting data, it can be argued that an international cooperative scheme, even a regional one, in creating favorable

---

75   *See supra*, note 44 and accompanying texts.

conditions for the conduct of marine scientific research in the marine environment should not have a discriminatory effect against States outside the region and their scientists who are willing and able to conduct such research in that region. Thus, the States Parties to UNCLOS, including non-Arctic States Parties, have a legal interest to ensure that their scientists be treated on a par with those from the eight Arctic States in a forthcoming scientific cooperation scheme applicable to the Arctic Ocean.

Thirdly, the nondiscriminatory treatment of scientists and research institutions in Arctic science has long been recognized in the Arctic scientific community, represented by the IASC, the ICSU, and the 2010 workshop on the IPY legacies supported by the Arctic Council. More concretely, the community recognizes nondiscriminatory treatment, irrespective of nationality and place of organization, in scientists' participation in the development of Arctic international scientific policies; in their participation in Arctic scientific cooperative activities; and in their access to Arctic research areas, infrastructure, and data. The principles of openness and universality in Arctic science as endorsed by the Arctic scientific community can be said to generate the legitimate expectation among the scientists and research institutions willing and able to conduct Arctic science that they be treated on a par with others engaged in similar Arctic scientific endeavors.

The Oslo Draft offers the improved legal environment only to those 'joint activities' conducted by participants from two or more Parties and obliges the Parties, for example, to facilitate access to research areas by the other Parties and their nationals. These differentiations of treatment based on scientists' nationalities will offend the legitimate expectation of the non-Arctic States' scientists, and, therefore, should be rectified in the final Agreement. This legitimate expectation arises for those scientists and research institutions substantially engaged in Arctic scientific activities, not for scientists generally. The criteria of "significant Arctic research," as applied by the IASC in admitting members to its Council,[76] would be a useful guide for non-Arctic States when representing their interests at the level of State-to-State negotiation of the Agreement in the SCTF. Although the current membership of 15 non-Arctic countries in the IASC's Council is slightly larger than the 12 non-Arctic observer States in the Arctic Council,[77] the negotiation of the Agreement in the SCTF to allow substantive inputs from those non-Arctic States can be

---

76   *Supra*, note 65.

77   Austria, Czech Republic, Portugal and Switzerland are members of IASC's Council but are not yet observer States in the Arctic Council; whereas Singapore is an observer State in the Arctic Council but not a member of the IASC's Council. France, Germany, the Netherlands,

ENHANCING INTERNATIONAL ARCTIC SCIENTIFIC COOPERATION

considered legitimate. In other words, the legitimate expectation endorsed by the Arctic scientific community should now be recognized at the policy level in the context of negotiations of the Agreement involving the eight Arctic States on one hand and the non-Arctic observer States and observer organizations, such as the IASC, on the other. The latter would represent the legitimate interest of scientists and research institutions substantially engaged in Arctic scientific activities.[78]

Finally, in addition to negotiation, there is a concern about implementation of this Agreement: the non-Arctic States may have an interest in seeing that implementation is fair to their scientists. This interest should be clearly distinguished from the right of the Parties to legally claim the facilitation required under the Agreement against other Parties, and to make formal representation based on the Agreement if and when such facilitation has been troublesome. The non-Arctic States, being third parties, would not obtain such a right directly from the Agreement. The interest they may have relates to their scientists and research institutions deserving to be treated on a par with those of the eight Arctic States enjoying an improved legal environment. This interest of the non-Arctic States would best be ensured in the drafting of provisions on cooperation with non-Parties and on review. The interest may even extend to a right of the non-Arctic States to participate in the discussion and decision-making within the Agreement's implementation scheme.[79]

A brief report from the Copenhagen meeting in August 2015 states that "some observers gave statements and underlined the importance that non-Arctic States would somehow receive benefits under the Agreement" and,

---

Poland, Spain, the United Kingdom, China, Italy, Japan, the Republic of Korea, and India are observer States of the Arctic Council and also members of the IASC's Council.

78   It should be remembered that, when discussing the workshop report on IPY legacies in October 2010, the Senior Arctic Officials of the eight Arctic States supported only the general content of the report, and no consensus was achieved as to its specific recommendations. Meeting of Senior Arctic Officials, Final Report, Faroe Island, 19–20 October 2010, Torshavn, 15. The participation of indigenous peoples both in the negotiation and the substance of the Agreement is another important issue, on which this paper cannot address. *See supra*, note 6.

79   Betsy Baker and Brooks Yeager do see a possibility, and even the need, to incorporate non-Arctic States in the decision-making under their proposed Arctic Ocean Coordinating Agreement. Betsy Baker and Brooks Yeager, "Coordinated Ocean Stewardship in the Arctic: Needs, Challenges and Possible Models for an Arctic Ocean Coordinating Agreement," *Transnational Environmental Law* 4 (2015): 35.

significantly, "this notion was supported by several Arctic States."[80] At the Reykjavik meeting in December 2015, it is reported that the "Task Force also emphasized the importance of scientific cooperation with the non-Arctic States. A Joint Statement prepared in advance of the meeting by the accredited Arctic Council Observers: France, Germany, and the United Kingdom contributed to the discussion on the draft agreement."[81] It is gratifying to see that, as this paper urges, some non-Arctic observer States substantially engaged in Arctic science have now raised the issue of two-category system potentially created by the Agreement and, together with the eight Arctic States, have begun to address this concern within the SCTF.

---

80   Arctic Council Task Force on Scientific Cooperation, VI meeting, Copenhagen, August 19–20, 2015, Summary submitted by the co-chairs (October 1, 2015) (on file with the authors).
81   "Scientific Cooperation Task Force meets in Reykjavik" (January 20, 2016), Arctic Council Secretariat News and Events.

THE YEARBOOK OF POLAR LAW VIII (2016) 163–186

The Impact of Choice-of-Law Rules in Cross-Border Pollution Damage Caused by Petroleum Spills from Offshore Rigs and Installations: The Case of the Barents Sea

Kristoffer Svendsen[a]

Abstract

The article examines the impact of choice-of-law rules in cross-border pollution damage caused by petroleum spills from offshore rigs and installations in the Barents Sea. Norway and Russia share the Barents Sea, and the ocean currents go from West to East. Therefore, the article examines the impact of an oil spill from a Norwegian licensee on the Norwegian side of the Barents Sea on a Russian party harmed by the spill on the Russian side of the Barents Sea. The article shows the procedural hurdles a Russian harmed party would need to jump in order to access Norwegian courts. The question of venue is clear. *Lex loci damni* is the principle enacted in the Norwegian Petroleum Act. It contains a unilateral extension of protection in delict law to Norwegian interests harmed in Russia, which is not extended to injured Russian parties harmed within the Russian jurisdiction, for situations where the source of harm is located on the Norwegian side of the Barents Sea. An injured Russian party forced to pursue a legal claim against a Norwegian licensee without assets in Russia may receive no compensation because no agreement exists between Norway and Russia regarding recognition and enforcement of foreign court judgments.

Keywords

Delict – choice-of-law – Barents Sea – Norwegian law – Russian law – oil spill

---

a Dr. Kristoffer Svendsen, LL.B. (Bond), LL.M. (Bond), LL.M. (MGIMO-University of MFA), and Ph.D. (UiT – the Arctic University of Norway) is a post doctorate researcher at the K.G. Jebsen Centre for the Law of the Sea, Faculty of Law, UiT – the Arctic University of Norway.

© KONINKLIJKE BRILL NV, LEIDEN, 2017 | DOI 10.1163/22116427_008010010

1   Introduction

Choice-of-law rules are national rules regulating whether to apply national or foreign law to a dispute heard in a national court. It is not uncommon that national courts hear cases governed by foreign law. A national court uses its national choice-of-law rules to determine the applicable law. The implication of applying one set of national delict rules compared to another set of national delict rules can play a significant role in the outcome.

Norway and Russia share the Barents Sea. Chapter 7 of the Norwegian *Petroleum Act*[1] sets forth specific choice-of-law rules applicable only to delict compensation for pollution damage caused by petroleum spills from offshore installations. This is different from the Russian *Federal Continental Shelf Law*[2] and the Russian *Federal Internal Waters and Territorial Seas Law*,[3] which do not contain specific choice-of-law rules regulating the issue specifically. Instead the Russia *Civil Code*[4] contains general choice-of-law rules (called collision-of-law rules) for delict compensation involving a foreign element. This article examines the application and effect of these choice-of-law rules to the scenario of cross-border pollution caused by a petroleum spill on the Norwegian side of the Barents Sea, inflicting harm on the Russian side of the Barents Sea. The article focuses on this scenario because the ocean currents go from West to East in the Barents Sea.[5]

---

1   Lov om petroleumsvirksomhet (November 29, 1996, Nr. 72).

2   Федеральный закон "О континентальном шельфе Российской Федерации" N 187-ФЗ (November 30, 1995).

3   Федеральный закон "О внутренних морских водах, территориальном море и прилежащей зоне Российской Федерации" N 155-ФЗ (July 31, 1998).

4   Гражданский кодекс РФ (ГК РФ) от 26.11.2001 N 146-ФЗ – Часть 3 (November 26, 2001).

5   The effect of cross-border pollution caused by a petroleum spill on the Russian side of the Barents Sea inflicting harm on the Norwegian side of the Barents Sea, *see* Chapter 5.4 of Kristoffer Svendsen, Compensable damage ex delicto as a result of harm in the Barents Sea caused by petroleum spills from offshore installations. A Norwegian and Russian comparative legal analysis of conflict of laws, the concept of harm, losses suffered by third parties, and environmental damage and its valuation and calculation, caused by petroleum spills from offshore oil rigs and installations in the Barents Sea (2015) Tromsø Ph.D., in law, Faculty of Law, UiT – Arctic University of Norway).

THE CASE OF THE BARENTS SEA 165

2   Procedural Access to Norwegian Courts and the Application
     of the Lugano Convention

A harmed Russian party, injured in Russia as a result of cross-border pollution, initiating legal action against a Norwegian harm-doer domiciled in Norway, has access to Norwegian courts under the *Lugano Convention*, or in the alternative, the Norwegian *Civil Procedure Act*. A foreign party, initiating legal action in Norway, must fulfill the court's requirements for general jurisdiction in §4–4 to §4–6 of the Norwegian *Civil Procedure Act*,[6] the specific rule on jurisdiction over a dispute of international character in §4–3,[7] and the accompanying *Lugano Convention*.[8] The *Lugano Convention* is a "parallel convention" to the *Brussels Regulation*[9] and part of the *Civil Procedure Act*.[10] The Convention prevails when in conflict with, for example, the rules in §4–1 to §4–8.[11]

For the present situation, §4–4 of the *Civil Procedure Act* sets forth the general rule of jurisdiction that legal action against a Norwegian company is initiated at the company's main office according to the Register of Business Enterprises. The Supreme Court has confirmed that when a defendant is sued at his domicile according to the general rules of jurisdiction, Norwegian courts are competent to hear the case, unless the facts of the case remove the case from Norwegian courts.[12] The first paragraph of §4–3 requires the facts of a case of international character "... to possess an adequate connection to

---

6   Lov om mekling og rettergang i sivile tvister (tvisteloven) (June 17, 2005 nr 90).

7   Tore Schei, et al., Tvisteloven Kommentarutgave Bind I (Universitetsforlaget, Oslo, 2013), 139, note 4.

8   Convention on jurisdiction and the enforcement of judgments in civil and commercial matters, Lugano (October 30, 2007).

9   European Communities, Council Regulation (EC) No 44/2001 of December 22, 2000 on jurisdiction and the recognition and enforcement of judgments in civil and commercial matters (EC ed. December 22, 2000).

10   Lov om mekling og rettergang i sivile tvister (tvisteloven) (June 17, 2005 nr 90), §4–8. The *Lugano Convention* is attached to the *Civil Procedure Act* through §4–8, which was implemented by the Ministry of Justice and Public Security, Lov om endringer i tvisteloven m.m. og om samtykke til ratifikasjon av Luganokonvensjonen 2007 om domsmyndighet og om anerkjennelse og fullbyrdelse av dommer i sivile og kommersielle saker (June 19, 2009 Nr. 79).

11   Lov om mekling og rettergang i sivile tvister (tvisteloven) (June 17, 2005 nr 90), §1–2.

12   The Supreme Court confirmed the Appellate Court's statement in Tricodommen – (third appeal) (LG 2013), 3127 (Gulating Appellate Court). In its rejection Tricodommen (third appeal rejected) (Rt. 2013), 1089 (Appeals Selection Committee of the Supreme Court of Norway).

Norway"[13] and to be read in the negative. The 'adequate connection' element is not an additional requirement *per se* when domicile is established under §4–4, but there must be no distinct reasons to remove the case from Norwegian courts.[14] The Norwegian Supreme Court supports this view, and the Court has stated that it should be difficult for a Norwegian company domiciled according to the general rules of jurisdiction to avoid legal action in Norway.[15] Thus, if the facts of the present scenario fall within §4–3 and outside the scope of the *Lugano Convention*, the scenario will likely be granted access to a Norwegian court and not removed based upon the defendant's domicile in Norway, large-scale economic activity in Norway, harm-causing event in Norway, and pollution damage in Norway.[16]

If a Norwegian court is competent to hear the case under *Lugano Convention*, then the adequate connection element in §4–3 is not applicable.[17] Section 1 of the *Lugano Convention* sets forth rules of general jurisdiction, of which the defendant's domicile in a State bound by the Convention, "... hinges on a

---

13   Lov om mekling og rettergang i sivile tvister (tvisteloven) (June 17, 2005 nr 90), §4–3.

14   Tricodommen (third appeal rejected) (Rt. 2013 p. 1089) (Appeals Selection Committee of the Supreme Court of Norway).

15   *Ibid.* Citing Tricodommen (second appeal) (Rt. 2012 p. 1951) (Supreme Court of Norway). #(88).

16   The *Operafjell* case was removed from Norwegian courts' jurisdiction. The defendant in the case was a Russian insurance company domiciled in Russia. The harmed parties were from Russia, Moldavia, and Ukraine, in which their losses materialized. The airliner was domiciled in Russia. There was no connection to Norway but for the harm-causing event that occurred on Svalbard, for which the Supreme Court refused to hear the case in a Norwegian court; *see* Operafjelldommen (Rt. 1998 p. 1647) (Appeals Selection Committee of the Supreme Court of Norway). According to Supreme Court Justice Skoghøy disputes about property rights in real property in another country, disputes about incorporation and dissolution of foreign companies, and disputes about rights based on registration in foreign registrars are some examples of facts exempt from being heard in Norway, even though the defendant had a domicile according to the general rules of jurisdiction. *See* Jens Edvin A. Skoghøy, "Tvisteloven og Lugano-konvensjonen – duplikk til Frantzen," 51 (7) Lov og Rett (2012): 439. *See* the full discussion as initiated by Jens Edvin A. Skoghøy, "Tvisteloven og Lugano-konvensjonen," 51 (4) Lov Og Rett (2012): 193–194. And the reply in Torstein Frantzen, Tvisteloven og Luganokonvensjonen. En replikk til Skoghøy, 51 (6) Lov Og Rett (2012): 379–381.

17   Tore Schei, et al., Tvisteloven Kommentarutgave Bind I (2013), 140. *See also* (Rt. 2012), 57 (Appeals Selection Committee of the Supreme Court). The case concerned whether Norwegian courts possess jurisdiction over an international dispute about shipbroker commission. The Supreme Court stated that the *Lugano Convention* is *lex specialis* and prevails over §4–3 first paragraph of the *Civil Procedure Act* when applicable, at 18.

THE CASE OF THE BARENTS SEA

factor connecting the defendant to the court…".[18] Section 2 of the Convention concerns special jurisdiction, which allows the plaintiff to bring an action in another State bound by the Convention. Even though the Convention pushes the required adequate connection in §4–3 out of play, the general jurisdiction rules arguably require some connection requirement,[19] but the special rules do reintroduce an adequate connection requirement as a requirement for a sufficient connection:

> …the special rules recognise a link between the dispute itself and the court which may be called upon to hear it…and will be justified only when there is a sufficient connection in terms of the proceedings between the dispute and the court before which the matter is to be brought…[20]

Does the *Lugano Convention* apply to the current scenario? The *Lugano Convention* applies to private and commercial disputes of international character,[21] which include delict compensation[22] for pollution damage. The general rule of jurisdiction is that "…persons domiciled in a State bound

---

18   Fausto Pocar, Notices from European Union Institutions and Bodies, Council, Convention on jurisdiction and the recognition and enforcement of judgments in civil and commercial matters, signed in Lugano on October 30, 2007, Explanatory Report (2009/C 319/01), December 23, 2009, #(39).

19   In the Trico case the minority (2 of 5) expressly stated that article 2 of the *Lugano Convention* does not contain an additional requirement of some connection to the Contracting State, (52) while the majority understood article 2 to contain a condition of adequate connection to the Convention State through a natural interpretation of the Convention (79). The Trico case concerned a company from Singapore, which initiated legal action in a Norwegian court for the fulfilment of a broker contract for broker commission as a result of the sale of two vessels, entered into in Singapore. The case's only connection to Norway was that the defendant's domicile was in Norway as a Norwegian Limited Liability Company with its main office in Norway. Tricodommen (second appeal) (Rt. 2012 p. 1951) (Supreme Court of Norway).

20   Pocar, Notices from European Union Institutions and Bodies, Council, Convention on jurisdiction and the recognition and enforcement of judgments in civil and commercial matters, signed in Lugano on October 30, 2007, Explanatory Report (2009/C 319/01). December 23, 2009. #(39).

21   The Ministry of Police and Public Justice, Ot.prp.nr. 89 (2008–2009) Om lov om endringer i tvisteloven m.m. og om samtykke til ratifikasjon av Luganokonvensjonen 2007 om domsmyndighet og om anerkjennelse og fullbyrdelse av dommer i sivile og kommersielle saker (8 May 2009), 15.

22   Convention on jurisdiction and the enforcement of judgments in civil and commercial matters, Lugano (October 30, 2007). Art. 5(3).

by this Convention shall, whatever their nationality, be sued in the courts of that State."[23] The Convention also contains a rule on jurisdiction of delict matters.[24] A legal person is domiciled at the place where he or she has a statutory seat, central administration, or principal place of business.[25] There is no requirement however that the plaintiff must be domiciled in a Convention State.[26] The European Union (EU)-courts' practice of the *Lugano Convention*, and the parallel *Brussels Regulation*, is an important source of law when interpreting the application of the *Lugano Convention* in Norway.[27] Based on EU-court practice, the *Lugano Convention* and not the *Civil Procedure Act* generally applies to an international dispute in which the defendant is a domicile of Norway (or another European Economic Area State) (EEA) regardless of whether the plaintiff is domiciled outside of the EEA, in another EEA country, or in Norway,[28] with possibly one exception expressed by the Supreme Court in the Trico case.[29] The majority of the Supreme Court in the Trico case examined the then-current EU-court practice, which had no precedent, with the same facts as the facts of the case in question. The majority decided that a plaintiff not domiciled in an EEA country cannot initiate legal action under the *Lugano Convention* against a defendant domiciled in Norway when the facts of the case have no further connection to the EEA-area but for the defendant's domicile.[30]

---

23   *Ibid.* at art. 2.1.

24   *Ibid.* at art. 5(3). See a discussion of choice of law and jurisdiction for delict compensation claims: Ivar Alvik, "Lovvalg og jurisdiksjon for ikke-kontraktuelle erstatningskrav," 40 (5–6) *Lov og Rett* (2005): 281–304.

25   Convention on jurisdiction and the enforcement of judgments in civil and commercial matters, Lugano (Oct. 30, 2007). Art. 60.1.

26   Case C-412/98 (Group Josi) (July 13, 2000) (Court of Justice of the European Union).

27   (Rt. 2007 p. 1759) (Appeals Selection Committee of the Supreme Court of Norway). #(42). (Rt. 2011 p. 897) (Supreme Court of Norway). #(35). (Rt. 2011 p. 1532) (Appeals Selection Committee of the Supreme Court of Norway). #(21). Tricodommen (second appeal) (Rt. 2012 p. 1951) (Supreme Court of Norway). Stated by minority in (34)–(35) and confirmed by majority in (68). *See also* Giuditta Cordero-Moss, *Internasjonal Privatrett på formurettens område* (Universitetsforlaget, Oslo, 2013), 31, with the accompanying footnote 43.

28   This is controversial and Cordero-Moss summaries the parties' view on page 33; however, special attention should be directed to *infra*, notes 50 and 51 in Cordero-Moss, *supra* note 27.

29   Tricodommen (second appeal) (Rt. 2012 p. 1951) (Supreme Court of Norway). For an in-depth discussion of the Trico case, *see* Cordero-Moss, *supra* note 27, 33–39.

30   Tricodommen (second appeal) (Rt. 2012 p. 1951) (Supreme Court of Norway). #(70) ff.

THE CASE OF THE BARENTS SEA

In the present scenario, a Russian not domiciled in an EEA country and initiating legal action in Norway against a company domiciled in Norway would possibly fall within the *Lugano Convention*, if the Russian can show a connection to Norway but for the company's domicile. If not, the legal action falls within the *Civil Procedure Act's* requirement in §4–4 and §4–3 as discussed above. Furthermore, as mentioned above, there are many factors in addition to the company's domicile, that connect the facts of the case to Norway. For the sake of this exercise, it may be assumed that the same factors suggested under §4–3 would also contribute to satisfy the connection requirement between the facts of the case and the jurisdiction established by the Supreme Court, resulting in application of the *Lugano Convention*. In the opposite, if the connection requirement is not satisfied, the facts of the case can be heard in a Norwegian court anyway, due to the fulfillment of §4–4 and §4–3.

3   Venue

Venue is "[t]he territory, such as a country or other political subdivision, over which a trial court has jurisdiction."[31] Chapter 7 of the *Petroleum Act* contains specific rules on venue in section 7–8, which applies the term "legal venue" (*verneting*):

> Legal action for compensation for pollution damage shall be brought before the courts in the court district where the effluence or discharge of petroleum has taken place or where damage has been caused.[32]

Section 7–8 amends the general rules on venue. To illustrate, claims for compensation of damage to real estate are generally initiated in the court district in which the real estate is located.[33] The proper venue for legal claims arising

---

31   Bryan A. Gardner, Black's Law Dictionary (West 2009), 1695, 'Venue.'

32   There are, however, some exemptions where the Ministry may decide where the action shall be brought, such as: "a) the effluence or discharge has taken place or the damage has been caused outside the area of any court district; b) it cannot be demonstrated within which court district the effluence or discharge has taken place or damage has been caused; c) the effluence or discharge has taken place in one court district and the damage is caused in another court district; d) damage has been caused in more than one court district." Lov om petroleumsvirksomhet (November 29, 1996 Nr. 72). §4–8.

33   Lov om mekling og rettergang i sivile tvister (tvisteloven) (June 17, 2005 nr 90), §4–5(1). *See also* Petroleum Committee, NOU: Erstatningsansvar for forurensningsskade som følge av petroleumsvirksomhet på norsk kontinentalsokkel (1981:33), 42–43.

from delict compensation for pollution damage is the court district where the effluence or discharge of petroleum has taken place or where damage has been caused. This also applies to the current scenario. The *Court Act*[34] opens for court districts having jurisdiction over facilities and constructions for exploration, extraction, storage, and transportation of submarine natural resources on the Norwegian continental shelf and in the Norwegian economic zone.[35] Regulation from 17 December 1999 Nr. 1391 grants jurisdiction over facilities and constructions when located north of 68th latitude and 30 minutes (roughly in between Bodø and Tromsø) to Nord-Troms District Court[36] and Hålogaland Court of Appeal.[37] Even though the regulation does not specify which court districts hold jurisdiction over pollution damage, it would be natural and reasonable to also apply the regulation to the location of pollution damage, as defined in section 7–1 of the *Norwegian Petroleum Act*.

4 Choice-of-Law Rules

4.1 *Introduction*

This part of the article examines the choice-of-law rules in section 7–2 of the Norwegian *Petroleum Act*, and the consequences of its application to a Russian party's delict claim for compensation of harm inflicted by a Norwegian company. The choice-of-law rules in §7–2 state that the place of harm governs the application of Chapter 7, and not where the delict was committed. The choice-of-law rules grant Norwegian interests harmed in adjacent seas a unilateral extension of protection in delict law. As a result of international obligations, this unilateral extension currently discriminates against only Russian interests harmed in Russia by a harm-doer on the Norwegian side of the Barents Sea. These harmed Russian interests are not compensable under Chapter 7 and must seek a remedy in the Russian jurisdiction. In these situations, Russian

---

34   The Ministry of Police and Public Security, Lov om domstolene (domstolloven) (13 August 1915 Nr. 5).

35   *Ibid.* at §26a. *See also* Tore Schei, et al., Tvisteloven Kommentarutgave Bind I (2013), 138.

36   Nord-Troms District Court include the following municipalities: Tromsø, Balsfjord, Karlsøy, Lyngen, Storfjord, Kåfjord, Skjervøy, Nordreisa, Kvænangen. The Ministry of Police and Public Security, Forskrift om domssogns- og lagdømmeinndeling (December 16, 2005 Nr. 1494).

37   The Ministry of Police and Public Security, Forskrift om politidistrikt, namsmannsdistrikt, lagdømme og domssogn for utøvelse av politimyndighet, namsmannsmyndighet og domsmyndighet på kontinentalsokkelen og i norsk økonomisk sone, samt politimyndighet i havområdet utenfor Svalbards territorialfarvann (December 17, 1999 Nr. 1391). §1.

THE CASE OF THE BARENTS SEA   171

harmed parties will receive a court judgment from a Russian court. However, the court judgment will not be recognized or enforced by a Norwegian court because there is no agreement about recognition and enforcement of foreign judgments between Russia and Norway.[38]

Section 7–2 of the Act 'scope and choice-of-law' is divided into three paragraphs. The first paragraph outlines the main rules of the scope of Chapter 7, which implicitly indicates choice-of-law rules. The second paragraph relates to damage occurring onshore or offshore a member of the *Nordic Convention on Environment Protection* of 1974.[39] The Convention grants an injured party in one convention state the ability to choose between the laws of either the place of harm or the place of the activity, as long as the activity is located in a convention state.[40] In the scenario at issue here, Russia is not a party to this convention and therefore the second paragraph is not discussed further. The third, and last, paragraph focuses on the Government's ability to enter into an agreement with another state about liability for pollution damage.[41]

4.2   *The Geographic Scope of Chapter 7 of the Petroleum Act*

Section 7–2 of the *Petroleum Act* regulates the scope of Chapter 7, while §1–4 of the *Petroleum Act* regulates the scope of the Act generally. The *Act's* §7–2 indicates whether Norwegian courts should decide a case of compensation for pollution damage according to Norwegian or a foreign state's law.[42] Chapter 7

---

38   *See* chapter 6 of Svendsen, Compensable damage ex delicto as a result of harm in the Barents Sea caused by petroleum spills from offshore installations. A Norwegian and Russian comparative legal analysis of conflict of laws, the concept of harm, losses suffered by third parties, and environmental damage and its valuation and calculation, caused by petroleum spills from offshore oil rigs and installations in the Barents Sea. 2015.

39   The Nordic Environmental Protection Convention (and Protocol), Stockholm. Implemented in Norwegian law through "Lov av 9. april 1976 nr 21 om gjennomføring i norsk rett av miljøvernkonvensjon mellom Norge, Danmark, Finland og Sverige, undertegnet 19 februar 1974" (February 19, 1974).

40   *Ibid.* at art. 3.

41   This paragraph of the section was intended to facilitate a possibly bilateral agreement with Great Britain on delict compensation rules for pollution damage as a result of oil activities or on ratification of Convention on Civil Liability for Oil Pollution Damage Resulting from Exploration for and Exploitation of Seabed Mineral Resources, London. London (May 1, 1977). *See* Committee, NOU: Erstatningsansvar for forurensningsskade som følge av petroleumsvirksomhet på norsk kontinentalsokkel, (1981: 33), 37.

42   U. Hammer, et al., *Petroleumsloven* (Universitetsforlaget, Oslo, 2009), 542.

of the *Petroleum Act* is '... applicable to liability for pollution damage from a facility...'[43] when occurring:

> ... in Norway[44] or inside the outer limits of the Norwegian continental shelf[45] or affects a Norwegian vessel, Norwegian hunting or catching equipment or Norwegian facility in adjacent sea areas. With regard to measures to avert or limit pollution damage it is sufficient that damage may occur in such area.[46]

The applicability of Chapter 7 rules is limited to the geographic area of Norway and all waters up to but not including the outer limits of the Norwegian continental shelf. Additionally, only Norwegian interests outside of this area enjoy the protection of Chapter 7 rules. In contrast, the Chapter 7 'liability without fault' rule applies to installations and not geographic areas.[47]

4.3 *The Law of the Place of Damage or Harm*

The place of harm (*lex loci damni*) governs the application of Chapter 7 of the Act,[48] and not where the delict was committed (*lex loci delicti commissi*). This makes the geographic location of the source of harm irrelevant. Thus, the connecting factor is the place of harm. Based on *lex loci damni*, harm caused outside of the legislative scope of §7–2 is compensated according to the delict compensation rules of the state in which the harm occurred.

---

43 Lov om petroleumsvirksomhet (November 29, 1996 Nr. 72), §7–2.

44 The term 'in Norway' (i *riket*) includes mainland Norway, which includes Svalbard and Jan Mayen (Svalbard and Jan Mayen are excluded from the general scope of the Act in §1–4), and Norwegian internal waters. *See* Ministry of Petroleum and Energy, Ot.prp.nr. 72. Lov om petroleumsvirksomhet. (1982–1983), 70.

45 Lov om petroleumsvirksomhet (29 November 1996 Nr. 72), §1–6l) defines the terminology Norwegian continental shelf.

46 *Ibid.* at §7–2. It should be noted that this is not the full citation of §7–2. The second paragraph of §7–2 explains the scope of the Act as applicable to The Nordic Environmental Protection Convention (and Protocol), Stockholm. Implemented in Norwegian law through "Lov av 9. april 1976 nr 21 om gjennomføring i norsk rett av miljøvernkonvensjon mellom Norge, Danmark, Finland og Sverige, undertegnet 19 februar 1974." February 19, 1974. The third paragraph of §7–2 grants the State the ability to "... issue rules relating to liability for pollution damage caused by petroleum activities pursuant to this Act...." by agreement with a foreign State. Thus, the State may enter into a treaty about liability for pollution damage with a foreign State, and implement the convention into Norwegian law.

47 Lov om petroleumsvirksomhet (November 29, 1996 Nr. 72), §7–3.

48 *Ibid.* at §7–2.

THE CASE OF THE BARENTS SEA 173

The Norwegian Government intentionally removed any requirement for a geographic location of the facility,[49] and to also include pollution damage inflicted by facilities located on other states' continental shelves and the open sea.[50] Therefore, it is not decisive where the facility is located; for example: whether the harm-inflicting facility is located within the outer limits of the Norwegian continental shelf or within the outer limits of another state's continental shelf, such as the Russian continental shelf.[51] This ability to impose liability for pollution damage within the outer limits of the Norwegian continental shelf due to the occurrence of harm on the Russian continental shelf is the implication of the extended definition of scope by §7–2 compared to the *Petroleum Act's* general definition of scope in §1–4.

Section 7–2 continues §38 of the old and repealed 1985 *Petroleum Act.*[52] If the legislation had continued the same wording of §38 in full, the rules would have been clearer. Section 38 clarifies situations where the *Nordic Convention on Environment Protection* of 1974 and other bilateral treaties do not apply:

> For pollution damage that occurs outside the areas as specified in the first and second paragraphs shall the delict compensation rules in that state in which the harm occurred apply.[53]

Keeping this enactment in §7–2 was "…according to the Ministry's view unnecessary next to the rule in §7–2 third paragraph…"[54] because the Government can enter into agreements about compensation for pollution damage with other countries.

The current §7–2 does not contain any requirement for a connecting factor between a Norwegian harm-doing company and harm inflicted in countries outside the *Nordic Convention on Environment Protection*, such as Russia.[55] Thus, the removal of §38 reduces the ability to cover all choice-of-law scenarios and to an extent amputates the choice-of-law heading of §7–2.

---

49   Department of Industry and Energy, Ot.prp.nr. 43. Om lov om petroleumsvirksomhet (1995–1996), 56.

50   Energy, Ot.prp.nr. 72. Lov om petroleumsvirksomhet (1982–1983), 70.

51   It should be noted that §7–2 also includes pollution from facilities located onshore. This was an extension of the 1985 Act, which only applied to pollution from offshore facilities. *See* Energy, Ot.prp.nr. 43. Om lov om petroleumsvirksomhet. 1995–1996. P. 56.

52   Lov om petroleumsvirksomhet (repealed) (March 22, 1985 nr. 11).

53   *Ibid.* at §38.

54   Energy, Ot.prp.nr. 43. Om lov om petroleumsvirksomhet (1995–1996), 56.

55   Cordero-Moss, Internasjonal Privatrett på formurettens område, (2013), 357.

4.4 Compensation of Pollution Damage to Norwegian Interests Only in Adjacent Sea Areas

Section 7–2 contains a unilateral extension of privilege granting 'Norwegian interests' protection in delict law under Chapter 7 for pollution damage suffered in adjacent sea areas.[56] The terminology 'Norwegian interests' means the three groups eligible for compensation under §7–2 when pollution damage is suffered in adjacent waters, by: 1) a Norwegian vessel, 2) Norwegian hunting or catching equipment, or 3) a Norwegian[57] facility. The preparatory works emphasize that harm and injury to personnel and/or equipment located on a vessel (group 1) or a facility (group 3) are included in the scope of §7–2.[58]

This privilege started as discrimination against all countries, except countries adhering to the *Nordic Convention on Environment Protection*. The *Lugano Convention*[59] granted their members equal footing, which left Russian interests as the only unprotected interests under Chapter 7. Chapter 8 of the *Petroleum Act* contains a similar unilateral extension of privilege expressly requiring fishermen to be Norwegian to claim delict compensation for inconveniences as a result of petroleum activities.[60] The application of Chapter 7 rules does

---

56　Lov om petroleumsvirksomhet (November 29, 1996 Nr. 72), §7–2.

57　Neither the *Petroleum Act* nor the preparatory works define the terminology 'Norwegian' with respect to vessels and facilities. However, the *Norwegian Maritime Code* sets out conditions for nationality of vessels (§1), drilling ships (§4), and drilling platforms and similar mobile constructions (§507). The general rule requires registration of vessels and facilities in the Norwegian Ordinary Ship Register (NOR) or the Norwegian International Ship Register (NIS) (§§11 and 507), *see* Norwegian Maritime Authority, NIS-NOR, The Norwegian International Ship Register (Norwegian Maritime Authority ed.). Section 7–2 does not appear to require actual registration in one of the registers as long as the conditions for nationality are fulfilled. However, for further information on the issue of registration and fulfilment of the conditions of nationality, as well as the non-appliance of the conditions of nationality to fixed facilities, *see* Hammer, et al., Petroleumsloven,(2009), 540, and H.J. Bull T. Falkanger, Sjørett (Sjørettsfondet Akademisk, Oslo, 2010), Chapter 2.

58　Energy, Ot.prp.nr. 72. Lov om petroleumsvirksomhet (1982–1983), 71. Neither §7–2 nor the preparatory works differentiate between Norwegian or foreign nationals. Thus, nationality does not affect a claim for personal injury or damage to equipment when on a Norwegian vessel or Norwegian facility (within the Norwegian- or other state's continental shelf). However, both Norwegian and foreign nationals would be ineligible to claim for personal injury and damage to equipment if located on a foreign vessel or facility outside the Norwegian continental shelf. *See* Hammer, et al., Petroleumsloven (2009), 541.

59　Convention on jurisdiction and the enforcement of judgments in civil and commercial matters, Lugano (30 October 2007).

60　Chapter 8 of the *Petroleum Act* does discriminate with respect to nationality when compensating fishermen for inconveniences as a result of petroleum activities. The Chapter

THE CASE OF THE BARENTS SEA

not discriminate as to ownership or nationality when harm is inflicted in Norway or within the outer limits of the Norwegian continental shelf, but only when Norwegian and Russian interests are harmed in the Russian jurisdiction. As a result, Chapter 7 only applies to and protects Norwegian interests harmed in the Russian jurisdiction, while the harmed Russian interests cannot rely in Chapter 7 and must seek remedy in Russian legislation. The harmed Russian interests are left without legal enforcement of remedies granted under Russian law, because there is no agreement between Norway and Russia about enforcement of foreign court judgments.

The terminology "...in adjacent sea areas...." received some attention by the entities entitled to comment on the bill when passed through the legislative process, since many found the terminology confusing.[61] The authors of the preparatory works stated that the terminology 'sea areas' which border the Norwegian continental shelf includes "...other states' continental shelves[62] that have a common dividing line with the Norwegian continental shelf... [as well as]... nearest adjoining states' continental shelves, and the immediate high seas (*frie havområder*)."[63] Norway's Ministry of Petroleum and Energy emphasized that the terminology 'adjacent sea areas' "...does not only think about the sea areas to the states that have a common dividing line with the Norwegian continental shelf, but also other parts of the North Sea, Norwegian Sea and the Barents Sea."[64] These statements were made long before the Norwegian-Russian delimitation agreement came into effect, and appear to ensure that the unsettled dividing-line-dispute was included in the scope of the *Petroleum Act*. Based on these clarifications and the fact that the source of pollution may be located outside the Norwegian continental shelf (for example on another country's continental shelf), the rules in Chapter 7 reach widely.

---

only applies Norwegian fishermen, which are "...persons registered in the registration list of fishermen and owners of vessels listed in the registry of Norwegian fishing vessels subject to registration licences." Chapter 8 does not apply to Chapter 7 pollution damage, and compensate financial losses for: one, occupation of fishing fields; two, pollution and waste; or three, damage caused by a facility or actions in connection with the placing of a facility. *See* Lov om petroleumsvirksomhet (November 29, 1996 Nr. 72), §8–1.

61   Energy, Ot.prp.nr. 72. Lov om petroleumsvirksomhet (1982–1983), 71.

62   The committee considers the continental shelf of other states to include "...the assumed territorial waters and the internal waters...." *See* Hammer, et al., Petroleumsloven (2009), 540.

63   Committee, NOU: Erstatningsansvar for forurensningsskade som følge av petroleumsvirksomhet på norsk kontinentalsokkel (1981:33), 36.

64   Energy, Ot.prp.nr. 72. Lov om petroleumsvirksomhet (1982–1983), 71.

4.5 Compensation of Measures to Avert or Limit Pollution Damage to the Norwegian Jurisdiction when Initiated in Russia

A factor in compensating reasonable measures[65] executed to avert or limit pollution damage is the intention to encourage the execution of necessary measures to limit the extent of pollution damage.[66] "[I]t is sufficient that damage may occur in such area."[67] As discussed earlier, 'such area' includes adjacent sea areas.[68] Measures executed in adjacent sea areas seem compensable when executed to avert or limit pollution damage to within the Norwegian jurisdiction. The preparatory works of the *Petroleum Act* state that:

> ... expenses for measures to avert or limit pollution damage should also be covered by the act when the measure is initiated in adjacent sea areas to hinder that pollution damage occurs ... [in internal waters, territorial waters, the continental shelf ...] or on Norwegian mainland.[69]

The preparatory works of the *Petroleum Act* further state that the licensee should compensate expenses for measures to avert or limit pollution damage of a source located outside the Norwegian continental shelf, for which the measures are initiated to combat petroleum pollution before the petroleum enters the Norwegian continental shelf.[70] The same applies if petroleum from within the Norwegian continental shelf drifts outside the Norwegian continental shelf, and threatens to drift back into the Norwegian continental shelf.[71] The first example appears problematic. If Russian fishermen or Coast Guard execute measures that avert or limit damage, that may occur on the Norwegian continental shelf from a Russian oil rig on the Russian side of the Barents Sea, §7–2 opens the possibility of Russian claims for compensation in a Norwegian court against a Russian licensee. Enforcing a Norwegian court judgment against a Russian licensee in Russia is difficult, as is enforcing a court judgment in Norway against a Russian licensee without assets in Norway. Likewise, if Norwegian fishermen and/or the Norwegian Coast Guard

---

65 §7–1 defines pollution damage as, amongst others, "... costs of reasonable measures to avert or limit such damage or such loss...." Lov om petroleumsvirksomhet (November 29, 1996 Nr. 72).

66 Energy, Ot.prp.nr. 72. Lov om petroleumsvirksomhet (1982–1983), 71.

67 Lov om petroleumsvirksomhet (November 29, 1996 Nr. 72), §7–2.

68 Section 4.4 *supra*.

69 Energy, Ot.prp.nr. 72. Lov om petroleumsvirksomhet (1982–1983), 71.

70 *Ibid.*, at 71.

71 *Ibid.*

THE CASE OF THE BARENTS SEA

cross the sea border to assist their Russian colleagues in the liquidation of an oil spill, the Norwegian participants may then claim compensation for measures in a Norwegian court with the same challenge, namely, to enforce a Norwegian judgment against a Russian licensee in Russia.

Measures executed in the Russian jurisdiction to avert or limit pollution damage to Norwegian interests (three groups) located in the Russian jurisdictions (seas) appear not compensable. As such and under the law as currently written, it would be better for these Norwegian interests to suffer damage rather than move to avert damage. As an example, a Norwegian trawler accruing expenses to save its trawl from pollution damage in the Russian part of the Barents Sea is excluded from compensation under Chapter 7.[72] Similarly, if a foreign trawler salvages Norwegian fishing equipment in the Russian jurisdiction, the expenses are likely not compensable.[73] If the foreign trawler suffers pollution damage (such as property damage), the trawler is likely also not eligible for compensation under Chapter 7.[74] It is unlikely that these results reflect legislative intent, which seems to encourage the executive of necessary measures.[75]

4.6   *Choice of Law by Analogy*

The effect of the choice-of-law rule is discrimination against Russian interests harmed in Russia by a spill on the Norwegian side of the Barents Sea, while Norwegian interests harmed in Russia enjoy the protection of Chapter 7. There are currently three different applicable choice-of-law-rule regimes to delict compensation for pollution damage scenarios (*Pollution Control Act, Petroleum Act*, and the *Nordic Convention on Environment Protection*). The Ministry of Justice have indicated a desire to amend these regimes, but with no success. The Ministry has also indicated a desire to harmonize the EU's international private law rules with the rules of Norway. Legal literature has expressed a need to adhere to the principles and rules of European international private law due to legal uniformity between Norway and Europe.[76] Applying the general choice-of-law rule in the *Pollution Control Act* can correct this discrimination.

The provisions of §54 of the *Pollution Control Act* apply to pollution damage occurring in two areas: 1) Norway or the Norwegian Economic Zone; or

---

72   Hammer, et al., Petroleumsloven (2009), 541.

73   *Ibid.*, at 541.

74   *Ibid.*, at 541.

75   Energy, Ot.prp.nr. 72. Lov om petroleumsvirksomhet (1982–1983), 71.

76   Cordero-Moss summarises the literature expressing this view in *supra*, note 20 at 27 in Cordero-Moss, Internasjonal Privatrett på formurettens område (2013).

2) outside Norway or the Norwegian Economic Zone if the damage is caused by an incident or activity within Norwegian sea or land territory. When the second situation occurs, the foreign injured party has the option to apply either Norwegian law or that party's foreign law.[77] Article 7 of the *Rome II regulation*[78] similarly states that an injured party may choose to apply the law of the country in which the damage occurred or the event giving rise to the damage occurred, to his or her claim for delict compensation arising out of environmental damage.[79,80]

The *Rome II regulation* is a part of the EU's judicial cooperation on civil matters and is therefore not implemented in Norwegian law, as EU's judicial cooperation is not included in the EEA agreement.[81] The Ministry of Justice and Police[82] indicated already in 1985 the importance of EU international private law for Norwegian international private law because of the already similar rules and the need for legal uniformity to avoid forum shopping.[83] When the EU started to explore changes to the *Rome Convention*[84] approximately twenty

---

77   The rules of the geographic scope and choice-of-law rules presented in §54 only applies to Chapter 8 of the *Pollution Control Act*, which regulates compensation for pollution damage.

78   European Parliament and the Council, Regulation (EC) No. 864/2007 of the European Parliament and of the Council on the law applicable to non-contractual obligations (Rome II) (July 11, 2007).

79   Environmental damage is considered under the regulation as "...adverse change in a natural resource, such as water, land, or air, impairment of a function performed by that resource for the benefit of another natural resource or the public, or impairment of the variability among living organisms." Council, Regulation (EC) No. 864/2007 of the European Parliament and of the Council on the law applicable to non-contractual obliga- tions (Rome II). July 11, 2007, Preamble (24).

80   A summary of environmental damage under article 7 at 86–88 in Claus Wilhelm Fröhlich, The Private International Law of Non-Contractual Obligations According to the Rome-II Regulation: a comparative study of the choice of law rules in tort under European, English and German law (Verlag Dr. Kovač, Hamburg, 2008).

81   For a summary of areas excluded from the EEA agreement, *see* Halvard Haukeland Fredriksen and Gjermund Mathisen, *EØS-rett* (Fagbokforlaget, Bergen, 2012), 31–33.

82   The Ministry of Justice and Police consists of a legal department, which acts as an expert legal body for the Government and its ministries. The expert legal body has the main responsibility for a plethora of legal areas, and to ensure technical quality in their legislation.

83   Høringsnotat – Utkast til lov om interlegale lovvalgsregler på formuerettens område. Jnr 1450/85 E BN/uwg (May 20, 1985), 1. For a discussion, *see* Cordero-Moss, *supra* note 27, at 25–27.

84   EC, Convention 80/934/ECC on the law applicable to contractual obligations opened for signature in Rome on June 19, 1980 (June 19, 1980).

THE CASE OF THE BARENTS SEA   179

years later,[85] this importance was confirmed as the Ministry expressed plans to examine and possibly codify the non-statutory choice-of-law rules of contract law and stated the EU amendments would have "... big importance for the shaping of Norwegian law."[86]

What has the Norwegian legislator stated regarding the legislative inconsistency between the *Petroleum Act* and the *Pollution Control Act*? The Ministry, in passing the first edition of the *Petroleum Act*, indicated a desire to harmonize the rules based on a need for legal uniformity:

> ... it is not reasonable that for example the Brits should receive a continuing right to compensation if the pollution stems from an installation on the Norwegian shelf than if it stems from an installation on the British [shelf]. When damage in the Great Britain it should therefore be the British rules that take effect.[87]

The main reason for the third paragraph in §38 appears to be Great Britain's unwillingness to ratify the Convention of Civil Liability for Oil Pollution Damage resulting from Exploration for and Exploitation of Seabed Mineral Resources, (CLEE) 1977,[88] and therefore it is not open for reciprocity of Norwegian liability rules applying inside and outside Norwegian territory.[89] It seems apparent that the Norwegian legislator intentionally created a regime of inequality as they made sure to implement the equality principle of the Nordic Convention on Environment Protection to Chapter 7 pollution damage stating "[t]he question of compensation shall not be judged by rules which are less favorable to the injured party than the rules of compensation of the State in which the activities are being carried out."[90] This left Great Britain,

---

85   European Commission, Green paper on the conversion of the Rome Convention of 1980 on the law applicable to contractual obligations into a Community instrument and its modernisation (2002).

86   Høringsbrev – Høring – Grønnbok om mulige endringer i Roma-konvensjonen 19. juni 1980 om lovvalg på kontraktsrettens område. 200206128 EP HCH/IHO/bj. (June 13, 2003). For an extensive discussion, *see* Giuditta Cordero-Moss, "Den nye europeiske internasjonale formueretten og norsk internasjonal formuerett," 48(2) Lov og Rett (2009): 69–70.

87   Energy, Ot.prp.nr. 72. Lov om petroleumsvirksomhet (1982–1983), 71.

88   Convention on Civil Liability for Oil Pollution Damage Resulting from Exploration for and Exploitation of Seabed Mineral Resources, London. London (May 1, 1977).

89   Ministry of Justice and Public Security, Ot.prp.nr. 33 (1988–1989) Om lov om endringer i lov 13 mars 1981 nr 6 om vern mot forurensninger og om avfall (forurensningsloven) m.v (Erstatningsansvar ved forurensningsskade) ((1988–1989)), 27.

90   The Nordic Environmental Protection Convention (and Protocol), Stockholm. Implemented in Norwegian law through "Lov av 9. april 1976 nr 21 om gjennomføring i

Russia, and Iceland (which is not a party to the Nordic Convention on Environment Protection) in a different position.

The choice-of-law rules in §54 of the *Pollution Control Act* were enacted in 1989.[91] Therefore, the introduction was before the removal of §38. The Ministry of Justice states in the preparatory works to the 1989 enactment of the *Petroleum Act* that it agrees with the rules in the *Petroleum Act* and leaves no doubt that compensation for issues regarding petroleum activity is regulated by the *Petroleum Act*.[92] The Ministry of Finance and the Ministry of Petroleum and Energy both suggest the same regime reflected by §38. The Ministry of Justice suggests a regime of choice (§54) to prevent a Norwegian harm-doer from possibly escaping the stricter compensation rules, granting the injured party optimal protection, and remains open to enforcement of a judgment against a foreign harm-doer if he or she holds assets in Norway.[93] The Ministry of Justice then expressed its dismay toward the more restrictive choice-of-law regulation in the *Petroleum Act*. The Ministry did recognize the broader scope of the *Pollution Control Act* and emphasized "...a clear need to more closely harmonize..."[94] the choice-of-law rules in the *Pollution Control Act* and the *Petroleum Act*. The Ministry continued in further criticism of the two-regime regulation of pollution damage:

> The Ministry views it nevertheless as not natural to operate with different rules about the scope/choice of law – according to the type of effluence/ pollution that occurs on the shelf etc. It is in other words not obvious [that] oil spill damage inflicted to the English coast as a result of petroleum activity on the Norwegian shelf should not follow Norwegian law, while the solution should be different for air pollution in England due to for example an incinerator ship which is located in the Norwegian economic zone.[95]

---

norsk rett av miljøvernkonvensjon mellom Norge, Danmark, Finland og Sverige, undertegnet 19 februar 1974." February 19, 1974, Art. 3.

91 Ministry of Police and Public Safety, Lov om endringer i lov av 13. mars 1981 nr. 6 om vern mot forurensninger og om avfall (forurensningsloven) m.v. (June 16, 1989 nr 67).

92 Security, Ot.prp.nr. 33 (1988–1989) Om lov om endringer i lov 13 mars 1981 nr 6 om vern mot forurensninger og om avfall (forurensningsloven) m.v (Erstatningsansvar ved forurensningsskade). (1988–1989), 27.

93 *Ibid.*, at 26.

94 *Ibid.*, at 27.

95 *Ibid.*, at 27.

THE CASE OF THE BARENTS SEA

Nonetheless, when §38 was removed from the 1996 *Petroleum Act*, the Ministry's only reason for removal was that it found the sentence unnecessary, and did not signal any indication of harmonization towards the *Pollution Control Act* regime. Thus, even though the third paragraph of §38 was eliminated, the Norwegian legislator did not touch the regime.

What is the Norwegian courts' take on a possible harmonization with the rules laid down in *Rome II*? The Supreme Court stated that the starting point for a choice-of-law assessment is: "...law, custom or other more fixed rules which regulate the question...[and with the absence of these]...find the way to the state that the case after a total assessment has its strongest or closest connection to ('the Irma-Mignon formula[/consideration]'[96])".[97] The Court confirmed its view as expressed earlier in the *Bookseller*[98] case.[99] In both cases the Supreme Court stated in *obiter dictum* that the main rule for deciding a

---

96   Irma-Mignon-saken (Rt. 1923 II p. 58) (Supreme Court of Norway). The case first adopted the so-called proximity principle, the closeness principle, or the aggregate-contacts test; but more a consideration of factors than a formula. The devil is known by many names. The case concerned the collision of two vessels, Irma and Mignon. The vessels were both Norwegian and collided in British waters due to the pilot on board of Irma, who maneuvered incorrectly. The Supreme Court made an exemption from the main rule, *lex loci delict*, and applied Norwegian law based on the fact of closest proximity to Norway. For an extensive discussion of this case, *see* Lars Anders Heimdal, Rettsvalg ved erstatning for krenkende ytringer (2012) Bergen PhD, Faculty of Law, University of Bergen), 146 ff. (case and development) and its critic, *id.* at 54 ff. Cordero-Moss lists critical legal literature about the 'formula,' *see supra* note 27, at 87 in Cordero-Moss, Internasjonal Privatrett på formurettens område (2013).

97   Krigsforbryterdommen (Rt. 2011 p. 531) (Supreme Court of Norway). #(29).

98   Bokhandlerdommen (Rt. 2009 p. 1537) (Supreme Court of Norway). The case concerned a Norwegian journalist, who lived with an Afghan bookseller's family for some time. The journalist wrote a book about the stay, on which she was later sued for delict compensation for infringement of the right to privacy. The choice-of-law issue was decided on Norwegian law due to the special circumstances of not gathering reliable information about Afghan law. The case is extensively discussed in Lone Veel Midtbø and Siv Myrvold Isabell Fjetland, "Lovvalg ved påståtte personvernkrenkelser," 3(20) *EuroRett* (2009); Giuditta Cordero-Moss, "Lovvalg i erstatningsrett – personlighetskrenkelse – ytringsfrihet – Høyesteretts dom 2. desember 2009 (HR-2009–2266-A)," 1 *Nytt i privatretten* (2010): 21–23; Hans Petter Graver, *Fortellinger om en bok og et besøk – noen kommentarer til lovvalgsdommen i saken om «Bokhandleren i Kabul»*, *see Ibid.* at Cordero-Moss, Internasjonal Privatrett på formurettens område (2013), 27–30; and Heimdal, Rettsvalg ved erstatning for krenkende ytringer (2012), 10–12, 53, 56, 143–146, 175–176, 198–199, 224–225, 275–276, 300, 389–390, 418–423.

99   Bokhandlerdommen (Rt. 2009 p. 1537) (Supreme Court of Norway). #(32) as put forth in Krigsforbryterdommen (Rt. 2011 p. 531) (Supreme Court of Norway). #(29).

claim for compensation is *lex loci delicti* (the law of the place where the event giving rise to the damage occurred),[100] while the *Petroleum Act* enacted *lex loci damni* (the law of the place where the damage occurred).

The Court in the *Bookseller* case continued, stating that when the place of action and the place of effect are located in different countries, the question arises as to which place is the place of harm.[101] The Norwegian Supreme Court mentioned that the *Rome II* regulation applies to this scenario for EU countries and that Norway is not bound by the regulation.[102] Further, the Court emphasized in *obiter dictum* the importance of the EU's international private law rules in Norwegian legal methodology and sources of law:

> To the extent we do not have deviating legal regulation, the consideration for legal uniformity however advocates that we when deciding choice-of-law questions place weight on that solution which the EU-countries has chosen.[103]

As such, the *Rome II* regulation cannot hold weight if the Norwegian legislator has enacted contradictory rules to the *Rome II regulation*. In a later case, the Supreme Court commented on the *Bookseller* case's *obiter dictum* and stated that even though the *Rome II regulation* does not apply, the *Bookseller* case relies on the fact that "... the regulation's choice-of-law rules ought to apply in Norwegian international private law based on the consideration as regards the need for legal uniformity with the EU."[104] The Supreme Court appears to indicate that the current position in Norwegian international private law is that the *Rome II regulation* should be applied as long as it does not contradict a different position taken by the Norwegian legislator.

---

100   Krigsforbryterdommen (Rt. 2011 p. 531) (Supreme Court of Norway). #(29), and Bokhandlerdommen (Rt. 2009 p. 1537) (Supreme Court of Norway). #(33).

101   Bokhandlerdommen (Rt. 2009 p. 1537) (Supreme Court of Norway). #(33).

102   *Ibid.* at #(33)–#(34).

103   *Ibid.* at #(34).

104   Krigsforbryterdommen (Rt. 2011 p. 531) (Supreme Court of Norway). #(46). The *Rome II regulation* was not applied in the current case due to the criminal actions in dispute occurred before the regulation came into effect and the court doubted the application of the regulation to delict claims based on a criminal act. Criticism and discussion of the case, *see* Marie Nesvik, "Lovvalg, erstatning for straffbare handlinger begått av utlending i utlandet. Rt. 2011 s. 531, 2011," 4 *Nytt i privatretten* (2011): 25–26; and Cordero-Moss, *supra* note 27, 336–341.

THE CASE OF THE BARENTS SEA

"Jurisdictional arbitrage is, as the name suggests, a matter of profiting from differences in the laws of different jurisdictions."[105] Jurisdictional arbitrage can be practiced for several reasons. For example, an oil company can operate a cross-border oil field located in the most stable and tax-beneficial jurisdiction, or an oil company can operate in a low-level protection country to avoid higher levels of protection in a neighboring country. The latter is the reason for granting the injured party the ability to choose the applicable law in article 7 of the *Rome II regulation*. The article is based on, among other things, liability without fault, and the policy of prevention:

> obliging operators established in countries with a low level of protection to abide by the higher levels of protection in neighbouring countries, which removes the incentive for an operator to opt for low-protection countries. The rule thus contributes to raising the general level of environmental protection.[106]

Are there any policy considerations against a harmonization of the two regimes in the two Norwegian Act? The law of the place of damage or harm is the starting point in delict compensation cases in Norway and also in the *Petroleum Act*. The considerations for this are, among other things, fairness and "... the need of potential harm-doers for the greatest possible foreseeability about their potential liability, particularly with a view to prevent liability and spreading the risk of liability [pulverizing liability] through insurance, etc."[107] The EU found that applying exclusively the law of the place where the damage is sustained could give an operator an incentive to establish his facility in such a place that in the event of an accident, the harm could have a higher likelihood of inflicting within the benefiting country and enjoy the benefit of the neighboring country's more forgiving rules.[108] "This solution would be contrary to the underlying philosophy of the European substantive law of the environment and the 'polluter pays' principle."[109] The current legal solutions

---

105   Annelise Riles, "Managing Regulatory Arbitrage: A Conflict of Laws Approach," 47(1) *Cornell International Law Journal* (2014): 12.

106   Comission of the European Communities, Proposal for a Regulation of the European Parliament and the Council on the law applicable to non-contractual obligations ("ROME II"): explanatory memorandum. Brussels (July 22, 2003), 19.

107   Krigsforbryterdommen (Rt. 2011 p. 531) (Supreme Court of Norway). #(31).

108   Communities, Proposal for a Regulation of the European Parliament and the Council on the law applicable to non-contractual obligations ("ROME II"): explanatory memorandum. July 22, 2003, 19–20.

109   *Ibid.* at 20.

for specific Russian parties in specific scenarios will likely leave these parties without a remedy. This situation could present an incentive to resist assisting, for example, in clean-up and other preventative measures limiting pollution damage within a Norwegian jurisdiction.

4.7 *Author's Recommendations*

This choice between place of harm and place of event giving rise to harm grants the less powerful party – the victim – not the courts the determination of the law that is most favorable to him or her. It does not appear, however, to be in breach of the fairness consideration. The powerful party, the licensee, will be aware of the legislative amendment and impact. That party can take the necessary precautions through, for example, insurance. At the same time, this choice sets a higher standard encouraging the injured party to sue in the jurisdiction awarding a higher reward, achieving a deterrence effect against pollution.

Importantly, such an amendment to the scope of Chapter 7 would also remove any issues of lack of recognition and enforcement of foreign judgments because a Russian party can then sue a Norwegian company in a Norwegian court; and, receive access to the Norwegian company's assets in Norway (assuming the company has no assets in Russia).[110]

Harmonization of the two regimes will create internal and external legal equality and uniformity as well as simplicity through reducing the number of applicable legal regimes. Nevertheless, it could be said that enacting the suggested choice-of-law option, where the injured party elects to apply the law of the country in which the damage occurred or the event giving rise to the damage occurred, could create an unbalance between the Norwegian and the Russian legal system. The option could grant Russian citizens more benefits within the Norwegian legal system without reciprocity. The amendment could also grant better protection of life, property, and environment in Norway through increased protection of measures initiated in the Russian jurisdiction, to avert or limit pollution damage within the Norwegian jurisdiction, and to Norwegian interests (and hopefully harmed interests in the execution of these measures).

Furthermore, article 7 of the *Rome II regulation* does not take into account whether the injury occurred in the state was foreseeable, as article 7 assumes

---

110   The procedural aspect however of dealing with foreign law in a Norwegian court is not discussed in the thesis. Beate Sjåfjell-Hansen, På Fremmed Grunn. Den Sivilprosessuelle Behandlingen av Saker med Utenlandsk Rett ved Norske Domstoler (Juristforbundets Forlag, Oslo, 2000).

THE CASE OF THE BARENTS SEA   185

that foreseeability either does not make a difference or that it is always present regardless of distance with respect to cross-border environmental damage.[111] In addition, the Norwegian *Petroleum Act* does not incorporate an objective foreseeability proviso in its choice-of-law section. However, delict law examines foreseeability when examining the extent of damage compensable.

Therefore, in light of recent oil spill accidents, proximity will likely be the gist of the issue in delict law, and not foreseeability.

The Supreme Court strongly indicates harmonization with the *Rome II regulation*, the preparatory works express a discomfort with the current gap between the Acts, and the literature suggest conformity with the *Pollution Control Act* and the *Rome II regulation*, due to, for example, the close ties between Norway and the EU. There appears to be little contradiction in suggesting a need to amend §7–2 to adhere to §54 and article 7. This legal choice-of-law amendment of §7–2 will be in line with the European international private law development, create internal and external (with the EU) harmonization of the choice-of-law rules, and it corresponds with the equality principle of the *Nordic Convention on Environment Protection*.

5   Conclusion

The article shows that there are small but significant hurdles to jump for a Russian harmed party to get access to Norwegian courts procedurally for the scenario where Russian parties on the Russian side of the Barents Sea are harmed by a Norwegian oil company on the Norwegian side of the Barents Sea. The question of venue is clear. *Lex loci damni* is the principle enacted in Chapter 7, with a unilateral extension of protection in delict law to Norwegian interests harmed in Russia, which is not extended to Russian injured parties harmed within the Russian jurisdiction, for situations where the source of harm is located on the Norwegian side of the Barents Sea. This privilege has resulted in discrimination only against Russian interests, which in some situations do not enjoy delict law protection under Chapter 7. A Russian injured party forced to pursue a legal claim against a Norwegian licensee without assets in Russia may receive no compensation because there is no agreement about recognition and enforcement of foreign court judgments between Norway and Russia. The best of reasons argues for a legislative amendment by the Norwegian Parliament to harmonies §54 of the *Pollution Control Act* and §7–2

---

111   Symeon C. Symeonides, "Rome II and Tort Conflicts: A Missed Opportunity," *American Journal of Comparative Law* 56 (2008): 38, http://ssrn.com/abstract=1031803.

of the *Petroleum Act* in favor of the wording in §54. This approach would apply the delict rules in Chapter 7 to pollution damage occurring: 1) in Norway or inside of the outer limits of the Norwegian continental shelf, or 2) outside the areas mentioned in 1), if the damage is caused by an incident or activity within Norwegian seas or land territory. When 2) is fulfilled, the foreign injured party should have the option to apply either Norwegian law or his or her foreign law. This proposed amendment would follow the wording in §54 and remove the discrimination against injured Russian interests harmed as a result of an accident, such as a blowout, on the Norwegian side of the Barents Sea. This ability to forum shop could have preventive and restorative functions.[112] Such a choice could have a positive effect on limiting cross-border pollution, from which the neighboring country will have difficulty protecting itself.[113]

Furthermore, reasonable measures, executed in the Russian jurisdiction, seem compensable under current law when executed to avert or limit pollution damage within the Norwegian jurisdiction. This creates two problems: first, Russian parties executing measures to avert or limit possible pollution damage in the Norwegian jurisdiction from a Russian oil rig on the Russian side of the Barents Sea could face difficulties enforcing a Norwegian court judgment against a Russian licensee in Russia, as well as enforcing a court judgment in Norway against a Russian licensee without assets in Norway. Likewise, if Norwegian parties cross into Russian jurisdiction to assist their Russian colleagues in the liquidation of the oil spill, Norwegian claimants may then face the same challenge of enforcing a Norwegian judgment against a Russian licensee in Russia.

Second, measures executed in the Russian jurisdiction to avert or limit pollution damage to Norwegian interests (three groups) located in the Russian jurisdictions (seas) appear not compensable. For example, a Norwegian trawler accruing expenses to save its trawl from pollution damage in the Russian part of the Barents Sea is excluded from compensation under Chapter 7.[114] Similarly, a foreign trawler salvaging Norwegian fishing equipment in the Russian jurisdiction is likely not eligible for compensation. Thus, a legislative amendment should be made to facilitate for compensation of expenses for measures to limit or avert pollution damage of all parties within the general scope of §7–2 and the parties assisting in such measures.

---

112 Ministry of Justice and Police, NOU: Generelle lovregler om erstatning for forurensningsskade. (1982: 19), 49.

113 *Ibid.* at p. 50.

114 Hammer et al., Petroleumsloven (2009), 541.

The Recent Arctic Council Assessments: Influential Tools in Policy-Making in the Council and Beyond?

Małgorzata Śmieszek,[a] Adam Stępień,[b] and Paula Kankaanpää[c]

Abstract

The scientific assessments of the Arctic Council (AC) have been widely regarded as the most effective products of the AC. Yet, so far comparatively little scholarly attention has been given to this primary area of the Council's work. This paper examines the most recent assessment work within the Arctic Council. In order to do this, we build on the literature on global environmental assessments to analyze whether this work exhibits design features and is carried out in a way that enhances the potential for AC assessments to be effective. We understand the effectiveness of assessments to influence decision and policy-making in the Arctic Council itself, but we also look beyond its structures. This paper focuses on four case studies: Arctic Biodiversity Assessment (ABA), Arctic Human Development Report-II (ADHR-II), Arctic Resilience Report/Arctic Resilience Assessment (ARR/ARA) and Adaptation Actions for a Changing Arctic (AACA). Whereas detailed examination of such influence is at this point not possible due to either very short time from their completion (ABA, ADHR-II) or the fact that the projects are still ongoing (ARA, AACA), the analysis of those assessments through the lens of a series of their design features provides us with some guidance in relation to their expected effectiveness in bridging science with decision-making in the AC and beyond. The article finds that whereas different processes exhibit different individual characteristics, all the studied assessments rank from relatively high to very high in terms of how their design may affect their salience, credibility and legitimacy. However, their actual policy influence will depend first and foremost on the political will of those ordering the assessments and wielding decision-making power in the Arctic Council.

---

a Arctic Centre, University of Lapland.
b Arctic Centre, University of Lapland.
c Marine Research Centre, Finnish Environment Institute (SYKE).

Keywords

Arctic Council – assessments – governance – science-policy interface

1 Introduction

The Arctic Council (AC or "Council") is today widely recognized as the primary body for circumpolar cooperation. This high-level forum was established in 1996 to promote cooperation, coordination, and interaction among the Arctic states with the involvement of indigenous representatives. The AC came to being in a time when, with demise of the Cold War, the interest in the Arctic was in decline and the world's attention turned to other more conflicting and demanding parts of the globe. Since its establishment, the bulk of Arctic Council work revolved around the conduct of scientific assessments, which collected information on the Arctic biophysical environment and human and social development in the region under conditions of accelerating change. The assessments such as the Arctic Climate Impact Assessment (ACIA) or those on persistent organic pollutants (POPs) have become hallmarks of the Arctic Council and played an important role in the Arctic's region-building process.[1] They have also contributed to raising awareness of the changes in the Arctic in the outside world and influenced certain policy-making developments. Eventually, they could be claimed to have legitimized the Arctic Council itself and ensure its unique position in the emerging circumpolar governance structures.[2]

Today, nearly two decades after the AC's founding, the Arctic is again the focus of the international community. The region's profound transformation is driven primarily by interacting forces of globalization and climate change, drawing the attention of many non-arctic actors interested in the potential economic opportunities arising with the opening of the Arctic Ocean, and in the consequences that the changing Arctic climate bears for the southern

---

1 David L. Downie and Terry Fenge, ed., *Northern Lights against POPs: Combating Toxic Threats in the Arctic* (Montreal and Kingston: McGill-Queen's University Press, 2003); Annika E. Nilsson "Knowing the Arctic: The Arctic Council as a Cognitive Forerunner," in *The Arctic Council: Its Place in the Future of Arctic Governance*, ed., Thomas S. Axworthy, Timo Koivurova, and Waliul Hasanat (Munk-Gordon Arctic Security Program, 2012), 190–224.

2 Koivurova Timo, Paula Kankaanpää, and Adam Stępień, "Innovative Environmental Protection: Lessons from the Arctic," *Journal of Environmental Law* 27, no. 2 (2015): 285–311.

latitudes.[3] Due to rising interconnectivity between the Arctic and rest of the world, and resulting growing interest of the outside actors in the region's governance, the question arises to what extent the Council will be able to maintain and secure its role in these circumstances. The Arctic Council responded to the challenges connected with Arctic change and the international interest in the region by strengthening its structures and incorporating a broader array of actors.[4] Nevertheless, this paper posits that as in the past, for the foreseeable future the assessments will remain the dominant activity of the Council. Yet, so far comparatively little attention has been given to this primary area of the AC's work in the discussion on the changing role of the Arctic Council in the Arctic governance. Can the recent and ongoing AC assessments be influential in policy-making processes within the AC and beyond? Will they prove effective? Conceivably, answers to those questions matter not only as regards the effective bridging of science with decision-making in the Council, but also to importance of assessments in future activities of the AC steadily increasing array of its fields of interests and deployed instruments. It is through the lens of effectiveness and influence on policymaking that the role of assessments in Arctic governance can be evaluated.

The overall aim of this paper is to examine the most recent work within the Arctic Council in order to highlight the current trends in science-policy interface and assessment methodologies. However, the focus on recent or ongoing assessments means that the above questions on effectiveness and influence cannot be answered directly. What can be done instead – and what thus constitutes the specific objective of this article – is the evaluation of the way these assessments are designed and carried out, and isolating features that topical literature identifies as potentially enhancing or inhibiting assessments' ability to bear impact on policy-making.

The article begins with the overview of the position of the Arctic Council in the Arctic governance as well as a discussion on the role of the AC as a knowledge producer and cognitive forerunner in the Arctic, and focuses in

---

3   Stępień, Adam, Timo Koivurova, and Paula Kankaanpää, ed., *Strategic Assessment of Development of the Arctic: Assessment Conducted for the European Union* (Arctic Centre, University of Lapland, 2014); Aki Tonami, "The Arctic Policy of China and Japan: Multilayered Economic and Strategic Motivations," *The Polar Journal* 4 (2014): 105; Duncan Depledge, "Emerging UK Arctic Policy," *International Affairs* 89, no. 6 (2013): 1445–1457.

4   Piotr Graczyk and Timo Koivurova, "A New Era in the Arctic Council's External Relations? Broader Consequences of the Nuuk Observer Rules for Arctic Governance," *Polar Record* 50, no. 3 (2014): 225–236; Erik Molenaar, "Current and Prospective Roles of the Arctic Council System within the Context of the Law of the Sea," *International Journal of Marine and Coastal Law* 27 (2012): 553–595.

190   ŚMIESZEK, STĘPIEŃ AND KANKAANPÄÄ

this last respect on assessments as the most recognized and valued products of the AC. Next, to set a broader stage for reflecting on AC scientific assessments, it sheds some light on global and regional environmental assessments, their development and theoretical underpinnings of their effectiveness. The article continues with a more in-depth study of four recent AC assessments selected to present wide spectrum of the Arctic Council's activities and then, analyses these assessments through the lens of a series of design features based on the body of literature on the conduct of scientific assessments. These assessments include Arctic Resilience Report/ Arctic Resilience Assessment (ARR/ARA),[5] Arctic Biodiversity Assessment (ABA),[6] Arctic Human Development Report-II (ADHR-II),[7] and Adaptation Actions for a Changing Arctic (AACA). The paper concludes by pondering over potential effectiveness and influence of the studied assessments on future policy-making in the Arctic Council.

2   Role of the Arctic Council in Arctic Governance

The Arctic Council is a primary circumpolar body dealing with matters pertaining to the Arctic. It was established in 1996 as a successor to the Arctic Environmental Protection Strategy (AEPS) to broaden the scope of cooperation among eight Arctic states from its earlier emphasis on the protection of environment to address issues of sustainable development in the Arctic.[8] Since the AEPS was incorporated into the newly formed Council, a new body inherited most of the operational practices and structural elements from its predecessor, including, *inter alia*, four working groups[9] and a position of Senior

---

5   Arctic Council, *Arctic Resilience Interim Report* (Stockholm Environment Institute and Stockholm Resilience Centre, Stockholm: 2013).

6   *See* report: CAFF (Conservation of Arctic Flora and Fauna), *Arctic Biodiversity Assessment: Status and trends in Arctic biodiversity* (2013), accessed February 18, 2016, www.arcticbiodiversity.is.

7   *See* final report: Joan. N. Larsen and Gail Fondahl, ed., *Arctic Human Development Report: Regional Processes and Global Linkages* (TemaNord, 2014): 567.

8   E. Carina H. Keskitalo, *Negotiating the Arctic. The Construction of an International Region* (New York, London: Routledge, 2004). In fact, the AEPS also worked on sustainable development issues via its task force on sustainable development and utilization (TFSDU), which had in its agenda more high level and controversial sustainable development issues that the SDWG eventually came to deal with.

9   Conservation of Arctic Flora and Fauna (CAFF), Arctic Monitoring and Assessment Programme (AMAP), Emergency Prevention, Preparedness and Response (EPPR), and the Protection of Arctic Marine Environment (PAME). A new working group, Sustainable

THE RECENT ARCTIC COUNCIL ASSESSMENTS 191

Arctic Affairs officials (SAAOs, renamed later to SAOs, Senior Arctic Officials) to coordinate work within the Council. Furthermore, similarly to the AEPS, the Arctic Council was established through a signed declaration (*Declaration on the Establishment of the Arctic Council*, hereinafter *Ottawa Declaration*) and not by an international treaty, thus reflecting political – but not legal – commitment of Arctic states towards enhanced cooperation in the region.[10] That resulted in the emergence of soft law arrangement rather than an international organization. Finally, the relatively low profile of the Council at that time was reflected in its lack of permanent funding and secretariat, and the AC did not take on in its agenda any controversial matters, instead gradually focusing on providing scientific expertise on environmental and social changes in the region.

Despite this unpromising beginning, the Arctic Council has succeeded beyond the expectations of most of those involved in its creation[11] and managed to position itself as the central player in the Arctic.[12] In fact, as Koivurova et al.[13] argue, it is exactly the institutional structure and the soft-law mechanism of the Arctic regional cooperation – together with the commitment of epistemic community which gradually grew around the Arctic Council – that enabled trust-building and bottom-up evolution of the Council's working structures and practices, contributing to its success. The AC has been highly appraised for its distinct, adopted mode of involvement of indigenous organizations as Permanent Participants, providing for their active participation and full

---

Development Working Group (SDWG) was established to address the part of the mandate on the sustainable development.

10 Evan T. Bloom, "Establishment of the Arctic Council," *American Journal of International Law* 93, no. 3 (1999): 712–22; Timo Koivurova, "Limits and Possibilities of the Arctic Council in a Rapidly Changing Scene of Arctic Governance," *Polar Record* 46, no. 02 (2010): 146–156.

11 Arctic Governance Project, *Arctic Governance in an Era of Transformative Change: Critical Questions, Governance Principles, Ways Forward* (2010), accessed March 20, 2016, http://www.arcticgovernance.org/.

12 Timo Koivurova, and David VanderZwaag, "The Arctic Council and 10 Years: Retrospect and Prospects," *University of British Columbia Law Review* 40, no. 1 (2007): 121–94; Thomas S. Axworthy, Timo Koivurova, and Waliul Hasanat, ed., *The Arctic Council: Its Place in the Future of Arctic Governance.... Arctic Security Program & ... Munk-Gordon Arctic Security Program* (2012); Paula Kankaanpää, and Oran R. Young, "The Effectiveness of the Arctic Council," *Polar Research* 31 (2012): 1–14; Olav Schram Stokke, and Geir Hønneland, ed., *International Cooperation and Arctic Governance. Regime Effectiveness and Northern Region Building* (London: Routledge, 2007).

13 Koivurova et al. (2015), *supra*, note 2.

consultation in all decision-making.[14] Finally, the forum has found its 'cognitive niche' by collecting knowledge and producing large-scale scientific assessments, including recommendations primarily directed at the Arctic countries' governments. Those assessments have been regarded as the most effective products of the AC[15] and played a key role in raising the Council's profile within and beyond the region. They have been instrumental in identifying Arctic pollution problems, influential in international environmental policy-making processes,[16] and have paved the way for recognition of the Arctic as a distinct region in the international political consciousness.[17] In this last respect, the Arctic Climate Impact Assessment (ACIA) stands out as it drew attention to the profound consequences of climate change for the Arctic and its indigenous inhabitants, and strongly contributed to the view of the region undergoing a thorough transformation,[18] influencing the perception of the Arctic within the Arctic countries and beyond.

The foundations of Arctic formalized cooperation were coined at times when the Arctic was a matter of only regional, not global interest.[19] However,

---

14 Indigenous contributions to works of the Arctic Council include traditional knowledge and strengthening of the messages delivered to the public by Council's assessments, thus enhancing the legitimacy of the AC in dealing with environmental matters (*see* Timo Koivurova, and Leena Heinämäki, "The Participation of Indigenous Peoples in International Norm-Making in the Arctic," *Polar Record* 42, no. 221 (2006): 101–9; Monica Tennberg, *Arctic Environmental Cooperation. A Study in Governmentality*, (Rovaniemi: University of Lapland Press, 1999); Koivurova 2010, *supra*, note 10).

15 Kankaanpää and Young, *supra*, note 12.

16 Lars-Otto Reiersen, Simon Wilson, and Vitaly Kimstack, "Circumpolar Perspectives on Persistent Organic Pollutants: The Arctic Monitoring and Assessment Programme," in *Northern Lights against POPs: Combating Toxic Threats in the Arctic*, ed. by D.L. Downie and T. Fenge (Montreal and Kingston: McGill-Queen's University Press, 2003).

17 Nilsson, *supra*, note 1.

18 Perhaps paradoxically, the assessments the Council has been, and is, sponsoring are further consolidating the view of the 'Arctic in change,' which in turn energize the redrawing of Arctic policies by Arctic actors and agencies in the face of possible regime change, *see* Koivurova 2010, *supra*, note 10.

19 According to Oran Young, the Arctic in the last three decades has experienced two fundamental state changes, each of them having major consequences for Arctic policymaking and governance in broader terms. The first change, 'a delinking or decoupling shift,' took place in the late 1980s/early 1990s and was closely linked to the waning of cold war and the collapse of the Soviet Union. It resulted in launch of numerous formalized structures of collaboration, was marked by a strong focus on Arctic-specific matters and allowed for gradual development of 'the idea of the Arctic as distinctive region with a policy agenda of its own.' At the same time this process brought in also 'a separation between Arctic

THE RECENT ARCTIC COUNCIL ASSESSMENTS 193

the scientific outlook for Arctic climate change, the widely reported 2007 Arctic sea-ice minimum, as well as the planting of the Russian flag on the seabed under the North Pole in the summer of same year all sparked speculation about geopolitical tensions as well as economic opportunities in the opening Arctic Ocean. That led to a change in the international perception of the region and resulted in increasing public focus on the Arctic. This growing interest of the outside world has presented new challenges to the Arctic Council, reflected, *inter alia*, in the influx of both state and non-state non-Arctic actors willing to join the AC as observers. The AC on its side took numerous efforts to address these challenges, among others, through elaborating on criteria for admission of new observers in Nuuk in 2011 and accepting six new states as observers at the Ministerial meeting in Kiruna in 2013, opening of a permanent secretariat in Tromsø in 2013 and recently facilitating the creation of the Arctic Economic Council.[20] In order to address issues of growing concern in the region, it has also provided a venue for negotiation of two legally-binding international agreements, on cooperation on aeronautical and maritime search and rescue that was concluded in 2011 and on marine oil pollution preparedness and response adopted in 2013,[21] with the third one – on scientific cooperation in the region – presently under way.

As Koivurova and two authors of this paper point out, the strength of the AC in adapting to the changing circumstances lies in the flexibility of its institutional design and operation modes, 'certain degree of informality of co-operation'[22] and finding a niche of increasing knowledge on the circumpolar

---

governance and the pursuit of governance on a global scale.' The second state change, 'a linking change' began in the Arctic in the early 2000s and continues until today, and it has been to large extent driven by processes of global environmental change and globalization, a mix of forces of environmental and socioeconomic character. *See* Oran R. Young, "The Arctic in Play: Governance in a Time of Rapid Change," *The International Journal of Marine and Coastal Law* 24 (2009): 423–442.

20 Arctic Economic Council brings together businesses, including those representing indigenous livelihoods, from eight Arctic states. Although developed under the auspices of the Arctic Council and having as one of its goals bringing the voice of Arctic private sector to Arctic Council work, it is a fully autonomous institution.

21 Agreement on Cooperation on Aeronautical and Maritime Search and Rescue in the Arctic (signed in Nuuk on May 12, 2011, entered into force January 19, 2013) 50 I.L.M. 1119 (2011) (SAR Agreement); Agreement on Cooperation on Marine Oil Pollution, Preparedness and Response in the Arctic (signed in Kiruna on May 15, 2013), accessed December 2, 1014, www.arctic-council.org/eppr (Oil Spills Agreement).

22 Koivurova et al. (2015), *supra*, note 2.

Arctic both within and beyond the region.[23] To this end they identify the large-scale scientific assessments as the best policy-shaping instruments that the Council has at its disposal. As laid out, assessments have been of utmost importance in the Council's past but the question arises if they will play also the same role in the future and whether they can exert further influence over AC decision-making. To answer this question, we will first revert to the broader discussion on global and regional environmental assessments, which in last few decades have become an increasingly common element of both international and national policy-making, so that the study on the proper conduct of such assessments can give us important hints in how to look at present AC projects.

3   Global and Regional Assessments

The increasing interest in global and regional assessments of different kinds stems primarily from concerns for better-informed, more effective, more efficient, and more transparent policy-making;[24] and can be linked to international and cross-boundary nature of many present environmental problems. Since air and water pollution, climate change, or loss of biodiversity know no jurisdictional limits, addressing them effectively requires cooperation among countries with inclusion of actors from all levels, from the local to the global,[25] as well as interaction between scientists and policy-makers. Assessments have become one form of such interaction. They can be understood as collective and organized efforts aiming at assembling scientific information for the use of policy-makers at all stages of decision-making, both within public and private sectors. As Clark et al. elaborate,[26] the increasing role of assessments has had its roots in a view that better and more widely shared information

---

23   *See* for example Stokke and Hønneland, *supra*, note 12.

24   Gerald Berger, "Sustainability Impact Assessment: Approaches and Applications in Europe," ESDN *Quarterly Report* (June 2007).

25   Elinor Ostrom, *Governing the Commons: The Evolution of Institutions for Collective Action* (Cambridge: Cambridge University Press, 1990); Oran R. Young, *The Institutional Dimensions of Environmental Change: Fit, Interplay, and Scale* (Cambridge, Massachusetts: MIT Press, 2002).

26   William C. Clark, Ronald B. Mitchell, and David W. Cash. "Evaluating the Influence of Global Environmental Assessments," in *Global Environmental Assessments. Information and Influence*, ed. Ronald B. Mitchell, William C. Clark, David W. Cash, and Nancy M. Dickson, (Cambridge, Massachusetts: MIT Press, 2006), 1–28.

THE RECENT ARCTIC COUNCIL ASSESSMENTS   195

can add to a more effective management of complex, transnational inter-actions between humans and nature. In addition, the reasoning behind assess-ments supposes that a better understanding of impacts of human actions, decisions and behaviours, presented with options for alleviation of these impacts, can provide incentives for political, social, and economic decision-makers to carry out their policies in a more sustainable way.

The assessments are considered a key interface between science and policy. As such, they may influence the formulation, implementation, and evaluation of public policy. Hence they are of interest not only to actors involved in them, but also to business, non-governmental organizations, regulatory offices etc.[27] Yet, the influence of assessments over policy-making is by no means straight-forward. Assessments may vary to a great extent as regards the type of influence they exert. To comprehend better the influence of assessments it is not enough to look at their scientific output and the products they deliver, frequently in the form of a report or publication. The report (like the ones released by, for example, the International Panel on Climate Change IPCC) is only the con-cluding stage of what can be much better understood as a social process:

> in which scientists, policymakers, and other stakeholders are (or are not) gathering data, conducting analyses, explaining, debating, learning, and interacting with each other around the issue on which the assessment focuses... From the time at which a few scientists, policymakers, and/ or stakeholders initiate an assessment, it is this process of interactions by which knowledge is created and transmitted among actors that deter-mines whether... the [assessment] will be influential.[28]

4   Assessments' Effectiveness and Evaluation

In general, the main aim of assessments is to inform decisions taken with regard to an issue under consideration. In other words, assessment's influ-ence refers in principle to its ability to lead actors to adopt policies and behaviours different to the ones they would undertake if no assessment was

---

27   Clark A. Miller, "The Design and Management of International Scientific Assessments. Lessons from Climate Regime," in *Assessments of Regional and Global Environmental Risks. Designing Processes for the Effective Use of Science in Decision-making* (Washington, DC: RFF Press, 2006), 187–205.

28   Clark et al., *supra*, note 26 at 14.

carried out.[29] However, being influential does not have to mean necessarily, as is often assumed, direct translation into adopted formal legislative or regulatory practices. When evaluating the assessment's effectiveness,[30] one should look instead at the entire issue domain including not only actors, but also their interests, beliefs, and resources; the institutional settings that enable and constrain interactions among those actors; the actors' behaviours such as decisions, policies or agreements; and, finally impacts of these behaviours on the outside world. Such approach is justified if we consider that a change in the issue domain is a continuous process. It may start by introduction of a new understanding of issues, which may consequently affect beliefs of participants to the process and over time – usually very long one – lead to shifts in interests related to problems addressed by the assessment.

The assessments may vary a great extent in their ability to affect policy-making. The existing literature suggests that these discrepancies stem from the level of fit into scientific and political contexts in which the assessments are conducted, the diversity of their goals and scope of their mandates, as well as a time scale upon which their effectiveness is being evaluated. Perhaps most importantly, such discrepancies can be associated with the way how different actors' distinct perspectives and interests affect their particular evaluation of assessments. Regardless of these variations, consensus exists among large group of scholars[31] that the general determinants of effectiveness of assessments can be found in the attributes of their salience, credibility, and legitimacy.

Salience, or relevance, relates to the ability of the assessment and its results to address particular concerns and needs of its user, whether this user finds it as providing information on issues over which they have control, in a form and at a time, which makes this information applicable for them in practice.

Credibility of the assessment refers to its scientific believability, of the quality of data as well as of utilized methods and approaches. In other words, the

---

29   Clark et al., *supra*, note 26.

30   This paper follows a simple definition of effectiveness proposed within the Global Environmental Assessment Project according to which 'more effective assessments are more likely to have significant influences on the corresponding issue domain and its development.' *See* Alexander E. Farrell, Jill Jäger, and Stacy D. VanDeveer, "Overview: Understanding Design Choices," in *Assessments of Regional and Global Environmental Risks. Designing Processes for the Effective Use of Science in Decision-making*, ed. Alexander E. Farrell and Jill Jäger (Washington, DC: RFF Press, 2006), 1–24.

31   Clark et al., *supra*, note 26; National Research Council, *Analysis of Global Change Assessments: Lessons Learned* (Washington, DC: The National Academies Press, 2007).

assessment's audience has to believe that the scientific content is 'true' or at least that it is more credible than the competing information.

Finally, legitimacy is a matter of perceived fairness and political acceptability of the assessment, giving due consideration to concerns, values and perspectives of assessment's various users. It is strongly tied to questions of participation and exclusion from the process as well as causes, impacts and policy options taken into account – one of the key observations from research on global environmental assessments was that "an assessment cannot promote knowledge regarding facts and causal beliefs without simultaneously, if often implicitly, promoting certain goals and values over others."[32]

It should be stressed that the three above-listed elements, identified as essential in raising potential effectiveness of an assessment, are not objectively existent factors per se, but are ascribed to assessments by their users. They are a matter of a subjective judgement made by the final users of the information on the basis of the process that led to creation or collection of this information. In sum, the assessment viewed by its audience as more salient, more credible and more legitimate, is more likely to induce change in this audience's beliefs and consequently be more effective and influential.[33] At the same time, evaluation of an assessment's effectiveness is not a straightforward task since any discernible changes in policy-makers' views or behaviour often become visible only in the long run. Moreover, acceptance of assessments' scientific output frequently depends on values, stakes as well as political, social and economic factors not explicitly related to the assessment itself. Finally, the formulation of policy responses is a result of on-going interactions between various people, groups and organizations, and within these broader dynamics assessment's scientific outputs are one element among many other forces.

It is not to say that the effectiveness of assessments relies completely upon external factors. On the contrary, a number of design elements have been identified which can foster or, if addressed inadequately, inhibit the users' perception of the assessment as salient, credible, and legitimate. For example, the effectiveness of assessment can be severely impeded by focusing on questions relevant from the perspective of the scientific community, but not important for final users of the collected information or by adopting too broad scale without tailoring the collected knowledge to fit the users' needs and concerns. Yet, such flaws can (and should) be avoided through the proper design of the assessment process, through paying careful consideration to elements like

---

32 Farrell et al., *supra*, note 30 at 8.

33 Therefore, the goal should be to increase number of stakeholders who find and consider the assessment as salient, credible, and legitimate.

framing of the process, the science-policy interface, engaging stakeholders, and treatment of uncertainty.

Since any evaluation of the assessment's effectiveness needs to encompass the entire issue domain and requires much longer time perspective, the aim of the authors of this paper does not lie in evaluating the tangible influence of the most recent assessment activities of the AC over decision-making processes in the Council. First, such an attempt would not be possible at this point in time where two of selected projects are still ongoing and two others have been only recently completed. Second, proper accounting for change in the issue domain shall take into account a highly compound nature of the process with different actors, ideas and interests involved, in which causal influence may oftentimes be indirect and where elements of an issue domain can change over time in response to non-assessment factors such as norms or the availability of technical solutions, an undertaking that lies beyond the scope of this article.[34]

Instead, building on the academic work and literature on global and regional environmental assessments, the authors selected a series of design features that have bearing on the potential influence of the AC assessments on policy-making and their expected effectiveness in bridging science with decision-making in the Council and beyond. Chosen elements are: ownership of the process; level of fit and time congruence; identification of the target audience; methodology; stakeholder participation/ engagement; and, the follow-up activities.

The *ownership of the process* relates to legitimacy and salience of the project and it allows for investigation of whether the assessment came from the broad consensus (in case of the Arctic Council – of the Arctic states and Permanent Participants), or if it was an initiative stemming from perhaps a narrower group that defined the goals of the process, which could consequently affect the effectiveness of the whole activity.

The *level of fit* and *time congruence* factor looks at whether the assessment seeks to be salient to its users by including the information responsive to local and regional conditions and specificities (so with regard to the Arctic – not only adopting the circumpolar perspective), focusing on issues over which assessment's users have control, and taking into account the time factor, so correspondence with other policy-making processes or larger developments in the issue domain (like the work on establishing or reviewing international arrangements).

---

34   Clark et al., *supra*, note 26.

The *identification of the target audience* is closely linked to applied communication and outreach strategies, diversification of formats of the final products and presentation of findings of the projects, whether they seek to resonate with local communities but also broader international society.

The *methodology* factor refers to assessment's scientific credibility, and consequently, legitimacy in the eyes of its users.[35]

The *stakeholder participation and engagement* has been often identified in the literature as one of the most significant factors affecting the influence of assessments. It allows for incorporation into the process stakeholders' knowledge and expertise (often very precise and context-specific). What is more, it repositions them from being mere objects of a given impact to the role of active agents. Here it should be remembered that the definition of a stakeholder depends to a large extent on the assessment domain and focus.

Finally, the *follow-up activities* constitute the element which is quite frequently neglected, e.g. due to a lack of sufficient funding and decreasing interest of the processes' participants upon completion of the main report, and which, if not addressed adequately and not incorporated into the assessment process, may strongly inhibit the assessment's overall impact.

In order to scrutinize each of the above factors the authors defined a list of auxiliary questions on which basis we attempted to examine the potential influence of ABA, ADHR-II, ARR, and AACA on their corresponding issue domains and development of these domains. The assessments have been selected to present a wide spectrum of the AC activities and topics taken up in the Council's work. Whereas the four cases under consideration do not provide a representative sample of multitude of projects carried out under the AC's auspices, each of them has been conducted under a different AC working group and altogether they represent a variety of concepts, aims and applied methodological approaches. The overview below presents the main findings and strongest points identified in each of the assessments under consideration.

---

35 "... [M]ethodology is related to ... answers to i.e. following questions: what is the geographical scope of the assessment? What are the sources of information and how was it accessed or obtained? Is TEK mentioned in the methodology of the assessment? Is the assessment based on any new concepts or rather well-established models and standards? Does it follow more disciplinary approach or seeks to promote an integrated one? Was there a review of the assessment product? Often, giving answers to all these interrogations is not possible. Nevertheless, it is worth to keep them in mind when investigating the Arctic Council assessments and searching for foundation of their potential impact." Paula Kankaanpää and Malgorzata Smieszek, eds. *Assessments in Policy-Making: Case Studies from the Arctic Council* (Arctic Centre, University of Lapland, 2014), 66.

200   ŚMIESZEK, STĘPIEŃ AND KANKAANPÄÄ

5   Recent Assessments of the Arctic Council

"There is consensus on the proposition that what the AC has done best is to identify emerging issues, carry out scientific assessments addressing these issues and use the results of the assessments both to frame issues for consideration and to set the agenda in policy settings."[36] Examples of such assessments include already mentioned ACIA as well as the Arctic Marine Shipping Assessment (AMSA) which in 2009 provided an influential study of shipping sector in the Arctic and the overview of its possible future developments.

5.1   *Arctic Biodiversity Assessment (ABA)*

The ABA, whose final report was presented in the Ministerial meeting in May 2013, was carried out as a support to one of the key findings and recommendations of the Arctic Climate Impact Assessment. In response to calls for an expansion and enhancement of monitoring of Arctic biodiversity, the Conservation of the Arctic Flora and Fauna (CAFF) Working Group of the AC launched an assessment of Arctic biodiversity in order to synthesize and assess the status and trends of biological diversity in the Arctic; and to inform, guide and serve as a baseline for future works of the AC and other international bodies. Though the process itself began in 2006, the final report came to be one of the main deliverables of the Swedish Chairmanship of the Arctic Council when it was presented in Kiruna in May 2013. It was the major assessment ever carried by CAFF and overall included contributions from more than 250 scientists from 15 Arctic and non-Arctic countries. It has provided up-to-date knowledge on Arctic biodiversity retrieved from scientific publications and complemented with inputs from traditional ecological knowledge (TEK), ensured by two appointed TEK coordinators. Overall, ABA consists of five components: *Arctic Biodiversity Trends 2010: Selected indicators of change;*[37] *Arctic Biodiversity Assessment: status and trends in Arctic biodiversity;*[38] *Arctic Biodiversity Assessment: synthesis;*[39] *Arctic Biodiversity Assessment: report for*

---

36   Kankaanpää and Young, *supra*, note 12.

37   Conservation of Arctic Flora and Fauna Working Group (thereafter CAFF), *Arctic Biodiversity Trends 2010: Selected indicators of change* (Arctic Council, Akureyri, Iceland, 2010).

38   CAFF, *Arctic Biodiversity Assessment. Status and Trends in Arctic Biodiversity* (Akureyri, Iceland, 2013).

39   CAFF, *Arctic Biodiversity Assessment: Synthesis.* Conservation of Arctic Flora and Fauna (Akureyri, Iceland, 2013).

THE RECENT ARCTIC COUNCIL ASSESSMENTS   201

policy makers;[40] and *Life Linked to Ice: a guide to sea-ice-associated biodiversity in this time of rapid change.*[41]

With regard to level of fit and time congruence, ABA's process was well aligned with other international developments in its field and its preliminary report from 2010 served as the contribution of the Arctic Council to the United Nations 2010 Biodiversity Target, to the International Biodiversity Year of 2010, and to the Convention of Biological Diversity (CBD) and its third Global Biodiversity Report. Such outreach ensured much broader audience for ABA which findings otherwise aim primarily at the Arctic states' governments and which many recommendations correspond with those of other AC projects. Moreover, great attention has been paid to delivery of assessment materials in various formats and languages, to enhance their resonance with the public. To this end next to the full scientific assessment and its synthesis, a report for policy makers was produced along with a movie on status and trends in Arctic biodiversity. In addition, a series of postcards with key ABA findings was made accessible in nine languages, among them Even, Inuktitut, Sakha and Yukagir and before that a summary of the Arctic biodiversity report was presented at the Convention on Biological Diversity COP10 in 2010 in Chinese, Danish, English, Greenlandic, German, Icelandic, Norwegian, and Russian.

The *Arctic Biodiversity Assessment. Report for Policy Makers* presented under 6 headlines its 17 recommendations for addressing the nine key findings of ABA.[42] They were all approved in the Kiruna Declaration by the AC Ministers, who also encouraged Arctic States to follow up on them.[43] Consequently, the Arctic Biodiversity Assessment team brought about a meticulous implementation plan for the ABA recommendations. Not only in this development CAFF has been searching for complementarities between ongoing works and new actions of the Arctic Council to address and implement ABA's

---

40 CAFF, *Arctic Biodiversity Assessment: Report for Policy Makers.* Conservation of Arctic Flora and Fauna (Akureyri, Iceland, 2013).

41 CAFF. *Life Linked to Ice: A Guide to Sea-ice Associated Biodiversity in this Time of Rapid Change.* Conservation of Arctic Flora and Fauna (Iceland, 2013).

42 Six headlines included: climate change; ecosystem-based management; mainstreaming biodiversity; identifying and safeguarding important areas for biodiversity; addressing individual stressors for biodiversity and improving knowledge and public awareness. CAFF. *Actions for Arctic Biodiversity, 2013–2021: Implementing the recommendations of the Arctic Biodiversity Assessment. Conservation of Arctic Flora and Fauna* (Akureyri, Iceland, 2015).

43 Arctic Council. *Kiruna Declaration, on the occasion of the Eighth Ministerial Meeting of the Arctic Council.* Arctic Council Secretariat(Kiruna, Sweden, May 15, 2013).

endorsements, but in an effort to ensure the input from a bigger and open group of stakeholders it organized in December 2014 the Arctic Biodiversity Congress – the largest gathering in the AC history with more than 450 participants – in Trondheim, Norway where scientific, indigenous, policy, NGO, academia, and industry audiences had the opportunity to discuss themes around ABA. The ABA implementation plan, *Actions for Biodiversity 2013–2021: implementing the recommendations of the Arctic Biodiversity Assessment*, which came as a result of these consultations and discussions among the AC Members, Permanent Participants, Working Groups, Task Forces and Observers was presented in the AC Ministerial Meeting in April 2015. For each of 17 ABA recommendations CAFF identified main gaps and needs, along with specific implementation options to address them. Whereas the ABA recommendations are directed to the Arctic Council as a whole, some recommendations are intended to be implemented through CAFF, while others are to be led in full, or in part, by other AC working groups and subsidiary bodies, and still some will require action by national authorities, stakeholders, and international organizations.[44] The eight-year implementation plan including those options is meant as a living document that will be reviewed and updated every two-years (from 2013 to 2021), corresponding to the cycle of rotation of the chairmanship of Arctic Council and CAFF – the right idea aiming to ensure smooth alignment of priorities, allocation of resources and reporting within the AC.

5.2 Arctic Human Development Report-II (ADHR-II)

The second Arctic Human Development Report (AHDR-II)[45] was published ten years after its predecessor. The Arctic Human Development Report (AHDR) in 2004 provided a first comprehensive overview of human development in the Arctic in terms of demographics, economy, culture, health and well-being, gender, legal and political issues. The ADHR-I had been considered a success as it established a baseline of knowledge on social matters in the region and contributed to the shift in the way how human development in the North was approached. The AHDR constituted one of the milestones in the evolution of Arctic cooperation from the AEPS's focus on environmental conservation to ever-increasing attention to questions of sustainable development,[46] and from the perception of the Arctic region as a "frozen desert"[47] and a wilderness

---

44   *See supra*, note 38.
45   Larsen and Fondahl, *supra*, note 7.
46   Koivurova and VanderZwaag, *supra*, note 12 at 151.
47   Koivurova (2010), *supra*, note 10.

towards the vision of the Arctic as a "region in change" and a homeland for indigenous and non-indigenous inhabitants.[48]

Like the ADHR-I, the AHDR-II was carried out under the auspices of the SDWG and initiated by the Stefansson Arctic Institute from Iceland. It was presented for endorsement to the AC in 2011, prepared by a group of 25 lead authors with a number of contributing experts, and eventually published in 2015 by the Nordic Council of Ministers. The latter also provided bulk of assessment funding. The volume focuses on changes, which took place since 2004 in social environments in the Arctic, to enable comparisons and identify major current and emerging trends in human development in the region. At least in principle, the AHDR-II had complemented well the emerging discussion on Arctic economic developments. The follow-up of the first AHDR, namely the process to develop tailored to regional specifics Arctic Social Indicators (ASI),[49] brings AHDR-related work closer to the global and regional assessment processes carried out by, *inter alia*, the United Nations Development Programme (UNDP).[50] However, AHDR, ASI, and AHDR-II are not linked directly to any larger international processes.

Arctic Human Development Report-II has a fair chance to build upon a success of the first AHDR as its focus on social dimension of developments in the Arctic is crucial within the Arctic Council's policy-shaping role in the region. The editors hope that "[a]s a second circumpolar assessment of human development and quality of life in the Arctic that identifies important and emerging issues relating to sustainable human development in the Arctic, the report provides a basis for the development of policies and actions to address these issues."[51] The high quality of the final product has been guaranteed by the participation of key Arctic experts. The draft chapters were externally peer-reviewed with a help of the International Arctic Science Committee (IASC).

---

48   The perception of "Arctic as a homeland" goes back some decades earlier, at the very least to 1977 Berger report *Northern Frontier, Northern Homeland*, in Canada.

49   Joan N. Larsen, Gail Fondahl, and Peter Schweitzer, *Arctic Social Indicators: A follow-up to the Arctic Human Development Report*, 2010, accessed March 15, 2016, http://norden .diva-portal.org/smash/record.jsf?pid=diva2%3A701571&dswid=-3421. The ASI were developed under the auspices of the SDWG and the Nordic Council of Ministers. The phase II of the ASI applied the developed framework of indicators to chosen case studies. *See* Arctic Social Indicators: ASI II: Implementation (TemaNord 2014): 568, Nordic Council of Ministers, accessed March 15, 2016, http://sdwg.org/wp-content/uploads/2015/02/ ASI-II.pdf.

50   *See* human development reports on UNDP website, accessed March 15, 2016, http://hdr.undp.org/en.

51   Larsen and Fondahl, *supra*, note 7, Preface at 13.

The AHDR-II is "an academic report" aiming to "help inform ... work [of the AC] and that of the SDWG in particular, in furthering sustainable development in the Arctic."[52] Whereas it clearly has a potential to deliver this goal, there are certain elements, which might have been addressed better throughout the process of preparing the report to enhance its resonance among wider public and while policy-makers and governments are mentioned as key audience,[53] design features that could increase assessment's influence over those groups – as identified in earlier sections of this article – appear not to have been addressed properly.

The stakeholder engagement was not particularly underlined, a shortcoming that was only partly mitigated by diverse authorship bringing together scholars from all Arctic states, including indigenous authors. The results of the project are available only in a form of academic report written in English, without any summaries translated into other languages (in particular, the lack of Russian version should be noted).

So far, no follow-up activities are scheduled, although actions connected to AHDR-II are proposed in the report, including dissemination via "well-targeted town hall meetings," production of dissemination materials targeting Arctic youth, the implementation of the Arctic Social Indicators monitoring system, as well as drafting an "AHDR-II science plan" addressing gaps in knowledge.[54] Perhaps most importantly from the perspective of the potential of AHDR-II to exert influence, several policy-relevant conclusions are proposed. These, significantly, include well-known in research community but largely absent from public discourse issues such as multidimensionality of the Arctic change (going beyond climate-induced changes), moderate view of economic developments, increasing role of urbanization processes, and Arctic governance innovations. These ideas have been reiterated in other assessments focused on social questions,[55] and highlighting them can be seen as yet another attempt to shift discussion (and ultimately, policy-making) in the Arctic from the

---

52 *Ibid.*

53 *Ibid.; see also* Arctic Human Development Report II: Regional Processes and Global Linkages (Proposal to SDWG),(2010, revised August 2011); Stefansson Arctic Institute, SAO Meeting(Lulea, November 2011); SAO Meeting Reports: Torshavn, October 2010; Copenhagen, March 2011; Lulea November 2011; Sustainable Development Working Group (SDWG).

54 The report identifies a number of knowledge gaps, including problems of youth and elderly, gender, food, water and energy security, Arctic urban development, as well as Arctic-global socio-economic linkages.

55 Stepien et al., *supra*, note 3; Ole R. Rasmussen, ed. *Megatrends* (TemaNord 2011): 527, Nordregio (Nordic Centre for Spatial Development) and Nordic Council of Ministers, 2011.

emphasis on strategic competition and large-scale economic developments towards human-centered development thinking. However, the AHDR has not produced clear and specific policy recommendations. There was no – typical for the Arctic Council – process of developing recommendations jointly by scientists and state officials (in the AC represented by SAOs and national representatives within the working groups).

The science-politics interaction proved to be particularly challenging for the AHDR-II process. The utmost care paid to scientific content of the report did not prevent representatives of some of the Arctic states to raise reservations with regard to certain chapters of the report. In their views, some parts and statements included in the ADHR-II – if endorsed by the Arctic Council – could have been interpreted as positions of the Arctic states to which there was no official consent. Eventually, to proceed with the project and preserve the scientific integrity of the report it was decided that the final volume was not officially endorsed by the Arctic Council, which instead "note[ed] the work done for the Arctic Council through the second Arctic Human Development Report."[56] This illustrates well the complexities of science-policy interface of which assessments are the major tools, and challenges, which should be overcome to enable better communication and long-term impact of assessment processes.

In sum, the AHDR-II takes up important but often overlooked socio-economic issues and trends and could be an important voice in debates on development in the Arctic, contributing to the way how policy-makers see the region. What supports the potential for influence of the AHDR-II is the methodology, which highlights key trends and changes since 2004 and links the assessment to the ASI process, time congruence with the ongoing multidimensional debate on Arctic development and with Canada's AC chairmanship that highlighted community development, and the credibility of highly-respected authors. However, the outreach capacity of the report to policy-makers is not convincing. Lack of straightforward recommendations and ambiguous link to the Arctic Council limits assessment's potential to reach policy-makers, and in particular those associated with the Council itself. Absence of broader stakeholder engagement adversely affects legitimacy of the assessment and positions it chiefly as an academic endeavour. Proposed dissemination actions, while interesting and potentially effective, have not been implemented. In fact, the dissemination has been so far limited to AHDR-II editors' presentations at various conferences. Overall, the potential of AHDR-II

---

56   Arctic Council. *Iqaluit Declaration on the occasion of the Ninth Ministerial Meeting of the Arctic Council*, Iqaluit, April 24, 2015, para. 19.

to influence discourses and policy-making is constrained, despite the very high quality of its final output (i.e. the report).

5.3   *Arctic Resilience Report/Arctic Resilience Assessment (ARR/ARA)*

The ARR/ARA[57] presents an interesting example of the Arctic Council's assessment conducted not by any of its working groups, but by the external institutions – the Stockholm Environment Institute and the Stockholm Resilience Center. The project came about as one of the priorities of Swedish chairmanship in the AC 2011–2013 term, and was initiated by the Swedish Ministry of the Environment in order to research and assess capacity and resilience of Arctic nature and communities in face of occurring and intensifying disturbances. Originally it was meant to be a part of AACA (see more below) but eventually, to speed up the process of its approval, it was taken out of this bigger scheme and accepted as a stand-alone project during the meeting of Senior Arctic Officials in November 2011.

Initially the ARR was to comprise of two phases, divided between two successive AC chairmanships, the Swedish and Canadian (2013–2015) chairmanships and the Arctic Resilience Interim Report[58] was delivered during the Ministerial meeting in May 2013. It received fairly good media coverage as it was mentioned among others in the New York Times and BBC pieces from the event, somewhat in contrast to final report of ABA that did not find its place in the mainstream media though was presented at the same meeting. In October 2014, the U.S. joined Sweden to co-chair the ARA, making strong engagement for resilience an important part of its own Arctic Council Chairmanship (2015–2017) program as well as trying to actively secure support for the resilience framework beyond 2017, into Finnish and Icelandic AC chairmanships. Coming outputs include a scientific assessment report in mid-2016, a synthesis for policy-makers in 2017 and a resilience-related contribution to the AACA.[59]

With regard to methodology, the Arctic Resilience Report project uses the integrative concept of resilience to contribute to systematic understanding of

---

57   The name has been changed from ARR to ARA during the course of the preparation of the scientific report of the project to be more reflective of the scope of effort as well as to signal the intention to continue work on the resilience framework into the future in some fashion.

58   Arctic Council (2013), *supra*, note 5.

59   *Arctic Resilience Report Trifold*, accessed March 25, 2016, http://arctic-council.org/arr/wp-content/uploads/2016/02/150603-Revision-of-Arctic-Resilience-leaflet-Final.pdf.

THE RECENT ARCTIC COUNCIL ASSESSMENTS   207

developments in the Arctic, including a very complex issue of the cumulative impacts of interacting drivers of change in the region. The applied conception describes the long-term capacity of a social-ecological system (SES) to deal with change and disturbance, and responding to and recovering from them in ways that maintain system's essential functions and identity. It offers not only the potential for integration of different kinds of knowledge, pivotal from the perspective of adaptation capacities of the Arctic SES, but also of various levels of governance where decisions on adaptation actions are taken. To its advantage, the ARR includes also a number of case studies, *inter alia*, on the reindeer herding in the Yamal Peninsula in Russia, coastal erosion and community relocation in Newtok, Alaska, and Skolt Sámi salmon finishing and restoration in the Näätämö River in Finland – to be further developed with the project. Those case studies allow not only for enhanced comprehension of the idea of resilience in practice, but provide a localized context that is very important as a realistic and applicable assessment that could be of use to its potential final users.

However, to this last point, of probable resonance and influence of the assessment, the ARR project so far has not aligned much with larger ongoing processes, has not included much stakeholder participation, and the materials produced up-to-now are primarily in English (with the notable exception of one part of the study on China's views on the Arctic, available both in English and Chinese) and available only in a form of report and online presentations. These deficiencies raise questions about the applicability and direct usefulness of the ARR to local and regional decision-makers in different parts of the Arctic, but as the project is still ongoing there is a chance to address those points. In addition, since the project is not a part of any regular process within AC, it was clearly undertaken upon the Swedish initiative and has been carried out by external institutions. However, there have been efforts to strengthen links between the ARR and AC working groups to ensure some institutional continuity of the project beyond its completion date. One example has been exploration by the ARR and the AACA teams of opportunities to coordinate outreach efforts to clarify and amplify key messages. The commonality between the two assessment processes, which allows for such concerted action, is that they both seek to move beyond identifying or describing the state of science related to specific characteristics of a given Arctic system and instead provide information how to address the impacts associated with rapidly changing Arctic. Their difference lies in the applied methodology, while the ARR "draws on a substantial set of recent case studies where major thresholds (or tipping points) are already apparent, in order to identify properties that make systems more resilient to both anticipated and unanticipated changes,"[60] the AACA examines adaptation opportunities based on projections well into the future.

6 Adaptation Actions for a Changing Arctic (AACA)

The AACA constitutes a major programme of the Arctic Council intended to provide more timely and focused information to guide actions and policies related to adaptation in the situation of rapid transformation of the Arctic.[61] The project is comprised of three phases. The first two included the overview of findings from other AC assessments as well as compendium of existing national, regional, and local adaptation efforts in the region and they formed the basis for the main phase of the project (AACA-C) which is run by the Arctic Monitoring and Assessment Programme (AMAP) and planned to be completed by 2017. In the AACA-C three regional case studies are carried out: in the Barents region, the Baffin Bay/ Davis Strait and in the Bering/Chukchi/ Beaufort Seas. They all represent integrated assessments where relevant environmental, social, cultural and economic dimensions are taken into account to inform the development and implementation of local-specific adaptation actions in various parts of the Arctic.

Concerning its targeted audience, AACA, like most others AC assessments, is prepared for the Arctic countries' officials gathering in the Arctic Council. However, its main users are defined as authorities of various levels as well as local and indigenous peoples. The chair of the AACA, Tom Armstrong stated that "[d]eveloping a comprehensive knowledge base of how the drivers of

---

60 *Adaptation and Resilience in the Arctic: A Primer on the Arctic Resilience Report and the Adaptation Actions for a Changing Arctic Report* distributed ahead of the Arctic Council Resilience Workshop organized in Fairbanks on March 14, 2016 during the Arctic Science Summit Week and ahead of the AC Senior Arctic Officials' meeting, where initial results from the meeting were reported.

61 *Adaptation Actions for a Changing Arctic*, Arctic Council, March 15, 2016, http://www .arctic-council.org/index.php/en/our-work2/8-news-and-events/346-adaptation-actions -for-a-changing-arctic-aaca; Adaptation of Actions for a Changing Arctic. DMM 02-15 May 2012-Stockholm, Sweden. Item 4, www.arctic-council.org; Shearer, Russel (AMAP Chair); Adaptation Actions for a Changing Arctic. Presentation at SAO Meeting, Haparanda, November 14, 2012, www.arctic-council.org; Adaptation Actions for a Changing Arctic (A), Draft Synthesis Report, 8 April 2013; Arctic Monitoring and Assessment Programme, Working Group Meeting Minutes, accessed March 15, 2016, www.amap.no: AMAP Report 2011: 3, Moscow, Russia, October 3–5, 2011; AMAP Report 2012: 2, Stockholm, Sweden, October 3–5, 2012; AMAP Report 2013: 2, Torshavn, Faroe Islands, September 16–18, 2013.

THE RECENT ARCTIC COUNCIL ASSESSMENTS 209

the rapidly changing Arctic interact will provide decision makers with the resources they need to respond to the challenges and prudently take advantage of opportunities."[62] Their engagement in the process constitutes a significant element of the AACA assessment work and their involvement as stakeholders is realized, among others, by workshops organized in each of the studied regions. Stakeholders are tasked, in principle, with defining key sectors of interest, issues, and questions, which they consider relevant and would like to see addressed by policy- and decision-makers. Consequently, such approach not only ensures focus on local specificities, but also enhances communication and a more open, two-way dialogue between scientists and assessment's end users. In contrast to AHDR-II, the broad stakeholder engagement makes it more likely that various social groups in the chosen assessment regions are aware of the AACA process and might take interest in its outcomes when they become available in 2017.

The project's team intends to deliver AACA results in various formats, including laymen's report, policy-makers report, press kits, and a film.

Even though at the time of completing this article, there is still one year until completion of the project (scheduled for 2017 Ministerial Meeting), the AACA is said to propose to the Arctic Council follow-up activities, which will relate to its key policy-relevant findings (as in the case of Arctic Biodiversity Assessment or Arctic Marine Shipping Assessment completed in 2009 and appraised for its follow-up practices).[63] One potential limitation is that the regional recommendations may take the format of policy-relevant key findings, somewhat softer than policy recommendations.[64]

As the project is still running, it is impossible to properly assess even its potential influence over future developments in the AC. However, already at this stage the assessment can be considered a cutting-edge in its efforts to bridge local adaptation planning with global level information on climate change and co-production of knowledge. The "general principles" adopted for AACA-C assessments[65] reflect the key factors for assessment's influence we identified above:

– The science report utilizes up-to-date science results from multiple disciplines;

62　*Adaptation Actions for a Changing Arctic*, Arctic Council, *supra*, note 61.

63　AMAP (October 1, 2013). Draft Implementation Plan. Version 1.1, Adaptation Actions for a Changing Arctic part C (AACA-C), accessed 20 November 2015, www.arctic-council.org.

64　*Ibid.*; also personal communication with one of the regional assessment leaders.

65　AMAP, *supra*, note 63, at 34.

- The analyses must utilize standardized approaches (methodologies must be defined)
- Multiple ways of knowing must be utilized (i.e., traditional and local knowledge, scientific information);
- Report in written in an acceptable style for non-specialists;
- Results and recommendations must be formulated and integrated so they address issues of regional (including decision makers) and stakeholder identified concerns and needs;
- Provides a synthesis of findings to inform possible adaptation options of use to decision-makers.

Nonetheless, the potential constraint on the AACA's influence as an assessment is the fact that its main aim is to capture the multidimensionality of Arctic change. Multiple drivers and three studied regions suggest that the final report will deliver a highly complex picture. Therefore, much depends on the way, how final report is formulated and how its key findings will be presented, reconciling the complexity of outcomes and the clarity of messages. Clarity and simplicity of message may be key to attracting attention and influencing the way of thinking of time-constraint and information-overloaded policymakers.

7 Conclusions

We have looked at four recent Arctic Council assessments to examine whether the way they are designed and produced enhance or inhibit their potential to influence policy-making. Our focus was mostly on the assessment process that led up to the final outcome (i.e. assessment report) as well as on (implemented or planned) forms of dissemination of collected information and follow-up activities. For this purpose, we drew upon the analytical framework developed in the literature on global environmental assessments that finds attributes of salience, legitimacy and credibility as determinants of effectiveness of assessments. These attributes bear upon the assessments' ability to change the beliefs of their participants or users; and, to induce change in the issue domain. Importantly, these three determinants are not factors that are objectively existent elements of any assessment. Instead, they are attributions made by assessment users. In order to enhance the effectiveness of an assessment, the aim of its designers and participants should be therefore to increase the number of users who view this assessment as salient, legitimate, and credible. They can promote these properties through choices they make with regard

THE RECENT ARCTIC COUNCIL ASSESSMENTS   211

to design of the assessment and its design features. For the purpose of this analysis the authors selected six of them: ownership of the process, level of fit and time congruence, identification of target audience, applied methodology, stakeholder participation, and follow-up activities. While the choice was necessarily partly arbitrary, these features offer some guidance in relation to the expected effectiveness of ABA, AHDR-II, ARA/ARR, and AACA in bridging science with decision-making in the Council and beyond.

Each of the analysed assessments has its specific characteristics. They are located under the auspices of different AC working groups and conducted through different institutional arrangements. The AMAP is a working group of the Arctic Council, which has the greatest experience in the conduct of scientific assessments. That allowed AMAP to develop own practices and learn through experience.[66] This learning process is visible for example in the way the AACA process has been designed and conducted, clearly in order to incorporate elements that increase the potential effectiveness of the assessment.

The assessments can influence both general policy-making of the Arctic states (represented in the AC by foreign affairs and sectoral ministries' officials) as well as further activities of the Arctic Council itself. Processes that are fully integrated into the AC structures are therefore more likely to make a difference. The AHDR-II and to some extent ARR (pre-2013 phase of the ARA entirely led by Swedish institutions) point to the limitations for assessments located outside of the Council structures, which in turn speak to the importance of the ownership of the assessment processes.

While assessments may sometimes exert more direct influence over decision-making, their potential to affect discourses and the issue framing should not be underestimated. For that reason, assessments like ARA and AHDR-II may prove to be the most influential over the long course of time through shaping public or policy discourses and through affecting indirectly policy processes, as the latter are hoped to incorporate more strongly the notions of resilience and Arctic human development, highlighted in ARA and AHDR respectively.

Analysed assessments generally meet high standards when it comes to the quality of the process; in terms of well-designed methodology, respected and diverse authorship, identification of target groups, and time congruence. However, two aspects appear more problematic: stakeholder participation and follow-up activities.

Stakeholder participation is currently often seen as an indispensable aspect of assessment work, but it is also a major challenge for those carrying out

---

66   Koivurova et al. (2015), *supra*, note 2.

assessments. Arctic Council projects typically include involvement (or at least invitation for) indigenous peoples' representatives. While in the Arctic context involvement of indigenous organizations is indispensable, currently it can be seen as insufficient to meet expectations for the desired broader stakeholder participation. For the AHDR-II, the *de facto* lack of stakeholder involvement (apart from case studies in one chapter) was a clear-cut shortcoming. In contrast, for AACA, stakeholder involvement is at the very core of the assessment and engaging stakeholders has proven so far relatively successful.[67]

Lack of clear and robust follow-up processes are likely to limit the long-term influence of the AHDR-II, while the process carried out after publication of the ABA in 2013 gives hope for the assessment to make imprint on policy-making. Next steps regarding the ARA still remain to be seen as at time of this writing the assessment's team concentrates its efforts not only on timely delivery of a scientific report, but also on ensuring the continued application of resilience framework in the work of the Arctic Council – beyond the project duration and perhaps in some combination with follow-up steps of the AACA.

In sum, assessments of the Arctic Council remain at the forefront of both regional and global efforts that aim to provide the best available and relevant knowledge to inform policy-making processes on the Arctic. Whereas different processes exhibit different individual characteristics, all the assessments analysed in this article rank from relatively high to very high in terms of design features that can enhance their salience, credibility, and legitimacy. However, once again, it should not be forgotten that those attributes are ascribed to assessments by their users – and hence it is important to increase the numbers of those who will find them salient, credible, and legitimate. In this respect, in the past, one of the main shortcomings of the Arctic Council assessment works was the fact that they remained relatively unknown to the audience outside of Arctic Council circles, both within the Arctic states and in the countries outside of the region. This fact should be addressed, particularly in light of a growing number of actors interested in Arctic developments and equipped in capacity to influence many Arctic-related issues. The problem of dissemination of results of assessment work carried out in the AC comes closely with the one of lack of monitoring of not only how the AC assessments are disseminated but also implemented at sub-national and national levels, and followed at the international ones.[68]

---

67   Personal communication, one of leaders of Barents regional assessment, March 2016.

68   For the interesting study of the World Bank on how its policy reports meet the stated objective of informing the public debate please *see* Doerte Doemeland and James Trevino, *Which World Bank reports are widely read?* Policy Research working paper,

This consequently brings us to the question of translating collected knowledge into action. Effective handling of this issue could be one of the main challenges ahead of the Arctic Council as the forum – according to some commentators[69] – turns from policy-shaping into more a policy-making kind of body. The interest in more action-oriented Arctic Council could be seen in increasing attention paid to the AC task forces which work on specific issues, within a given mandate and for a limited time, and from which two first of legally-binding agreements negotiated under the auspices of the AC came. Both agreements (and the third one, on scientific cooperation, currently under negotiation) gained a lot of coverage among observers of the Arctic affairs. That resulted in a debate concerning future directions of development of the Council, in terms of the possible matching of growing expectations on the AC and what the forum can actually deliver. However, this debate should not overshadow the bulk of work that has been going on in the Arctic Council that generates and constantly deepens our knowledge on the rapidly changing region. As shown in this article, the AC assessments provide very good examples of lessons learnt and best available practices in such endeavors. Acting upon and following-up the assessments' recommendations is nevertheless a different question. The appropriate addressing of qualities of salience, credibility, and legitimacy makes assessments more effective and usable as instruments of policy influence. However, the actual policy influence of these assessments depends first and foremost on the political will of those who order them and who wield decision-making power in the Arctic Council. Policy-makers have to make a political choice to act upon information aggregated and presented in AC assessments. The responsibility for making assessments matter lies therefore primarily with the eight Arctic states – both as regards future activities of the Council as well as the Arctic states' international, national and subnational decision-making.

WPS 6851 (Washington, DC: Worl Bank Group, 2014), accessed March 15, 2016, http://documents.worldbank.org/curated/en/2014/05/19456376/world-bank-reports-widely-read-world-bank-reports-widely-read.

69 Kankaanpää and Young, *supra*, note 12; Young, *supra*, note 19.

The Nordic Welfare State and the Development of Northern Finland

Matti Niemivuo[a] and Lotta Viikari[b]

Abstract

This article provides an overview of the legal regulation involved in building – and dismantling – the Nordic welfare state in Finland. Within this context this article details how legislative reforms have been reflected in the development of Northern Finland, as well as the effects on the Sámi population and a comparison between Nordic countries.

The Nordic welfare state was implemented in Finland primarily through parliamentary legislation. Human and fundamental rights played no role in the process of building the welfare state. The beginning of the 1990s marked the end of what had been massive build-up of the public sector. Over the last 20 years or so we have seen cutbacks in municipal services such as schools, healthcare centres, and social services.

The future of municipal government in Finland looks very different than it did when the welfare state was being created. We may well be facing a bleak future with weaker municipalities, fewer public services, less state funding for municipalities, less manoeuvring space in relation to the state, and more privatisations. Wise structural reforms might be the way ahead if we want to create functional regional and local governance and thus to guarantee the future of the Nordic welfare state in Finland.

Keywords

municipal government – Nordic countries – Northern Finland – regional policy – Sámi people – welfare state

---

a Professor Emeritus, Public Law, University of Lapland.
b Professor, Public International Law, University of Lapland.

1 Introduction

The five Nordic countries – Denmark, Finland, Iceland, Norway and Sweden – all built welfare states after the Second World War; while this work proceeded at somewhat different paces, the Nordic welfare state reached what may be considered its fruition at the beginning of the 1990s. In these countries, it is mainly the local government that is responsible for providing welfare services, key among these being education, health care, and social welfare. Government's tasks and obligations in the provision of such services are laid down in the law, and residents of municipalities are entitled by law to certain other services as well, such as libraries and other cultural services. Since the early 1990s, the number and scope of public services has been reduced through cuts in public spending. Economic considerations have figured in this development: the severe recession that began in the country in the early 1990s prompted cutbacks in services. Ideological factors have had a part to play as well. In every Nordic country, the parties in parliament who built the welfare state have lost support to parties whose platforms emphasize privatization and reductions in the public sector in general.

This article discusses the building and dismantling of the Finnish welfare state, looking at these processes from the perspective of legal regulation. The particular focus will be the core public welfare services. A second principal aim of this paper is to demonstrate how the welfare state has shaped conditions in northern and remote areas. Although we will be concentrating on the Finnish system, we will offer a comparative look at the systems of regional and local governments in the other Nordic countries that provide the core public services there.

In the next section, we proceed to define the key concept we draw on in our analysis: the Nordic welfare state. In sections 3 and 4, we take up the legislative reforms in Finland that have contributed to the building of the welfare state and those that have brought about its decline; in the process, we illustrate the trends to be seen in the focal legislation. In section 5, we go on to describe in some detail how the welfare state has affected the development of Northern Finland. Section 6 proceeds with a comparative look at regional and local government in the other Nordic countries. In closing, we present our principal conclusions and put forward an assessment of what developments the near future may hold.

2 What Is the Nordic Welfare State?

All five Nordic countries share common and distinguishing features regarding their legal and political systems. The reasons for the differences they exhibit lie in history and geography. Today, all of the Nordic countries have a government based on parliamentary democracy even though some (Denmark, Norway, and Sweden) are monarchies and some (Finland and Iceland) republics. Three of the countries are members of the EU – Denmark,[1] Sweden and Finland – but only the last is in the monetary union. Norway has rejected membership in the EU twice in referendums (1973 and 1995) but it belongs to the European Economic Area, as does Iceland.

It is difficult to define the Nordic welfare state, or even to characterize it in general terms.[2] Ongoing developments concerning multiculturalism, democracy, and the growing significance of human and fundamental rights in particular, considerably reshape the Nordic welfare state. With these considerations in mind, we have chosen to emphasize the following four features of the Nordic welfare state:

1. The formal and substantive characteristics of the *constitutional state* (rule of law) feature prominently;
2. *Democracy* is realized in the exercise of power and as a substantive principle at the level of state and municipal government;

---

1 The Faroe Island, which is a self-governing part of Denmark, is not part of the European Union, mainly because of its fishery policy. Greenland is an Overseas Countries and Territories (OCT) of the EU. Originally, Greenland joined the EC with Denmark in 1973, but it left the Community in 1985. Both the Faroe Islands and Greenland are self-governing territories of the Kingdom of Denmark.

2 In recent years the status of the welfare state in Finland, its problems, and future prospects have attracted the interest of growing numbers of decision makers and researchers. *See, e.g.,* Juho Saari, ed. *Tulevaisuuden voittajat – Hyvinvointivaltion mahdollisuudet Suomessa* [The Winners of the Future – the Prospects of the Welfare State in Finland] (Eduskunnan tulevaisuusvaliokunnan julkaisu 5/2010), accessed December 8, 2015, https://www.eduskunta.fi/FI/tietoaeduskunnasta/julkaisut/Documents/tuvj_5+2010.pdf; *see also* Juho Saari, ed. *Hyvinvointivaltio. Suomen mallia analysoimassa* [The Welfare State. Analyzing the Finnish Model] (Helsinki: Gaudeamus, 2009); Elina Aaltio, *Hyvinvoinnin uusi järjestys* [The Welfare's New Order] (Helsinki: Gaudeamus, 2013); and Juho Saari, *Huono-osaiset. Elämän edellytykset yhteiskunnan pohjalla* [The Poor. The Conditions for Life at the Bottom of Society] (Helsinki: Gaudeamus, 2015).

THE NORDIC WELFARE STATE & DEVELOPMENT OF NORTHERN FINLAND 217

3. *Government* takes principal responsibility, primarily through tax revenues, for providing social benefits and essential educational, social and health care services to the population; and

4. *International solidarity* plays a significant role in issues relating to immigration and refugee rights.

Elaborating on these features in turn, we would point out that the Nordic welfare state is fundamentally a *constitutional state*. Historically, the concept "constitutional state" (Rechtstaat) is fundamentally German in origin,[3] although it has a certain affinity with the familiar common law concepts "rule of law" and "due process of law."

In the Nordic countries, the concept of the constitutional state was long viewed in *formal terms*: the state derived its power from the legal order and it acted within the boundaries set by that order. Another essential element of the constitutional state was a functional system of legal protection, one grounded in an independent judiciary. The courts were complemented by a system of parliamentary ombudsmen.[4] A third basic pillar of the constitutional state was the desire and readiness of citizens to obey legal norms that they considered acceptable and reasonable.[5]

Gradually, in fact not until the 1990s, human and fundamental rights began to endow the concept of constitutional state with a *substantive content*. Traditionally, fundamental rights guaranteed individuals human dignity and protected citizens, primarily from actions taken by the state. Fundamental rights also formally guaranteed that individuals were equal before the law. Later on, a major change could be seen in demands that the implementation of equality was to result in actual equality.

Enshrining economic, social, and educational rights in the Constitution marked an essential change in Finland. These rights required affirmative measures on the part of the state: government now had to promote the realization of these rights. Fundamental rights were increasingly taken into account not only in legislation but also in government and the courts. At the same time,

---

3 *See* Kaarlo Tuori, "Oikeusvaltiokäsitteestä ja sen historiasta" [The Concept of the Constitutional State and its History], in *Oikeusvaltio ja hyvinvointivaltio* [The Constitutional State and the Welfare State], ed. Niklas Bruun (Helsinki: 1981), 6–23.

4 *See* Kirsi Kuusikko, *Oikeusasiamiesinstituutio* [The Institution of the Ombudsman] (Helsinki: Suomalaisen Lakimiesyhdistyksen julkaisuja E-sarja N:o 22, 2011). All the Nordic countries have a parliamentary ombudsman. Finland and Sweden also have chancellors of justice.

5 *See* Lars Erik Taxell, *Rätt – Individ – Samhälle* (Helsingfors: Föreningen Konstsamfundet publikationsserie v, 1989), 143–144.

attitudes towards international human rights instruments changed: the provisions in them began finding their way into decisions made in government and the courts. One could well speak of a change in Finnish legal culture.

The second distinctive feature of the Nordic welfare state that we would emphasize is *democracy*, which is realized in government on different levels: national, regional and local. Political power is based first and foremost on representative democracy, with this complemented to a certain extent by other forms of participation, such as national and local referendums. Decisions made by democratically elected bodies are based on the principle of majority rule: where the views of representatives elected by the people differ, the opinion of the majority prevails. Human and fundamental rights guarantee the minority certain inviolable rights that cannot be infringed by majority decisions even in times of crisis.

In the Nordic countries, democracy is more than a form of power. The countries emphasize that one of the functions of the state is to guarantee citizens the largest degree of equality possible. Accordingly, the state has become heavily involved, through legislation, in the country's economic system and other societal structures. Not surprisingly, the principal value informing the welfare state is equality, a value which can only be realized if the state has a strong presence. One particular dimension of this in the Nordic countries has been the promotion of equality between men and women in working life.

The third principal feature that merits consideration in analyzing the Nordic welfare state is the role of *government* as the body responsible for providing social benefits, as well as the central educational, social, and health care services for the entire population. Government here is understood as embracing not only the state but also municipal and provincial authorities. Municipal self-government is markedly strong in all of the Nordic countries. Among the functions of municipal government, health care in particular has been heavily outsourced to the private sector, but the state provides support even where private services are used.

The fourth characteristic of the Nordic welfare state that we would like to mention is the importance they give to *international solidarity*. This can be seen quite clearly in the form of tolerance in determining the position of refugees and immigrants. Considerable differences can be found between the Nordic countries on this issue, with Sweden bearing more of the burden than the others. All of these countries have seen mounting criticism of multiculturalism and this has figured as an issue in recent elections.[6]

---

6   The Nordic welfare state differs from other welfare states. *See e.g.*, Gösta Esping-Andersen, *The Three Worlds of Welfare Capitalism* (Princeton, New Jersey: Princeton University Press, 1991), 26–29.

THE NORDIC WELFARE STATE & DEVELOPMENT OF NORTHERN FINLAND

3   Legislative Reforms: Building the Finnish Welfare State

3.1   *Background Factors*

Finland changed rapidly after the Second World War, with a particularly drastic change in the country's economic structure. Agriculture and forestry declined in importance; industry grew but growth was comparatively slow; and the share of the service industries in the economy increased markedly. With the changes in the structure of the economy came a regrouping and redirection of economic resources. The cumulative effect of resources in particular regions, a trend that had started even before the wars, continued and even intensified. This resulted in a strong concentration of the population in urban areas (urbanization) and the formation of strong regional centers. The change in society was also reflected as uneven development among regions. In particular, the northern and eastern parts of the country did not enjoy the same level of economic development as the more industrialized south.

The period surrounding the Second World War had brought strong involvement by the state in virtually every aspect of life in society. The state continued to play a prominent role after the wars as well, a sign that Keynesian ideas had begun to gain ground in Finnish social thought, as they had elsewhere. Also of focal importance was the emphasis on economic growth and demands for a higher standard of living.[7] The importance of the national government in the regulation of different sectors of society grew with the development of national planning systems, such as country planning and the system of central hospitals.

After the Second World War, the greatest change that occurred in political life was the ascension of all political groups to the level of decision-makers. Here, the demands for equality found far more fertile ground than they had previously. The legislative reforms undertaken were the work of governments led by the Agrarian League/Centre Party and the Social Democrats. In addition, labor market organizations gained a strong position as means-based social insurance and social assistance took shape. When the country entered the 1980s, the era of short-lived governments was over: a single government now worked over the entire four-year electoral period, which ensured long-term legislative work.

3.2   *Changes in Legal Regulation and Legislative Drafting*

The state, its functions and legislation, have been closely interrelated. The traditional tasks of the state – public order and security, national defense,

---

7   The most important declaration of welfare policy in Finland was Pekka Kuusi's work, *60-luvun sosiaalipolitiikka* [Social Policy in the 1960s] (Helsinki: WSOY, 1961).

taxation, and the basic structures underlying the relationship between the state and its citizens – figured very prominently in Finland until as late as the 1950s and 1960s. It was only after this period that one began to hear the state described as a welfare state whose principal tasks were the provision of education, social welfare, and health care.

The regulation governing the traditional functions of the state in Finland was based on commands and prohibitions generally directed to citizens and communities. Government authorities then oversaw compliance with these orders. In the 1960s, alongside this traditional regulation, emerged the framework laws, development laws, planning laws and goal-setting laws. A common feature of all these types of acts is that they provided a loose structure for planning and development, and did not specify in detail how the societal goal in question was to be achieved.

All in all, laws changed their nature. In a sense, they contained less, but in a sense also more, than traditional laws. In the case of a framework law, the legislature contented itself with setting out the general bases of an activity rather than regulating it in fine detail, and gave authorization for determining the details through implementation provisions and administrative measures. One would not do justice to framework, development and planning laws if one described them merely as flexible. A second typical feature of such laws was that they were heavily programmatic. A law might well have set out clear substantive goals regarding the reform work to be done, perhaps even expressed in quantitative terms. A law might also have limited the means available, define the timetable, and created a monitoring system for the work involved.[8]

New forms of regulation were introduced alongside and to a certain extent in place of legislation.[9] Finland began using public-law agreements as well as a variety of relatively less formal arrangements between the government and different interest groups. The extensive statutory planning system, one spanning many different areas of government, acquired a significant status.

---

8 See Jaakko Nousiainen, Lainsäädäntöperustelut parlamentaarisen ohjauksen välineenä, Politiikka (1982), 6.

9 Driving this development was an effort to use softer means (soft law), which were employed extensively in international regulation. On the role of soft law in public international law, see e.g., Commitment and Compliance: The Role of Non-Binding Norms in the International Legal System, ed. Dinah Shelton (Oxford: Oxford University Press, 2003). This type of regulation was in use in other areas as well and took the form of various recommendations, guidelines, arrangements and negotiations. See the publication of the Legislative Drafting Department 5/1987: 92. In addition, the discussion of what is known as reflexive law addresses issues of soft law. See e.g., Günther Teubner, Reflexives Recht, Archiv für Rechts- und Sozialphilosophie (1982), 13–59.

Development meant that the state was no longer giving orders from on high but was also a party distributing resources, steering, and in some instances, negotiating and making agreements.

The regulation exercised by the government – despite the increase in welfare overall – was not perceived as positive. Criticism pointed to a variety concerns: the excessive growth in the number of statutes, the unanticipated and unwelcome impacts caused by the statutes, the vagueness of the regulation, the complexity and ambiguity of statutes, and the complexity of legal language as a whole.

The increase in legal regulation was strong: three times as many statutes were enacted in the 1970s as in the 1920s. The number of statutes adopted annually did not increase between the mid-1970s and the late 1980s, when it began rising again.

The statistics clearly show the increase in regulation that took place until the beginning of the 1990s, the period when one can consider the Finnish welfare state to have reached its full extent. The number of acts passed by Parliament had also increased steadily: in 1980 Parliament passed one-fourth of all statutes as acts and in 1990 one-third. Yet, the increase in regulation was not as dramatic as the figures taken alone might suggest. Some of the statutes contained no more than amendments to existing statutes and thus did not increase the number in force at the time or at least not significantly. Moreover, many statutes repealed existing ones and thus directly reduced the quantity of regulation on the books. What is more, a significant proportion of the statutes were

The Number of Statutes Published in the Statute Book of Finland in the Period 1920–1990.

Year	Statutes	Acts of Parliament	Percent of all statutes	No. of pages in Statute Book
1920	338	53	16	897
1930	410	79	19	1232
1940	826	158	19	1685
1950	680	127	19	1195
1960	558	140	25	1415
1970	917	255	27	1693
1980	1107	274	25	2404
1990	1394	463	33	2981

short, consisting of an amendment no more than several sections in length. Also worth noting is that a very small part of the statutes applied directly to everyone. Indeed, most of them pertained to government organizations and their activities.

Many reasons can be put forward as to why regulation increased. Developing the welfare state called for rules that brought together resources as well as rules governing how these resources were to be distributed. The changes brought about by science, technology, economics, and culture all occasioned a need for regulation. The underpinnings of the constitutional state, in particular the principle of legality in government, also required regulation. Likewise changes in the values and mores of society called for a change in legislation deemed outdated. Much regulation was enacted for symbolic purposes, that is, to convey a particular impression, with no intention of bringing about an actual change. Yet another factor driving the growth in regulation nationally was the increase in international cooperation, necessitating the implementation of international standards as well as the adoption of other types of new norms at the national level to facilitate such cooperation.

Adopting framework laws and similar flexible statutes led to an explosive increase in the issuance of norms by government authorities in the 1970s and 1980s. Particularly prolific in this regard were the central agencies, which issued very detailed orders and guidelines. In the 1980s, this came to be considered a serious shortcoming and, not surprisingly, led to a reassessment of administrative authorities' issuance of rules and regulations with no constitutional basis and to extensive efforts to repeal them.[10] This resulted in thousands of statutes being repealed that were deemed unnecessary. The situation became clearer and more stable with the adoption in 1989 of what was known as the Norms Act (786/1989). The law was in effect until the coming into force of the 2000 Constitution, which sets out the legal basis for norms laid down by government authorities (Constitution, § 80.2).

Until as late as the 1960s, legislative drafting in Finland was understood largely as the drafting of sections – also referred to as 'tinkering with sections' – and thus a task that naturally fell to lawyers. In practice the drafting of reform proposals began with the drafting of sections without deeper consideration of neither the aims of the reform in question nor the practical means to achieve it. In addition, precious little effort was put into anticipating the impacts of the new legislation.

---

10   For more detail, *see* Matti Niemivuo, *Hallintoviranomaisten norminanto* [Issuance of Norms by Administrative Authorities] (Rovaniemi: Lapin korkeakoulun julkaisuja, Sarja B:12, 1988).

THE NORDIC WELFARE STATE & DEVELOPMENT OF NORTHERN FINLAND 223

The beginning of the 1970s saw increased attention turned to the nature and societal significance of legislative drafting. In a break with the past, drafting gradually came to be seen fundamentally as sociopolitical planning. The task of drafters was to plan and prepare reforms that would then be implemented through legislation. No longer were drafters drawn exclusively from the ranks of lawyers; others were deemed qualified for the job provided they had the research and planning skills drafting required.

Two other considerations also figured significantly in legislative drafting. The first was the importance of academic research and of using it to advantage. The second was the emerging emphasis on the transparency of legislative drafting.

Furthermore, it was understood more clearly than before that legislative drafting was important in societal terms. With the essential structures and rules of conduct in society defined in legislation, how provisions were drafted became crucial. Previously, little or no attention had been paid to the rationale for bills in the government's legislative proposals. As a rule the rationales were short; even in the important government bills they were only a few pages long. More extensive rationales for bills, which also became more informative, had bearing on the use of legislative power in Parliament, because the improvements enhanced Parliament's opportunities to bring about real change in doing reform work. More detailed rationales were naturally important to those applying the legislation as well.

When the realization occurred that legislative drafting was work central to the development of society, special concern arose for drafting and how it could be improved. This was reflected in the issuance of guidelines for how to draft government bills and in the beginning of a training program in drafting in the mid-1970s.

Back in the 1960s, government ministries had rather limited staff and for this reason societally important reforms were generally prepared in multimember bodies: committees appointed by the government and by the ministries. The period when the welfare state was built was very much the golden age of committees – different sectors of government had numerous committees and they produced their proposals for reform in quite a timely manner.

3.3 *Principal Reforms of Public Services and their Impacts*

Reforms affecting education, health care and social welfare occupied center stage when the Finnish welfare state was being built. After the Second World War, the school system had to be developed apace to meet the needs of the large age groups at the time. The 1950s saw intensive construction of primary schools. This was then followed in the late 1950s and 1960s by a wave of school closures; hundreds of small village schools were shut in a change precipitated by the depopulation of rural regions and the concentration of population in urban areas. Where educational policy was concerned, the principal change came in 1968, when the Framework Act on Comprehensive-School Reform was enacted (467/1968). The government approved regional implementation plans for the reform in 1972. The reform meant increased equality in education, for all the children born in a given year were offered the opportunity to attend the nine-year comprehensive school.

In the area of health care, construction of hospitals received a boost in the 1950s with the enactment of the Planning Act for Central Hospitals (337/1950). The legislation on state aid at the time had created an imbalance in health care policy in the relative proportions of outpatient and residential services. The robust construction of hospital facilities, extensive even by international standards, resulted in the development of public health work and outpatient care in general lagging seriously behind. The Public Health Act, a frame-work law enacted in 1971, introduced planning systems that subsequently made it possible to correct the structural imbalance between basic and specialized care.

The impact of the new legislation was considerable. The number of staff at health care centers doubled in less than three years. The share of state health care expenditures for public health care work rose from 10 to 30 percent. In an additional development, the regional imbalance in the delivery of basic care had been corrected to a significant extent towards the end of the 1970s. Investments in health care and hiring of new staff were channeled to areas where the need for health care services was greatest.

A third crucial reform (in addition to the 1968 Framework Act on Comprehensive School Reform and the 1971 Public Health Act) took place in 1973 with the passage of the Children's Daycare Act (36/1973). The impact of the legislation was profound. In 1986, there were some 285,000 children in municipal daycare. Although many more women had begun working outside the home back in the 1960s, only one-fourth of mothers with children did so. Towards the beginning of the 1990s, 79 percent of mothers were already members of the workforce.

The regulation of children's daycare is based on the fact that guardians of children under school age have a subjective right either to a place in public day-care or to support when caring for children at home or arranging private daycare for them. The implication of the right is that a municipality cannot refuse to grant a child under school age a place in daycare, for example by appealing to a lack of funding. This is a real subjective right, which the children's

THE NORDIC WELFARE STATE & DEVELOPMENT OF NORTHERN FINLAND   225

guardians are able to effectively assert by initiating procedures for damages or lodging a complaint with the Parliamentary Ombudsman, for instance.

4   Legislative Reforms: Dismantling the Finnish Welfare State

4.1   *The Recession and State Budget Cuts*

A recession took Finland by surprise in the early years of the 1990s. When a new government was being formed after the 1991 parliamentary elections, no one had an inkling of the kind of recession, banking crisis, and record unemployment the country was headed towards. The recession was at its worst in 1993, with over half a million unemployed at a rate of 18 percent. It changed the way people thought: they felt there was no going back to the old welfare state. People also began to view things differently. One saw a whole new terminology at work.[11] There was talk of change, competitiveness, flexibility, technology, innovation, know-how, and incentive.

The response to the recession and the difficulties in financing government spending was to cut public expenditures. This was accomplished through what were known as the *austerity acts*, whose principal purpose was to curb government spending. Before 1992, the number of such laws was very small; their number and economic importance later grew substantially. The budget cuts carried out during the government of Prime Minister Esko Aho (1991–1995) primarily affected education and children's daycare. Efforts were made to cut unemployment benefits and job security but these failed due to opposition by the unions. The next government, led by Prime Minister Paavo Lipponen (1995–1999), brought cuts to benefits paid to individuals, such as student financial aid, child allowances, housing allowances, and support for home care. The minister of finance under both governments was Mr. Iiro Viinanen. Budget cuts were absolutely necessary in his view: between 1991 and 1999, austerity acts had cut government spending by some 55 billion marks, or 9 billion euros in today's money. No additional austerity acts proper were adopted in the 2000s – until the 2008 financial crisis hit, that is.

Cuts in government spending were made possible by the transition undertaken in the early 1990s to *normal parliamentarianism*, a change affected by removing from the Constitution the provisions making it possible to leave

---

11   Anu Kantola, *Markkinakuri ja managerivalta. Poliittinen hallinta Suomen 1990-luvun talouskriisissä* [Market discipline and managerial power. Political governance in Finland during the economic crisis of the 1990s] (Helsinki: Pallas-sarja, Lokikirjat, 2002).

ordinary laws in abeyance until the next Parliament is convoked. What this legislative institution entailed was that a vote by 67 of the 200 Members of Parliament could postpone the consideration of any law until after the next parliamentary elections and thus prevent, for example, passage of budget-related bills brought before Parliament by the government. Initially this change was carried out through a temporary constitutional amendment, but it became permanent six months later with the amendment to the Constitution that came into force on September 1, 1992.

The civil servant[12] who presented the legislative change to the Government assessed the impact of removing the abeyance provisions as follows: "[t]he almost total repeal of the abeyance provisions would make the parliamentary system clearer and more effective. With the support of a simple majority in Parliament being enough to bring ordinary laws into force immediately, a government that enjoys the confidence of Parliament could implement its political line in a consistent manner. In light of recent experiences, one crucial impact of the change would seem to be improved functioning of our decision-making machinery, for example during an economic recession. Approving the proposed change would also bring clarity to the division of political power and responsibility and might increase citizens' interest in politics."

Today, almost a quarter of a century since the 1990s transition to normal parliamentarianism, one can see problems as well in this reform. Needless to say, the old system gave 67 MPs too much power in allowing them to torpedo reforms proposed by the government. Yet, the system forced the government to negotiate with the Opposition on reforms in order to ensure they would be adopted. Then again, the change was perhaps not all that dramatic after all. Without it, adjusting government expenditures to the conditions prevailing during the recession would have undoubtedly been harder.

4.2 Changes in the Legal Culture

The state and legal regulation are very much intertwined. Gone is the day when the nation-state enjoyed sovereignty in the exercise of concentrated legislative power. The changes that had taken place were also reflected in Finnish legal regulation as the 1990s came to an end. The decade preceding the millennium meant radical and profound changes. These stemmed from international factors on the one hand, and national factors on the other. Of the former, perhaps the foremost in significance was Finland's accession to the Council of Europe and its European Convention on Human Rights. Accession was a

---

12   See Matti Niemivuo, *Kansallinen lainvalmistelu* [National Legislative Drafting] (Helsinki: Talentum, 2002), 143.

very painful experience for many Finns, who had considered their country a model constitutional state. Before Finland could accede to the Convention, its domestic legislation had to be amended in many respects.[13] Accession to the Council of Europe meant substantial changes in jurisdiction and in attitudes towards state sovereignty.

Accession to the Human Rights Convention also prompted a reform of fundamental rights, an undertaking which had been on ice for years. At the beginning of August 1995, a new, modern catalogue of fundamental rights was brought into force as a partial reform of the Constitution. This catalogue and related provisions were then incorporated virtually as such (only titles were added) into the 2000 Constitution as its Chapter 2. In terms of substance, the fundamental rights covers the obligations imposed by the Human Rights Convention; what is more, the chapter contains provisions whose enactment was prompted by domestic considerations, such as educational and social rights (§16–19), the environment (§20), and good administration (§21).

The point of departure for the constitutional provisions on fundamental rights is the principle, enshrined in section 1, subsection 2 of the Constitution, of the inviolability of human dignity and the freedom and rights of the individual. The provision has a clear connection with the European Human Rights Convention and other human rights conventions. Both the cited provision in the Finnish Constitution and the human rights conventions refer to protection of the same human being from infringements of his or her human rights.

A more profound impact on legal regulation, however, was brought about by European integration. Accession to the European Economic Area (EEA) constituted an intermediate stage in the process of Finland becoming a full member of the European Union. The EEA Agreement required an enormous amount of legislative work: several hundred laws had to be amended and this had to be done fast. The Finnish constitutional system had to be amended twice as well; the most salient changes were those pertaining to how the Parliament participated in the consideration of integration-related affairs.

Accession to the European Union had numerous indirect consequences for Finland, ones which above all affected financial basis of the welfare state. Accession to the European Monetary Union (EMU), as well as the Stability and Growth Pact, markedly constrained the choices available in domestic economic policy. In addition, the increasingly international character of the economy – globalization – had changed the conditions under which companies operated and limited what could be done under national economic and financial policy.

---

13   *See* Matti Pellonpää – Monica Gullans – Pasi Pölönen – Antti Tapanila, *Euroopan ihmisoi-keussopimus* [Convention on Human Rights] (Helsinki: Talentum, 2012), 6–8, 60–63.

Doubtless the effects of Finland joining the EU were also felt on the ideological level. Indeed, membership was invoked as one argument for privatizing what had been public provision of services. These factors left less and less scope for independent decision making when efforts were made to reform the Nordic welfare state, which first and foremost had been a national project.[14]

4.3 Changes in Legislative Work

The 2000 Constitution gave the Finnish government a strong role in leading work on legislation. It further clarified the procedure for bringing international agreements into force. The procedure specified that the most important international agreements were to be brought before Parliament for consideration in the form of a government legislative proposal. The partial reform of the Constitution in 2012 strengthened the exercise of legislative power vis-à-vis the President of the Republic.[15]

As Finland entered the 2000s, legal regulation in the country had changed considerably. At least the following features could be distinguished:

- an increase in international regulation or in domestic regulation prompted by international regulation;
- more frequent codification of legislation;
- an increase in regulation at the level of acts of Parliament, a trend prompted by, among other things, the reform of fundamental rights and of the authority to issue decrees; and
- discontinuation of detailed regulation in, among other contexts, guidance for municipal government.

Legislative drafting had changed fundamentally. Extensive social policy reforms were no longer prepared by committees; rather, responsibility for this work was given to working groups led by civil servants. Sound legislative drafting, once considered a value in its own right, fell into decline, although at the same time effort was invested in developing drafting and training for drafters.

---

14 For more detail, *see* Kaarlo Tuori – Toomas Kotkas, *Sosiaalioikeus* [Social Law] (Helsinki: WSOYpro, 2008), 101–109.

15 *See* KM (Committee Report) 9/2010 and HE (Government Bill) 60/2010 vp.

THE NORDIC WELFARE STATE & DEVELOPMENT OF NORTHERN FINLAND   229

5   The Welfare State and Northern Finland

5.1   *Regional Policy*

After the Lapland War (1944–1945), Northern Finland lay in ruins. The people gradually returned home and rebuilding of the province began. In 1952, Urho Kekkonen, who was to become the country's longest-serving president (1956–1981), published a book titled "Does our country have the patience to prosper?", in which he put forward a detailed program of development for the northern part of the country.[16] Responsibility for the plan would lie primarily with the state. Prior to the end of the 1950s, support measures by the state such as loans to small industry, state loan guarantees and employment loans – had lacked focus and coordination.

The late 1950s marked the beginning of what might be considered a conscious *regional policy* in Finland.[17] One concrete sign of the effort was the Tax Abatement Act (190/1958) adopted in 1958, which provided a variety of tax abatements designed to revive the economy in the two northernmost provinces of Finland: the provinces of Lapland and Oulu. At that same time, considerations of regional policy prompted the state to locate enterprises in Northern Finland rather than in the southern part of the country. A similar decentralization occurred in higher education, with the University of Oulu opening its doors in the late 1950s.

Trends in domestic migration led to depopulation of undeveloped areas on the one hand and congestion in population centers on the other. In order to check this undesirable development in the northern and eastern parts of the country, the first laws on undeveloped regions were enacted, designed to cover the period 1966–1970. The Framework Act to promote economic development in undeveloped areas (243/1966) laid down provisions on the goals, means and territorial divisions that would guide regional policy and on the principles to be followed in planning and development. The concrete support measures, ranging from tax abatements and investment credits, were set out in two other laws.[18] Despite the new legislation, uneven regional development continued in the 1960s, and even intensified. The next body of regional policy legislation, enacted for the period 1970–1975, also failed to stop undesirable trends. People working in agriculture and forestry, particularly in northern and eastern

---

16   Urho Kekkonen, *Onko maallamme malttia vaurastua?* (Helsinki: Otava, 1952), 97 ff.

17   Initially it was called "policy for developing regions".

18   Act concerning tax abatements for industries in undeveloped areas (244/1966) and Act concerning investment credits for industries and certain other livelihoods in undeveloped areas (246/1966).

Finland, found themselves forced to move to the South faster than industry and services there could employ them. At the same time, migration abroad, to Sweden in particular, took on worrisome proportions. The seriousness of the situation prompted the establishment in 1972 of a Regional Policy Department at the Office of the Prime Minister to improve the effectiveness and coordinate the planning of regional policy.

A third series of laws was passed to cover the years 1976–1979, this time after heated debate in Parliament. The laws defined the object of regional policy to be the entire country, not just the undeveloped regions. The laws were subsequently extended, remaining in force until the end 1981. The new regional policy laws adopted for the period 1982–1989 sought to promote a balanced welfare state. The idea embraced at the time was that not all regions had to be alike. It was no longer necessary to develop all regions using the same formula, for they had different needs and faced different challenges. In 1984, responsibility for regional policy was transferred to the Ministry of the Interior.

The most profound reforms of legislation on regional policy were to be seen in the laws adopted for the periods 1989–1993 and 1994–2002. These laws were built on program-based regional policy, and subsequent legislation: the sets of reformed regional policy laws adopted in 2002, 2006 and 2009 which had here to the same approach. Following Finland's accession to the European Union (EU), the EU began to set the pace of regional policy in the country, which brought a radical change in how things were done in Finnish society. For example, one no longer heard discussion of industry in Northern Finland. Nor was there any defense of the welfare society in any genuine sense. What began to occur was an extensive series of programs and special programs designed for particular regions, focusing on particular problems and being run by civil servants. Complementing government civil servants as partners, were actors including the EU, municipalities, businesses, civic organizations, and citizens. The work of the programs was steered through EU funding, with the state required to contribute matching funds to the activities.

The regional development that ensued was not what was hoped for. Northern Finland, for example, has lost thousands of jobs to the South. In fact, given that the new regional policy has made previously strong regions even stronger, the direction of development has been backward. The idea was to lessen not increase the differences in degree of development between regions. A largely market-driven regional policy has led to prosperous regions becoming even more prosperous.

Regional policy in a broad sense can boast many other decisions that have favorably affected public services and government in Northern Finland. When the welfare state was under construction, one important policy decision was to

THE NORDIC WELFARE STATE & DEVELOPMENT OF NORTHERN FINLAND   231

begin the comprehensive school reform in Lapland, from where it proceeded in stages to other parts of the country. Another favorable development was the founding, in 1979, of the University of Lapland in Rovaniemi. That same year saw the establishment of the Rovaniemi Court of Appeal, which from the very outset has worked closely with the Faculty of Law at the University. Other sectors of government as well ended up being amply represented in the capital of the province.

Northern Finland was spared when provincial government was downsized in 1997: where this level of government was reduced by half elsewhere in the country, the provinces of Oulu and Lapland retained their governments. In a similar vein, the comprehensive reform of regional government that took place at the beginning of 2010 made Rovaniemi the seat of new authorities, the Regional State Administrative Agency and the regional Centre for Economic Development, Transport and the Environment.

Later years brought some negative developments. In 2014, the Rovaniemi Administrative Court was discontinued. In addition, reorganization of the police administration reduced the number of police stations and other law enforcement resources available in Lapland.

Notwithstanding the recent developments, the goal that should be embraced in developing Northern Finland is to narrow the differences between it and other regions. The need to reduce inequality is also made amply clear in the report of the Organisation for Economic Co-operation and Development (OECD) on Finland:

> Disparities have also been increasing across regions, particularly in labour market outcomes. This reflects the dramatic structural change that has occurred since the early 1990s, and the lack of policy success in tackling this transition. These growing disparities in regional labour market outcomes have contributed to serious demographic imbalances building up in the regions. These are especially prevalent in the smaller municipalities and challenge the very sustainability of these entities.[19]

The government of Prime Minister Jyrki Katainen (2011–2014) expressed the view in its statements that Finland as a whole is an Arctic country.[20] Other

---

19   *See* OECD Economic Surveys: Finland 2010, Vol. 2010/4: 105, 106–120.

20   Accordingly, pursuant to *Finland's Strategy for the Arctic Region 2013* (Government resolution on 23 August 2013, Prime Minister's Office Publications 16/2013), 7, 17: "Underlying the review of Finland's Strategy for the Arctic Region is ... a growing perception of the whole of Finland as an Arctic country"; "Finland as a whole is a truly Arctic country."

positive steps that can be cited are the formulation of a new development plan for Eastern and Northern Finland, the tentative policy recommendations of a working group appointed by the Ministry of Employment and the Economy,[21] and group's final report, titled "Looking North," completed in January 2013.[22] The development program is an important document for Northern Finland. A second significant one is the Lapland provincial plan for 2030, "Lapland as the North's creative success story," approved by the Regional Council of Lapland in November 2009. The plan sets out the long-term goals for developing Lapland as well as the strategy for achieving the goals.

5.2   Municipal Reform and the Sámi

One important issue that will bear on the structures of government in Northern Finland is the outcome of the pending reform of municipalities, an effect of which will be to redraw municipal borders. At present there are over 300 municipalities in the country, but plans call for reducing the number in particular and substantially; Northern Finland will be no exception. Over the last decade, the number of municipalities has declined by over a hundred. The trend has affected Lapland as well, where a significant merger of the city of Rovaniemi (the administrative capital of Lapland) and the Rural Municipality of Rovaniemi took place in 2006.

The previous governments (2011–2015) sought to continue the reform, the principal impetus for doing so being economic considerations rather than the furthering of self-government. The rhetoric heard as part of the effort stressed concepts such as cost effectiveness, productivity, competitiveness, and market-drivers.

The efforts to redraw municipal borders have not given due consideration to the special conditions in Northern Finland. Sheer size, long distances, a harsh climate and sparse population are factors which distinguish the municipalities in Lapland from those elsewhere in the country.

One particularly problematic issue is how the municipal reform will affect the status of the Sámi, the EU only indigenous people. For the municipalities in the Sámi homeland region – Enontekiö, Utsjoki, Inari and Sodankylä – the potential that a new, larger municipality would have to offer services would be weakened due to the long distances involved. Larger municipalities would also in many cases weaken the resulting municipalities' economies and sustainability. Changes in the present municipal borders and the development of services should be based on elements relevant for the municipality in

---

21   Background memorandum of the "Looking North" policy recommendations.
22   Reports of the Ministry of Employment and the Economy 2/2013.

THE NORDIC WELFARE STATE & DEVELOPMENT OF NORTHERN FINLAND 233

question. Particularly at risk is the municipality of Utsjoki, which does not have the capacity to develop into a strong and vital municipality if its borders are redrawn. What the municipal reform would be well advised to do is to examine an alternative whereby the municipalities' in Lapland would work with their neighbors on the Norwegian side of the border. Such cooperation has long historical traditions in the areas of business, public services and culture. Having a common Sámi language has also done much to enhance contacts across the border.

The government formed in Finland after the 2015 parliamentary elections has promised in its program "to promote voluntary mergers of municipalities" and to repeal the legislative measures enacted under the previous government regarding the number and size of municipalities. In practice, this most likely means that no dramatic changes will take place in Lapland where municipal boundaries are concerned.

The position of the Sámi is otherwise difficult in Finland, where the ratification of the ILO 169 Convention has been in progress almost 25 years. In 2014, despite dissenting opinions on ratification[23], the Government submitted the Convention to Parliament for ratification after it had reached a compromise on the definition of the Sámi.[24] In March 2015, legislative proceedings on the matter were interrupted, because the Parliament was not willing to accept the new definition of the Sámi. It is possible, but not very likely, that Prime Minister Sipilä's government will continue consideration of the matter.

The Nordic Sámi Convention project received a boost in November 2010 when the Nordic ministers in charge of Sámi affairs and the Sámi parliamentary chairpersons agreed on the establishment of a negotiating delegation for the purpose of preparing a Nordic Sámi Convention. The work itself was initially launched in the spring of 2011. The expert working group's 2005 report notes that the goal of the Nordic Sámi Convention is to improve the position of the Sámi as an indigenous people as well as strengthen and consolidate Sámi rights.[25] The purpose is to bring the discussions to a close in 2016.

---

23 *See Oikeusministeriön mietintöjä ja lausuntoja* [Reports and statements of the Ministry of Justice] 40/2014. For example, the Sámi Parliament regards ratification as important. In its opinion, the ratification nevertheless requires clarifications and legislative amendments, in particular, with respect to Sámi land rights.

24 Government Proposal 264/2014. According to the government program approved in 2014 by Prime Minister Alexander Stubb's government, "ILO convention 169 shall be ratified during the autumn on condition that mutual understanding is achieved within the government on the Sámi definition."

25 On the Nordic Sámi Convention in more detail, *see, e.g.*, Niemivuo Matti, "Human and Fundamental Rights of the Sámi," in *The Yearbook of Polar Law* 7 (2015): 290–316.

Undoubtedly, the most difficult question in Finland is the Sámi people's relationship with lands and waters.[26] The Finnish Government has very much to learn from other countries – like from Norway – how indigenous property right question could be solved. Another good example is the Territory of Nunavut established in 1999 in Canada.[27]

6 Comparison of Governmental Structures: Regional and Local Government in the Other Nordic Countries

6.1 A Nordic Model?

In recent decades, regional and local government in the Nordic countries has been the target of a veritable flurry of reform. The reforms to be seen have generally had their origin in national considerations and in legal instruments of the Council of Europe. Undoubtedly, one common denominator that can be found in the reforms is a transition from a legalistic system to a market-oriented one, in the neoliberalist spirit, which the EU and EEA have brought with them.

One often hears talk of "the Nordic model". This is primarily a reference to the fact that the Nordic countries have strong municipal self-government if

---

26 See *The Proposed Nordic Saami Convention. National and International Dimensions of Indigenous Property Rights*, ed. Nigel Bankes and Timo Koivurova (Oxford and Portland, Oregon: Hart Publishing, 2013). The Finnish Government accepted a proposal for a new Act on Metsähallitus (Finnish Forest and Park Service) on December 3, 2015. The legislative proposal encountered fierce criticism for several reasons, including the fact that the Sámi homeland region was not given any role in the proposal. For instance, there were no references to even recognition, let alone protection of the rights of the Sámi to practice traditional indigenous land uses, such as reindeer herding. The Parliament of Finland accepted the Act (234/2016) on Metsähallitus which entered into force on April 15, 2016.

27 See *e.g.*, André Légaré, "Canada's Experiment with Aboriginal Self-Determination in Nunavut: From Vision to Illusion," in *International Journal on Minority and Group Rights* 15 (2008): 335–367. Despite the somewhat pessimistic assessment by Légaré, Nunavut may well have a bright future. A positive pointer to this is the population growth in Nunavut, being twice as much as elsewhere in Canada. The mere establishment of the territory of Nunavut marks a historic moment in the relationship between governments and indigenous peoples worldwide as it is the first time that an indigenous population forming a minority in a sovereign state forms a standard governmental entity (a territory, in this case) in a modern Western state. *See* Laurence C. Smith, *Uusi Pohjoinen – Maailma vuonna 2050* [*The World in 2050: Four Forces Shaping Civilization's Northern Future*], trans. Tuukka Perhoniemi (Helsinki: URSA, 2011), 251–253.

THE NORDIC WELFARE STATE & DEVELOPMENT OF NORTHERN FINLAND   235

compared to other states in Europe.[28] The municipalities in the region tend
to be rather large but one nevertheless sees variation within and between
the countries. It is in the structure of regional government in particular that
we find differences between them. Iceland has none at all. And Finland has
no regional self-government in the proper sense of the word; in its place we see
regional confederations of municipalities.

In what follows we will examine the systems of regional and local self-
government in Sweden, Norway and Denmark. Iceland has been left out of the
review, for it differs significantly from the other countries in this regard.

6.2   *Sweden*

One can see the beginnings of a welfare state in Sweden in the 1930s, but it was
not until the decades after the Second World War that the real breakthrough
in its development appeared. The system gives extensive responsibility for
people's welfare to the public sector, which then does its best to even out disparities in welfare among them. Citizens' confidence in the system, as well as
the high tax rate required to maintain it, remained robust well into the 2000s.
Later in the decade, after a centre-right alliance came into power, pressures
have increased to lower taxes and privatize public services. The present government, led by Social Democrats, has had to focus much of its attention on
the country's immigration policy, which traditionally has been very tolerant.

On the regional level, the Swedish system of government includes state
(national) and municipal bodies. The state is represented by county governments, in an arrangement that boasts a long history. Today Sweden is divided
into 21 counties, each of which has a government that answers directly to the
state. County governments are general administrative authorities with a broad
spectrum of responsibilities ranging from general elections to environmental
protection.

Municipal self-government is one of the pillars of the state as it is understood in Sweden. Sweden has municipalities on both the regional and local
levels. The status of these entities was consolidated through an amendment to
the Constitution that came into effect in 2011.[29] The government justified the
change on the grounds that municipal self-government forms a crucial component of the country's democratic system.[30]

---

28   *See Local and Regional Democracy in Europe*, ed. John Loughlin, Frank Hendriks, and
Anders Lidström (Oxford: Oxford University Press, 2011).

29   *See, e.g.*, Joakim Nergelius, *Svensk statsrätt*, 3. uppl. (Studentlitteratur 2014), 341–359.

30   Prop. 2009/10, 208.

In short, Sweden has a two-tier system of municipal government. On the local level, the country is divided into 290 municipalities; on the regional level it comprises 20 counties.[31] The municipalities of Gotland, Malmö, and Gothenburg fall outside the division of the country into counties and handle the responsibilities of basic municipalities as well as counties. The population of the counties varies between 130,000 and 1,500,000 inhabitants.

Like basic municipalities, counties have general authority: they may take on and carry out tasks which have not been assigned to other authorities in special acts. The maneuvering room available to self-government is nevertheless relatively limited because the county authorities must carry out demanding statutory duties prescribed in special legislation. The counties' principal responsibility is health care, which covers both hospital care and basic public health care. They are also responsible for the provision of public transportation.[32]

Counties' public expenditures are covered from the same sources as those of the basic municipalities. The principal source of revenue is county and municipal taxes. Other sources include state aid, payments received through the Swedish Social Insurance Agency, fees, and loans.

In 2007, a committee suggested in its report[33] that the present counties should be replaced by between six and nine regions. These would have councils chosen in direct elections and would handle the present responsibilities of the counties, in particular health care. They would also take care of tasks relating to regional development. Furthermore, the regions would have the right to levy taxes. There has been extensive debate on these reforms for years but little or no progress has been made to date.

6.3   *Norway*

Norway has two-tiered municipal government comprising 19 counties and 429 municipalities. The capital, Oslo, plays a dual role: as both a county and a municipality. One striking feature of the Norwegian system is the large number of small municipalities, with 55 percent having fewer than 5,000 inhabitants.

---

31   Of the counties, Skåne, Halland and Västra Götaland are counties in a legal sense. However, they also have the right to use the designation "region" as they have more responsibility for regional development than the other counties do.

32   *See* Matti Niemivuo, Aluehallinto ja aluepoliittinen lainsäädäntö [Regional Government and Regulation of Regional Policy] (Vantaa: Lakimiesliiton Kustannus, 2013), 207–208.

33   Ansvarskommittén, SOU (Statens Offentliga Utredningar, Swedish Government Official Reports) 2007: 10.

THE NORDIC WELFARE STATE & DEVELOPMENT OF NORTHERN FINLAND   237

On the other hand, three-fourths of the country's population lives in its three largest cities (Oslo, Bergen, and Trondheim).

At various times, Norway, like the other Nordic countries, has seen its share of debate on the size of municipalities and counties. Attempts at reform of the communal system were made in 1995 and 2005, but at the end of the day nothing came of them.

Both municipalities and counties have similar organizational structures. The highest decision-making body is an elected council. The preparation of matters and implementation of decisions is the responsibility of an executive board. County and municipal elections are held at the same time every four years. The voter turnout in Norwegian elections had traditionally been quite high; nevertheless, it dropped to 62 percent in 1995. The same downward trend continued in the two subsequent elections. In an effort to strengthen democracy, reports were commissioned and issues were debated in public, even on the level of the Stortinget (the Norwegian Parliament). In the 2011 elections, a number of municipalities experimented with lowering the voting age to 16 years and with utilizing electronic voting.[34]

Division of responsibilities between state and municipalities and counties is set out in special legislation. In Norway hospitals and specialized medical care are assured/provided by the state. The counties have duties relating to secondary education, land use planning, and regional development. The other welfare-related tasks are handled by the municipalities.

Norway can well be described as a decentralized state. Particularly in the period between 1970 and 1990, public tasks were steadily transferred to municipal government. Thereafter the direction changed. Quite a few tasks were transferred back to the state or to semi-public organizations. The counties in particular lost a considerable number of the responsibilities they had been given. The first to go were those relating to economic development. Later, in 2002, they lost to the state what had been their most important responsibility – hospitals and specialized medical care. The only change running counter to the trend was one carried out in 2010 in which maintenance of national roads was made a responsibility of the counties.

Discussion of the division of responsibilities between central government and county and municipal government sharply divides opinions. There are those who speak out in favor or the system of self-government on the grounds that residents' needs can best be taken into account regionally and locally.

---

34   Ks. NOU (Official Norwegian Reports) 2005:6, NOU 2006:7 and St. meld. nr. 33 (2007–2008).

Others advocate an expanded model giving the state more control, because it better guarantees equality among the populace.[35]

6.4 Denmark

Denmark implemented a radical reform of regional and local government in 2007. In the first phase, 271 municipalities were combined into 98, which meant their size increased by one-third. The second phase was to change the country's 14 counties into 5 new regions. The population of the regions varies considerably – from 600,000 to 1,600,000 (the capital region). Copenhagen became part of the capital region and this part came to form one of the new municipalities.

The reform brought with it a sizeable change in the division of responsibilities. What had been the tasks of the former counties – with the exception of health care – were divided between central government and the new municipalities. The change was also radical where financing was concerned: the new counties no longer had the right to levy taxes. In contrast, the new municipalities were still allowed to tax residents but, at the same time, a system of fiscal equalization was introduced to balance out economic disparities between municipalities.

The municipalities are run by an organization consisting of a council of between 9 and 31 members, a number of committees and a municipal manager. The organization of government on the regional level differs substantially from the municipal model. The highest decision-making body is the county council, which has 41 members. Counties also have a regional chairperson, whose task is comparable to that of a municipal manager. Regions do not have a system of committees, however. They may have an executive committee but, unlike municipalities, may not establish sectoral committees.

The principal task of regions is the maintenance of hospitals and basic health care. In addition they have coordinating tasks in regional development. Regions finance their work primarily through the various forms of assistance that they receive from the state and the municipalities. Another crucial source of revenue is the fees which municipalities pay for the use of regional hospitals and social institutions. Regions and municipalities have to make agreements in order to coordinate activities; these agreements are political, not legal, in nature.

The reform has left the new regions rather weak entities. Earlier counties had a general authority: they could take on and handle a task if this was not expressly prohibited by law. New counties do not have this authority, but

---

35   See Niemivuo, *supra*, note 34 at 209–211.

THE NORDIC WELFARE STATE & DEVELOPMENT OF NORTHERN FINLAND   239

rather may only handle tasks expressly assigned to them in the law. These are restricted to basic health care and specialized hospital care.

The structure of political decision making is also modest, with a region having only a council and an executive committee. This being said, the chair of the region has a strong position, given that he or she is the only full-time regional politician.

The regions have severely limited independence. They no longer have the right to levy taxes, which makes them dependent on central government and the contributions they receive from their constituent municipalities. Another consideration is that there is no longer any linkage between decision-making authority and fiscal responsibility.[36]

On balance, with the narrow scope of the responsibilities and authority now given them, the new regions are vulnerable and face an uncertain future.

7   Conclusions and Prospects for the Future

Law as we see it today has become not only more societally driven and more of a means than an end, but also increasingly European and global in nature. A look at virtually any sector of social policy makes these changes evident. We have a constant need for new regulation that will enable us to control new problems in society. At the same time, however, we have to invest effort in repealing old and unnecessary regulation in like measure so that the body of regulation on the books does not end up being unmanageable and thus too heavy a burden for people, authorities and business. Yet, we cannot concur with the views being put forward in many quarters in Finland which claim that solely by repealing legal norms – everyone pitching in to get rid of unneeded norms – we will find ourselves in an improved society. This has been made one of most important projects in Government Programme of Prime Minister Juha Sipilä, which came to power after the 2015 parliamentary elections. Legal norms can be found in many sectors – working life and consumer protection to name two – where they are designed to provide security for the weaker party. There seems to be a great deal of wisdom in the words of former Minister of Justice Christoffer Taxell, who said, "We have too many laws on the books, but yet not enough."

Our government has set out to balance the state budget by *cutting back public services*. The measures it has proposed are strongly reminiscent of those taken during the recession in the 1990s, which proved largely ineffective and

---

36   *See* Niemivuo, *supra*, note 34 at 212–213.

240 NIEMIVUO AND VIIKARI

unfair. The most drastic cutbacks in public services targeted education and children's daycare. The government also plans sharp cuts in funding for developmental aid, a measure that will seriously undermine its commitment to international solidarity – one of the pillars of the Nordic welfare state.

In recent years, legislative work in Finland has faltered badly. The Centre Party pushed through a reform of *regional state administration*, which came into force in 2010. The debate in Parliament on passage of the bill was agonizing. It was referred to as a "fiasco" and even the government's own MPs used unusually strong language ("What a mess", "This is not going to be one of the best bills on record" and "a botched job").[37] Then again, such a debate in Parliament is by no means exceptional. The legislation to reform regional government have always aroused strong emotions and been difficult to draft. Things have become sharply confrontational, particularly where adjusting the borders of administrative regions is concerned. Implementing reforms once approved has proven even more difficult.

In the following four years, in the governments of Prime Ministers Jyrki Katainen and Alexander Stubb, the National Coalition Party and the Social Democrats tried to hurry two reforms through Parliament: municipal restructuring and the reform of social and health care services. The municipal restructuring reform has been in the works since back in the 1960s. It is only in the last decade that it has made brisk progress – for economic reasons – and economic considerations in particular kept pressures on to make more headway. Here, the reforms carried out in the other Nordic countries have no doubt done much to speed up the pace of reform in Finland.

The municipal restructuring reform and reform of social and health care services have been prepared at different paces, despite their being interdependent. In the case of both, the drafting process has been criticized for its not including the Opposition. In addition, criticism has been levelled at the tight schedule set for the work, particularly in the case of the municipal reform.[38] For example, unconscionably little time was set aside for deliberation of the reform in Parliament despite the societal importance of the legislation. The Municipal Structure Act was passed by a parliamentary majority and came into force on 1 July 2013. The related reports of the Administration Committee and

---

37   *See* the speeches by Representatives Jacob Söderman (Social Democrats), Ville Niinistö (Greens), Ilkka Kanerva (National Coalition Party) and Håkan Nordman (Swedish People's Party).

38   *See Kuntarakennekirja* [Municipal Structures], ed. Ari Mölsä (Helsinki: Kunnallisalan kehittämissäätiö, 2012).

THE NORDIC WELFARE STATE & DEVELOPMENT OF NORTHERN FINLAND 241

the Constitutional Law Committee contained statements by the Opposition speaking out against the reforms.[39]

The system initially chosen in the reform of social and health care services, built on strong municipalities, was problematic in many respects. The administrative model chosen later, which had six regions, proved problematic as well. Given the form of municipal democracy they imposed and the expenses municipalities were burdened with, neither model fulfilled the requirements of the Constitution. As a result, no progress was made in the case of either of the reforms during the electoral term.

It appears that what we are seeing here is a political power game. The parties in power at any given time each push their own models of local and regional government. What will happen during the present term? The Government Programme of Prime Minister Sipilä states: "The Government will prepare a solution for the arrangement of social welfare and health care ... services based on autonomous areas larger than a municipality. There will be a maximum of 19 areas."[40] The Programme also states: "With respect to the coordination of the central government's regional administration and provincial administration, a separate decision will be made aimed at simplifying the arrangement of public regional administration (central government, regions and municipalities). The primary solution is centralising functions in terms of duties and authority in clear autonomous areas."[41]

In building the model of government, we could do well to look at how government has been structured in other Nordic countries. In Norway, the state has responsibility for hospitals, whereas in Sweden and Denmark hospital care is provided by the counties. The excerpt from the Government Programme above indicates that the planned reform may be based on regional self-government, as is the case in the Swedish model.[42] In Finland we have often adopted models for legislative drafting from the Swedish system. In the next few years, we would be well advised to again turn our sights to how county

---

39   *See* HE [Government bill] 31 and 53/2013 vp, HaVM [Report of the Administrative Committee] 11/2013 vp and PeVL [Report of the Constitutional Law Committee] 20/2013 vp.

40   Finland, a land of solutions, Strategic Programme of Prime Minister Juha Sipilä's Government May 29, 2015, Government Publications 12/2015, 30, accessed December 8, 2015, http://vnk.fi/documents/10616/1095776/Ratkaisujen+Suomi_EN.pdf/c2f3123a-d891-4451-884a-a8cb6c747ddd?version=1.0.

41   *Ibid.*, at 32.

42   We in fact have experiences of the model, gained from a project piloting regional government in Kainuu (2004–2012).

government is organized there, for this can offer the best solution for developing regional government at home.

If responsibility for specialized hospital care is going to be taken away from municipalities, it might be worthwhile to stop and think about the municipality of the future. One key starting point there would be that not all municipalities have to be alike. In particular, special arrangement should be created for the capital region. A sound basis for planning the municipality of the future and the tasks it will handle can be had in the proposal on the Municipal Act of the future that was published in Sweden in March 2015.[43]

Also the particularities of the northernmost areas of Finland, the Sámi homeland region included, need to be taken into account. At the same time, the growing influx of asylum-seekers, many of whom arrive in the provinces of Oulu and Lapland across the borders of Northern Finland, cannot be ignored. The manifold numbers of asylum-seekers and – later, in all likelihood – immigrants granted asylum is bound to have profound effects on various aspects of life in provinces and municipalities of the North, and not least where social and health care services are at stake.[44] The other Nordic countries currently face similar challenges, hence it would be wise to study closely their developments and solutions adopted by them.

Another highly relevant factor is the fact that general significance of the northernmost areas is increasing steadily. Lapland serves as our gate to the High Arctic. Our former Prime Minister Paavo Lipponen underlined in his recent report called "A Strategic Vision for the North" (commissioned by the Confederation of Finnish Industries EK) that Finland must take advantage of the great opportunities in the Arctic region. He argues that what is needed is more Nordic cooperation in general, and new infrastructure and building of railways in particular. Lipponen concludes:

> The Arctic and northern policy must be developed in close cooperation with the population centres in northern Finland, regional administration and in provinces, and by universities, research institutes and business

---

43   SOU [Statens Offentliga Utredningar, Swedish Government Official Reports] (2015), 24.

44   The number of asylum-seekers in Finland has reduced considerably from what it was in fall 2015: in Septermber 2015, Finland received nearly 11,000 asylum-seekers, while a year later the number was c. 500 per month. However, there is no reason to expect that migrants would stop crossing into Europe, northern Scandinavia included. Considering the current world situation, it seems most likely that the amount of people seeking asylum will increase again considerably sooner or later.

THE NORDIC WELFARE STATE & DEVELOPMENT OF NORTHERN FINLAND   243

life. The Sami population and non-governmental organisations must be included in decision-making.[45]

It is difficult to disagree with Lipponen's assessment.

On balance, the mind-set relating to regional policy has changed in Finland. The state has largely abandoned its application of regional policy on the national level. Its economic investment generally amounts to little more than the national contribution required as part of EU funding.[46] Given the pace at which the world is changing today, there hardly is any going back to the old approach to regions. At the same time, it seems obvious that the recent developments emphasizing the increasing over-all importance of the North call for the sharpening of our national regional policies – and, preferably, sooner than later. To begin with, we could start speaking again of *regional policy* instead of regional development. This would not cost a thing.

---

45   Paavo Lipponen, *A Strategic Vision for the North: Finland's Prospects for Economic Growth in the Arctic Region* (2015), 12, accessed December 8, 2015, http://ek.fi/wp-content/up loads/A-Strategic-Vision-for-the-North.pdf.

46   In two of his speeches at opening ceremonies for the academic year (2002 and 2005), former rector of the University of Lapland, *Esko Riepula*, sharply criticized the change that has occurred in regional policy. *See Juhlakirja: Esko Riepula 1941 – 2.2.2001*, ed. Ilpo Paaso (Tampere: Finnpublishers, 2001), 194–200, 233.

Poster Based Articles

How Satellites Can Support the Information Requirements of the Polar Code

Johnny Grøneng Aase[a] and Julia Jabour[b]

Abstract

In 2000, the International Maritime Organization (IMO) adopted a new requirement for all international and cargo ships exceeding a certain size, and all passenger ships, to carry Automatic Identification System (AIS) transponders capable of providing information about the ship to other ships and to coastal authorities automatically. The requirement became effective for all ships on 31 December 2004. AIS provides other vessels with information about, for example, a ship's identity, position, course, speed and destination.

The IMO is finalizing implementation of the Polar Code for the safety of vessels, which will apply in both polar waters and will require additional information about the profile of the fleets of ships operating there. However it must be noted that the AIS data is generally only available from legitimate operators (for example, licensed fishers, tourist operators and vessels on government service) and if the AIS transponder is turned off, the vessel becomes virtually invisible. This methodology, therefore, is not a stand-alone system.

Norway has currently two satellites in polar orbit capable of receiving AIS signals. AIS is an excellent tool to track tourist vessels and as such create situational awareness and assist in search and rescue operations in the Arctic. The paper presents findings from three regions in the High Arctic: east of the coast of Greenland, north of Svalbard and surrounding the Russian archipelago of Franz Joseph Land, for the years 2010 to 2014 about maritime activities in these regions with a focus on passenger and fishing vessels. It also suggests other satellite-based means for verifying the AIS data.

---

a Institute for Marine and Antarctic Studies, University of Tasmania, Hobart, Australia/ Norwegian Defence Cyber Academy, Lillehammer, Norway). Email johnny.aase@utas.edu.au.
b Institute for Marine and Antarctic Studies, University of Tasmania, Hobart, Australia. Email Julia.Jabour@utas.edu.au.

Keywords

Shipping – International Maritime Organization (IMO) – Satellite tracking – Arctic vessels

1 Introduction

The International Maritime Organization (IMO) has adopted the *International Code for Ships operating in Polar Waters* – the Polar Code.[1] It will enter into force on 1 January, 2017 for ships constructed after that date, and for existing vessels – by the first intermediate or renewal survey, whichever occurs first, after 1 January, 2018. It is expected that the Polar Code will increase the safety of maritime activities in polar areas and enhance protection of the marine environment. Instead of creating a new, independent convention, the IMO chose to make the Polar Code mandatory through amendments to three existing conventions – the 1974 *International Convention for the Safety of Life at Sea* (SOLAS); the 1973 *International Convention for the Prevention of Pollution from Ships*, as modified by the 1978 Protocol relating thereto (MARPOL); and the 1978 *International Convention on Standards of Training, Certification and Watchkeeping for Seafarers* as amended (STCW).[2]

Specific amendments will be made to these three conventions to prescribe additional requirements for polar operations. These amendments will provide, for example, specific guidance on ship structure, stability and integrity (Part 1-A); specific guidance on additional pollution prevention requirements (Part II-A); the process for acquiring additional training for ships' crews (Part 1-A). In relation to the latter, the often overlooked aspect of the Code sets out the labor regulations and functional requirements of crewing polar operating vessels.[3] Amendments to Chapter V of STCW are required to establish a training and certification program for masters and deck officers. A Polar

---

1 International Maritime Organization. *International Code for Ships Operating in Polar Waters* (Polar Code). Two IMO Resolutions establish and adopt the Polar Code: MSC.385 (94) (London, November 21, 2014) and MEPC.264 (68) (London, 15 May 2015).

2 The specific amendments to SOLAS are contained in IMO Resolution MSC.386 (94) (London, November 21, 2014), and to MARPOL Annexes I, II, IV, and V in Resolution MEPC.265 (68) (London, May 15, 2015). Chapter V of the International Maritime Organization, *International Convention on Standards of Training, Certification and Watchkeeping for Seafarers* will also be amended. http://www.imo.org/en/OurWork/HumanElement/TrainingCertification/Pages/STCW-Convention.aspx.

3 Polar Code, *supra* note 1, Chapter 12.

INFORMATION REQUIREMENTS OF POLAR CODE   249

Waters Certificate of Proficiency will be offered at both basic and advanced levels, with the probability of a phasing-in period while training programs get underway. The Master and Chief Mate of a tanker or passenger vessel operating in ice-covered waters, for example, both must have advanced training under the new STCW rules. The objective of this obligation is to ensure that officers "attain the abilities that are appropriate to the capacity to be filled and duties and responsibilities to be taken up" when a vessel is operating in polar waters."[4] Officers of the navigational watch need only basic training.

The Polar Code requires that sufficient information about the physical environment surrounding a vessel be available for the highly trained crew to undertake its safe operation. Some of this information will also be of interest to national authorities for purposes of situational awareness, particularly in relation to search and rescue.

Most vessels sailing in the vicinity of the Antarctic continent can communicate with the rest of the world using geostationary satellites. The Polar Code applies south of 60°S latitude. A geostationary satellite has a theoretical range to 81.3°N or S. Vessels sailing in the waters surrounding Antarctica will be within range of geostationary satellites and therefore will have few difficulties achieving satisfactory communications.

The situation is different in the Arctic, however. In the European Arctic, this latitude range corresponds approximately to the locations of Bear Island (Norwegian: Bjørnøya) and the main settlement on Svalbard, Longyearbyen. Vessels sailing in this region should not rely upon communication through geostationary satellites alone. The rule of thumb is that robust communication stops somewhere between 75°N and 78°N.[5] Aase and Jabour have shown that tourist vessels sailing north of the islands of Spitsbergen and Nordaustlandet have reached latitudes exceeding 82° N, which puts them out of the range of geostationary communication satellites and into dangerous waters.[6] In the Barents Sea and North Atlantic, the Polar Code will apply north of a set of straight lines drawn between Cape Kanin Mos in Russia, Bjørnøya (Bear Island), South Cape on the Norwegian island Jan Mayen and further to four points surrounding the coast of Greenland.

It is always challenging to sail in Arctic and Antarctic waters. It is dark during the winter months. The weather changes quickly. There is always the risk of

---

4   *Ibid.*, 12.2.

5   J.G. Aase and J. Jabour," Can Monitoring Maritime Activities in the European High Arctic by Satellite-Based Automatic Identification System Enhance Polar Search and Rescue?" *The Polar Journal* (2015): 1–17.

6   *Ibid.*

topside icing with potential reduction of stability and equipment functionality. A vessel will from time to time run into sea ice. The ice conditions may change fast. The communication infrastructure is limited, and some areas have not even been properly mapped. Access to rapid response in cases of emergency is also limited. To acknowledge and mitigate these unfavorable operating conditions, the Polar Code prescribes the classification of vessels according to their structure and operating capabilities, assessing risks in known and foreseeable areas of operation, and guiding the composition of a Polar Water Operational Manual[7] unique to each vessel. The status of communications is one of the key risk factors for operations in polar waters. This paper examines the information requirements of the Polar Code, and describes how satellites can be used to meet these requirements. While this paper will focus on the Arctic, it is acknowledged that the two polar regions have both common and different operating conditions and information challenges.

2   Search and Rescue in the Arctic

Each year there are a significant number of accidents and emergencies in polar waters involving all kinds of vessels – including those fishing, on government service, and tourist cruises. Details about these incidents were presented to the IMO Sub-Committee on Ship Design and Equipment (DE) during the development of the Polar Code.[8] Climate change has made the Arctic even more accessible, to the point where it has become a high-end tourist destination. For example, the cruise liner *Crystal Serenity* was the world's first luxury liner to sail from the Pacific to the Atlantic Ocean via the Canadian Northwest Passage during summer of 2016.[9] The plan was to have the *Crystal Serenity*, which has capacity for over 1,000 passengers, to be accompanied during the voyage by an escort vessel, which would carry additional safety and environmental protection equipment.

With the potential compromise to a vessel's ability to receive or transmit communications, and the impending re-classification of vessels operating in polar waters, the time was never more appropriate for the adoption of a

---

7   Polar Code, *supra* note 1, at Chapter 2.

8   IMO document DE 56/INF.9, "IAATO Polar Risk Assessment", submitted to the Sub-Committee on Ship Design and Equipment by Cruise Lines International Association, dated December 9, 2011.

9   *Crystal Serenity* Prepares for Arctic Voyages, http://www.marinelink.com/news/serenity-prepares-crystal407362.aspx, accessed April 10, 2016.

INFORMATION REQUIREMENTS OF POLAR CODE

search and rescue agreement specific to the Arctic. The *Agreement on Aeronautical and Maritime Search and Rescue in the Arctic* was signed during the Arctic Council's 2011 Ministerial Meeting in Nuuk, Greenland.[10] This Agreement delimitates the Arctic into search and rescue regions where each of the Arctic nations has special responsibilities.

The SAR Agreement made it clear, however, that delimitation of the search and rescue regions is not related to and does not prejudice the delimitation of any boundary between States or their sovereignty, sovereign rights or jurisdiction.[11]

Under the Convention, each Party is to promote the establishment, operation and maintenance of an adequate and effective SAR capability within its area of responsibility. If a SAR agency and or rescue coordination center (RCC) of a Party receives information that any person is, or appears to be, in distress, that Party is obliged to take urgent steps to ensure that the necessary assistance is provided.[12] If it has reason to believe that a person, a vessel or other craft or aircraft is in a state of emergency in the area of another Party, it is obliged to forward as soon as possible all available information to the Party or Parties concerned. A SAR agency and/or RCC of a party that has received such information may request assistance from the other Parties. The Party to whom a request for assistance is submitted must promptly decide on and inform the requesting Party whether or not it is in a position to render the assistance requested and will promptly indicate the scope and the terms of the assistance that can be rendered. Assistance must be provided to any person in distress, regardless of the nationality or status of such a person or the circumstances in which that person is found. A Party is obliged to provide all relevant information regarding the search and rescue of any person to the consular or diplomatic authorities concerned. Any party to the Agreement may, where appropriate, seek cooperation with States not party to the Agreement that may be able to contribute to the conduct of search and rescue operations, consistent with existing international agreements.[13]

A number of search and rescue exercises have been carried out in the Arctic with the objective of identifying strengths and weaknesses in SAR capabilities,

---

10   Agreement on Cooperation on Aeronautical and Maritime Search and Rescue in the Arctic (SAR Agreement) https://oaarchive.arctic-council.org/bitstream/handle/11374/531/Arctic_SAR_Agreement_EN_FINAL_for_signature_21-Apr-2011%20%281%29.pdf?sequence=1&isAllowed=y.

11   *Ibid.*, Article 3.

12   *Ibid.*, Article 7.

13   SAR Agreement, *supra* note 10, Article 18.

and how to use the lessons learned to ensure that the gaps are filled. Exercise SAREX Greenland Sea 2012, held in September that year, involved some 1,000 people from different organizations in the Arctic nations.[14] The scenario was centered on a cruise ship in distress in a remote part of the Arctic, which highlighted the challenges posed by geographic distances, local terrain and lack of infrastructure. The scenario involved a medium-sized cruise ship "Arctic Victory" with 160 passengers and crew. The "Arctic Victory" first went missing in the Greenland Sea and later ran aground in King Oscar's Fjord, followed by an explosion and resulting fires on board. "Arctic Victory" was simulated by the Danish Naval vessel HDMS *Triton*. King Oscar's Fjord is located to the west of the Norwegian island Jan Mayen.

The scenario included maritime search and rescue; firefighting at sea; evacuation by sea and air; deployment of emergency medical personnel, fire and rescue personnel, and police registration personnel; triage and emergency medical treatment by doctors and paramedics at sea and on land; establishing a reception facility for evacuees on land; establishing guard duty to protect evacuees against polar bear attacks; and continuous updating of SAR service's Person On Board (POB) list and the Police's Disaster Involved Registry (DIR) with identities and medical status of evacuees. The intent was to closely simulate the many challenges of coordinating a multinational search and rescue effort in the High Arctic.

The Area of Operation (AO) was the Greenland Sea, King Oscar's Fjord, Ella Island and Mestersvig Airstrip in northeastern Greenland. The main hubs for maritime and air assets proceeding into the AO were Reykjavik, and Keflavik airport on Iceland.

The Exercise Report highlights that the lack of communications played an important role during SAREX Greenland Sea 2012.[15] At sea, HF and VHF radio communications worked effectively despite bad weather conditions, with sea state of up to 10 meters. Satellite communications using Iridium telephone and internet services experienced losses of connectivity. Satellite communications were completely lost during the Rescue and Evacuation phases in King Oscar's Fjord. The mountains in the East Greenland fjords prevented connection to geostationary satellites and significantly degraded communications with Iridium satellites. Furthermore, the mountainous terrain in the fjord system hampered VHF connectivity between the participating units.

---

14   Greenland Command/ISCOMGREENLAND, Search and Rescue Exercise Greenland Sea 2012 (SAREX Greenland Sea 2012) Final Exercise Report, http://www.institutenorth .org/assets/images/uploads/attachments/SAREX_Greenland_Sea_2012_Final_Exercise_ Report.pdf, accessed April 10, 2016.

15   *Ibid.*, chapter 7.4 Communications.

INFORMATION REQUIREMENTS OF POLAR CODE

The exercise report suggests that deployable stations capable of relaying satellite and VHF communications should be placed on mountain-tops. Alternatively fixed wing aircraft should be deployed as radio relays.

Follow-up exercises were carried out in 2013 and 2015 and have provided useful learning opportunities for national SAR organizations.

3   The Polar Code

The International Maritime Organization (IMO) has adopted the new Polar Code, which applies both in the Arctic and Antarctic. In the lead-up to its implementation in 2017 and beyond, classification societies, ship insurers, flag states and ship operators are all keen to understand their responsibilities and the need for specific information to assist them in decision-making.

3.1   *Definitions*

The areas of application of the Polar Code for the Arctic and the Antarctic relate directly to their definitions outlined in SOLAS regulations XIV/1.2 and XIV/1.3 respectively, and MARPOL Annex I, regulation 11.46.2; Annex II, regulation 10.21.2; Annex IV, regulation 7.17.3; and Annex V, regulation 3.13.2. For the Antarctic, all waters south of 60° South are covered, but in the Arctic the demarcation is not as straightforward.[16]

Ships sailing in Arctic and Antarctic areas, as defined by the Polar Code, will require a Polar Ship Certificate,[17] which can be issued either by a classification society on behalf of a flag state, or by the flag state itself. The Polar Code defines three categories of vessels according to what kind of ice they are designed to operate in.[18] Category A ship means a ship designed for operation in polar waters in at least medium first-year ice, which may include old ice inclusions. Category B ship means a ship not included in category A, designed for operation in polar waters in at least thin first-year ice, which may include old ice inclusions. Category C ship means a ship designed in open water or in ice conditions less severe than those included in categories A and B.

Sea ice means any form of ice found at sea which has originated from the freezing of sea water.[19] First-year ice means sea ice of not more than one winter growth developing from young ice with thickness from 0.3 m to 2.0 m.[20]

---

16   Polar Code, note 1, Introduction, para 5.

17   *Ibid.*, para 1.3.1.

18   *Ibid.*, paras 2.1–3.

19   *Ibid.*, para 2.12.

20   *Ibid.*, para 2.4.

Medium first-year ice is defined as first-year ice of 70 to 120 cm thickness.[21] Thin first-year ice means first-year ice 30 cm to 70 cm thick.[22] Open water means a large area of freely navigable water in which sea ice is present in concentrations less than 1/10 and where no ice of land origin is present.[23] Old ice means sea ice that has survived at least one summer's melt, typical thickness up to 3 m or more. It is subdivided into residual first-year ice, second-year ice and multi-year ice.[24]

3.2 *Voyage Planning*

Chapter 11 of the Polar Code covers voyage planning in polar waters. The goal of this chapter is to ensure that the Company, Master and crew are provided with sufficient information to enable operations to be conducted with due consideration of the safety of the ship and persons on board and, as appropriate, the environment.

The voyage plan will take into account any potential hazards on the route of the intended voyage. When considering a route through polar waters, the master will take into account the following:

- Any limitations of the hydrographic information and aids to navigation available;
- Current information on the extent and type of ice and icebergs in the vicinity of the intended route;
- Statistical information on ice and temperatures from former years;
- Place of refuge;
- Current information and measures to be taken when marine mammals are encountered relating to known areas with densities of marine mammals, including seasonal migration areas;
- Current information on relevant ships' routing systems, speed recommendations and vessel traffic services relating to known areas with densities of marine mammals, including seasonal migrating areas;
- National and international designated protected areas along the route; and
- Operation in areas remote from search and rescue (SAR) capabilities.

All of these risk assessments will help inform the content of the Polar Water Operational Manual (PWOM), which will give clear instructions to the ship's

---

21   *Ibid.*, para 2.8.
22   *Ibid.*, para 2.15.
23   *Ibid.*, para 2.10.
24   *Ibid.*, para 2.9.

Master and crew about the capabilities and limitations of a vessel holding a Polar Ship Certificate. The procedures outlined in the PWOM are ultimately the responsibility of the ship's Master. Ideally the PWOM will be augmented by real-time access to updated ice and weather information.

4 Communication of Real Time Data

Clearly, communications are an essential element in the gathering of real time knowledge about operating conditions, as envisaged by the Polar Code. But communications in the high latitude polar regions are not without their problems. Both Canada and the United States have established internet portals providing aids to safe navigation, as discussed later in this article. The SAREX Greenland Sea 2012 exercise report highlighted that the mountains within the East Greenland fjords effectively disconnected the connection to geostationary satellites, as well as significantly degrading communications via satellites in polar orbit, i.e. Iridium. Robust communications are necessary to access the new navigation portals. Chapter 10 of the Polar Code outlines communications requirements. The goal of the chapter is "to provide for effective communications for ships and survival craft during normal operations and in emergency situations." Chapter 10.2.1 of the Polar Code outlines the functional requirements of ship communication:

– Two-way voice and/or data communications ship-to-ship and ship-to-shore shall be available at all points along the intended operating routes;
– Suitable means of communications shall be provided where escort and convoy operations are expected;
– Means for two-way on-scene and SAR coordination communications for search and rescue purposes including aeronautical frequencies shall be provided; and
– Appropriate communication equipment to enable tele-medical assistance in polar areas shall be provided. Section 10.3.1.4 states further that the communication equipment shall provide for two-way voice and data communication with a Tele-medical Assistance Service.[25]

---

25   Tele-medical service has the potential to save lives at sea and is of special interest to vessels that have no doctor on board, or vessels with young and inexperienced doctors or other medical personnel. In some areas in the High Arctic a seriously ill person may be evacuated by helicopter to a town with a hospital, such as Longyearbyen or Hammerfest, or to a vessel with hospital facilities. Due to the distances or weather conditions, helicopter

Ship-to-ship communications may be both line of sight and beyond line of sight. There are a number of communications options available to ships operating in polar waters.

4.1 Geostationary Communication Satellites

Most vessels embarking on international voyages are equipped with satellite communications equipment. An antenna connects the vessel to a satellite in geostationary orbit, approximately 36,000 km over the equator. In this orbit the period of the satellite equals the rotation period of the Earth, and it appears that the satellite is fixed in the same spot in the sky. Such communications links can provide almost limitless bandwidth and services. Geostationary satellites deliver TV channels, telephone services and broadband Internet. When using such a satellite, there are no restrictions on the amount of information accessible to the crew and passengers.

From this vantage point the global network of communication satellites can see most of the Earth's surface. The only exceptions are the polar areas. As one moves away from the equator, the geostationary satellites get closer to the horizon. The theoretical range is at 81.3° latitude. Above this latitude, the satellite will always be below the horizon. A rule of thumb is that one cannot expect to have robust satellite communications above 75–78° latitude. In the European Arctic, this corresponds approximately to the latitudes of Bear Island and Longyearbyen. The line of sight to the satellite in the Arctic or in Northern Europe is easily blocked by islands or mountains, or when sailing in fjord systems. In areas with satellite shadows there is no access to information.

This is a problem relevant for ships sailing in the Arctic. Ships operating in Antarctica will rarely reach latitudes where they lose contact with geostationary satellites.

4.2 Inclined Geostationary Communication Satellites

The gravitational pull from the Earth, Sun and the Moon force a geostationary satellite, over time, into a daily orbit that oscillates around a point on the equator. The orbit looks like the number 8. This is called an inclined orbit. The operator will usually use the satellite's thrusters to compensate for this movement, but when a working satellite approaches the expected end of life the operator may choose to stop compensating for the gravitational pull to save fuel and extend the lifetime and income from the satellite. In such an orbit,

evacuation may not be available. Telemedicine will enable experienced doctors at distant hospitals to guide personnel out in the field who have to perform emergency life-saving medical procedures.

INFORMATION REQUIREMENTS OF POLAR CODE

a satellite could be at 3° N latitude at noon, and 3° S latitude approximately 12 hours later. When the satellite is furthest north, it will see all the way to $(81.3 + 3)°$ N = 84.3° N. This comes at an expense in the south, where the satellite will only see to $(81.3–3)°$ S = 78.3° S. Approximately 12 hours later, the situation is reversed. (Please note that these calculations do not take into account that the Earth is not a perfect sphere, but flat at the poles. As a first approximation, and to illustrate principles, these numbers are however accurate enough.) A communications satellite in an inclined orbit can hence communicate with stations further north or south than geostationary satellites can do during predictable periods of the day.

When a satellite has an inclination of 8.7° degrees, the signals can be received at both the North and South Pole.

The Norwegian Cyber Defence Forces and the industrial company Airbus have tested communications at high latitude by using a geostationary satellite in inclined orbit. In April 2015 communications were established between the Coast Guard vessel *Svalbard* at 83.3° N and the Norwegian mainland. This communications link was only available when the satellite was above the horizon. The time slots get shorter the further north one gets. The time slots are however predictable, and by using a number of satellites in inclined orbits one may be able to establish continuous communications.

4.3   *Low Polar Orbit Communications Satellites*

Iridium is a constellation of 66 satellites orbiting the Earth in low polar orbits.[26] The constellation consists of six groups of 11 satellites orbiting after each other in the same orbital plane. The altitude is approximately 440 miles, and each satellite uses 100 minutes to orbit the Earth. The inclination of each orbital plane is approximately 86.4 degrees.[27] Iridium satellites are hence capable of providing satellite communications in areas where geostationary satellites can not, like the Polar areas.

The Norwegian Cyber Defense Forces carried out a series of practical tests of Iridium in the High European Arctic in 2015. The tests show that the service is expensive, slow and the connectivity is highly variable. But it is the only service that is almost continuously available in these areas. The situation may improve when the new Iridium NEXT constellation is launched in the second half of the 2010s. These satellites will use new technologies that are not available in the Iridium constellation.[28]

---

26   Iridium satellites, http://www.n2yo.com/satellites/?c=15, accessed April 10, 2016.

27   Iridium, http://www.astronautix.com/mfrs/iridium.htm, accessed April 10, 2016.

28   Iridium Next, https://www.iridium.com/network/iridiumnext, accessed April 10, 2016.

4.4 *Highly Elliptic Orbit Communications Satellites*

The best solution to improve communications in the High Arctic is to launch communication satellites into highly inclined elliptic orbits. From such an orbit a satellite will look into the Arctic basin for several hours of each orbit. At least two satellites are required to give robust 24/7 coverage.

The Soviet Union/Russia has been using communication satellites in such orbits since 1965.[29] The Molnija (12 hour period) and Tundra (24 hour period) satellites have been providing robust communication services to civilian and military users in the Russian Arctic.

There are currently no alternatives to the Russian satellites available in Western Europe and North America. Canada plans to launch the Polar Communication and Weather (PCW) constellation,[30] however this satellite constellation will probably not be in orbit before 2020. Space Norway is studying a similar constellation. Broadband services in the Arctic from Western satellites will not be available for several years. It is unknown to the authors if Russia plans to provide commercial services for international users with their Molnija or Tundra satellites.

4.5 *Ground Radio Chains*

In some areas the communications requirements can be met by using chains of radios and radio repeaters. VHF and UHF radios will only provide line of sight communications. HF radio has longer range.

5 Automatic Identification System (AIS)

Given the communication difficulties experienced in the high latitude Arctic, authorities need to rely on alternative means of locating vessels in the event of communication failure. The purpose of the Automatic Identification System (AIS) is to increase safety at sea.[31] It transmits information about the ship and voyage. All ships of 300 gross tonnage and upwards that are engaged on international voyages, cargo ships of 500 gross tonnage and upwards not engaged on international voyages, and all passenger ships irrespective of size must have and use AIS. The requirement became effective for all ships by 31 December

---

29 Molnija, http://www.astronautix.com/project/molniya.htm, accessed April 10, 2016.

30 The Polar Communications and Weather Mission, http://www.asc-csa.gc.ca/eng/satellites/pcw/, accessed April 10, 2016.

31 AIS transponders, http://www.imo.org/en/OurWork/Safety/Navigation/Pages/AIS.aspx, accessed April 10, 2016.

INFORMATION REQUIREMENTS OF POLAR CODE

2004. Ships equipped with an AIS transponder must maintain it in operation at all times except when international agreements, rules or standards provide for the protection of navigational information.

5.1 Types of AIS

AIS equipment Class A is ship-borne mobile equipment intended to meet all performance standards and carriage requirements adopted by the IMO.[32] Class A stations report their position autonomously every 2 to 10 seconds depending on the vessel's speed and/or course changes. Position messages are transmitted every three minutes or less when the vessel is at anchor or moored. The static and voyage related messages are transmitted every six minutes. Class A stations are capable of text messaging safety related information and AIS Application Specific Messages, such as meteorological and hydrological data, electronic broadcast Notice to Mariners, and other marine safety information.

AIS equipment Class B is ship-borne mobile equipment that is interoperable with all other AIS stations, but does not meet all the performance standards adopted by the IMO. Like Class A stations, they report every three minutes or less when moored or at anchor, but their position is reported less frequently or at less power than for Class A equipment. The vessel's static data is reported every six minutes. Class B equipment does not send any voyage related information. It can receive safety related text and application specific messages, but cannot transmit them.

Class A AIS position reports are transmitted as Messages 1, 2 and 3.[33] Such messages contain the vessel's Maritime Mobile Service Indicator (MMSI) number. This is a unique nine-digit number that identifies the vessel that transmits the message. These messages also inform about the vessel's navigational status, like "under way using engine", "at anchor", "restricted maneuverability", "moored" or "aground". In these messages one can also find information about the rate of turn, speed over ground, position accuracy, longitude, latitude, course over ground and true heading.

Class A AIS ship static and voyage related data are transmitted in AIS Messages 5. These messages contain the ship's MMSI number, and also the IMO number, call sign and ship name. They also inform about the type of ship and cargo type, overall dimension, type of electronic position fixing device, estimated time of arrival (ETA), maximum present static draught, and destination.

---

32   Types of Automatic Identification Systems (Per ITU-R M. 1371 and IEC Standards), http://www.navcen.uscg.gov/?pageName=typesAIS, accessed April 10, 2016.

33   AIS messages, http://www.navcen.uscg.gov/?pageName=AISMessages, accessed April 10, 2016.

Class B position reports are transmitted as AIS messages types 18 and 19. They include the vessel's MMSI number, speed over ground, position accuracy, longitude, latitude, course over ground, true heading and some technical information. Messages type 19 also include the ship's name and information about the type of ship and cargo.

Messages type 24 are Class B static data reports. They consist of two parts, A and B. Part A includes the MMSI number and the vessel's name. Part B also includes the MMSI number, in addition to the type of ship and cargo type, vendor ID, call sign, dimension of ship and type of electronic position fixing device.

5.2 Use of AIS

Vessels sailing close to land are tracked by AIS land stations, but such stations are unable to track a ship on the high seas. The Norwegian AISSat program was initialized to increase that country's situational awareness in the North Atlantic and Arctic Ocean. AIS receivers in polar orbit have revolutionized Norway's situational awareness in its areas of interest.

The two satellites currently in orbit have exceeded design and lifetime expectations, and now receive AIS messages over the entire surface of the Earth.

AISSat-1 was launched in July 2010,[34] and AISSat-2 in July 2014.[35] More satellites are scheduled be launched in 2016 and 2017. As of 10 April 2016, AISSat-1 orbits the Earth every 96.9 minutes. The altitude varies between 611.7 and 626.5 km. The orbit inclination is 98.0°. AISSat-2 flies in a slightly higher orbit, 630.7 × 630.7 km. The period of this satellite is hence slightly longer, 97.2 minutes. The orbital inclination of AISSat-2 is 98.3°.

The satellites automatically receive messages from vessels while orbiting the Earth. The messages are automatically downloaded when the satellites pass over a ground station on Svalbard and forwarded to authorities on the Norwegian mainland through fiberoptical cables dug into the ocean floor between Spitsbergen and the Norwegian mainland.

Aase and Jabour (2015) used data from the AISSat satellites to map maritime activities in three regions of the European High Arctic in 2010–2014. The AIS data sets showed that most tourist vessels visit the Arctic region few times a year. This may imply that they have limited experience with operating in the challenging Arctic environment. The data sets also showed that the Norwegian Coast Guard did not have a continuous presence in the waters north of

---

34   AISSat-1, http://www.n2yo.com/?s=36797, accessed April 10, 2016.

35   AISSat-2, http://www.n2yo.com/satellite/?s=40075, accessed April 10, 2016.

Svalbard. No military vessels were seen in the waters surrounding Franz Joseph Land, so it was impossible to assess the Russian SAR capabilities using those data sets. It should however be noted that military vessels are not obliged to transmit AIS messages.

In North America, the US Coast Guard have started the eNav and Nationwide AIS (NAIS) initiatives. NAIS[36] consists of approximately 200 VHF receiver sites located throughout the coastal continental United States, inland rivers, Alaska, Hawaii and Guam. It is designed to collect AIS transmissions from local vessels. The primary goal of NAIS is to increase Maritime Domain Awareness (MDA) through data dissemination via a network infrastructure, particularly focusing on improving maritime security, marine and national safety, SAR and environmental protection services. NAIS is based on AIS, a technology sanctioned by the IMO as the global standard for ship-to-ship, ship-to-shore and shore-to-ship communications. NAIS uses digital VHF waveforms to continually transmit and receive voiceless data.

The NAIS program was initiated in response to the Maritime Transportation Security Act of 2002. NAIS enhances maritime domain awareness with a focus on improving security, navigational safety, search and rescue, and environmental protection services. The system combines AIS data – such as vessel location, source and speed – with other government information and sensor data to form a holistic view of maritime vessel traffic near the continental U.S. and its territorial waters. Informed by a comprehensive view of traffic on the nation's waterways, decision makers are better positioned to respond to safety and security risks. NAIS improves the safety of vessels and ports through collision avoidance and strengthens national security through detection, identification and classification of potential threats while they are still offshore.

The NAIS program is implemented in increments, which will help to address technical, logistical and budgetary risks that would be more difficult to manage in a single step approach.

- Increment 1: The shore-based capability to receive AIS messages within the nation's 58 major ports and 11 most critical coastal areas is implemented by using existing government infrastructure and meeting cost and performance requirements.
- Increment 2: Transceiver capability, transmitting data out to 24 nautical miles and receiving data from out to 50 nautical miles is implemented.

---

36   Nationwide Automatic Identification System, http://navcen.uscg.gov/?pageName=NAIS main, accessed April 10, 2016.

Permanent transceivers combine with satellite coverage to observe traffic up to 2,000 miles from the coast.

The Canadian Coast Guard has created a web portal to aid in safe and efficient navigation in Canadian waters – E-Nav.[37] This portal contains information about marine weather, tides, currents, hazards, notices, ice conditions, charts and sailing conditions in Canadian waters.[38] The Northwest Passage is located in two regions, the Western Arctic and the Eastern Arctic. The portal also contains information about the location of Canadian Coast Guard units assigned to icebreaking services.

Land-based AIS is also available in Europe. Shelmerdine (2015)[39] used data from a single land-based AIS receiver on Shetland. The data set was broken down by sector into meaningful and usable data packets, which could be analyzed over time. Vessel tracks showed variation in vessel routes, especially around island groups. Additional uses of AIS data were addressed and included risk mapping for evasive non-native species, fisheries, and general statistics.

5.3 Weaknesses of the AIS System

AIS is a passive system, and has some weaknesses. It is not possible to verify the information being transmitted. It is also possible for the crew to turn off the transponder.

There are examples of AIS position data transmitted from a trawler apparently sailing deep in the Greenlandic ice sheet. The same trawler transmitted similar AIS messages in 2010, 2012 and 2014. In all three years the position data from the trawler shows that it is located deep into the Greenlandic ice sheet. This is obviously false. Some skepticism is required when using AIS data, and data from other sources should be used to verify AIS readings.

---

37 Fisheries and Oceans Canada – E-Navigation Portal, http://www.dfo-mpo.gc.ca/media/infocus-alaune/2015/ENav/index-eng.htm, accessed April 10, 2016.

38 E-Navigation Maritime Information Portal – Navigation by region, http://www.marinfo.gc.ca/e-nav/index-eng.php, accessed April 10, 2016.

39 R.L. Shelmerdine, "Teasing out the Detail: How our Understanding of Marine AIS Data can Better Inform Industries, Developments and Planning," Marine Policy, 54 (2015): 17–25, http://www.sciencedirect.com/science/article/pii/S0308597X14003479, accessed April 10, 2016.

INFORMATION REQUIREMENTS OF POLAR CODE

5.4   *Examples of the Use of Satellite-Based AIS*

The wealth of information embedded in the AIS messages makes it easy to follow a vessel's voyage. It is straightforward to plot the positions on maps and follow the voyages through the Northeast Passage and other waters.

6   Weather and Ice Maps

The risk assessments required by the Polar Code include substantial and real time knowledge about both weather and ice. Under the general heading of "Arrangements for receiving forecasts of environmental conditions," the Code requires that the means for obtaining this information, and the frequency with which both ice and weather data are available, be expressly laid out in the PWOM.[40] Ice is, of course, one of the defining features of polar waters, and its presence is one of the reasons why the Polar Code has been established to augment a ship's usual ISM Code (IMO 2016) when vessels are taken into polar waters. The ISM Code is designed to provide international standards for the safe management and operation of ships and for pollution prevention. Each ship operator is obliged to provide a manual – called the ISM Safety Management Manual – containing practical guidance for how to operate the vessel so that it complies with the requisite safe management practices and procedures. When the vessel enters polar waters, the situation changes and therefore PWOM was designed to be essentially a polar-specific version of this manual. Understanding and predicting safe navigation through ice, given difficult weather conditions, will be a major component of the day-to-day operations of ships in polar waters.

Ice forecast maps are made on a daily basis. These maps use data from the European and Canadian radar satellites Sentinel-1 and Radarsat-2. Radar satellites have a great advantage over optical satellites taking images of the Earth's surface. Radar satellites can obtain the required information even when it is cloudy or dark.

These maps show water temperature and regions with fast ice, very close drift ice, close drift ice, open drift ice, very open drift ice and open water.

National authorities and search and rescue coordination centers will have an interest in monitoring the maritime activities in their waters. Companies have an interest in following a vessel's voyage. Such situational awareness has several practical advantages. Combined with updated ice data it enables

---

40   Polar Code, *supra* note 1, Annex 6, Division 2, Chapter 2.

national authorities to ensure that a vessel is not heading for an area with more severe ice conditions than the vessel is certified for. The Polar Code Categories determine the kind of ice a vessel is permitted to operate in. A Category A ship, for example, means a ship designed for operation in polar waters in at least medium first-year ice, which may include old ice inclusions. Europe is currently launching a flotilla of Earth observation satellites through its Copernicus program, which will assist in ice and weather forecasting. It should be a goal of the scientific community to develop ice data products that are detailed enough to give data on thickness and age of ice. When AIS and such detailed data products are combined, both the vessel and national authorities can determine if the vessel is heading towards an area that exceeds the vessel's certification.

7 Conclusion

The Polar Code has been designed to increase the safety of maritime activities in polar waters and to enhance protection of the marine environment. It classifies a vessel according to its ability to withstand impact with ice of specific types. It requires that crew, particularly the higher ranking officers, undertake advanced training that will enhance their skills in navigating in polar waters. The Polar Code requires that ships carry a Polar Water Operational Manual that sets out how to operate the vessel safely and appropriately in polar waters. This means that sufficient information must be available for the vessel to be operated safely and in an environmentally responsible way by the specially trained crew. The quality of this information depends, to a degree, on the provision of a solid broadband communication infrastructure, for example to have the capacity to receive real time ice and meteorological data. This paper has shown that while vessels sailing in Antarctic waters can expect to be within range of geostationary communication satellites, which would facilitate the receipt of this crucial operating information, this might not be the case in the Arctic. Here the means of communication available, and the quality of broadcast, depend on latitude and geography. This will change when commercial communication services are available from satellites in Highly Elliptical Orbits, but this is unlikely to happen before 2020.

National authorities can use AIS to track a vessel. The AIS messages contain the vessel's MMSI number, which can also be used to identify the vessel. By establishing a database that contains the MMSI number, the Category, and the Polar Class Certificate Category it will be possible to determine if a vessel is heading into ice conditions for which it is not certified. If the cargo manifest is available, it will also be possible to determine the environmental risk that a ship poses. For example, in the Arctic it would be possible for Russian or Norwegian authorities to track a vessel along Kuril Islands and Kamchatka Peninsula, and identify questionable vessels well before they entered the Arctic Ocean through the Bering Strait. This would give both nations time to prepare for spills in the case of an emergency. However, information about the thickness and age of ice should be developed to increase safety at sea.

Essential Fish Habitat Regulation in the United States: Lessons for High Latitudes?

Aileen M. Nimick[a] and Bradley P. Harris[b]

Abstract

Commercial fisheries in the United States are managed by eight regional fisheries management councils operating under the authority of the National Marine Fisheries Service (NMFS, Department of Commerce) and governed by the Magnuson-Stevens Fisheries Conservation and Management Act and accompanying federal guidelines. The Act mandates that NMFS identify essential fish habitat (EFH) for fish stocks and minimize, to the extent practicable, adverse effects to EFH through the councils' fishery management plan development and revisions process. The statute and regulatory guidelines implicitly assume that NMFS and councils have the scientific information necessary to make informed EFH designations for all commercially harvested species, assess the realized or potential threats to EFH, and have the management tools to protect EFH. Further, the interpretation and implementation of several important, but ambiguous, terms in the guidelines are left to NMFS and the councils. Our thesis is that these factors (specifically, insufficient information support and regulatory ambiguities) can and are resulting in inconsistent and potentially sub-optimal fish habitat management throughout the country. As we enter an era of increased climate variability these factors may be having a disproportionally high impact in higher latitudes where change is expected to be more rapid. Here we provide a brief history of essential fish habitat regulations, explain the issues arising from the state of the science and regulatory ambiguities, and conclude with a discussion of the implications and recommendations for United States high latitude EFH management.

---

a M.Sc. student in the Fisheries, Aquatic Science & Technology (FAST) Lab at Alaska Pacific University (APU), email: animick@alaskapacific.edu.
b Director of the FAST Lab and Assistant Professor of Environmental Science at APU.

Keywords

essential fish habitat – Magnuson-Stevens Act – Sustainable Fisheries Act – fisheries management councils – regulatory ambiguity

1 Introduction

The Magnuson-Stevens Fishery Conservation and Management Act (MSA)[1] is the primary statute governing commercial fisheries in the United States federal waters.[2] It delegates authority to the National Marine Fisheries Service (NMFS), which is part of the National Oceanic and Atmospheric Administration (NOAA) in the Department of Commerce. The Secretary of Commerce (Secretary), through NMFS, promulgates the regulatory guidelines used to implement the MSA[3] mandates, which the eight regional fisheries management councils (councils) must follow.[4] Each council is responsible for maintaining the sustainability of the fishery resources within its management area.[5] Fish stocks[6] are managed through fishery management plans (FMPs), which contain stock status information and the rules pertaining to fishing each stock. FMPs are required to contain information regarding essential fish habitat (EFH) for each fish stock and any potential fishing or non-fishing threats to EFH.[7] FMPs and their amendments are submitted by councils to the Secretary for approval.

This paper begins with a brief history of EFH legislation followed by a review of the language in both the MSA and its associated regulatory guidelines, then proceeds to examine the potential problems arising from implicit assumptions about the state of the science available to support EFH analyses. This is followed by a discussion of the implications of current regulatory ambiguities

---

1 16 U.S.C. §§ 1801–1891 (2007).
2 Federal waters are those within the Exclusive Economic Zone (EEZ), defined as 3 nautical miles (nm) off the coast to 200 nm.
3 16 U.S.C. § 1851(b).
4 *Id.* § 1852(b)(1); the eight councils are New England Council, Mid-Atlantic Council, South Atlantic Council, Caribbean Council, Gulf of Mexico Council, Pacific Council, North Pacific Council, and Western Pacific Council.
5 For maps of council management areas see: http://www.nmfs.noaa.gov/sfa/management/councils/.
6 16 U.S.C. § 1852(h)(1).
7 *Id.* § 1802(10) defines essential fish habitat (EFH) as "those waters and substrate necessary to fish for spawning, breeding, feeding or growth to maturity."

on EFH policy. Generally, we contend that 1) the current state of the science is not sufficiently advanced to manage EFH as expected by Congress, and that 2) current regulatory ambiguities may be inhibiting optimal and consistent EFH management throughout the country. The paper then explores the idea that high latitude management areas may be particularly susceptible to these issues and concludes with recommendations for the future.

2   A Brief History of Essential Fish Habitat Legislation

The MSA was enacted in 1976, primarily in reaction to heavy fishing by foreign vessels off the coasts of the United States (US), and established, for the US, exclusive rights to all natural resources within 200 nm of the country's coast.[8] Fletcher and O'Shea summarized the previous attempts towards habitat legislation, explaining that habitat was included in the original MSA as something to be researched, but was not afforded explicit protections.[9] Amendments to the MSA in 1986 and 1990 added some habitat provisions – FMPs must include a habitat assessment that councils could use to comment on any federal action that may have potential to damage habitat.[10]

In 1996, the Sustainable Fisheries Act (SFA) introduced the EFH legislation of today.[11] All FMPs are required to identify and describe EFH for all life stages of each managed fish stock, identify any potential threats to EFH, and suggest actions that could enhance or conserve EFH.[12] Any project that is authorized or permitted by a federal agency that may adversely affect EFH requires an EFH Assessment, identifying the potential impacts and possible mitigation measures.[13] This consultation requires NMFS to provide EFH Conservation Recommendations, if applicable.[14]

The requirement to submit FMP EFH amendments to the Secretary for approval went into force two years (October 1998) after the SFA was passed.

---

8   James P. Walsh, "The Origins and Early Implementation of the Magnuson-Stevens Fishery Conservation and Management Act of 1976," *Coastal Management* 42, no. 5 (2014): 414, 418, accessed November 7, 2014, doi: 10.1080/08920753.2014.947227; the 200 nm zone later became the Exclusive Economic Zone.

9   Kristen M. Fletcher and Sharonne E. O'Shea, "Essential Fish Habitat: Does Calling It Essential Make It So?," *Environmental Law* 30, no. 51 (2000): 54–58.

10   *Id.* at 56.

11   16 U.S.C. § 1801–1884.

12   16 U.S.C. § 1853(a)(7) and 1855(b)(1)(B).

13   50 C.F.R. § 600.920(e)(2002).

14   *Id.* § 600.905(b).

ESSENTIAL FISH HABITAT REGULATION IN THE UNITED STATES   269

The Secretary approved all of the initial EFH amendments, but those submitted by the New England, Gulf of Mexico, North Pacific, Pacific, and Caribbean Councils were challenged in court for not complying with standards of the National Environmental Policy Act (NEPA).[15] As a result, these five councils were ordered to revise and resubmit their amendments, and thus the standard for the NEPA-based review of EFH was established.

3   Magnuson-Stevens Act Language

The MSA defines EFH as *"those waters and substrate necessary to fish for spawning, breeding, feeding or growth to maturity."*[16] *Fish* refers to any marine animal or plant, except marine mammals and birds.[17] Congress mandates that either the Secretary or the councils do three things with respect to EFH – (1) describe and identify EFH for all life stages of each species managed in an FMP; (2) identify and minimize to the extent practicable adverse effects caused by fishing; and (3) identify actions that will encourage the conservation and enhancement of each habitat.[18] The MSA also mandates that the Secretary or councils consider 'adverse impacts' on EFH, including fishing and non-fishing impacts.[19] Additionally,

> [e]ach federal agency shall consult with the Secretary with respect to any action authorized, funded, or undertaken, or proposed to be authorized, funded, or undertaken, by such agency that may adversely affect any essential fish habitat....[20]

4   Regulatory Guidelines Language

NMFS publishes regulatory guidelines that provide instructions to councils about how to include EFH provisions in FMPs. These regulations define an *'adverse effect'* as

---

15   *See* American Oceans Campaign v. William M. Daley, 183 F. Supp. 2d 1, 15 (D.D.C. 2000).

16   16 U.S.C. § 1802(10).

17   *Id.* § 1802(12).

18   *Id.* § 1853(a)(7).

19   *Id.* § 1855(b)(1)(B).

20   *Id.* § 1855(b)(2).

any impact that reduces quality and/or quantity of EFH. Adverse effects may include…loss of, or injury to, benthic organisms, prey species and their habitat…if such modifications reduce the quality and/or quantity of EFH.

The guidelines also state that

councils must act to prevent, mitigate, or minimize any adverse effects from fishing, to the extent practicable, if there is evidence that a fishing activity adversely affects EFH in a manner that is more than minimal and not temporary in nature.[21]

5   State of the Science Problem

Despite the 20 years which have lapsed since the SFA amendments were implemented and several decades of research on fishing-habitat interactions, the state of the science remains nascent.[22] Kaiser et al., working with 39 practitioners from the seafood industry and fishery management and 13 active fishing-impacts research scientists from 12 countries, determined the top 25 knowledge-needs for this field.[23] Five of the top 10 knowledge-needs are listed below. Note that this list includes foundational information about the types and locations of seabed habitats and fishing activities, the roles habitat features play in fish life history, and the vulnerability of these features to fishing impacts.

- What is the extent and distribution of different seabed habitat types? (Rank = 1)
- What are the habitat-related variables (e.g. biota, substratum type, current flow) that determine resilience (recovery time) to disturbance from different types of trawling and in different benthic habitats? (Rank = 4)

---

21   *Id.* § 600.815(a)(2)(ii).

22   Jonathan H. Grabowski et al., "Assessing the Vulnerability of Marine Benthos to Fishing Gear Impacts," *Reviews in Fisheries Science & Aquaculture* 22, no.2 (2014): 142–155, accessed May 21, 2014, doi: 10.1080/10641262.2013.846292.

23   Michel J. Kaiser et al., "Prioritization of Knowledge-Needs to Achieve Best Practices for Bottom Trawling in Relation to Seabed Habitats," *Fish and Fisheries* 16, no. 4 (2015): 668–683.

ESSENTIAL FISH HABITAT REGULATION IN THE UNITED STATES 271

- What is the spatial and temporal extent and variation in the intensity of bottom-trawling activity for all vessels? (Rank = 6)
- What kind of information do we need to quantify about seabed habitats, and about the mode of operation, prevailing environmental conditions and attributes of fishing gear to understand their interaction? (Rank = 7)
- What is the functional relationship between the biological and physical attributes of the seabed and the survival and reproduction of managed stocks? (Rank = 9)[24]

The EFH regulatory guidelines require FMPs to describe the physical, chemical, and biological properties of EFH for each life stage and the role those properties play in making EFH essential. Contrasting those requirements with the list above illustrates the gap between the state of EFH science and the information demands implicit in EFH policy.[25] The FMPs must also note the level and type of information supporting the EFH descriptions. There are four different levels described in the regulatory guidelines-

- Level 1: [Species] distribution data are available for some or all portions of the geographic range of the species.
- Level 2: Habitat-related densities of the species are available.
- Level 3: Growth, reproduction, or survival rates within habitats are available.
- Level 4: Production rates by habitat are available.[26]

The North Pacific Fisheries Management Council (NPFMC) manages over 60 stocks via six FMPs. Each fish stock has four to five life stages identified, resulting in more than 300 potential EFH assessments. During the 2010 EFH review, analysts in this region had Level 1 (fish distribution) information to work with for about half of the life stages for each stock and no information for the other life stages.[27] Three of the groundfish stocks in the Bering Sea Aleutian Islands (BSAI) area and three in the Gulf of Alaska (GOA) area had

---

24   *Id.* at 8.
25   50 C.F.R. § 600.815(a)(1)(i).
26   *Id.* § 600.815(a)(1)(iii)(A).
27   North Pacific Fisheries Management Council (NPFMC), Fishery Management Plan for Bering Sea/Aleutian Island King and Tanner Crabs, (Anchorage, AK: NPFMC, 2011): 135. NPFMC, Fishery Management Plan for Fish Resources of the Arctic Management Area, (Anchorage, AK: NPFMC, 2009): 80. [hereinafter FMP for the Arctic]. NPFMC, Fishery Management Plan for Groundfish of the Bering Sea and Aleutian Island Management Area, (Anchorage, AK: NPFMC, 2015): 86. [hereinafter FMP for Groundfish of the Bering Sea and Aleutian Island].

no habitat information available for any life stage.[28] This aligns with the top knowledge-needs highlighted by Kaiser et al.[29]

The underlying assumption of EFH legislation is that analysts have the information necessary to designate EFH, understand threats to its integrity, and to conserve it. These include knowing (1) the spatiotemporal distribution of commercially targeted fishes by life stages, (2) the spatiotemporal distribution of the habitat features, (3) how habitat features are connected to *"spawning, breeding, feeding or growth to maturity"*[30] of fishes, (4) the spatiotemporal distribution of the fishing and non-fishing activities at the scales of the activity-habitat feature interactions, and (5) how fishing and non-fishing activities alter the habitat features. As illustrated above, these questions still lack basic answers.

The limited state of the science is further complicated by well-meaning legal standards and precedents that are vulnerable to information deficits. McGuire and Harris identified what they termed 'back-ended' processes resulting from the interaction of the MSA and NEPA.[31] National Standard 2 of the MSA states that *"management measures shall be based upon the best scientific information available"*;[32] every FMP is a federal action and, therefore, subject to a NEPA review.[33] NEPA requires a 'hard look' at all available information, but the *doctrine of deference,*[34] which federal courts apply to executive branch (e.g. NMFS, council) science and scientific interpretations, limits judges' consideration

---

NPFMC, Fishery Management Plan for Groundfish of the Gulf of Alaska, (Anchorage, AK: NPFMC, 2015): 73. [hereinafter FMP for Groundfish of the Gulf of Alaska]. NPFMC, Fishery Management Plan for the Salmon Fisheries in the EEZ off Alaska, (Anchorage, AK: NPFMC, 2012). NPFMC, Fishery Management Plan for the Scallop Fishery off Alaska, (Anchorage, AK: NPFMC, 2014): 70.

28   FMP for Groundfish of the Bering Sea and Aleutian Island, *supra*, note 28 at 86.

FMP for Groundfish of the Gulf of Alaska, *supra*, note 28 at 73.

The stocks are sharks, octopuses, and forage fish complex (in both FMPs). Sharks and octopuses are managed as a fishery and the complex is considered an ecosystem component and is managed to prevent fishing and conserve those stocks as prey for marine mammals, seabirds, and fish.

29   Kaiser et al., *supra*, note 23 at 8.

30   16 U.S.C. § 1802(10).

31   Chad McGuire and Bradley P. Harris, *Some Back-Ended Legal and Political Issues in United States Fisheries Management,* Journal of Politics and Law 3, no. 2 (2010): 52–62.

32   16 U.S.C. § 1851(a)(2).

33   42 U.S.C. § 4321–4347.

34   The judicial interpretation of the Doctrine of Deference has been defined most recently by the U.S. Supreme Court decision in *Chevron U.S.A. Inc. v. Natural Resources Defense Council, Inc.,* 467 U.S. 837, 104 S.Ct. 2778, 81 L.Ed.2d 694 (1984).

of the scientific rigor of EFH information. This may result in scenarios where unreliable and/or unverified information becomes the basis for a major council action (e.g. EFH designations or protections like habitat closure areas), and the only recourse available to the public for critical review and accountability is constrained by precedent.[35]

6   Regulatory Ambiguity Problem

There are ambiguities present in the MSA and the EFH regulatory guidelines that ultimately leave the individual councils in control of the interpretation and implementation of critical aspects of EFH assessment and conservation. The MSA mandates that adverse impacts to EFH from fishing be minimized to the extent practicable.[36] In the guidelines, NMFS further clarifies that councils must act to mitigate, prevent, or minimize adverse fishing impacts if they are *"more than minimal and not temporary."*[37] The guidelines provide no further language defining 'minimal,' 'temporary,' or state whether the impacts in question are to a fish stock (e.g. reduced fish abundance) or to habitat features (e.g. reduced number of seabed structures). Multiple permissible interpretations of these guidelines may result in sub-optimal or ineffective EFH protections and inconsistent EFH management among councils.

The words 'minimal' and 'temporary' reflect Congress' aim to protect EFH from substantial permanent damage, but they are vague, relative terms open to subjective interpretation. A minimal impact is dependent on the feature of impact (the fish stock or the habitat features) and the spatial scale of the impacting event relative to that of the feature. For example, if 100% of the sponges in a given area (e.g. a local bed) are damaged, but the bed represents only 0.001% of all sponges in that region (e.g. Bering Sea), it is likely not a minimal impact to that bed, but it is probably minimal to the population of sponges. Further, the impacts of that event to fish depends on the spatial scale and specific ways in which a given fish species uses sponges at a particular life stage, which is generally not known (*sensu* Kaiser et al.).[38] Likewise, the temporal measurement ('temporary') is relative. A habitat feature could recover

---

35   For a full discussion on these issues, refer to McGuire and Harris, "Some *Back-Ended Legal and Political Issues in United States Fisheries Management.*"

36   16 U.S.C. § 1853(a)(7).

37   50 C.F.R. § 600.815(a)(2)(ii).

38   Kaiser et al., *supra*, note 24.

from an impact in a month, a year, 10 years, or in 100 years. All these scenarios could be considered temporary because recovery eventually happens.

The largest ambiguity, however, results from the implicit assumption that adversely impacted habitats result in reduced fish stock production. The language in the MSA makes it clear that Congress' intention with EFH management was to protect the sustainability of a harvested fish stock by conserving its habitat.[39] This assumes a real and measureable link between the two. The statute and regulatory guidelines, however, do not clarify whether impact to EFH, as assessed by the councils, should be measured by the 'health' of fish stocks or by some metric of impact to habitat features themselves (e.g. damaged proportion of a given habitat feature). Building on the previous example, in their 2010 EFH assessment, the NPFMC measured fishing impact by examining a metric of fish stock health. If an effect to EFH made a fish stock more likely to fall below the minimum stock size threshold (MSST), then that effect to EFH could be considered adverse ('more than minimal and not temporary').[40] While using MSST as a reference point for habitat impact has been criticized,[41]

---

39   16 U.S.C. § 1801(a)(2) says, "Congress finds and declares... certain stocks of fish have declined... as a consequence of... direct and indirect habitat losses which have resulted in a diminished capacity to *support existing fishing levels*." (emphasis added).

      Id. § 1801(a)(5) says, "... the fisheries can be conserved and maintained so as to provide *optimum yields* on a continuing basis." (emphasis added). *Id.* § 1801(a)(6) says, "A national program for the conservation and management of the fishery resources of the United States is necessary... to facilitate long-term protection of essential fish habitats, and to realize the *full potential* of the Nation's fishery resources." (emphasis added). *Id.* § 1801(b)(4) says, "The purposes of the Congress in this Act – to provide for the preparation and implementation, in accordance with national standards, of fishery management plans which will achieve and maintain, on a continuing basis, the optimum yield from each fishery...."

40   Minimum Stock Size Threshold (MSST) is the greater of (a) one half BMSY, or (b) the minimum stock size at which rebuilding to BMSY will occur within 10 years while fishing at the maximum fishing mortality threshold. MSST is measured in terms of spawning biomass or other appropriate measures of stock productive capacity. National Oceanic and Atmospheric Association (NOAA), *NOAA Fisheries Glossary*, NOAA Technical Memorandum NMFS-F/SPO-69 (Silver Spring, MD: NOAA, 2006), http://www.st.nmfs.gov/st4/documents/F_Glossary.pdf.

41   Center for Independent Experts (CIE), Center for Independent Experts (CIE) Review of Evaluation of Fishing Activities That May Adversely Affect Essential Fish Habitat Appendix B of Draft Environmental Impact Statement, by Asgeir Aglen (Fairbanks, AK: Northern Taiga Ventures, Inc. (NTVI), 2004): 2. CIE, Center for Independent Experts (CIE) Review of the National Marine Fisheries Service's Evaluation of the Effects of Fishing on Essential Fish Habitat in Alaska, by Pierre Pepin (Fairbanks, AK: NTVI, 2004): 1. CIE, Review of the Draft of Appendix B: Evaluation of Fishing Activities That May Adversely Affect

ESSENTIAL FISH HABITAT REGULATION IN THE UNITED STATES   275

it is important to note that the NPFMC declared a definition and implemented a standardized metric (most of the other councils have not). Having an explicit impact reference point makes EFH status determination and the expected results of EFH protections clear for the council and its constituents. The lack of a clear EFH impact criterion can result in confusing and protracted council EFH assessment and management processes that result in policy actions without clear measureable expected outcomes (e.g. the New England Council).

7   Compounded Difficulties in High Latitudes

High latitude management areas are particularly susceptible to these problems due to a relatively lower-level of fish-habitat research and increasing climate variability. Advancing the state of EFH science is particularly difficult in regions like the northern Bering, Chukchi, and Beaufort Seas due to their size, remoteness, seasonal ice cover, and lack of research infrastructure. Further, high latitude regions generally experience more energetic storms and a broader range of physical conditions resulting in more variable and intense natural disturbance regimes, making the effects of fishing vs. non-fishing disturbances on EFH harder to distinguish. This distinction is particularly important to EFH management because councils are only *required* to act if *fishing* impacts are 'more than minimal and not temporary.'[42]

Much attention is currently focused on the impacts of climate variability in Alaska's Arctic region. The predicted warming may result in increased stock vulnerability to harvest and, ultimately, the movement of fish and, therefore, fishing distributions northward into currently unfished areas (commercial fishing is currently not authorized in US Arctic federal waters).[43] This provides a unique opportunity to apply EFH lessons-learned and to develop EFH policies that are robust to the information and ambiguity issues raised here.

Essential Fish Habitat, Prepared by Scientists at the National Marine Fisheries Service, by K. Drinkwater (Fairbanks, AK: NTVI, 2004): 1. CIE, Review of the Draft Environmental Impact Statement for Essential Fish Habitat Identification and Conservation in Alaska, by J. Anthony Koslow (Fairbanks, AK: NTVI, 2004): 1. CIE, Review of the National Marine Fisheries Service and the North Pacific Fishery Management Council Draft Environmental Impact Statement with Respect to Essential Fish Habitat: Evaluation of Fishing Activities that May Adversely Affect Essential Fish Habitat, by Paul Snelgrove (Fairbanks, AK: NTVI, 2004): 2. CIE, Review Report: Evaluation of the Effects of Fishing on Essential Fish Habitat in Alaska, by Kenneth T. Frank (Fairbanks, AK: NTVI, 2004): 2.

42   50 C.F.R. § 600.815(a)(2)(ii).

43   FMP for the Arctic, *supra*, note 28 at ES-2.

Unlike most of the US continental shelf regions, Arctic benthic habitats have been subjected to very little to no fishing and, therefore, can provide baseline data on pre-fishing environments. Working now to establish baseline data on the spatiotemporal distributions of fish and their habitats will facilitate informed interpretations of fishing (and non-fishing) effects when fishing in the Arctic commences. The opportunity to conduct EFH studies before management measures are developed will allow managers and scientists to observe and track the direct and indirect impacts of anthropogenic stressors to a previously unfished environment. This would lend insight to the appropriate measure of habitat impact, potentially guiding law makers and fishery managers towards overcoming the regulatory ambiguities in the current EFH policy.

Non-fishing activities will also increase as sea ice melts. The potential of opening shipping routes has prompted the US Coast Guard to begin an initiative with NOAA to map the seafloor along the expected route for safe navigation purposes.[44] This lack of basic water depth data is a good example of the limited habitat information currently available. Shipping, oil and gas development, and several other non-fishing activities will initiate EFH consultations.[45] The efficacy of NMFS EFH consultations will depend on the state of the EFH science for the region, and while these consultation recommendations are only advisory,[46] this process provides an opportunity to encourage EFH data collection by non-fishery entities. For example, commercial ships have been used effectively as research vessels of opportunity.[47]

8   Recommendations and Conclusion

We contend that due to unrealistic expectations regarding the state of fish-habitat science during the development of the MSA, Congress and federal regulators promulgated language that left councils with ambiguous guidance leading to inconsistent and potentially ineffectual policy actions. The lesson-learned over the past 20 years of EFH policy is that if we are committed to

---

44 Yereth Rosen "NOAA, Coast Guard Team Up to Re-survey Arctic Waters", *Alaska Dispatch News*, March 17, 2015, http://www.adn.com/article/20150317/noaa-coast-guard-team-re-survey-arctic-waters, accessed Feb. 9, 2016.

45 16 U.S.C. § 1855(b)(2),(3),(4).

46 FMP for the Arctic, *supra*, note 28 at 86.

47 "Ship of Opportunity Program," last modified April 8, 2014, http://www.aoml.noaa.gov/phod/soop/index.php.

ESSENTIAL FISH HABITAT REGULATION IN THE UNITED STATES 277

understanding and mitigating the impacts of anthropogenic stressors on fish populations, then direct and substantial efforts to support fundamental research are required now. Therefore, investment in baseline habitat assessment and monitoring should be prioritized along with fishery stock assessments. Focusing on under-developed areas of research (e.g. as defined by Kaiser et al.)[48] that pertain to fishing and non-fishing effects on ocean habitat should be a top priority. Concurrently, emphasis should be put on developing advanced analytical work flows that are appropriate for both current and future EFH information. These tools should provide users with reliable (or at least reasonable) predictions of expected EFH dynamics while characterizing the substantial uncertainties associated with limited scientific information support. It is encouraging that several initiatives are underway by the Alaska Fisheries Science Center, including the cooperative Alaska EFH Research Plan.[49]

These investments would begin to address the state of the science issues inherent in the EFH policy but are not likely to produce substantial increases in fishing-fish-habitat science in the near-term. Congressional clarifications on the EFH legislation should be sought to the extent possible. A transparent conversation about how best to achieve EFH protections given the state of the science leading to clear guidance will result in consistent interpretations across councils. This will strengthen EFH management within the council process.

We contend that problems with the current EFH policy in the US are not insurmountable, but that substantive improvements in the EFH process depend on developing policies that are robust to the state of the science and on clarifying regulatory ambiguities. The state of scientific knowledge regarding fishing-fish-habitat interactions can and are actively being improved by workers around the world. As Kaiser et al. reveal, this work involves basic efforts to map habitat features, track fishing effort, and better understand gear-habitat interactions.[50] It is critical that funding agencies, managers, and the public at large understand that these projects are costly. Next, the regulatory ambiguities elucidated here are resulting in inconsistent EFH management throughout the US. These ambiguities and their associated implications can and should be explored and clarified by legislators and federal regulators.

---

48   Kaiser et al., *supra*, note 24.

49   Alaska Fisheries Science Center, Alaska Essential Fish Habitat Research Plan: A Research Plan for the National Marine Fisheries Service's Alaska Fisheries Science Center and Alaska Regional Office, by M.F. Sigler, M.F. Cameron, M.P. Eagleton, C.H. Faunce, J. Heifetz, T.E. Helser, B.J. Laurel, M.R. Lindeberg, R.A. McConnaughey, C.H. Ryer, and T.K. Wilderbuer, AFSC Processed Report 2012–06 (Juneau, AK: Alaska Fisheries Science Center, 2012).

50   *Id.*

A clear-eyed assessment of the state of fishing-fish-habitat science can lead to realistic expectations and will constitute a long-delayed step towards the effective EFH policy that Congress envisioned.

We have focused on a US domestic policy, but it is worth noting that the issues we raise are relevant to a number of other Arctic governments that have similar fish habitat regulations. Canada's Federal Fishing Act gives fish habitat protection and includes *"any permanent alteration to, or destruction of, fish habitat"* under the definition of *serious harm to fish*.[51] The European Union's Criteria and Methodological Standards on Good Environmental Status of Marine Waters state that *"the assessment of species also requires an integrated understanding of the distribution, extent and condition of their habitats... to make sure that there is a sufficiently large habitat to maintain its population, taking into consideration any threat of deterioration or loss of such habitats."*[52] It also identifies that *"the main concern for management purposes is the magnitude of impacts of human activities on seafloor substrates structuring the benthic habitat."*[53] Norway's Marine Resources Act directs the Ministry to prioritize "an ecosystem approach that takes into account habitats" when implementing management measures of marine resources.[54] Additionally, the Joint Norwegian–Russian Fisheries Commission manages the fish stocks in the Barents Sea, and it is beginning to prioritize more long-term management goals, which includes more ecosystem-based management.[55] All of these policies stress the importance of basing management decisions on the best available science. The knowledge needs highlighted by Kaiser et al.[56] were drawn from a *global* community, suggesting that the state of the science in these countries is limited as it is in the US, and EFH lessons learned in the US may be applied on an international level. We conclude that the state of the science and regulatory ambiguities may be present in international habitat policies, and the same recommendations can be made for these countries as for the US.

---

51   Revised Statutes of Canada (R.S.C.) 1985 c. F-14 § 2(2)(2016).

52   2010/477/EU: European Union Commission Decision of 1 September 2010 on criteria and methodological standards on good environmental status of marine waters (notified under document C (2010) 5956) § B (Descriptor 1) (2010).

53   *Id.* at 22.

54   Lov 2008-06-06 no 37: Act relating to Management of Living Marine Resources § 7(b)(2010).

55   Norwegian Ministry of Foreign Affairs, *The Norwegian Government's High North Strategy*, (Oslo, Norway, 2007): 52.

56   Kaiser et al., *supra*, note 24.

Printed in the United States
By Bookmasters